Tomb →

GEORGE WASHINGTON'S MOUNT VERNON

Oxford University Press

Oxford   New York
Athens   Auckland   Bangkok   Bogotá   Buenos Aires   Calcutta
Cape Town   Chennai   Dar es Salaam   Delhi   Florence   Hong Kong   Istanbul
Karachi   Kuala Lumpur   Madrid   Melbourne   Mexico City   Mumbai
Nairobi   Paris   São Paulo   Singapore   Taipei   Tokyo   Toronto   Warsaw
and associated companies in
Berlin   Ibadan

Library of Congress Cataloging-in-Publication Data
Dalzell, Robert F.
George Washington's Mount Vernon : at home in Revolutionary America /
Robert F. Dalzell, Jr., Lee Baldwin Dalzell.
p. cm.   Includes bibliographical references and index.
ISBN 0-19-512114-7
1. Mount Vernon (Va : Estate)   2. Washington, George, 1732–1799—
Homes and haunts—Virginia—Fairfax County.
I. Dalzell, Lee Baldwin.   II. Title
E312.5.D24   1998   975.5'292—dc21   98-23215

3 5 7 9 8 6 4 2
Printed in the United States of America
on acid-free paper

For A.D.B. and F.C.C.,
through whom we first came to know
George Washington,
all those years ago

Contents

List of Illustrations

Preface

SEVERAL MONTHS BEFORE the Battle of Yorktown, with military affairs already near full boil, George Washington received a singularly distressing piece of news from home. Believing that Mount Vernon was about to be burned to the ground by the British, its manager, Lund Washington, a distant relative, had gone on board the enemy warship anchored in the Potomac opposite the house. On receiving assurances that no hostile act was planned against Washington's property, he returned to shore and arranged to send— as he reported afterward to Washington—"sheep, hogs, and an abundant supply of other articles" out to the ship "as a present."

Embarrassingly enough, word of the incident also reached Washington from his dashing young friend and protégé, the marquis de Lafayette, who was moving south with a detachment of troops to oppose British forces in the area. The response came quickly. An angry letter went off to Lund with a copy and covering note to "My dear Marquis." "It would have been a less painful circumstance to me, to have heard, that in consequence of your non-compliance with their request, they had burnt my House, and laid the Plantation in ruins," fumed Washington to Lund, adding: "You ought to have considered yourself as my representative, and should have reflected on the bad example of communicating with the Enemy, and making a voluntary offer of refreshments to them with a view to prevent a conflagration."

These were strong words, and no doubt Washington meant them, though the letter reads more than a little as if it were written for wider circulation—and for Lafayette's eyes in particular. Perhaps Lund sensed this; even so, it would have been hard not to feel stung by his kinsman's outburst. Among other things, the house he hoped to save from burning was so important to Washington that despite the enormous difficulties involved, it had been under almost constant renovation since the beginning of the Revolution. More than once Lund had questioned the wisdom of spending so much time and money rebuilding a place that might at any moment be destroyed, but Washington insisted that the work continue.

In his covering note to Lafayette, Washington did make one comment that helps put the situation in perspective, though as often happened when he was anxious about something, the syntax was shaky. "A false idea arising from the consideration of his being my Steward and in that character was more the trustee and guardian of my property than the representative of my honor has misled his judgment and plunged him into error," he wrote in Lund's defense. Property and honor: two very different entities, and the point at which they intersected was Mount Vernon. It was a configuration that went to the core of Washington's feelings about his home. It is also central to this book about the making of George Washington's Mount Vernon and its place in his life and mind.

Inevitably thoughts about Washington conjure in the mind's eye a series of iconic pictures. Commanding troops in battle, crossing the Delaware in winter, presiding over the Constitutional Convention, taking the oath of office as president—the images flash by in grand and familiar sequence, and there he is at the center of each of them, steadfast, calm, and aloof, which is exactly how he meant to appear to the world at large. Yet in reality Washington was a person of intense emotions, and nothing engaged his emotions more deeply than Mount Vernon—the piece of earth he loved better than any other, the home he claimed to value above all the honors the world could bestow, the palpable result of a lifetime of effort and concern, but also something he was prepared to see destroyed if "honor" demanded it.

Feelings so powerful underline what was obvious to anyone who knew Washington: Mount Vernon was far more than simply a house. It was an extension of the man himself, a tangible emblem of his character, his personality, his hopes, his dreams. For more than four decades he served as its architect and chief planner, a role he shared with no one, not even Martha Washington. Deft at dealing with people of all sorts, she was a warm and vital presence at Mount Vernon, and its rooms and fields rang with the laughter of her children and grandchildren. But in the complex calculus of the relationship between husband and wife, the basic decisions about the style and design of the house and grounds were Washington's, always. Signature and self-portrait, Mount Vernon reflected at every turn his sense of himself and of his place in the larger world, and to this day it remains the most personal—the most intimate—expression of those things we have from his own hand.

Fully as interesting as what Mount Vernon can tell us about Washington's feelings, too, is what it reveals of his mind. Little given to abstract theorizing and inclined always to keep his innermost thoughts to himself, he rarely had much to say about the issues that animated the great events of his life. In an artfully crafted autobiography Benjamin Franklin transformed the story of his youth into an extended revery on the benefits of freedom. Washington never wrote an autobiography, and his diaries are largely confined to accounts of the weather and lists of the people who came to dinner. In Mount Vernon itself, however, he produced a text from which it is possible to coax a remarkably full sense of his political convictions and of how, over time, they changed.

To approach Mount Vernon in these terms—to see it as not only a "real" place, an actual structure on a piece of land that can be pinpointed on a map, but also as a cultural space, encompassing diverse imagery and meanings—is, after all, to do only what can be done with any house. In this case, however, the imagery and meanings were inextricably bound up, through Washington, with the whole process of nation-making in which he played so prominent a role. Along with Lexington and Concord, Boston and Philadelphia, Valley Forge and Yorktown, Mount Vernon was one of the sites where American independence was forged, in symbolic no less than in literal terms.

Recognizing the importance of the subject, both of Washington's principal biographers in this century, Douglas Southall Freeman and James Thomas Flexner, have called for studies of Mount Vernon, but to date nothing has appeared. This is surprising because the sources are unusually rich—so rich that it is possible to learn more about Washington's home during his lifetime than we know of any other eighteenth-century American house. Recently, too, as part of the growing interest in the material culture of the past—in *things* considered as historical evidence—houses have become the subject of intense scholarly investigation, often with impressive results, and studies of the material culture of colonial Virginia have been especially numerous. As the notes at the end of this book indicate, our debt to those studies is large.

Conceptually, two of the more interesting interpretations of Virginia's early material culture are those by Henry Glassie and Rhys Isaac. In *Folk Housing in Middle Virginia*, Glassie emphasizes the crucial importance of the shift from traditional domestic building forms to "Georgian" design, a shift that involved moving from "open" to closed house plans, and which he sees as marking "the point at which face-to-face community dies." In contrast, Isaac stresses the public uses of Georgian-style houses, at least among the gentry. Yet for both men the issue at bottom was control. Glassie's Louisa County farmers attempt to assert control by withdrawing from contact with other people; Isaac finds his gentry reinforcing its power through increasingly formal systems of social interaction.

Which analysis better fits the reality? Each focuses on a different group of individuals, but the truth is, it is easy enough to find houses that seem to reflect, simultaneously, both a desire for privacy and a taste for public ritual and ceremony, with little sense of the logical contradiction involved. In developing Mount Vernon over the years, Washington continued to add public as well as private spaces to the house, keeping the two separate from one another and allocating roughly the same square footage to each.

Both interpretations also assign a large role to emulation in shaping individual choices about things like architectural style, and certainly much of what Washington achieved at Mount Vernon can be explained in such terms, but not all of it can be. Eighteenth-century England witnessed a radical increase in the availability of goods imitating, at relatively low cost, styles set at the top of society, and the master of Mount Vernon was an eager participant in that "consumer revolution." Similarly, high-style architectural design reached an ever-expanding market through printed pattern books and builders' guides, and again that development is amply illustrated at Mount Vernon. Yet as time went by, Washington also showed himself to be notably more willing to strike out on his own—to ignore fashionable taste and build instead simply what pleased him. Nor, in such cases, does he seem to have been particularly concerned about control. The most striking innovation at Mount Vernon, the sweeping piazza that borders the east front of the house, is a remarkably open space in a social as well as a physical sense.

What, then, was Washington aiming at in arranging his personal material world as he did? Our conclusion is that over time he became distinctly less concerned, as an architect and builder, with the hegemonic functions of his home—with its use as an instrument of power—and more interested in what it said to him about himself. Ultimately what he wanted most from Mount Vernon was an affirmation of his sense of himself as a free man.

But freedom had more than one meaning during those years, and Washington also experienced Mount Vernon as more than just the result of the plans he made for it. Invariably once the process of building began it took on a life of its own. Try as he might, he could only control so much. There were too many different elements involved in building to keep it moving smoothly on track for long. And above all there were the people who did the work.

Washington's papers offer a good deal of information about who those people were and how they lived, and assiduous digging elsewhere has filled in many of the remaining gaps. The basic patterns of life in Virginia—in particular the combination of staple crop agriculture and African slavery and the growing inequality it fostered within the white population—were already well established when Washington reached maturity, and the terms of labor he set for his workers reflected those patterns. But his terms were not the only ones defining the relationship; the workers played an equally important role in the process. Also, his attitude toward Virginia's economy and society changed markedly over the years, a fact most prominently illustrated by his growing antipathy to slavery.

In part, the change registered a broader shift in values growing out of the Revolution. At least as important, however, was Washington's day-to-day experience building and running Mount Vernon. By nature he was a difficult and demanding taskmaster. Lund Washington was only one of dozens of individuals "at home" to feel the sting of his anger. Yet the anger Washington felt was matched on his workers' side by a resolute determination to use their labor for their ends as well as his. They would build his house and shape and tend his land, but they also had lives and dreams of their own to fulfill. Eventually Washington grew to understand this, and the knowledge had a subtle but profound effect on his thoughts about many subjects.

Broadly speaking, it is the thesis of this book that George Washington's Mount Vernon embodied, in succession, two quite distinct visions. The first was of an ordered society managed by an elite of virtuous, independent gentlemen; the second was of a nation characterized by equality of opportunity and independence for all. The first vision was fundamentally republican; the second, essentially democratic. As Gordon Wood argues in *The Radicalism of the American Revolution,* many Americans moved, as Washington did, from one to the other during those years. But for someone who seemed to embody so perfectly the republican ideal to have traveled that road is surprising. Indeed, most scholars, however sympathetic to Washington, have tended to depict him as permanently frozen in the classical republican mold. Yet to see him thus is to miss much of the meaning of the later part of his life, particularly as he lived it at home, at Mount Vernon. The book that follows seeks to remedy that situation—to recover the entire drama as Washington himself meant it to play, including the final act.

Appropriately enough, the book grew from an idea that first occurred to us at Mount Vernon, and for that and countless kindnesses over the years we owe a large debt to the superb staff there. On a January day in the early 1980s, while we were in Washington on a break from the normal academic routine, we prevailed upon our hostess to drive us out to Mount Vernon. It had snowed the night before, but the sky was blue, the sun was shining, and the place looked marvelously appealing. Better still, because we seemed to be the only people there that morning, the guide offered to take us through the entire house from top to bottom. We even climbed up in the cupola to see the view. Afterward, stopping by the gift shop to buy whatever book or books were available on Mount Vernon and its building, we were astonished to find nothing but the standard handbook. One of us had been thinking of writing a short, single-volume biography of Washington, but in that instant another idea suggested itself. Washington and Mount Vernon: that was the book that needed to be written, and we could do it together.

Unfortunately, we never learned the name of the guide who was so generous with her time that day, but there are other people at Mount Vernon we can thank here for the untold hours they have spent finding research materials for us, patiently discussing our ideas, and showing us around the place whenever we happened to be in town. They are: Christine Meadows, former curator of Mount Vernon; Ellen Clark McAllister, former librarian; King Laughlin, the present curator; Barbara McMillan, the present librarian, and her assistant, Rebecca Case; Karen Peters, photographic archivist; Marc A. LeFrançois, architectural conservator; and Dennis J. Pogue, director of restoration, who also read and commented insightfully on several chapters of the manuscript. To John P. Riley, historian and assistant to the director of Mount Vernon, we are especially grateful for any number of favors, including reading the entire manuscript and saving us from more than a few errors. His unfailing enthusiasm for the project has meant a great deal to us.

From the beginning, essential to our efforts has been a series of leaves, sabbatical and otherwise, granted through the generosity of the trustees of Williams College. The college has also helped liberally with funds for research and illustrations for the book.

The first of the leaves we spent in Charlottesville, at the University of Virginia, working in the offices where the Washington papers are being prepared for publication. In addition to the aid and encouragement of the staff, we were given full access to the extraordinarily rich collection of material assembled there. Though hardly set up to operate as a research library for scholars, "the Papers" made our work both a pleasure and far more efficient than traveling to dozens of different archives would have been. In the years since then, too, the staff has been consistently helpful in answering our questions and checking and rechecking innumerable facts. For their unfailing patience and goodwill, we wish to thank in particular William W. Abbot, former editor of the papers of George Washington, who also read and commented on several chapters of the manuscript; Dorothy Twohig, the current editor; and Beverly H. Runge and Philander D. Chase, associate editors.

Without libraries, scholars could not function. This is doubly true if you live and work in far western Massachusetts. The staff of the Williams College Library has been wonderfully supportive throughout every stage of the project. We would especially like to thank Phyllis L. Cutler, college librarian; Peter Giordano, Walter J. Komorowski, Rebecca O. Spencer, and Helena F. Warburg, reference librarians; and Alison R. O'Grady, interlibrary loan supervisor. Also at Williams, Robert L. Volz and Wayne G. Hammond, Jr., custodian and assistant librarian, respectively, of the Chapin Library, have provided much-appreciated help with research materials and illustrations. The Chapin is Williams's rare-books library. Relatively small in size but lavishly provided with treasures, it contains, among other things, George Washington's copy of the *Federalist Papers;* a complete list—in his own hand—of all his federal and state securities; and the account book of his estate.

Other libraries and institutions we wish to thank are: The Boston Athenaeum, Boston, Massachusetts; Alderman Library, University of Virginia, Charlottesville, Virginia; Lloyd House, Alexandria Public Library, Alexandria, Virginia; The Library of Congress, Washington, D.C.; The Huntington Library, San Marino, California; The National Trust Library, London, England; The National Portrait Gallery, London, England; Washington and Lee University, Lexington, Virginia; Colonial Williamsburg, Williamsburg, Virginia; The Mable Brady Garvan Collection, Yale University Art Gallery, New Haven, Connecticut; The Sterling and Francine Clark Art Institute, Williamstown, Massachusetts; The Museum and Library of Maryland History, Baltimore, Maryland; Gunston Hall Plantation, Lorton, Virginia; Pohick Episcopal Church, Lorton, Virginia; History Office, Fort Belvoir, Fort Belvoir, Virginia; Maryland State Archives, Baltimore, Maryland; and the Fluvana County Court House, Palmyra, Virginia.

In addition to several of the people already mentioned, there are others who have read all or part of the manuscript at different times. Their comments, criticisms, and suggestions have been invaluable, though in no sense should they be held responsible for any errors of fact or interpretation that remain in the book. Our blunders are our own. Colleagues at Williams who have served as readers are: the late Michael D. Bell of the English Department; Charles B. Dew, Patricia J. Tracy, and James B. Wood of the History Department; and James Nolan of the Anthropology/Sociology Department. Also, among the emeritus faculty at Williams, two individuals—William H. Pierson, Jr., and Frederick Rudolph—have both been warmly encouraging and usefully critical as readers. We owe them a great deal.

Other readers, all of whom have made helpful comments are: Joseph Ellis of Mount Holyoke College; William A. Flynt and Philip M. Zea of Historic Deerfield; Peter Burchard, freelance writer; John C. O'Brien of the Deerfield Academy English Department; Mrs. Sidney D. Ross, Williamstown, Massachusetts; and Judge Charles R. Alberti, ret., of the Superior Court of the Commonwealth of Massachusetts.

Our final and largest debt in this category is to Kevin M. Sweeney, of the History and American Studies Departments, Amherst College. He has read all of the manuscript once and much of it twice. His suggestions on issues of organization and interpretation—invariably thoughtful and imaginative—have helped shape the book in vital ways, making its argument both clearer and more forceful, for which we are deeply grateful.

Friends who point you to new sources of information, or provide food and lodging on research trips, or find places for you to live during leaves, or simply manage—at just the right time—to seem excited about what you are doing, also make a vital contribution to scholarship. For these and other favors we especially want to thank Beverly and John Sullivan, Peter Spang, Joyce and Michael Holt, Jim Cox, Warren Boeschenstein, Helen and Betty Livingston, Scott Swanson, Bill Pitt, Kate Briggs, Karen O'Brien, Ruth and

Arthur Localio, Jane and Leo Marx, and Eve and Bill Lilley, Tom Kohut, and Susan Dunn. We would also like to take this opportunity to express our gratitude to Frank Oakley, who both as a friend and as president of Williams College, 1985–93, has given the two of us constant support and encouragement.

Through countless drafts, a confusing jumble of pages—half handwritten, half computer-generated—was readied for publication by the Faculty Secretarial Office of Williams College, under the direction of Donna Chenail. The work itself was flawlessly done by Shirley Bushika, whose diligence and fortitude are boundless. And for faithfully checking and rechecking the quotations in the book we are indebted to two Williams College students, Margaret L. Ronald and Christia M. Mulvey.

We would also like to thank the staff at Oxford University Press and in particular our editor, Joyce Berry, whose "I get it"—frequently penciled in the margins of the manuscript together with suggestions for cuts—both amused us and noticeably improved the text. Special thanks, too, to Kim Torre-Tasso, our wonderfully efficient production editor.

When we began this project, three of our four children were still in school; now they lead busy lives in places that span the globe from Tokyo to Boston. Nevertheless, they continue to take a lively interest in our work, with Victoria and Alex cheering us on, and Fred, a professional historian, and Jeffery, an architect, each reading and commenting wisely on the entire manuscript. Jeffery also provided several of the drawings used as illustrations.

Lastly, we should say something about the collaborative nature of the project. Not only are the two of us in separate fields, but we are also differently trained and have different interests. Yet those differences seem—to us, at least—to have meshed in useful and productive ways. Several months after starting the research, we spent a long lunch outdoors, on a lovely autumn afternoon in Charlottesville, outlining in a rough way what the final book might look like. Then, taking the chapters we had agreed on, we each listed those we would like to write. When we compared the two lists, there were no duplications, and every chapter had been accounted for.

In completing the research and during the initial stages of writing we held to that design, working independently on our individual chapters. Next came the process of editing what we had written, and after that the complicated business of turning ten separate chapters into a single book. Happily, all of this seemed to get done without serious disagreement—perhaps because it was so important to us; perhaps, too, because we found the work so exciting and absorbing. In any case, we can honestly say we enjoyed writing the book together and look forward to collaborating again soon.

Sweden, Maine
Summer 1997

PART I

Landscapes of the Republic

PATTERNS

MOUNT VERNON was George Washington's home throughout his entire adult life. Today it is a national shrine visited by roughly a million people a year. If one wants to find the "real" man, surely here is an essential set of clues, a place where we can hope to discover the private side of this very public figure, to see beyond the all-too-familiar, rather stiff face he presented to the world at large.

Washington's contemporaries harbored much the same hope. Invited or not, they descended on Mount Vernon year after year in ever growing numbers. And Washington was ready for them, just as he always seemed ready—whatever his personal feelings—to play the hand that fate had dealt him. A lifelong lover of the theater, he set the stage quite carefully for his visitors, and much of what he acomplished in that regard remains intact today.

Yet for all Washington's assiduous management, Mount Vernon never became simply another public mask, and it continues to reveal a great deal about him precisely because he put so much of himself into it. From 1754 until his death in 1799, there was never a time when he was not at work on the place. Twice he all but completely rebuilt the main house, each time doubling it in size, and over the years he spent untold hours planning and carrying out other changes both in it and in the grounds, as well as in the larger plantation of which they were part.

Despite everything he invested in the effort, however, Washington's will was not the only agency shaping Mount Vernon. The place came to him with a history. It and he were also products of a particular society, and in his role as planner/builder he was continually maneuvering along the boundaries set by the traditions, practices, and beliefs of that society. The possibilities were not infinite. Part of Washington's achievement at Mount Vernon was ordained before he began: ordained by the past, no less than by the culture of eighteenth-century Virginia. So what we find there is layered, encrusted, in complex ways—a tantalizing set of clues, yes, but one that needs to be read with care and imagination.

CHAPTER I

An Uncommon Place

FEW OF US EVER BOTHER to examine the faces of old friends very closely, and so it is with Mount Vernon. If you visit Washington's home today, chances are you will come by car or bus along the George Washington Parkway. After purchasing tickets and entering, on foot, an imposing gateway, most people then follow a short avenue to the bottom of the flat expanse of lawn that the guidebooks identify as the bowling green. There, abruptly, the house comes into view, barely two hundred yards away, looking much as it must have in Washington's lifetime. Yet so familiar is it—so often has it been pictured in books, prints, and paintings (not to mention on postcards, coffee mugs, and dish towels)—that it is easy to stand before it and still not see the real thing.

By the same token, Mount Vernon tends to be everyone's picture-perfect, ideal "colonial" American home. The truth is, however, that even among eighteenth-century American houses of the grander sort it stands out as unusual. In Virginia such places were almost always built of brick; here only the chimneys, foundation, and garden walls are brick. The same houses make a notable show of "classical" architectural detail, yet Mount Vernon mixes its classicism with some decidedly nontraditional elements. Most such houses also went up in a single building campaign, but at Mount Vernon the process was more complicated and took much longer.

The distinctiveness of Washington's house was not lost on his contemporaries, though opinions on the subject varied. In the midst of the Revolution, while the house was undergoing major renovation, Bryan Fairfax, an old friend and neighbor, wrote Washington, "I was yesterday at Mt Vernon, where I hope it will please God to return you in time, & I like the House because it is uncommon for there has always appeared too great a Sameness in our Buildings."[1] Yet the "uncommon" house Bryan Fairfax admired left Baron Friedrich von Steuben—the man who did so much to mold Washington's troops into a properly drilled, European-style fighting force—singularly unimpressed. "If . . . Washington were not a better general than he was an architect the affairs of America would be in very bad condition," he confided to a friend after seeing Mount Vernon.[2]

There is no record of Washington's reaction to Fairfax's remark, and presumably von

Steuben's salvo never reached his commander's ears. The baron was right about one thing, however: Mount Vernon was George Washington's creation. The initial impression it made on visitors, too, was something on which he lavished a great deal of attention, and as it happens, the way today's tourists approach the house is not at all what he intended.

In the eighteenth century the main road to Mount Vernon ran from Alexandria inland, rather than along the river, as the modern parkway does. Much of the way was thickly wooded, and two steep hills had to be negotiated, but the road was reasonably good—at least in dry weather. Eventually came fields, orchards, and meadows belonging to Mount Vernon, and farther on, a pair of low wooden gates, above which, still the better part of a mile away, across a wide meadow loosely bordered by trees, appeared the house itself.

From that distance it would have been difficult to gauge its size precisely, but the many windows and doors suggested that it was quite substantial. From there also, the windows and doors would have seemed symmetrically placed, with the symmetry accentuated by the central pediment projecting from the low roof and, even more strongly, by

Mount Vernon, the west gate. Courtesy of the Mount Vernon Ladies' Association.

Mount Vernon, the west front. Courtesy of the Mount Vernon Ladies' Association.

the cupola rising above the entire composition. For unquestionably this *was* a composition: a carefully calculated combination of elements. And framed by the long belts of trees sweeping up from the foreground, it made a most attractive picture.

Beyond the wooden gates, a curving drive led through the trees, offering only an occasional glimpse of the house. The next full view came at the bottom of the bowling green, yet the effect remained much the same, with the size and symmetry of the house continuing to command attention, except that now, with less of the landscape intervening, the command became that much more insistent.

From the bottom of the bowling green a pair of matching serpentine drives wound their way to the house. These could be followed on foot, or the main drive could be taken in a wider arc past the stables and on toward the house. Again, trees and shrubbery covered much of the view, until the point where the plantings ended and the drives converged. Ahead lay an oval lawn set off from the cobblestones by a post and chain fence, and immediately beyond that stood the "great front door" of the mansion itself.

Mount Vernon, the river front. Courtesy of the Mount Vernon Ladies' Association.

Though this was the route most eighteenth-century visitors took to Mount Vernon, there was an alternative. To the east of the house the Potomac River stretched more than a mile wide across to Maryland. Along the Virginia side its shore was frequently broken by smaller streams and creeks, between which the land jutted out in a series of irregular promontories. It was on one of these that Mount Vernon stood, with the land in front of it falling away sharply to a substantial wharf below, which provided ready access by water.

At a height of one hundred and twenty-five feet above the river, the house could be seen from a considerable distance away, yet from any point its most arresting feature was the piazza. Covered by a flat extension of the main roof, the piazza rose a full two stories and ran the entire length of the east side of the house. Across the front the roof was supported by eight wooden pillars, square in shape and perfectly straight, with only the simplest of moldings. The pillars were also strikingly slender compared to the mass of the building, giving an overall impression of great height and lightness. Seen from the Potomac, Mount Vernon had an airy, almost magical quality.

But the view from the river was fleeting. In toward the shore the house slipped from sight, and the road to it led inland, up a steep bank planted with trees, to the west side of the building with its oval lawn. At that point the piazza was completely hidden from view, around the other side of the house.

Yet pausing by the oval lawn there were new things to notice, for clearly visible to left and right of the main house were two pairs of outbuildings. Along much of the way from both the west gate and the river they had been masked by trees, but once in view they defined a highly formal entrance courtyard. The pair nearest the house were linked to it by curved, covered arcades; the other pair stood close by them, facing, as their companions did, squarely into the central space. Like the main house, all four outbuildings were white, with dark red, wooden shingled roofs.

Again the impression was inescapable: symmetry, balance, the strong geometry of right angles and straight lines, only intermittently relieved by curves. But there were counterpoints to the composition that would have struck the eye almost as forcibly. The use of color—white walls, punctuated by green shutters at the windows and topped by the rich reddish-brown of the roofs—produced an effect of great liveliness. The arcades were also painted green, and rippling through their openings could be seen bits of the landscape beyond, softening the insistence on order implicit in the buildings.

Other details, too, suggested a kind of dissonance, or at any rate would have seemed surprising. If from a distance the west front of Mount Vernon appeared symmetrical, close at hand it looked anything but. The spaces separating the principal door and the windows on either side of it were noticeably unequal, with the greater space falling to the right. No doubt to divert attention from that fact, both the doorway and the pediment were placed slightly off-center relative to the cupola. Yet the ruse was largely unsuccessful, for the asymmetrical arrangement of the windows also meant that the left end of the pediment fell over the middle of a window, while the right end fell over a space between two windows. In addition, the pediment was placed so low on the roof that it had been necessary to eliminate the portions of the second-floor window-surrounds beneath it,

Outbuildings on either side of the west front of Mount Vernon. Courtesy of the Mount Vernon Ladies' Association.

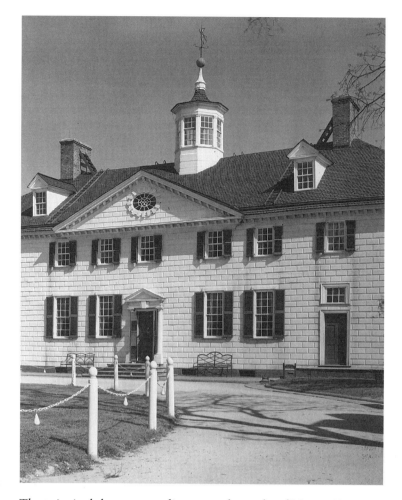

The principal doorway, pediment, and cupola of Mount Vernon, seen from the west. Courtesy of the Mount Vernon Ladies' Association.

emphasizing the asymmetry and making the pediment itself seem jammed onto the facade almost as an afterthought.

At this point it is easy enough to imagine von Steuben shaking his head. And still another problematic junction in the building occurred where the arcades met the main house, though there the difficulty was not too tight a fit but the reverse. For as they curved around from the flanking outbuildings, the arcades barely grazed the corners of the central structure. If their purpose was to provide cover from the elements, that could have been done either by carrying them squarely into the end walls of the house or by continuing them across the building to the two doors that stood on the left and right in front. But neither solution had been used. As a result, someone passing through the arcades—to get from the kitchen to the house, for example—had no choice but to cross the last twenty-five feet in the open.

Finally there was the material of the outside walls of the house. Their whiteness suggested that they were painted, and the use of paint on horizontal wooden clapboards was standard practice in Virginia, even then. Yet the walls of Mount Vernon were not clapboarded. Instead they displayed a pattern of rectangles, uniform in size and beveled at the edges, rising in courses from the foundation to the roof line, giving the impression of dressed stone masonry. In fact, however, the rectangles were made of wood, not stone, and painted white with sand added to the paint to further suggest the more expensive building material. In some lights the sham was more convincing than in others, but the merest tap, as one entered the house, would have revealed the truth.

In Washington's day visitors to Mount Vernon were greeted promptly, even when he was not at home, and people thought to be of any consequence were ushered into the central passage, which was not only the primary point of entry but also one of the house's most elaborately decorated spaces. In addition to walls completely covered with wooden paneling worked in a complicated pattern of rectangles, it boasted triangular pediments over four of its doorways, and to the west stood the great stairway with its curved railing,

The central passage and stairway of Mount Vernon. Courtesy of the Mount Vernon Ladies' Association.

turned spindles, and wide band of carving done in a Greek key pattern. After the Revolution all of this woodwork was painted brown and grained in contrasting tones to resemble mahogany, producing a rather somber effect. Decorated as it was and ringed with straightbacked chairs, the space was impressive and the work throughout was skillfully done, yet to a critical eye it might well have seemed that there was too much of it—too many elements, of too large a scale, in too small a space.

From the passage someone spending the night in the house would probably have been shown to one of the upstairs bedchambers. On the second and third floors there were no fewer than eight of those, but in keeping with their private character they were much more simply decorated than the rooms below. It was on the ground floor, in places like the passage, that Mount Vernon made its principal bid for the world's attention and respect.

But that did not mean all of the ground-floor rooms were alike. On the contrary, some were much more lavishly finished than others. Two that matched the passage in this respect were the large parlor and the dining room on the west side of the house. Of the two, the parlor was more like the passage, with paneling rising from floor to ceiling and pediments topping the doorways, which were further embellished with flanking

Mount Vernon, the west parlor. Courtesy of the Mount Vernon Ladies' Association.

Mount Vernon, the dining room. Courtesy of the Mount Vernon Ladies' Association.

pilasters finished with carved capitals. The *chef d'oeuvre* of the west parlor, however, was the chimneypiece. On either side of the fireplace opening, which was surrounded by marble, broad, carved scrolls reached from the floor to a frieze of carved arabesques abutting a pair of brackets supporting a shelf. Next came an overmantel with more scrollwork, within which was set a landscape painting done in oils, and above that a projecting, broken-scroll pediment centered with the Washington coat of arms. Completing the picture was the room's furniture, mostly mahogany chairs, and a multitude of family portraits.

Across the passage, the treatment of the dining room was different from that of the west parlor, yet fully as rich. Decorative carving surrounded the fireplace, but was even more finely done, with the motifs echoed above in an intricate cornice incorporating three separate bands of ornament. And on top of that, over the entire ceiling, spread a design deeply carved in raised plaster, alive with twisting, cascading scrolls, arabesques, and spiraling ropes of leaves, meeting an opposing pattern of festooned husks, surrounding a great wheel, also of husks, its sixteen spokes springing outward from a large central rosette. For pure dramatic impact, nothing at Mount Vernon matched the dining room.

*Mount Vernon, the small parlor. Courtesy of the Mount Vernon Ladies'
Association.*

The other two ground-floor rooms in this, the central core of the house, definitely
did not. Located on the eastward, river front of the building, both were distinctly plainer
than the rooms to the west. The simpler of the two served as an informal parlor or sitting room, and its only decorative detail consisted of a wooden chair rail and cornice, a
modest mantel, and a thin band of ornamental plasterwork around the ceiling. Furnished
as a bedchamber, the room across the passage had walls covered with paneling, yet the
chimneypiece and cornice were both relatively plain, and the ceiling had no decoration
at all.

As simple as these two rooms were, however, there remained the grandest space of
all at Mount Vernon—the very large room at the north end of the house. A full two
stories high, like the dining room it was richly ornamented with plasterwork. Swags
and garlanded husks decorated the entire ceiling, as well as the doorways and the outsized "Venetian" or Palladian window in the north wall. But unlike the dining room,
this one wore its splendors with an air of studied calm. So large was the space that it

could have absorbed even more decoration without appearing unduly burdened. The plasterwork was also notably flatter, done in lower relief, than in the dining room, and it was entirely contained within a pattern of geometric shapes, mostly rectangles, defined by molded borders. The same measured restraint, too, was evident in the room's furnishings. On either side of the Venetian window stood substantial mahogany sideboards, above which hung two very large mirrors, with simple gilt frames. There were also a pair of candlestands and a great many chairs, all of the same pattern. Except for rush matting, the floor was bare.

The last of the rooms on the ground floor of Mount Vernon was one few visitors ever saw. Located at the south end of the house, it was Washington's study. Two small spaces, which also acted as vestibules since they contained doors to the outside, buffered it from the adjoining dining room and bedchamber, and the room's furniture reinforced the impression that it was a private preserve: a desk; a dressing table; another small table, with a letterpress; and a large, freestanding globe. Along the east side of the room were built-in bookcases with glass doors. Only the fireplace wall, which included an over-

The large room at the north end of Mount Vernon. Courtesy of the Mount Vernon Ladies' Association.

Mount Vernon, Washington's study. The portrait is of Lawrence Washington, George Washington's older half-brother. Courtesy of the Mount Vernon Ladies' Association.

mantel somewhat awkwardly fitted into the space, was fully paneled. The other walls were plain plaster, painted white, with no ornament beyond a utilitarian chair rail. At some point the woodwork was false-grained in the same manner as the passage and remained that way as long as Washington lived.

Directly above the study and connected to it by a separate stairway in one of the vestibules was another very private space, the Washingtons' bedchamber. Usually referred to as "Mrs. Washington's room," it was even more plainly finished than the other bedchambers in the house, except for a pair of closets large enough to be used as dressing rooms, a luxury absent elsewhere at Mount Vernon.

While the study and the Washingtons' bedchamber went unseen by most of Mount Vernon's visitors, one space commented on in almost all accounts written at the time was the great open expanse of the piazza. Functioning as an integral part of the house and so placed that it invariably caught the breeze from the river, even on the hottest of Virginia summer days, it was a delightful place to sit, and seemed to be what almost everyone liked best about Mount Vernon. Today's tourists still linger contentedly in replicas of the sturdy, bottle-green Windsor chairs that Washington chose for it—linger and gaze out at the view, with its glorious sweep of river.

Could it be that for those tourists, no less than for their counterparts two centuries ago, the piazza offers a bit of welcome relief from the rest of the house? Compared to the relentless parade of contrasting, often highly decorated rooms inside, the simple square pillars that define the space look just substantial enough to do the work intended for them and hardly intrude at all on the view. Here light and air are everywhere. Here, too, is a generosity of scale, a commanding spaciousness commensurate with the character of the man whose house this was. Surely this is what one came to Mount Vernon expecting to find, hoping to find. Also, most of Washington's contemporaries had never seen anything like the piazza before and so were all the more charmed by it.

And seen it was, far oftener than the rest of the house. In later years Washington complained that he was endlessly bothered by visitors whenever he was at Mount Vernon. In truth many of them had been invited beforehand, and most of the rest carried proper letters of introduction. Yet the piazza was visible to anyone passing along the busy river. There it stood, rimming the east front of the building, half rustic and half sophisticated, making of it something simultaneously simple and grand, a fitting home for the greatest American of his generation, the model republican hero-statesman of the age. But then as

The view from the piazza at Mount Vernon. Courtesy of the Mount Vernon Ladies' Association.

Early engraving of Mount Vernon. Courtesy of the Chapin Library of Rare Books, Williams College.

suddenly as they materialized, miragelike in their bower of greenery, piazza and house together would disappear around the bend in the river.

This, then, was George Washington's home: an unusual house in a surpassingly beautiful setting. Yet once that has been said, going farther becomes difficult. In one sense, surely, Bryan Fairfax was right. Mount Vernon does have a distinctiveness and vitality often lacking in other houses of the period. But it is not a great monument of art history. It is no Monticello. It has none of the dazzling bravura and little of the finesse of Jefferson's masterpiece; its parts do not even cohere particularly well. In fact, the term "art" hardly seems to apply. Nor does the place appear to hold within it a single, neatly encoded message of any sort. It speaks in different tongues at different points, leaving us to blend the results as best we can.

One thing that does emerge with clarity, however, is a sense of will—of focused, purposeful choice. There is nothing casual or random about Mount Vernon. If its individual parts fail to cohere, one still senses that each of them was thoroughly thought out; that alternatives were considered and rejected; that what we see is what we were meant to see. And because of this, the place does seem to speak of the man whose will, choices, and objectives did so much to give it shape, and who was himself, after all, a singularly complex human being.

CHAPTER 2

The Washingtons of Virginia, 1657–1757

IN A LIFE BLESSED with more than a few fortuitous turns, it was no accident that Mount Vernon became George Washington's home. When he took it over at the age of twenty-two, it had already belonged to four generations of Washingtons, beginning with his great-grandfather John, who founded the family line in Virginia. In England, John Washington's clergyman father had been ousted from his living by Puritans, ostensibly for drinking too often in alehouses.[1] America was kinder. Restless, acquisitive, and ambitious, the family prospered from the start, early on becoming part of the colony's emerging elite. In the long run, however, it proved easier to rise into that group than it did to move upward through its ranks, and in that sense each generation discovered certain stubbornly persistent limits to its achievement. The principal problem was time. In Virginia, unlike the more orderly world "at home" in England, the pathways to raw opportunity lay ever open, and the Washingtons traveled tirelessly along them. Yet none of the men in the direct line from John to Augustine Washington, George's father, lived to the age of fifty. They all died with too many ventures incomplete, too much left undone.

In this history Mount Vernon played a changing role, and one that in its own way mirrored the Washingtons' fortunes. To the first two generations it was a wilderness tract of limited importance, a place that could be willed to younger children, but in time, as its value increased with the development of the area, the family's focus shifted there, at first tentatively, then decisively. Augustine Washington probably built the first permanent dwelling on the property, and his oldest son, George's half brother Lawrence, chose it as the center of his operations. It was George himself, however, who finally made it his home in the fullest sense, thereby linking it inextricably to his own destiny. But that was only after trying, without success, a very different means of establishing himself in life.

⸻

That first John Washington—"the immigrant," as he is sometimes called—decided to settle in Virginia in 1659 when the ship on which he was sailing as an officer and trading partner ran aground in the Potomac River. Evidently he liked what he saw of the area and perhaps found an added inducement to stay, because in no time at all he married Anne Pope, the daughter of a wealthy local planter. Over the next ten years he accumulated more than five thousand acres of land, much of it through headrights for servants brought over from England. Widowed twice, he remarried both times, acquiring more property with each marriage: a mill, a tavern, a shop, a prison, a courthouse. As an indication of his growing status he served as coroner and collector of taxes and eventually became a member of his parish vestry, a justice of the county court, a burgess, and a colonel in the militia. When Nathaniel Bacon's opposition to the policies of Governor William Berkeley flared into full-scale rebellion, John Washington sided with the governor and at one point led a party that butchered a small group of unarmed Indians. Afterward he proved equally assiduous in reclaiming land seized by Bacon's lieutenants.[2]

For land was and would remain the single most important key to success in Virginia. Colonists eager to increase their wealth sought out and patented tracts distant from their home plantations, then "seated" them, as the law required, with a rudimentary building or two and an initial planting of tobacco.[3] William Fitzhugh, one of the most successful Virginians of his generation, estimated in 1680 that it took the equivalent in value of thirty thousand pounds of tobacco to start a plantation,[4] but crops grown on newly developed land could yield impressive profits, provided the land was well located. Since tobacco packed in hogsheads was heavy, it was best to grow it near one of the deep rivers where its journey to market began. In Virginia four such rivers, each easily navigated by oceangoing ships, sliced through the eastern part of the colony between broad, fingerlike peninsulas. The Northern Neck, bounded by the Potomac and Rappahannock Rivers, was one of those peninsulas, and it was there, on the Potomac, that John Washington established himself.

Settlement in the region was still only in its first generation and had yet to move beyond the lower parts of the river to "The Freshes," as the area lying farther upstream, away from the salt water, was called. But the same year John Washington arrived in Virginia, several enterprising planters had secured patents as far up as Dogue Creek, which emptied into the Potomac two hundred eighty miles from Chesapeake Bay. One of those patents was for a piece of land running between Dogue and Little Hunting Creeks, on the south bank of the Potomac, opposite the Indian town of Piscataway. By 1669 the piece had already been patented twice, but no one had seated it. John Washington probably learned of it while acting as attorney for his widowed sister-in-law, whose husband had acquired the adjoining land, and with opportunity beckoning, he hurried to have a survey done in partnership with Nicholas Spencer, a fellow burgess.[5]

As eager as the two men were to proceed, they must have taken the step with some trepidation. A few years earlier, Charles II had granted proprietorship of the entire Northern Neck to seven of his former comrades in exile, provoking intense anxiety in Virginia over the status of the grants that the colony itself had made in the area. But perhaps Nicholas Spencer, who was already on his way to becoming a member of the governor's council, also knew of a modified version of the proprietorship that had only just been negotiated in England. Under its terms, all titles issued before 1661 would be recognized by the proprietors as long as the land claimed was in actual possession by May 8, 1669. The point for Washington and Spencer was this: if the current patentee, Richard

Chesapeake Bay, the Potomac River, and the Northern Neck, showing the location of Mount Vernon on the upper left, in Fairfax County. Taken from the map of Virginia in the 1786 French edition of Thomas Jefferson's Notes on Virginia. *Courtesy of the Chapin Library of Rare Books, Williams College.*

Lee, failed to seat the piece in question by May of that year (and it was already April), it would revert to the proprietorship and could be theirs if they wished to patent it.[6]

Lee did lose the property, but another five years passed before Washington and Spencer secured title to it. The agents initially sent over by the proprietors issued few new patents. Then, when the proprietors proceeded to insist on a resurvey of all land already taken up in the Northern Neck as headrights, many Virginians were concerned enough to try to buy them out. Finally a new agent arrived, who issued fifteen patents, including one to Washington and Spencer for the land they had surveyed plus an additional one thousand acres. The patent came at the direct order of Lord Thomas Culpepper, one of the proprietors, who also happened to be a cousin of Nicholas Spencer's and shortly afterward became governor of Virginia.

Thus the Little Hunting Creek tract, the nucleus of Mount Vernon, became the property of John Washington. But three years later, setting the pattern that was to haunt the family for decades, he died suddenly, while still relatively young. Whether he had seated the Little Hunting Creek tract is unclear. His will mentions the land but no improvements on it. The times were unsettled, and labor was chronically scarce in Virginia. Still, to seat a grant, one had to cultivate only a single acre, however indifferently, and put up the simplest sort of structure—"be it but an Hog-House, it serves the Turn"—so something was probably done after all.[7]

Lawrence Washington, John's principal heir, was just eighteen when his father died and may still have been in school in England at the time. Under the terms of the will, he inherited the plantation given to his father and mother by her father, as well as other land, including the Little Hunting Creek tract.[8] As befitted his position, he held a number of offices in the colony over the next two decades. By the age of twenty-one he was already a justice of the county court, and four years later he won election to the Virginia House of Burgesses. He married the daughter of a former Speaker of the House and probably traveled to England again after his marriage. In time, no doubt, he would have added considerably to his holdings, but he was to die at age thirty-eight, leaving three children—John, the eldest; Augustine; and Mildred, who was still an infant.[9]

Meanwhile, Nicholas Spencer had died in 1689, and to settle his estate, Lawrence Washington and Nicholas Spencer's widow had divided the Little Hunting Creek property the following year. The Mount Vernon archives contain a well-drawn plat, dated 1690, showing the division. As surveyed, the two portions were slightly unequal. When Lawrence offered Spencer's widow the choice of either piece, she took the larger, more valuable one and paid him twenty-five hundred pounds of tobacco as compensation.[10]

Whatever use Lawrence may have made of the Little Hunting Creek property, either before or after the division, is lost in a welter of confusing, if intriguing, evidence. The 1690 plat shows two houses on the piece. The depictions are stylized, and neither one of the two appears to be located where Mount Vernon stands today. In the cellar of the present house, however, are traces of two earlier foundations, one inside the other. The innermost, earliest set of walls is made of soft sandstone from the river, and imbedded in it is a rectangular stone (now a replica, the original having been removed for safekeeping) carved with a heart flanked by halberds and the initials "LW." The design appears to belong more to the seventeenth than to the eighteenth century, but the stone bears no date, and its original use is unclear. If, as is generally assumed, it was intended as a cornerstone, why is the date lacking?[11]

The cornerstone theory also suggests that at some point Lawrence may have—and with a certain amount of flourish—set his mark on the Little Hunting Creek property by erecting a fairly substantial building on it, yet in all likelihood this was not the case. Since he himself never lived at Little Hunting Creek, the only possible use for such a structure would have been to house tenants, two of whom were mentioned in his will: "Mrs. Elizabeth Minton and Mrs. Williams."[12] However, at that date it would have been extremely

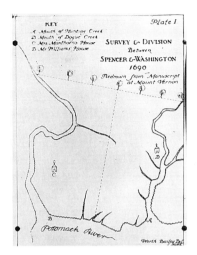 

Left: *Drawing based on the survey dividing the Little Hunting Creek property between Lawrence Washington and Madam Spencer. Courtesy of the Mount Vernon Ladies' Association.*

Right: *The "LW" stone, Mount Vernon. Courtesy of the Mount Vernon Ladies' Association.*

unusual to build housing for tenants substantial enough to have masonry foundations. Mrs. Minton and Mrs. Williams surely lived somewhere, but if either of them had a house where Mount Vernon stands today, no clearly identifiable trace of it remains.

———

Under the terms of Lawrence Washington's will, his infant daughter Mildred inherited the tract at Little Hunting Creek. His more valuable holdings, including the home plantation near Pope's Creek on the lower Potomac, went to his eldest son, John. Augustine, the second oldest—who would one day father George Washington—received eleven hundred acres, seven hundred of them subject to life tenancies, but since he was only three years old at the time, it would be a while before he could do much to develop that patrimony.[13]

In the intervening years, too, Virginia's economy and society underwent a series of momentous changes. In 1690 a prolonged depression in the price of tobacco began. Altogether fifty years would pass before Virginians enjoyed again the solid prosperity they had known through much of the seventeenth century. Many people suffered as a result, but for those with a solid toehold in the colony's plantation economy the opposite was sometimes true. Given enough good land and a little extra capital, or access to credit, enterprising planters could acquire what was rapidly becoming the *sine qua non* of profitable agriculture in the region: black slaves. With slaves to do the work, plantation operations became more efficient, and planters with large crews could patent added land for future generations. Slaves also brought leisure for other pursuits—holding office, for example, or cultivating those graces that defined a "gentle" man or woman.[14]

It was during these years, in fact, that a uniquely powerful gentry class came to dominate Virginia. Distancing themselves more and more in economic and social terms from those below them, a small group of families managed through intermarriage and other strategies to perpetuate their standing for a century and more. With the return of prosperity, when tobacco prices rose again after 1740, members of the group moved quickly to consolidate a virtual monopoly of political power in the colony, thanks to an adroitly constructed alliance with their yeoman farmer neighbors. A generation later, descendants of the same individuals would lead Virginians in the protracted struggle against Great Britain that resulted in American independence.

Despite everything the gentry class achieved, however, at no time could its position simply be taken for granted. Often at odds with the colony's governor, it also faced repeated challenges from below. At the same time, its members had to contend with all the problems inherent in dependence on a single staple crop. To combat falling tobacco prices the gentry worked to limit the supply of tobacco and improve its quality through various legally mandated warehousing and inspection schemes. While the necessary legislation passed, opposition from small planters ran high and in some cases led to open violence. Nor could any act of government alter tobacco's greatest liability—its tendency to sap the fertility of even the best soil after a few seasons. To solve that problem the gentry needed a steady supply of virgin land, and the result was an unending, often ruthless, scramble after ever larger holdings of fresh acreage.

Not a little of that activity focused on the proprietorship lands in the Northern Neck. In 1702 Robert "King" Carter, ironically enough once an outspoken opponent of encroachments on colonists' rights by the proprietorship, became its agent and began at once to patent huge amounts of property for himself and his family. Briefly sidetracked when Thomas Lee (who proved equally tireless at feathering his own nest) served for a time as agent, Carter was reappointed in 1719. By then he had become the richest, most powerful man in the Northern Neck, but his acquisitive instincts remained as boundless as ever. Over the next five years he assigned fully 90,000 acres to himself, his children, and grandchildren, a total to which he managed to add another 118,000 acres by 1731. And Carter was hardly alone in such pursuits. In the midst of negotiating a treaty to clear the territory south of the Rapidan River of Indians, Governor Alexander Spotswood had his agents grab 68,000 acres of prime land in the area, while his associates were helping themselves to another 54,000 acres.[15]

Most of these vast holdings were intended for later resale or for growing tobacco, but their owners were also quick to discover that other opportunities lay within their reach, opportunities not dependent on future land values or tobacco prices. With the growth in British manufactures, the demand for iron had risen steadily, causing investors to eye with increasing interest the iron ore deposits then being discovered in Maryland and Virginia. Governor Spotswood had plans to develop the area north of Fredericksburg, where rich veins of iron had been found, and on retiring from office he began importing German families to set up the mines and furnaces needed to produce pig iron.[16] Farther up the Potomac near Little Falls, King Carter and Thomas Lee were both prospecting for ore. In those activities, moreover, they were soon to be joined by Augustine Washington, though in other respects he was scarcely in their league.[17]

The most appealing of the early Washingtons, George Washington's father, "Gus," as he was known, proved to be both more energetic than his father, Lawrence, and more successful at adding to his wealth. Yet in his restless drive to increase his holdings he also spread himself—and his resources—dangerously thin at times. Certainly that was true of his mining and manufacturing operations, which were never meant to be more than profitable sidelines.

An imposing figure of a man, Gus made a good match in Jane Butler and soon afterward bought property close to where his grandfather had settled, on Pope's Creek in Westmoreland County. By 1722 he was having a house built there for his family, plus a mill nearby. Meanwhile, he also began speculating in land that might turn out to be rich in iron ore. Following the discovery of deposits on several tracts along Accokeek Creek above Fredericksburg, one of which he had already patented, he added 349 acres to his holdings and, in exchange for a share in the enterprise, leased the property to a London-based company called Principio Iron Works. Had he been more cautious he might have stopped there. Instead, by July 1726 he had acquired and leased another 1,600 acres to Principio. In return, the other investors agreed to build a furnace and share their profits with Washington, but there were also certain imperfectly spelled-out responsibilities he committed himself to beyond providing the land.[18]

In fact, so muddled was the second Principio contract that Washington twice traveled to England to clarify its terms. Moreover, to protect his interests he came to play a growing role in actually operating the works at Accokeek. Yet his primary occupation remained tobacco-growing, as he proved when, in the midst of his negotiations with Principio, he bought the Little Hunting Creek tract from his sister, Mildred.

In many ways the timing of the purchase was curious. Augustine was still developing his plantation at Pope's Creek. His new house there was just being finished. But land was land, and perhaps he sensed that the less thoroughly cultivated tract farther up the Potomac was going to be worth more than the £180 he paid his sister for it. In any case, it had become his by October 1726. At about the same time it also came to be called Eppsewasson, after a small creek on the property, and in less than a decade, hoping perhaps to capitalize on his earlier decision to buy the place, Augustine took his family there to live. Meanwhile, his first wife had died, and he had found another, Mary Ball. The oldest child of that union, born at Pope's Creek in 1732, was given the name George. As young as he was when the Washingtons left Westmoreland County, he cannot have had many memories of the place. Nor would the move from Pope's Creek to Eppsewasson be the family's last. In 1738, barely three years after settling there, Augustine transferred operations again, this time to a newly purchased plantation near Fredericksburg, which had the advantage of being closer to the iron furnace at Accokeek Run, where he was finding it necessary to spend more and more time.[19]

When the Washingtons moved to the Fredericksburg property, a fairly substantial house already stood on it. The most they could have found earlier at Eppsewasson was a tenant's quarter, which almost certainly would not have met their needs. So a fair amount of building must have preceded that initial move, and in all likelihood the result was a house, sitting on the stone foundations still partially visible in the cellar of Mount Vernon. It appears to have consisted of two rooms and possibly a passage on the first floor, topped by a half story above containing another two rooms, squeezed in under the eaves. There would also have been several adjacent outbuildings, including a separate kitchen. Such was the establishment that constituted the kernel of what eventually became George Washington's home.

The house in Fredericksburg provided more ample quarters, with as many as seven rooms, though still in a structure only a story and a half high.[20] In turn, too, that house located the Washingtons quite accurately in the colony's emerging social landscape. While such places were becoming more common by the middle of the eighteenth century, they remained far superior to what an ordinary yeoman farmer would have owned. However, the differences were just as great looking at a wholly new kind of house that had begun to appear in Virginia during those years—one far more imposing than anything seen up to then.

Before 1725, Virginians built their houses almost exclusively of wood. Because it was plentiful and could be moved and worked easily, building in wood cost much less than building in stone or brick. For most of the seventeenth century, few people even bothered with masonry foundations. Instead they made do with various types of "earthfast" construction, utilizing timbers set directly on or in the ground. Elsewhere in America earthfast houses were considered temporary expedients to be replaced as soon as resources permitted. Their major drawback was their relatively short life: wood soon rots if left in contact with damp earth. But in Virginia the trade-off for anything more permanent was likely to be fewer funds for new purchases of land and slaves. Also, given the rate at which tobacco exhausted the soil, making the most of one's chances often meant having to relocate every ten or twelve years. In that situation, what difference did it make whether a house lasted twenty years or a hundred? Like most Virginians of his generation, George Washington was born in an earthfast house.[21]

Nevertheless, at some point the colony's rising grandees' thoughts about housing began to shift in favor of permanence. The concerns that led to the change were primarily political and cultural, not financial. Impermanent housing continued to make good economic sense in Virginia, but at the upper levels of society there were other imperatives to consider. At home in England an appropriate family "seat" had long been a badge of membership in the ruling class. Politically as well as socially the effect was to legitimize family power by simultaneously giving substance to its roots in the land and elevating it, on that foundation, to the level of national prominence. For a group like the Virginia gentry, eager to consolidate its position yet still facing stiff opposition over issues such as tobacco inspection, here was a telling lesson in how superior power might be represented to the world at large. In England, too, the aristocratic family seat was no urban palace or town house but a place quintessentially in and of the countryside, a figure in the rural landscape, the only arrangement possible in Virginia.

To be sure, the scale of things was different. There would be no tidewater Hatfield Houses or Castle Howards, no attempts to duplicate the grandeur and opulence of the enormous piles belonging to those in the premier ranks of Britain's aristocracy. Instead, it was the substantial sort of house favored by the prosperous British gentry that the new

Westover, the Byrd family seat on the James River. Photograph by William H. Pierson.

"mansions" of the Virginia elite would most closely resemble. Still, in a world of one- or two-room earthfast houses generally unpainted and often in poor condition, the message was clear. Brick-built, foursquare, with symmetrically ordered facades, deep roofs, and flanking brick dependencies, such houses spoke unmistakably of permanence and power.[22]

Also, by the time the gentry began the effort, the Governor's Palace in the new capital city of Williamsburg was available as a model. One of three major focal points in a town plan that itself configured power in elaborately precise ways, it was the first house in Virginia to combine brick construction, a two-and-one-half-story, five-bay elevation, and "classical" architectural details.[23] No private dwelling would copy it *in toto*, but well over one hundred houses built in the colony over the next two generations would incorporate all or most of these features. Nor was this simply a matter of imitating the latest style. In the high-stakes game the gentry class was playing, the opposition of the governor could be every bit as troublesome as resistance from below. Brick houses might not prevent such an eventuality, but they would at least make clear how seriously the gentry took its prerogatives and how little inclined its members were to rate anyone else's power—including the governor's—above their own.

For the family of Gus Washington, however, there were to be no brick houses. In his hectic pursuit of the main chance, he moved too often to establish a proper "seat." He

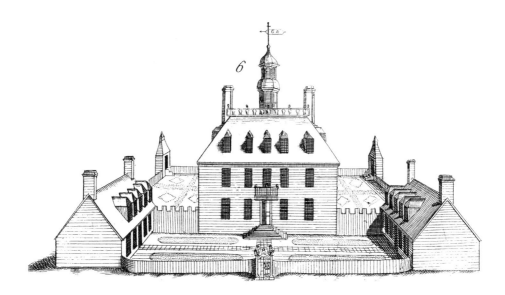

Early view of the Governor's Palace, Williamsburg, taken from an engraving discovered in the Bodleian Library, Oxford University. The engraving was used as the basis for the twentieth-century reconstruction of the building. Courtesy of the Colonial Williamsburg Foundation.

also lacked the means. Though he was not unsuccessful in what he set out to do, at his death in 1743 none of his scattered ventures had reached maturity. He left some ten thousand acres in at least seven different tracts, which was more than respectable, yet "King" Carter had managed to lay his hands on twenty times that much.[24] And where Carter had owned more than seven hundred slaves when he died, Augustine Washington's inventory listed only forty-nine, too few by half to place him in the first rank of Virginia's slave owners.

Neither were such holdings large enough to support an equal division among the seven surviving children of Augustine's two marriages. Instead, what amounted to the lion's share of the estate, including both Eppsewasson on Little Hunting Creek and the interest in the iron furnace at Accokeek Run, went to Lawrence, the eldest son of the first marriage. In contrast, George, as the eldest son of the second marriage, received only the much smaller holding at Fredericksburg, several pieces of undeveloped land, and ten slaves.[25]

As it happened, George Washington never took much of an interest in the Fredericksburg property. During the decade after Augustine's death he was increasingly at Eppsewasson—or Mount Vernon, as it was now renamed—where his half brother Lawrence lived. Never particularly close to his mother, George seems to have idolized Lawrence, who, like his father and grandfather before him, had been educated in England, as George himself might have been had his father lived. Lawrence Washington could also claim the distinction of having served under Admiral Edward Vernon in the Caribbean, hence the new name for Eppsewasson. But even more important, being at Mount Vernon during those years offered certain tantalizing opportunities to someone setting out in life—as George Washington was—with nothing more than a modest inheritance to his name.

The palpable sign of those opportunities had appeared in the early 1740s, in the form of an imposing brick "great house," built on the point of land just south of the Little Hunting Creek property. The first such house in the neighborhood, it must have caused a considerable stir, but then everything about its owner and his family would have aroused intense curiosity, for Colonel William Fairfax was no ordinary newcomer to the Northern Neck, or to Virginia. In 1733 he had been chosen to serve as chief agent for his cousin Thomas, sixth Baron Fairfax, who, as a result of his grandmother's marriage to Lord Culpepper, was now the sole proprietor of the Northern Neck. Wise in the ways of the world, the colonel had depended all his life on the favor of richer, more powerful men. He remained ambitious for himself and his children, but perhaps because of his own experience he could also be a generous and thoughtful patron.[26]

From the start, too, the presence of the Fairfaxes at Belvoir, as their new home was called, was to prove singularly advantageous for both Lawrence Washington and his brother George. With the colonel and his family came a whole new style of life, made manifest in Belvoir itself, which was very much the kind of place leading Virginians were building during those years.[27] With the Fairfaxes also came multiple ties to the world

Conjectural drawing of the Fairfax family's Belvoir. Courtesy U.S. Army Garrison, Fort Belvoir.

beyond the Northern Neck, not only to the proprietor in England, with his vast holdings in the west, but to the government in Williamsburg, where the colonel was a member of the governor's council, as well as to British officialdom throughout America. And for the Washingtons those ties soon became family ties, thanks to Lawrence's marriage to Anne Fairfax, or Nancy, as she was called, one of the colonel's daughters.[28]

That piece of good fortune was followed by others. In 1745 Lord Thomas Fairfax reached a final, highly favorable agreement with the crown, settling the previously disputed boundaries of the proprietorship and confirming his exclusive right to dispose of more than five million acres between the headsprings of the Rappahannock and Potomac Rivers.[29] At the same time the Fairfaxes, along with Lawrence Washington and a group of partners that included influential London investors and Governor Robert Dinwiddie of Virginia, were joining forces to seek a grant of five hundred thousand acres in the Ohio Valley. By settling families there, they hoped both to secure the area against the French and to establish a profitable fur trade with the Indians. Closer to home, when the new town of Alexandria was organized, Lawrence served as one of its trustees. He also won appointment as adjutant general of the colony and eventually took his place in the House of Burgesses.[30]

In the space of a few years, in short, Lawrence Washington became a person of considerable consequence. In keeping with his rising stature, at some point he also decided to rebuild the house at Little Hunting Creek that he had inherited from his father, and once he decided to rebuild, he proceeded boldly. In a single, clean sweep, he eliminated everything his father had built aboveground. Then he had the existing sandstone foundation, now laid bare, enlarged along its outside perimeter with additions of brick and rubble (including, perhaps, the "LW" stone), plus a completely new set of brick foundation walls extending to the north. These changes made it possible both to widen the footprint of the house slightly and to add as much as eight feet to its length. On top of the altered foundation, new wooden framing then went up as well as new chimneys to provide corner fireplaces on the interior, and with the framing in place, the walls were closed in and covered with clapboards.

All of this work appears to have been done in considerable haste. The extension of the foundation to the north enclosed only a crawl space, not a full cellar. The expanded foundation posed serious problems later, when changes were made in the structure. Also, inside the house the rooms seem to have been finished with nothing more than plain plaster walls, baseboards, chair rails, and simple window, door, and fireplace surrounds—at least initially.[31]

The reason why Lawrence was in such a hurry to rebuild the house is unclear, but he may well have been rushing to get it ready for his new bride. That would put the changes in 1743, the year of his marriage to Anne Fairfax. His father had died only a few months before, and possibly he made the two decisions—to marry and to rebuild—together, counting on his inheritance to cover the costs.

The house in its new configuration contained a passage and four ground-floor rooms, which in the inventory of Lawrence's estate were listed as "The Hall," "Parlour & Passage," "The Red Room," and "Mrs. Lee's Room" (Lee being the name of Anne Fairfax Washington's second husband). In addition, there were four small rooms above, on the second floor.[32] Outside, on the east and west fronts, the windows were symmetrically arranged in the best classical manner.[33] Though the house was still only a story and a half high, it was at least as large as Gus Washington's house in Fredericksburg and would have cut a decidedly more impressive figure than the one he had built earlier at Eppsewasson—the structure Lawrence started with.

This, then, was the place Lawrence proudly renamed "Mount Vernon," in honor of his former commander. Though not everything its owner, or his bride, might have wished, it was a beginning, and in time much could have been done to improve it. By the end of the decade, however, Lawrence was already seriously ill, and the most he may have accomplished, beyond the initial expansion of the house, was fitting the ground-floor room in the southeastern corner with elaborate wood paneling.

In George Washington's day the same room served as a downstairs bedchamber and was at the back of the house relative to the principal entrance, which was on the western—or land—side. But in earlier years the main entrance may well have been on the east, facing the river. At a time when most traffic in Virginia still moved by water, this would not have been unusual. And the elaborate decoration of the room in question is consistent with its having been given pride of place, next to the main entrance. In that place and decorated as it was, it could well have served as Lawrence's "Hall."[34]

Halls had once been multipurpose rooms in which all the basic functions of domestic life went on, including cooking, eating, and sleeping. Over time many of those functions, at least in larger houses, had migrated to other spaces, leaving halls to be used primarily for entertaining guests.[35] Listed in the hall in the inventory of Lawrence's estate were several tables of various sizes, a large number of chairs, and numerous dishes, glasses, and silver eating utensils, all of which point to entertaining as the primary use of the space.[36] And as a hall, this particular room would have acquitted itself quite respectably, with its fully paneled walls, crisp chair rail and cornice, and handsome chimneypiece. Though the cornice is unenriched with any sort of added, classical styling, and details like the chair rail follow patterns rarely used in Virginia after 1750 (thus the early dating of the room's finish), each of these elements was carefully planned, and planned in relation to the others, so that together they form an integrated whole. All of the shapes are geometric, and for the most part rectilinear. The material throughout is wood, but its identity and character are masked by paint. Human will controls everything the eye sees, and a highly disciplined, calculating will at that. Here, unmistakably, is the rational mind of the eighteenth century at work. If the room existed in this state when George Washington remade the ground floor of Mount Vernon, changing almost everything about it, this was one space that survived intact.

But even if Lawrence did refinish the room as his hall, much else remains unclear. When did he order the work done, and how did it relate to the other changes he had made, or might have been planning to make, at Mount Vernon? Was it the final flourish of his earlier building campaign, or was he contemplating additional changes, in which a newly decorated hall would be only a first step?

Of the latter two possibilities, the second seems more likely, for in Lawrence's world the stakes had continued to mount with regard to houses. When Augustine Washington moved to Eppsewasson, the Fairfaxes' Belvoir had not yet been built; a decade later it

Mount Vernon, the ground-floor bedchamber which initially may have been Lawrence Washington's hall. Courtesy of the Mount Vernon Ladies' Association.

was the only place of its kind in the neighborhood. Within five years, however, similar houses had begun to appear, including one in nearby Alexandria built entirely of dressed stone by another Fairfax son-in-law, John Carlyle. Under the circumstances it is hard to imagine Lawrence not wondering what more he could do with his own house—wondering and perhaps even making plans for another general overhaul.

Yet all the while his health continued to deteriorate. The problem was tuberculosis. A trip to England for medical advice, months spent trying to regain his strength, first in Barbados, with George as company, then in Bermuda—nothing seemed to help. His cough only grew worse; he grew steadily weaker. On June 20, 1752, four days after returning from Bermuda, he signed his will. He died a little more than a month later, on July 26.[37]

The record hints that even then, work on Mount Vernon may have been under way. Of the three men who witnessed Lawrence's will, two were "joyners."[38] One of them, William Waite, so impressed John Mercer, the Washingtons' lawyer, that within a year he had apprenticed his son to him for architectural training.[39] In the accounts drawn up after Lawrence's death, both Waite and the other joiner/witness, John North, were listed among those to whom money was owed.[40] So too was Colonel Richard Blackburn, a builder or "undertaker" who lived nearby and sometimes styled himself as an architect. Nowhere in any of the documents is there mentioned a specific project on which these individuals might have been working, however. It could have been the refurbished hall; it could have been the beginning of something more ambitious; in the case of Waite and North it could also have been something as immediately needful as Lawrence's coffin.

According to the terms of Lawrence's will, his widow, Anne, was to have life interest in Mount Vernon, and Sarah, the only one of their four children still living, would inherit after her.[41] If Sarah died without issue, the property would go, as Gus Washington had stipulated in his will ten years before, to George, the oldest son of his second marriage, and essentially that is what happened.[42] Within six months of her husband's death, Anne Washington had remarried and moved to Westmoreland County. Her daughter Sarah died two years later, in 1754, and before the year was out, George had arranged to lease Mount Vernon for the full term of his sister-in-law's life interest.[43]

So with the stroke of a pen, George Washington—at age twenty-two—became master of Mount Vernon. Of the many roles he was to play in life, it would be simultaneously, perhaps, the most pleasurable and the most frustrating. For the moment, however, he had other things to think about. War, long anticipated, had finally broken out, and his own future remained in every way unsettled. Unsettled, yet by no means bleak, for characteristically he had used the time since his father's death to good advantage.

By the age of fifteen he had already become the sort of person other people noticed. Tall and blessed with a strong physique, he excelled at horsemanship and loved hunting. He had taken up dancing and learned to play a good hand of cards. Although his schooling was rudimentary, he had dutifully copied assorted rules of polite conduct from Francis Hawkins's *Youth's Behavior*. At some point he had read *The Spectator* and a history of England, perhaps at the suggestion of Colonel Fairfax, whose library was impressive. For a visit to Belvoir in 1748, his packing list included a razor, nine shirts, six linen waistcoats, four neck cloths, and seven caps.[44] Clothes mattered. They were part of the impression one made, and the circle at Belvoir had recently been joined by no less a personage than Lord Thomas Fairfax, the great proprietor himself.

Yet as important as linen waistcoats and rules of polite conduct might have seemed, they were hardly enough to build a life on. Earlier there had been talk of George's going to sea to make his fortune, but his mother had balked. That left the land, and no doubt at first because it seemed a good way to earn some ready money, he had learned to use a set of surveyor's tools left in one of the storehouses in Fredericksburg by his father. Soon he was taking in enough cash to serve occasionally, in a small way, as banker for his friends and relatives.[45]

He also seems to have genuinely enjoyed surveying, which after all was far more than simply a way of keeping a young man's pockets full. In a society where the ownership of land was everything and where, from a few days' ride away, the wilderness stretched on seemingly forever, surveying was a vital tool for transforming the natural world into wealth. Streams, hills, outcroppings of rock, stands of ancient timber—all of them could become points between which lines could be run, dividing the landscape into neat, acquirable segments, transmuting it into the stuff of ownership, of profit, of riches. Here truly was a set of skills to conjure with, an alchemy for grabbing hold of the promise that seemed everywhere in the air, as men like the colonel and Lord Fairfax talked of vast tracts to the north, to the west, and beyond, in the Ohio Valley.

Some of all this Washington had a chance to see firsthand—while honing his skills as a surveyor—in 1748, the year after Lord Fairfax's arrival in Virginia, when he was asked to accompany the colonel's oldest son, George William, and a small company on an exploration of the back country of the Northern Neck. On the third day out, on the other side of the Blue Ridge Mountains, Washington wrote in his journal, "Rode to his Lordships Quarter about 4 Miles higher up the River we went through most beautiful Groves of Sugar Trees & spent the best part of the Day in admiring the Trees & richness of the land."[46] There were to be other, similar trips to the west, including one with Lawrence to Berkeley Springs, where together they looked for likely pieces of land to buy. Surveying also brought Washington his first official appointment. On July 20, 1749, after swearing the requisite oaths, he became surveyor of Culpepper County. And with the money he made applying his skills there and elsewhere he began buying land for himself, an activity that became yet another lifelong preoccupation.

During these years, too, he was discovering that the world could be surveyed in more ways than one. Societies had hills and valleys just as the natural landscape did, and one could measure the heights and depths there, too. While he was in Barbados during that last, futile attempt of Lawrence's to regain his health, they stayed in private houses because the island had no public inns. Reflecting on what he found, George noted in his journal that everyone seemed to be either very rich or very poor: "there are few who may be calld midling people."[47]

As the owner of a minor, relatively unfertile farm, he himself was certainly not rich. On the other hand, he had already picked up several thousand acres of land in the back country, aligning his interests with those of the Fairfaxes as well as those of the Ohio Company, and significant developments were occurring on that front. Governor Dinwiddie, one of the Ohio Company's members, was trying to secure the area against French claims and the constant threat of Indian raids so that homesteaders could settle along the fertile river valleys. In part his activities reflected his personal stake in the matter, but he also cherished a sweeping imperial vision that saw British power spreading ever more broadly across the continent. Like other visionaries, too, he could be thoroughly ruthless in pursuit of his objectives, though in company he was usually genial enough. When Washington returned from Barbados, he rode to Williamsburg to deliver letters to the governor, who asked him to stay and dine at the palace. The subject of the back country would surely have come up then.[48]

Six months later Lawrence was dead, and as much as he had tried to put his affairs in order after returning to Mount Vernon, there were debts and tangles of conflicting claims that took time to settle. On three separate occasions John Mercer, the family's lawyer, had to go to Williamsburg to represent the estate in legal actions. George, as one of the executors (along with John Carlyle and George William Fairfax), acted as bookkeeper, making careful lists of all accounts outstanding. In September 1752 appraisers were appointed, and the inventory was completed by December, the same month that Anne Washington left to embark on a new life in Westmoreland County.

In due course, all of the items in Lawrence's estate were distributed, but there was

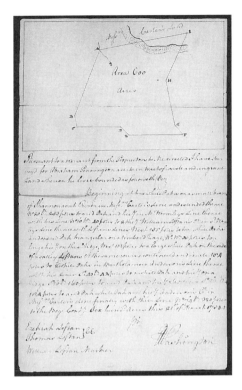

LEFT: *Early survey plat drawn by George Washington. Courtesy of the Chapin Library of Rare Books, Williams College.*

RIGHT: *Governor Robert Dinwiddie, by an unknown artist. Courtesy of the National Portrait Gallery, London, England*

one thing, not on any list, that had belonged to his brother that George particularly coveted—the adjutancy of the colony. If surveying nurtured visions of wealth, military service offered rewards of a different sort, above all a chance for personal glory and renown. This too was a passion that would drive Washington for years to come. The adjutancy was a modest enough beginning, a part-time position that involved little more than reviewing local militia units and raising troops for the colony, if any were needed. Yet who could tell what might come of such a post in less peaceful times?

Washington's bid for the adjutancy had the support of the Fairfaxes, but perhaps because of Dinwiddie's anxiety over the western territories, or the large number of candidates, he decided to split the position in three, with each adjutant having responsibility for a separate district. Several months later the council went even further and divided the colony into four military districts. Finally word came that George had been named adjutant for the southern district, which stretched from the James River to the borders of North Carolina. He would have preferred the Northern Neck, and eventually the change was made, but in the meantime he needed a uniform, and an order went off to a London merchant via John Carlyle in Alexandria for the makings of one: a gold shoulder knot, gold lace, twenty-four inches of "rich gold Embroidd Loops," a "Rich Crimson Ingr[ained] silk Sash," four dozen gilt coat buttons, a hat with gold lace, three and a half yards of scarlet cloth, two yards of blue, and so on. With the attendant expenses, including searchers' fees in London, entry fees, freight, lading, and commissions, the bill came to £28.10.3, a hefty sum, but apparently the dignity of Washington's new position demanded nothing less.[49]

In the meantime, the situation on the western frontier had become increasingly tense, as French forces moved into territory claimed by England at the headwaters of the Ohio River. Prompted by repeated warnings from Dinwiddie, London finally authorized a mission to the area formally calling on the French to withdraw. Sensing a rare opportunity, Washington hurried to Williamsburg and volunteered to carry the message, an offer the governor's council readily accepted. Thus in the autumn of 1753, Washington began his role as Dinwiddie's agent in securing the backlands for Britain.

The expedition proved to be a great adventure, appropriately full of hazard. The French, though polite to the British party, clearly had every intention of strengthening their position on the Ohio. The Indians were sometimes helpful and sometimes not. The weather was dreadful. On the return trip, proceeding ahead of his party on foot, Washington survived not only an assassination attempt by his Indian guide but also a death-defying plunge into the icy waters of the Monongahela. All of this was duly described in his report to Dinwiddie, which was rushed into print as soon as he returned to Williamsburg.[50]

The publication of Washington's journal won him a certain amount of fame, and he was placed on active pay as a captain, in addition to what he already earned as adjutant. Dinwiddie's position was also considerably strengthened. After bargaining with the burgesses, he was finally authorized in February 1754 to raise a regiment to protect a small contingent he had sent out earlier to build a fort where the Monongahela and the Allegheny Rivers joined to form the Ohio. Washington, as lieutenant colonel, would be second in command to Joshua Fry, but he would have only a Virginia commission, not one in the regular British army, which seemed acutely unfair. Colonel Fairfax persuaded him to accept the offer, however, and agreed to use his influence to have the pay increased.[51]

In mid-March Dinwiddie, feeling that time was of the essence, urged Washington to begin his march to the Ohio at once. Fry planned to follow as soon as possible, yet word came later that he had died as a result of a fall from his horse, so Washington remained in effective command of the Virginia Regiment throughout the expedition. Unfortunately, he had neither the experience nor the material resources to meet the challenges ahead.

The regiment set out early in April, but progress was maddeningly slow. Then came news that the party Dinwiddie had sent off earlier to build a fort at the head of the Ohio had abandoned the effort after a much larger French force, bent on the same mission, appeared in the area. Still, Washington chose to press on, and when he was told by friendly Indians of a group of Frenchmen camped nearby, he hurried to the spot. In the ensuing skirmish ten Frenchmen were killed, and the survivors surrendered, but they claimed they were on a diplomatic mission and accused their captors of murdering their leader.[52]

From there Washington's difficulties multiplied steadily. His Indian allies began to disappear. His supplies ran low. Meanwhile, there were constant reports of a massive French fort being built at the forks of the Ohio. And when he and his troops tried to establish a defensive position of their own, they ended by taking refuge in a pitifully weak, badly sited fort, which they hurried to enlarge and then named for exactly what it represented: Necessity. Finally, on July 3, the French moved to avenge the earlier ambush of their compatriots. Fort Necessity was attacked, and after holding out for the better part of a day Washington agreed to surrender and signed a document in French, which he may not have fully understood, confessing that his troops had killed an ambassador.[53]

Since France and England were still technically at peace, Washington's attack on the French had indeed been illegal. Considering the weakness of his forces, it was also reckless and ill-advised. Nevertheless, to his officers, as well as to many of those who had risked less and stayed at home, he was a hero. Rash he may have been, but his ardor, his steadfastness and endurance, and his superhuman energy all seemed ideally suited to frontier warfare. However, Governor Dinwiddie had other calculations to make, and so did his masters in England. With the French solidly entrenched on the Ohio, nothing short of a major effort would dislodge them. Unless England stepped in, the enterprise was doomed. Of course, England's involvement would mean war, and it would also mean control of military operations by the English. Yet as Dinwiddie saw it, that was the only alternative they had. Provincial sources of supply, provincial troops—and, yes, provincial officers—had proved inadequate for the task.

What all of this would mean for Washington became apparent in the months after his surrender of Fort Necessity. In the fall came word that the Virginia Regiment was to be broken into independent companies. As commander of one of them, Washington would be a mere captain, whereas formerly he had the rank of colonel, and he would still be without a royal commission, with all the humiliation that would entail. "In short," he wrote, "every Captain, bearing the King's Commission; every half-pay Officer, or other, appearing with such commission, would rank before me."[54] Plainly this was unacceptable. He had enjoyed his military service and had tasted the glory it could bring, but in November 1754 he resigned his place in the Virginia Regiment.[55]

Perhaps coincidentally, and perhaps not, it was just a month later that he signed the agreement to lease Mount Vernon from Anne Washington Lee (as she had become). Here was an alternative to military campaigning; here, too, was a realm where no one was likely to challenge his authority. The annual rent of fifteen thousand pounds of tobacco a year—about half his salary as adjutant—would give him the use of the estate and its eighteen resident slaves. He also paid £55 for "sundrys" left behind in the house.[56]

Meanwhile, he had begun thinking about repairs even before signing the lease, paying a joiner "for his advice upon sawing," perhaps in an effort to train one of the plantation's slaves as a carpenter. In December his ledger showed a debit to George William Fairfax for four days' labor from the Belvoir carpenters and a painter. John Patterson, a local joiner, started working at Mount Vernon in January 1755, and in February Washington bought Kit, a slave carpenter, for £29.5.[57]

But February also brought word of Major General Edward Braddock's arrival in the colonies. For months rumors had been circulating about military preparations. Now there was definitive proof that the British were committed to a major military effort against the French. Braddock was to be commander in chief of all forces in North America, and once ashore, he went immediately to Williamsburg to confer with Dinwiddie.[58]

To Washington, the coming of so important a figure, on so vital a mission, was bound to seem momentous. And so it proved to be. After a series of eminently polite exchanges, Washington was offered and accepted a place as a volunteer on Braddock's personal staff. The general needed his knowledge of the back country, and in return the arrangement would give Washington both the opportunity to learn the ways of proper European warfare and another chance at military glory. Also, his volunteer status promised to eliminate all embarrassment with regard to rank. By April his preparations were well along. He had been in command at Mount Vernon for just four months, but his younger brother Jack agreed to come and oversee things there. At Winchester, with the march inland about to begin, Washington's thoughts turned to home, and he wrote Jack by courier asking him to report regularly on the state of things there.[59] It was the first of many such requests, made over a lifetime.

Tragically, Braddock knew nothing of frontier fighting. Supplying an army when farmers were reluctant to lend their horses and wagons was an incomprehensible nightmare, as was the terrain over which heavy guns had to be hauled. Building a road that was up to British military standards took more time than the weather allowed. But the nadir was to come after Braddock's army had made its tortuous progress to a point on the Monongahela River just below Fort Duquesne. There, on July 9, the red-uniformed, precisely formed columns of British troops collided with an enemy force, and instead of taking cover in the trees, they panicked and were either slaughtered or ran off. Braddock himself was fatally wounded. In the chaotic retreat that followed, Washington worked mightily to bring as many of the survivors as possible to safety, and it was he who saw to the burial of Braddock in the road, directing the wagons to run over the grave so it would not be discovered by the Indians.[60]

In the colonies Washington was lauded for the role he had played in the debacle on the Monongahela, but Britain blamed the provincials for what had happened and seemed to have no immediate plans for renewing the campaign to take back the Ohio. As a result the Virginia frontier lay open to Indian raids, and soon enough they began, with particular ferocity. In Williamsburg Dinwiddie hurried to resurrect the Virginia Regiment, and in August Washington was offered sole command of it. If he accepted, it would mean more time away from Mount Vernon, but dreams of glory continued to beckon, and the terms of the offer were generous. He would be furnished with an aide and a secretary, plus 30 shillings a day, £100 a year for his table, an allowance for servants, and a commission of 2 percent on all the funds he handled. Still, his acceptance was not easily won, and by now the problem was familiar: this was not to be a commission in the regular army. In the end Washington acquiesced, but the issue of his rank continued to fester.[61]

One of the Virginia Regiment's responsibilities, in addition to protecting the scattered homesteads of settlers on the frontier, was to strengthen the garrison at Fort Cumberland, just over the Maryland border. In command there was Captain John Dagworthy, who, with his king's commission, outranked Washington, and who regularly undermined his authority by diverting supplies meant for the Virginia Regiment and issuing orders to its officers. Appeals to Dinwiddie and then from Dinwiddie to Governor William Shirley of Massachusetts, who was serving temporarily as commander in chief of British forces in America, proved unavailing. Finally, feeling that nothing would do but a personal appeal from him, Washington left his post and rode, in the dead of winter, eleven hundred miles with a pair of aides and two body servants to see Shirley.[62]

After stopping in Philadelphia long enough to shop for clothes, he reached New York City by mid-February. There he visited Beverly Robinson, the son of John Robinson, the Speaker of the Virginia House of Burgesses and treasurer of the colony, who was married to Susannah Phillipse. Her family was one of the wealthiest in New York, and apparently her younger sister Polly had a special attraction for Washington. Could she become mistress of Mount Vernon? It seems he did not ask her, but he did linger with the Phillipses for five days. From New York the small expedition made its way to New London, Connecticut, staying with another friend, Joseph Chew, and Washington's interest in Polly Phillipse is clearly indicated in a jovial letter Chew wrote the following year, describing her as "in the same Condition & situation as you saw her."[63] Three months later he wrote again, urging Washington to press his suit, even though Polly was subject to the attentions of another admirer.[64]

After leaving New London, the party proceeded by boat, probably stopping at Newport and staying with another Virginian, Godfrey Malbone, and then moved on to Boston. All along the way the newspapers reported on the progress of the young colonel from Virginia, but the accounts were unclear as to the reason for his journey, and Washington himself was silent on the subject.[65] Neither do his impressions of the places he saw along the way survive, but certainly there was no shortage of things to notice. Philadelphia and New York were large cities, and Boston was so urban that people remarked it looked like London. New buildings and new building styles were also everywhere, and some of them would eventually be reflected at Mount Vernon. Particularly noteworthy was the work of Newport architect Peter Harrison, the designer of the impressive Redwood Library in that city. To dress up the building, he had the exterior walls covered with boards shaped to look like stone, with sand added to the paint covering the boards to heighten the effect. Much the same treatment was used at Governor Shirley's new mansion at Roxbury, which Harrison may also have designed and which Washington almost certainly saw.[66]

More immediately to the point, Shirley agreed, when Washington met with him, to write a letter to Governor Sharpe of Maryland endorsing Washington's command over Dagworthy. There were to be no royal commissions for the Virginia officers, but as long as British forces were not present, Dagworthy was to act solely in his capacity as a provincial captain. With his mission at least partially accomplished, Washington set out for Virginia, and after reporting to Dinwiddie, left to rejoin his men.

The months that followed were marked by repeated crises. The small forts along the frontier did little to avert Indian attacks, and the militia units raised to lend support proved unreliable. On the other hand, Britain had at long last declared war against France, and a new commander in chief of North American forces, the earl of Loudoun,

*Early engraving of the Redwood Library, Newport, Rhode Island, Peter Harrison,
architect. Along with the building's handsome exterior, the engraving shows the rusticated boards used to cover its exterior, which may have provided the model for those
used later at Mount Vernon. Courtesy of the Williams College Art Department.*

had been appointed. In a carefully worded report to Loudoun, Washington argued that
a properly supplied force of three thousand men could take and destroy Fort Duquesne.
He also took up the perennial question of rank. Both Braddock and Shirley had promised
to advance him to a "better Establishment"; he hoped Loudoun would see the justice of
doing so as well.[67]

The next step was to meet the great man in person, and the opportunity to do so
came in March 1757. At Loudoun's request a council of governors gathered at Philadelphia to coordinate strategy, and Washington asked permission to attend. Grudgingly
Dinwiddie consented, and the meeting between the two commanders took place with
appropriate cordiality, but no definite promises of anything. Meanwhile, behind closed
doors Loudoun and the governors agreed that there would be no move against Fort
Duquesne that year. Instead the primary British thrust would be directed at French positions on the Great Lakes and would originate in the north. Washington was told none of
this, but had there been plans for a significant offensive in his area, he would have
known it soon enough. Plainly, his advice had not been followed.

On April 15, 1757, three weeks after the council in Philadelphia had concluded its business, Washington placed an order for a longish list of items with Richard Washington, a
London merchant to whom he had first written in December 1755.[68] The purpose of
that earlier letter had been to open a regular commercial relationship of the sort that

wealthy Virginians typically relied on for marketing their tobacco and supplying themselves with goods from abroad. Evidently Washington had chosen Richard Washington as his agent under the mistaken impression that they were related. There had been no correspondence since then, nor did Washington mention what he intended to do with the "Sundries" on his list, but the answer was simple enough: they were to be used for rebuilding and substantially enlarging Mount Vernon. For two years, ever since Braddock's expedition, Washington's energies had been wholly focused on war. Now Mount Vernon had entered his thoughts again, just as the Philadelphia council's decision not to attack Fort Duquesne was becoming clear. Significantly, in his letter to Richard Washington he both mentioned the subject and made his views quite clear: "From what strange Causes I know not, no attempt this Season will be made I fear, to destroy this Hold of Barbarians."[69]

These were strong words, but so were the emotions that lay behind them. As long as the French remained in place at Fort Duquesne, the raids on the Virginia frontier would continue, and Washington would have to deal with them as best he could. It was a service that offered no chance for glory, as another campaign on the Ohio would have, only an endless, grinding succession of stopgap holding actions in which the most that could be hoped for was a temporary standoff. Even so, it might all have been worthwhile if the rewards had included what for Washington had become a matter of transcendent significance—a commission in the regular British army.

During the weeks while he was waiting to see Loudoun, he had busied himself drafting appeals, both on his own behalf and on behalf of his fellow officers in the Virginia Regiment, stating yet again the case for their "preferments." In one particularly impassioned plea to Dinwiddie he enumerated at length the regiment's many services, including the fact that it had been "the first in arms of any Troops upon the Continent." Disregarding such a record, he believed, would surely tend "to discourage Merit and lessen that generous Emulation, spirit, and laudable ambition so necessary to prevail in an Army." And if the problem was that they were Americans, Washington had a ready answer: "We cant conceive, that being Americans shoud deprive us of the benefits of British Subjects." With such arguments he earnestly hoped to enlist Dinwiddie's help— "your Honours Patronage"—in winning Lord Loudoun to their cause.[70]

The truth was, however, that Dinwiddie had little to gain, and much to lose, if Washington succeeded in his quest. The governor needed the Virginia Regiment on the frontier, and Washington had shown himself to be a resourceful and energetic commander as well as an exceedingly ambitious one. With a royal commission in hand he was likely to want to go where the stakes were highest, and by the spring of 1757, as Dinwiddie knew, the British were committed to striking at the heart of French power in Canada. Thus, promoting Washington might well cost Virginia his services, and though the final decision was Loudoun's, a quiet word from the governor would have settled the issue easily enough. So much for "your Honours Patronage."

Yet Washington was as able as Dinwiddie to read the direction of the wind and calculate his options accordingly. Perhaps the time had come to resign his command and leave the military. But if not the military, then what? His renewed interest in Mount Vernon seemed to suggest that he might be willing to take his chances as a Virginia planter,

Portrait of Martha Dandridge Custis as a young matron, painted by John Wollaston. Courtesy of the Mount Vernon Ladies' Association.

and indeed that was the direction in which he now began to move. More than a year and a half would pass before he finally relinquished his command, however, and by then Fort Duquesne lay in ruins, burned by the French themselves. By then, too, Washington had completely transformed Mount Vernon and won the hand of Martha Dandridge Custis.

Because Washington's marriage and the rebuilding of Mount Vernon were so nearly concurrent in time, it is easy to assume the two were related, and they were, but Mount Vernon was not in fact rebuilt to provide a home for Martha Custis and her children. As the "List of Sundries" sent to Richard Washington proves, plans for the work to be done on the house were already well along in April 1757, and at that point Martha's first husband, Daniel Parke Custis, was still very much alive. He died suddenly three months later, and it was not until March of the following year that Washington began recording tips for the Custis servants in his cash accounts, indicating that he was visiting and presumably courting her.[71]

If he had anyone in mind as a prospective bride when he sent off the order to Richard Washington, it was probably Polly Phillipse, who Joseph Chew had just assured him was still available. But Polly was a week's ride away in New York, and there was an added complication. Living for years in close proximity to the Fairfaxes, Washington had come to know all the members of the family well; in one case, however, his feelings had grown far beyond ordinary friendship. With Sally Cary Fairfax—the vivacious, sophisticated wife of his close friend George William—he had fallen deeply in love. In the end everyone's good sense prevailed, and nothing serious came of what could have been a profoundly awkward situation.[72] Still, with Sally so near, it may have been difficult for Washington to keep his attention focused on Polly. Martha Custis, on the other hand, lived just outside Williamsburg. By all accounts, too, she was a thoroughly amiable person.

But Martha Custis had more to recommend her than simply her good nature, for she also was one of the richest women in Virginia, and it would be naive to suppose that Washington was oblivious to that fact. Because Daniel Custis died intestate, she had inherited one third of his estate, which included plantations in six counties in Virginia and personal property and slaves valued at £30,000. In addition, she had the right to charge the balance of the estate for her children's expenses as long as they remained minors.[73]

The difference all this promised to make in Washington's life was dramatic. Overnight he would become part of that small circle of Virginians at the very pinnacle of the colony's society. Had he, then, planned it all from the beginning? There is a saying, which may have been old even in Washington's day, that good luck comes to those who count on it. To have resigned his command merely to become an ordinary planter would have been a poor exchange, and marriage in Virginia had long been a way of increasing one's assets. Significantly, too, the changes he was planning to make at Mount Vernon would take nearly all the money he had made in the army, leaving him in the bargain with a much more elaborate establishment to maintain. In fact it is difficult to imagine how he expected to foot the bill without some sort of windfall. But, of course, he had no way of knowing that Daniel Custis would die when he did.

Nor did his good fortune in winning the widow Custis's hand in any way change his plans for Mount Vernon. The basic decisions had all been made in the spring of 1757, though as the date of his wedding approached he became increasingly eager to see the work completed. On both points his thinking was probably the same. Had he married well and waited until afterward to rebuild Mount Vernon, the supposition would have been that he had done so with his wife's money and was thus beholden to her for the very roof over his head. As it was, he could stand before the world as an independent gentleman possessed of just such a home as might appeal to a woman of means.

All of which suggests how central Mount Vernon had become to Washington's calculations during these years—the *new* Mount Vernon, that had first begun to take shape in the list of window glass and wallpaper, "fashionable Locks" and "neat and strong Mahogany Chairs" he drew up to send Richard Washington in the spring of 1757.[74] He had tried soldiering; he had tried the thick of battle and the fickle patronage of great men. And he had not come away empty-handed, but neither had he won all that he dreamed of. If he was ever to break the pattern and move beyond the point the Washingtons had reached in their stalled, New World rise, he would have to find another way of doing so. Mount Vernon was his ace in the hole; the time had come to play that card.

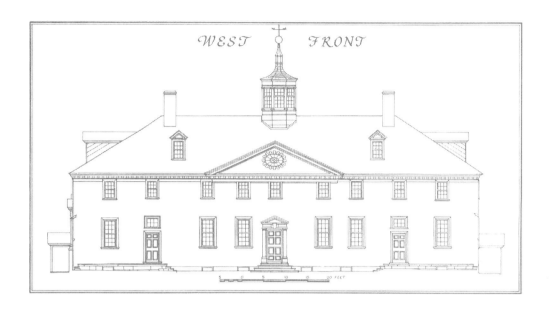

WEST FRONT

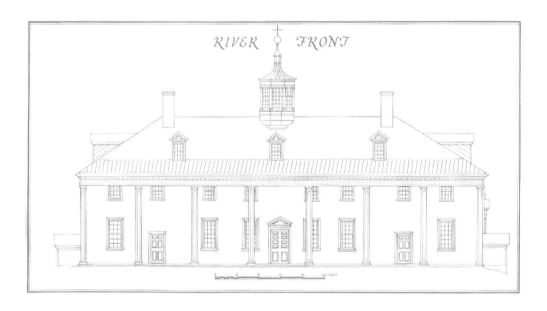

RIVER FRONT

BUILDING

THOUGH OFTEN FRUSTRATED by the process, Washington derived deep satisfaction from building. Planning what was to be built, collecting the necessary materials from dozens of different sources, and directing the workers in their myriad tasks were all exercises in creative organization and management. They also carried with them a distinct frisson of risk, for building in Virginia was very much a public performance. To manage successfully everything that had to be managed, with the community looking on and speculating about the results, could be a fine demonstration of personal control. But roofs that leaked, corners that were not plumb, chimneys that did not draw properly—not to mention rotted frames that had been left uncovered too long—told an altogether different story. And the more ambitious the undertaking, the riskier the performance became.

Raising the stakes even higher in Washington's case was the fact that both of his major rebuildings of Mount Vernon occurred at critical points in his life. The first coincided with the end of his military service during the French and Indian War; the second began in the years just prior to the Revolution. In both cases, too, he was absent for the bulk of the actual construction, making the issue of control that much more problematic.

In other respects, however, the two rebuildings were quite different. The first marked Washington's decision to turn from military to civilian life, but the factors behind the second were more complex. Architecturally the second rebuilding was also bolder, more original than the first, and it took longer to complete. Even before it was finished, too, Washington began altering the result in significant ways—altering it to take account of the torrent of change, both in his own life and in the life of the nation, released by the American Revolution.

CHAPTER 3

A New Mount Vernon, 1758–1773

You must have the House very well cleand, & were you to make Fires in the Rooms below it, wd Air them—You must get two of the best Bedsteads put up—one in the Hall Room, and the other in the little dining Room that use to be, & have Beds made on them against we come—you must also get out the Chairs and Tables, & have them very well rubd & Cleand—the Stair case ought also to be polishd in order to make it look well.[1]

ALMOST THREE MONTHS after their wedding, George Washington was finally bringing his bride home to Mount Vernon, and his anxiety was clear in the hastily penned instructions he rushed on ahead to John Alton, one of his workers. Equally clear was the fact that while the house may have been habitable, it was not much more than that. The furniture was still being kept wherever it had been stored during the long months of construction, and apparently there had been no time to give the place a proper cleaning, or so Washington feared. One imagines scraps of wood, sawhorses, paint pots, bits of wallpaper, and plaster dust everywhere. And since he had given Alton only a day's notice of the family's pending arrival, it would have been no small feat to get things ready in time.

Yet such were the dramas of ordinary domestic life, and of house building, as Washington would have ample opportunity to discover in the years ahead, for the rebuilding of Mount Vernon that had begun with the plans he made in 1757 would prove to be a never-ending enterprise, extending ultimately far beyond the main house that stood waiting to receive the family that spring. Each new project would beget another, multiplying both the pleasures and the frustrations of building. Some of the frustrations, too, would turn out to be surprisingly reminiscent of the difficulties Washington had encountered as a military commander, including the most annoying one of all: British arrogance and insensitivity to what he took to be due his personal dignity and character. Coincidentally, these were also the years leading to the American Revolution, and in crucial ways Washington's experience as master of Mount Vernon would both resonate with and reinforce his response to the deepening crisis in Anglo-American relations.

In the spring of 1759 all that lay in the future, however. There was a new house to

47

settle into, and even Washington seemed a bit uncertain about how to proceed on that front. In his instructions to John Alton he asked to have beds set up in two of the principal ground-floor rooms. Did he imagine that the family would be sleeping in those rooms permanently, or was this a temporary arrangement, to be changed later, when the house was more settled? In his father's day the parlor in Fredericksburg had contained a bed, but the parlor at the Fairfaxes' Belvoir most definitely would not have.

Though the evidence is unclear on the point, in all likelihood the two rooms Washington referred to as "the Hall Room" and "the little dining Room that use to be" were those on the east side of the ground floor. Perhaps he meant to let Martha decide how they were ultimately to be used, as well as where the family would sleep. But about the other two rooms on the ground floor there was no uncertainty; he knew how he was going to use them. The one in the northwest corner of the house was to be his best room, or parlor, as it came to be called. To mark its importance its walls had been completely covered in paneling, with projecting pediments above the doorways, supported by fluted pilasters. Also, two years earlier he had ordered "A Neat Landskip . . . for a Chimy" from Richard Washington, which item, done in oil paint and described as "after Claude Lorrain," had been duly installed over the mantel in the

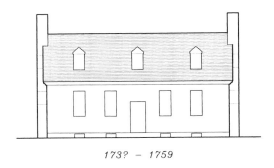

173? – 1759

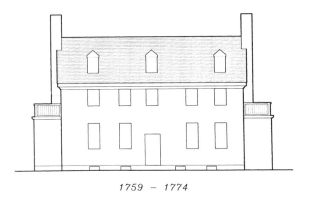

1759 – 1774

Conjectural drawing of Lawrence Washington's Mount Vernon and the house as rebuilt by George Washington in 1758–59. Drawing by Jeffery F. C. Dalzell.

room, immediately below a carved replica of the Washington family coat of arms. And at the same time, he had asked for "paper of a very good kind and colour for a Dining Room 18 by 16." It too had arrived—a "Crimson embost paper wte Masaic"—and presumably was already on the walls of the room across the passage, in the southwest corner of the house.[2]

A new best room as well as a new dining room, leaving their predecessors to be used for purposes he himself may not have known: that was part of what Washington had done to change Mount Vernon, but only part. There was also the new staircase he was so eager to have "polishd in order to make it look well," plus a remade central passage, again covered in elaborate paneling, to go with it. The most dramatic change lay above, on the second floor, however, for the entire house had been raised a full story. Where before there had been four small rooms, wedged in under the eaves, now there were five, all of "8 feet pitch," as he indicated in ordering wallpaper for them.[3] Essentially, the house had been doubled in size, and with its newly embellished interior and exterior it had become a very different place. If still not quite in the same category as great brick mansions like the Fairfaxes' Belvoir or William Byrd's Westover, at least it resembled them more closely than before. Certainly no one would have doubted that it was the home of someone of consequence.

None of it had come easily, however. In addition to all the problems invariably associated with house building, there was the speed with which Washington wanted everything done. Also, during the entire time construction was under way, he was absent from Mount Vernon, participating in the final campaign against the French at Fort Duquesne. Fortunately he was well served by those overseeing things on the spot. Still, there must have been moments when getting the job done seemed almost as complicated as commanding troops in the wilderness.

At the outset things went slowly because of illness among the workers, but by mid-June 1758 the framing for the heightened walls was cut and mostly assembled on the ground, according to John Patterson, the Alexandria house carpenter who was acting as manager or "undertaker" for the project. To build the new roof, the Mount Vernon slaves had searched the woods for the sturdy white oak needed to make the laths that would serve as underpinning for the shingles.[4] As a precaution, the old roof was temporarily left in place, but the outside walls would remain vulnerable to the whims of the weather until the new weatherboarding was painted, even though, as it turned out, this particular summer was notably dry, with no rain to speak of until the end of August.[5]

By the beginning of July the framing for the new second floor had been raised and fixed in place on top of the existing frame of the first floor with heavy iron spikes. The roof laths were also ready. Meanwhile, under the supervision of William Triplett, sixteen thousand bricks had been made to enlarge the chimneys at either end of the house and to bolster its foundations, which would now have to carry the weight of the additional story. Triplett would also be responsible for plastering the interior walls.[6]

Later that same month—in yet another step taken in preparation for his new life—Washington was chosen by the voters of Frederick County to represent them in the

House of Burgesses. George William Fairfax, just back from a quick trip to England to settle his father's estate, had gone to Winchester with John Carlyle on election day to see his friend successfully elected (Washington being detained at camp).[7] Also, at Washington's entreaty sent by courier, Fairfax began riding over to Mount Vernon regularly to check on the progress of the building and give Patterson whatever help and advice he could. Anxious about the unpainted state of the weatherboarding and sensing that the carpenters had enough work to do, Fairfax hired a worker to coat the exterior of the house. On the second floor, some of the floorboards, once cleaned, proved to be uneven or defective. In addition, a completely new floor was needed for the passage on the first floor if Washington wished to eliminate the nail holes left when a partition that divided the space in Lawrence's day was eliminated.[8] Washington had already noticed the holes and wrote Fairfax: "The Floor of my Passage is really an Eye sore to me, I woud therefore take it up if good & Seasond Plank coud be laid in its place."[9] But Patterson doubted whether he could find planking to make a floor that was any better looking.[10]

In the same letter, Patterson wrote that plank was still needed for a pair of "Closets" to go at either end of the house, but otherwise the exterior was almost complete.[11] Apart from its greater bulk, the most striking change in its outward appearance was the elegant new covering of row upon row of beveled boards, used instead of ordinary, horizontal clapboards. When the boards were painted, sand would be thrown at them while the final coat was still wet to heighten the likeness to stone, a detail Washington had undoubtedly seen on his trip to New England in the winter of 1756.[12] Above the beveled boards, around the entire house, ran a stylish modillioned cornice. Then came the newly shingled roof, crowned by heightened chimneys. Only the windows were lacking—the glass panes for them having arrived from England at a landing on the York River instead of the upper Potomac.[13]

With the outside of the house nearly finished, the focus shifted to the inside. The rich paneling and chimneypieces for refurbishing the two rooms on the west side of the ground floor; a new, wider, and more ambitiously embellished staircase; and the paneling in the central passage all had to be done. Doubtless to save time, rather than stripping the existing trim, plaster, and lath in those rooms, the crew simply covered the old wall surfaces with new ones. The flooring, chimneypieces, baseboards, trim around the windows and doors, and ceiling and chair rail moldings for the second-floor bedchambers also had to be made, given a coat of paint, and put in place before Triplett's men could plaster the walls. Before the plastering was done, too, lath had to be made and fastened to the studs.

It was clear to John Patterson that he would have to recruit more workers, since those who had come earlier to assist in raising the house had other commitments. And when he showed Triplett a plan of Washington's (perhaps drawn up during odd moments in camp) for two new dependencies and a "yard wall" to be built next to the house, Triplett told him that he was too busy to take on the extra work that year. He would finish only what he had already agreed to do.[14]

On September 1 George William Fairfax, in response to two separate inquiries from Washington, wrote that the plank for the new floors still had not arrived, nor had the shipment containing the glass panes for the windows. The latter was not expected for another three weeks.[15] Hurrying over to Mount Vernon later that same day ("indeed the Oftener I come over the more I think it really necessary"), Fairfax consulted with Patterson and wrote a second letter after returning home. The space on the second floor at the head of the stairway, he suggested, could be partitioned so that the old stairs, having been disassembled and rebuilt above to give access to the third floor, would become a "retired Stair," leaving an eight-by-twelve-foot room with a window, to be used for guests if needed. Should this be done? And did Washington want the upstairs landing wallpapered, or should it be plastered like the landing at Belvoir? The rest of the letter contained discouraging news. Triplett still had not finished his work, yet declared that he had other jobs and could do nothing more before the first frost, which in Virginia usually comes in November. Since it was important that the lathing for the plastering be finished by then, Washington's own labor force would have to do that. Also, Fairfax had either looked around outside himself, or had been enlightened by the conscientious Patterson, and wrote that all the outbuildings needed repairs. "But enough of this for fear you should be uneasy"—a remark hardly calculated to produce calm.[16]

The next day Patterson himself wrote. Still in transit were the goods that had arrived on the York River, which included—besides the window glass—the landscape painting to be installed above the mantel in the west parlor, hinges and locks for the interior doors, all the wallpaper for the house, and premolded ceiling ornaments for two of the refurbished rooms on the ground floor. On the other hand, the doors themselves were almost ready, and "Col. Fairfax" had been able to locate plank for the floors. Triplett had finished the chimneytops and had assured Patterson that he would come again by the end of November, after finishing a project for Colonel West. And because there was still so much joiners' work to do on the interior woodwork of the house, Patterson had hired a man to do the painting for 4 shillings a day. He was trying to find more help, but if no accidents occurred he still hoped "with the Men I have got to finish the House towards the last of Novr."[17]

In mid-September, while Washington waited in camp for the march to Fort Duquesne to begin, Fairfax wrote again from Belvoir. The shipment with the window glass still had not arrived, which was causing serious problems. "The detention of your goods is really a very great disappt for nothing can be done (I mean finished) till the Glass is in, consequently you cant expect the Work can be done by the time you expected." Progress was also delayed by the absence of Triplett, who, Fairfax thought, "might have put the work a good deal forwarder by doing only a part of his." He was glad Washington approved of their ideas for the stairs to the third floor, but they were still uncertain what to do about the floorboards in the passage below.[18]

Over the next month, preparations for the assault on Fort Duquesne were finally completed, and in the middle of October the march westward began.[19] In charge of the expedition was yet another British general, John Forbes, but the Virginia forces remained under Washington's command, and it had been agreed that he would not be outranked by British officers below the grade of colonel.[20] However, his advice about the route to be followed to Fort Duquesne had not been taken, and his service under what he considered misguided leadership became more frustrating and disagreeable with each passing day. "So miserably has this Expedition been managd, that I expect after a Months further tryal, and the loss of many more Men by the Sword, Cold, and Perhaps Famine, we shall give the Expedition over as Impracticable this Season and retire to the Inhabitants condemnd by the World."[21] Ultimately Washington's prediction proved wrong. The expedition did get through, but the result of that final grueling march to the forks of the Ohio was anything but glorious. On November 25 a scouting party reached the smoldering ruins of the same fort that Forbes's forces had for so long been preparing to attack. The French, cut off from their supply source upstream, had retreated and burned what they had been forced to leave behind. The campaign was over. The British could now disengage their troops, leaving the provincials to man the fortifications along the frontier.[22] Presumably throughout this time the work on Mount Vernon continued, but any letters sent from home after September have not survived.

At the end of 1758 Washington formally resigned command of the Virginia Regiment.[23] In January he and Martha Custis were married, and he became stepfather and guardian to her two young children, Jackie, almost four years old, and Patsy, his younger sister.[24] For all of that first winter the family stayed either at Martha's plantation or at her house in Williamsburg. There was much for Washington to do: attending his first sessions as a member of the House of Burgesses; refining and cataloging the division of property between himself (as Martha's consort he controlled her part of the Custis inheritance) and the children; assuming responsibility for the farms belonging to Martha and to Jackie; and seeing to the outstanding loans Martha had made to friends as a young widow.[25] There was also the matter of an order to Robert Cary & Co., Martha's London agent, and a letter explaining her new situation.[26]

The choice of Mount Vernon as the place to center their lives may also have been at issue during those months. But if it was, Washington carried the day, which would have made it all the more important to have the house finished when Martha arrived. Yet that was not to be. Triplett had probably finished the plastering inside, since Washington's ledger shows that he was paid in February.[27] But not until the end of the summer would a joiner from Alexandria named Going Lanphier be reimbursed for "turnery"—no doubt for the spindles of the grand new staircase.[28] Also, Patterson did not receive his principal payment until September, suggesting that his work was unfinished as well. Most telling of all, however, is an entry in Washington's ledger from the middle of the summer.[29] Whatever Martha saw when she arrived at Mount Vernon that April, it was not a fully painted house, as a furious note scribbled in the margin of the ledger proves: "Jno Winter before he had near finished Painting my House, Stole a good deal of Paint & Oyl and apprehensive of Justice ran off."[30] With the outside of the house still unfinished, the painter had left, taking Washington's paint and oil in the bargain!

Despite all the delays and mishaps, however, one thing would have gone according to plan that April day. Regardless of the route they took, the Washingtons would have arrived on the west side of the house, which henceforth was to be its principal entrance front. Lawrence's most important rooms—and probably his main entrance as well—had faced the Potomac. The placement of Washington's elegant new parlor and dining room on the other side of the ground floor reversed that orientation, which symbolically may have been the most important of all the changes he made at Mount Vernon.[31]

For Lawrence, facing the river—and beyond it the Chesapeake and ultimately the

Atlantic itself—meant facing "home." His great-grandfather had come to Virginia from England, and each generation since then had been educated there. He himself had gone to school in England, and his military service had taken him to the Caribbean under Admiral Vernon, whose name he memorialized by giving it to his home. He had even hoped to send young George to sea, but that was not to be.[32]

Instead, except for that single, brief trip to the Barbados, George never left what he would describe to a London merchant in 1760 as the "Infant Woody Country"[33] of his birth, and it was the land that captured his imagination, not the sea. He was more at home on a horse than he would ever be on water. With his surveyor's eye, he would always be fascinated with, and almost fanatically eager to acquire, rich river bottom-lands, reaching far into the interior. His military experience, too, had been grounded in the forest wilderness of the back country. How fitting, then, that his Mount Vernon should face the land, should face west.

And there is another sense in which such a reorientation of the house would have seemed appropriate. Washington's long struggle to have his military service rewarded with a proper king's commission had ended as it began, in frustration. How much bitterness he harbored as a result he alone knew, but indications are that it ran deep. Deep enough to strain his fundamental loyalty to "home"—to England and the entire system that had proved so niggardly in dealing with "provincial" claims to preferment? No doubt such a question would have shocked him, but perhaps unwittingly, in turning his back on the river and the sea, he had answered it anyway. To be sure, it was no rebel camp that he had brought Martha home to, but neither was it, any longer, the home of a simple English gentleman.

Having taken up life as a Virginia planter, Washington meant to proceed in an orderly, businesslike fashion. He would conduct his own affairs, attending to them in a timely way. Complicated questions like whether to replace floorboards or what to do when tradesmen failed to appear on schedule would be tackled firsthand. Workmanship and work habits could be supervised on the spot. The land would also be taken in hand, and tobacco growing, the lifeblood of the place, would be more profitably managed.

One of the first decisions he made was to dispense with the services of Richard Washington.[34] It was that gentleman's shipment of window glass and other items to the wrong Virginia river that had caused such delays for those struggling to finish the work on Mount Vernon on time. Even without that annoying mishap, however, it would have made sense for Washington to switch his trade to Martha's agent, Robert Cary, since he already had detailed knowledge of her financial affairs.

The relationship Washington contemplated with Cary amounted to a textbook example of mercantilist policy at work: manufactured goods from the home country, paid for with money earned by exports of a colonial commodity, tobacco. As a rule, the nature of the exchange depended on the size of the transactions. Most planters sold their tobacco in Virginia, but the richest of them (and Washington was now among their number) dealt directly with one or more of the London or Bristol houses specializing in colonial trade, because the profits were thought to be higher.[35]

The merchants kept the accounts. On one side of the ledger went credits from tobacco sales and any other income; on the other side, charges for the myriad items wealthy Virginians wanted and needed to sustain the lives they led. When an individual planter's requests reached an English merchant, his agents shopped for the items listed, arrangements were made for packing and shipping, and invoices were drawn up that included charges for both the goods themselves and the services involved. With luck there would be a balance in the account large enough to cover the charges, and eventually a shipment containing the right goods would arrive at the right landing on the right river in Virginia.

In reality things seldom went so smoothly. Shipments regularly arrived later than expected and in the wrong place. Goods were frequently spoiled or damaged, and items urgently needed sometimes never appeared at all. The sizes were wrong, the materials inferior, and the workmanship poor—or so Virginians constantly complained. Also, the prices invariably seemed too high, and often there was not enough in the account to cover them, so over the years negative balances tended to grow, sometimes at an alarming rate.

There was another problem with the system as well. When Washington ordered items from abroad, he frequently used words like "fashionable" and "in the newest taste" to describe what he wanted.[36] Such requests were common, and in making them Virginians were participating in a phenomenon that was transforming the entire British economy— the rapidly growing market for consumer goods of all kinds. Fueled by rising incomes and falling prices, the drive to consume was also closely linked to changes in fashion. Once the province of the aristocracy, taste was now being established in the marketplace by middle-class consumers, as innovative manufacturers like Josiah Wedgwood recognized. To own clothing, tableware, and furniture in the latest style was something thousands of people could hope to do and wanted to do, including colonists an ocean away.[37]

The difficulty was that most colonists had to depend on other people to choose consumer goods for them. Only the few who traveled in England could gauge for themselves how the winds of fashion blew. Nevertheless, Virginia planters—because they operated as individuals in their dealings with English merchants—liked to think that their requests for only "neat and fashionable" goods would carry particular weight. Unfortunately, all too often their commercial "friends" in England disappointed them. The goods sent were old-fashioned, outmoded, and not in the latest taste at all, which only made a difficult situation worse. That the planters had to depend on others to make such important choices for them was already problematic because it compromised their independence. To find themselves so ill treated in the bargain was doubly annoying. Evidently English merchants thought any old thing was good enough to send to the colonies. But the items in question were not going just to the colonies; they were going to proud Virginia planters who believed they were entitled to the very best that money could buy.

Still, off to Robert Cary went all the Washingtons' orders for London finery, and in those first few months the couple seemed to require a veritable niagara of goods: six dozen metal plates engraved with the family coat of arms; dessert glasses and stands for sweetmeats; knives and forks with handles of ivory bound in silver; twenty-two pairs of men's stockings of assorted kinds; half a dozen pairs of men's shoes with high heels; half a dozen pairs of men's gloves; two beaver hats and a red morocco sword belt; six pairs of women's kid gloves and a black mask; a dozen chambray handkerchiefs and six pounds of snuff; six pounds of perfumed powder and two dozen sponge toothbrushes; pickles, olives, capers, and a bottle of Indian mangoes; a large Cheshire cheese and four pounds of green tea; twenty-five pounds of raisins and the same amount of almonds; fifty pounds of candles; twenty loaves of sugar, twenty sacks of salt, and twenty-five pounds of soap; yard upon yard of cloth for making slaves' clothing; and an extensive supply of medicines, including six bottles of "Greenhouse Tincture"—plus more, much more.

In addition to the plates, glassware, and cutlery, there were bulkier items for the house. At the time he took over Mount Vernon, Washington had purchased some of Lawrence's furniture from his widow and on several occasions since then had ordered tables, chairs, and bedsteads from England. Now he and Martha decided to add Wilton carpets for two bedchambers; fifty yards of floor matting; a pair of fire screens; "1 Large, neat, and easy Couch for a Passage" (the one Cary sent was described as a neat mahogany Marlborough couch "with a Roll head & Leathr Casters . . . stufft up in the best mannr & covd with black Leathr"); a mahogany stool "in the newest taste" with a place for a chamber pot; two lanterns; and an assortment of ornaments, including eight busts of famous military figures and "2 Wild Beasts."

There was also a request for a new tester bedstead "7 1/2 feet pitch" with blue and white curtains, chosen to harmonize with an enclosed sample of wallpaper, plus window curtains and chair-seat covers in the same fabric, "in order to make the whole furniture of this Room uniformly handsome and genteel." Even more elaborately detailed than the rest of Washington's instructions, these almost certainly pertained to the bedchamber he and Martha would share, and the seven-and-a-half-foot height of the bedstead indicates that it was destined for the second floor of Mount Vernon, which had lower ceilings than the first.[38] Apparently Martha preferred sleeping upstairs. Her influence was evident as well in the careful attention to details like color and pattern that Washington had never before been specific about in orders to England.

Altogether Cary's charges for the large shipment he eventually put together in response to the first two orders that year came to £151.5.10. In making up the shipment, his agents had purchased goods from seventeen different establishments in London. Searchers' fees and shipping charges totaled £1.8.6, freight £3.19, and insurance £11.5.[39] The following spring he sent an even larger shipment,[40] and it was a rare year thereafter that Washington was not billed at least £300 for goods bought, crated, and shipped to the Potomac.

Occasionally Cary's searchers failed to find items Washington requested. For example, the eight busts of military figures completely defeated them, though the "Wild Beasts," described as "Two Lyons after the Antique Lyon's in Italy finisht. Neat & bronzd with Copper," were sent. If Washington still wanted the busts (which perhaps he hoped to put in the pediments over the doorways in the passage), he was told they could be made for four guineas each. Or, if he was willing to forgo the likes of Julius Caesar, Alexander the Great, and the duke of Marlborough, he could choose from a long list of ready-made busts of other worthies, including Homer, Virgil, Shakespeare, Pope, Locke, and Newton.[41] Apparently neither alternative suited, for the next and final time he mentioned the busts was to tell Cary, "a future day will determine my choice of them if any are wrote for."[42]

But even when things were sent as ordered, problems began to arise almost at once. As early as the summer of 1760, Washington was complaining to Cary that some of the items he received were "mean in quality but not in price, for in this they excel indeed, far above any I have ever had." And a month later he remarked even more caustically: "You may believe me when I tell you that instead of getting things good and fashionable in their several kind we often have Articles sent Us that coud only have been usd by our Forefathers in the days of yore."[43]

Probably the single most annoying transaction in Washington's dealings with Cary occurred the following year, when an invoice arrived for a long list of goods ordered the previous September, including a mahogany case with sixteen square glass bottles, each to hold a gallon of liquid. Washington had described what he wanted in considerable detail, specifying that the case should be supported by four legs; that it should be two feet, four inches high; and that the bottles should be "very Strong."[44] Since the chances of finding

The case and decanters ordered by Washington from Robert Cary & Co., the price of which seemed so outrageously high. Courtesy of the Mount Vernon Ladies' Association.

such a thing ready-made were nil, Cary went ahead and had it done to order, complete with brass casters and brass lifting handles. The bill came to a stunning £17.17.[45] Furious, Washington wrote back saying that surely there had been some mistake, or this was "as great an Imposition as ever was offerd by a Tradesman." He could have had the case made in Virginia "of the same stuff, and equally as neat for less than four Guineas." That left 10 guineas for the bottles—a ridiculous price![46]

Evidently there had been no mistake, however, and here again, as in all such transactions, Washington was in the same position as other Virginia planters. Many of the items he wanted were simply not available locally. Also, doing business in Virginia would have required cash he did not always have on hand. Still, he believed Cary had a duty to act faithfully and responsibly in his behalf. Not to do so was to break a trust, and trust between gentlemen was everything. Without it the only guides to action were power and profit, and Washington, for one, was not about to settle meekly for inferior standing on either count, any more than he had been willing to let British officers of inferior rank lord it over him on the frontier. But for the time being he continued to order from Cary, despite his growing dissatisfaction with the system.

Two categories of goods that all of Washington's orders included and that would have been difficult to find locally were tools and certain kinds of building materials. No doubt he saw in his mind's eye an end to building, a moment when all tools could be laid aside and he at last looked out on a finished creation. But the fact was that such work would remain as much a part of life at Mount Vernon as the great river that washed the shore before it.

High on Washington's list of priorities when he arrived with Martha in the spring of 1759 was putting up the new outbuildings he had hoped to have completed the year before. At the time he took over Mount Vernon, there were already several outbuildings on the property, including a pair with stone foundations on the west side of the house. He proposed to add a second pair to those two, built of wood on brick foundations. The plan shown to Triplett in the summer of 1758 had also called for low brick walls, topped by wooden fences, linking the four structures to the main house. An array of symmetrically placed outbuildings, flanking a central great house: it was a design sanctioned by decades of use in the Tidewater. Belvoir was similarly laid out, and as much as anything Washington had done to Mount Vernon, that configuration of buildings promised to give tangible expression to his ambitions for the place.

As usual there were delays, however. Because of other work they had to do, the bargain with William Triplett and his brother Thomas was not struck until March 1760, though between them the two did contract to do the entire job, building "the two houses in the Front of my House," as Washington noted in his diary, plus the walls connecting the outbuildings to the main house. The price agreed on was £18.[47] In preparation for the project, bricks had already been fired at Mount Vernon, then cooled and stacked, at a site near the landing on the river, and limestone had been burned for the mortar that would be needed.[48] In mid-April the Tripletts began work.[49]

But ultimately a great house needed more than just symmetrically placed outbuildings to cut a proper figure in the world. As important as what people saw was how they saw it—the total sequence of experiences that began the moment the house first came into view. Above all there had to be a suitably imposing approach, and over the next decade Washington would work continuously to formalize, embellish, and extend the drive leading to the west front of Mount Vernon. In a related effort, he also developed large, enclosed gardens on that side of the house.

Much of Washington's initial interest in gardening consisted of experiments in cultivating various species of native plants for practical purposes. In 1760 he described in his diary using one end of his garden as well as the area between the garden and the stable to plant different grass seeds to test how well they would grow. Shortly afterward he had pine trees planted at the head of "my Cherry Walk" and three days later others "in the Fencd place at the Cornr. of the Garden," after some of the livestock ("Creatures") had trampled on the first ones.[50]

In time, as the mention of a "Cherry Walk" suggests, Washington also came to see the ornamental possibilities in gardening, which again may well have been due to Martha's influence. An early order to Cary included "Langleys Book of Gardening," which remained in Washington's library as long as he lived.[51] Written by Batty Langley, the author of several widely used builders' guides, and first published in 1728, the book had as its full title *New Principles of Gardening: Or the Laying Out and Planting [of] Parterres, Groves, Wildernesses, Labyrinths, Avenues, Parks, etc. After a More Grand and Rural Manner, than has been done before; With Experimental Directions For raising the several Kinds of Fruit-Trees, Forest-Trees, Ever-Greens and Flowering Shrubs with which Gardens are adorn'd. To which is added The various Names, Descriptions, Temperatures, Medical Virtues, Uses and Cultivations of several Roots, Pulse, Herbs, etc. of the Kitchen and Physick Gardens, that are absolutely necessary for the Service of Families in general.*

Doubtless such a title was meant to inspire confidence among even the least knowledgeable of gardeners, but Mount Vernon confronted Washington with certain conditions that no amount of landscaping could alter. The usual place for a garden would have been on the opposite side of the house from the principal entrance. Gardens so placed were both screened from public view by the house and readily accessible from it, making them in effect private worlds for the enjoyment of owners and their guests. The gardens of great houses in Europe were routinely laid out in this way, and so was the garden at nearby Gunston Hall, the home of Washington's friend George Mason.[52] Yet at Mount Vernon such an arrangement was out of the question because the land on the east side of the house sloped too steeply toward the river.

Actually, Batty Langley would probably have applauded a plan that left the splendid view of the Potomac unencumbered by extensive formal gardens. The newness of his *New Principles of Gardening* consisted chiefly of stressing the beauty of "natural" as opposed to artificial landscape effects; such was the *More Grand and Rural Manner* he wished to promote. The plan Washington adopted followed a very different aesthetic, however. The only flat land near the house lay to the west; thus the garden would have to go there. Necessity also dictated that it should be fenced in some way to keep "Creatures" out, and brick walls, rather than ordinary fencing, would both accomplish that and provide greater privacy. But since nothing could be allowed to block the view of the

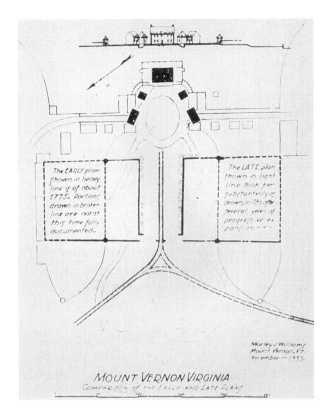

Conjectural drawing of Washington's initial development of the approach to Mount Vernon from the west. Courtesy of the Mount Vernon Ladies' Association.

house, the garden with its walls would have to be set off either to the left or right, an awkward, asymmetrical arrangement, unless, of course, there were two gardens, one on each side. This, indeed, was how it was eventually done: with a pair of gardens, identical in size and rectangular in shape, surrounded by high brick walls on three sides, with lower walls, topped by wooden fencing, facing in toward the center. Punctuating the four points where the higher and lower walls met were octagonal, wooden "garden houses" set on brick foundations, and in front of the lower walls stretched twin rectangular expanses of clipped, green lawn. Between those, neatly bisecting the entire composition, ran the drive to the house.[53]

The result was an imaginative solution to a difficult problem, though Langley would certainly not have approved of its undisguised imposition of human will on nature. For the most salient feature of the approach Washington had designed to his house was its artificiality. All symmetry and precise geometric shapes, like the paneling on the walls of so many of the rooms inside Mount Vernon, it was equally uncompromising in its rationality. It was also very much a surveyor's landscape, and as such spoke unmistakably of dominion—Washington's dominion—over everything one saw, moving up that wide, straight drive.

Along with its other virtues, too, the altered landscape made a great show of brick, the material of which so many leading Virginians had built their houses, and at long last Washington had found someone other than William Triplett to do the work. On May 3, 1762, Guy, a slave bricklayer hired from a nearby plantation, arrived at Mount Vernon.[54] He worked first on the kitchen, building a new oven, laying a hearth, and repairing the area behind it, but in a week's time he was ready to begin the garden walls, which proved to be a much longer project. By the end of July he had enclosed three sides of one of the gardens.[55] Eventually Philip Fletcher, a white artisan, came to make more bricks, seventy-eight thousand of them.[56] According to Washington's diary, the kiln was fired on October 23, and the holes were plugged to begin the cooling four days later.[57] Also, Guy's labor was purchased for another twelve months, which was not cheap. Washington paid his master, William Dangerfield, at the rate of £30 a year plus room and board.[58] Work on the garden walls would continue for several years longer, but during the winter of 1769, at a time when hands could be spared from the fields, trees were cleared to create an "Avenue" reaching across the land toward the main road, thus lengthening the central axis and giving those arriving at the house a more distant vista of it.[59]

While all this activity was going on outside, enhancements within the house had kept pace, as orders to Cary went off each fall and again in early summer. In 1762 mahogany knife cases were ordered for the top of the dining room sideboard, and two years later Cary sent fourteen leather chairs and six Windsor chairs painted green—the latter, perhaps, for one of the garden houses so the family and visitors could sit and catch the breeze on hot afternoons.[60] That summer, too, the Washingtons ordered, from a different source, still more chairs—two arm or "Elbow" and ten "common sitting Chairs for an Entertaining Room" to be "large neat and fashionable."[61]

Other additions of furniture followed, but basically by the end of the 1760s the new Mount Vernon stood complete, inside and out. Altogether it had taken more than ten years of work, yet in that time Washington had wholly remade not only the house but also the landscape around it. In the spring of 1761 Anne Fairfax Washington Lee had died, giving him outright ownership of the property, but the change made little difference. He had known since the death of Lawrence's sole surviving child in 1754 that he had only to outlive his brother's widow to inherit Mount Vernon, and by the time she died, he had already gone far toward making the place his own in every way. Now that process was finished, or so it might have seemed. By 1773, however, Washington was already planning a second major rebuilding of the house, and in the ensuing fifteen years he would radically alter its setting, tearing up and reshaping much of the landscape that had been so painstakingly created up to then. But before all that happened, certain other important events were to occur, both at Mount Vernon and in the larger world beyond it.

In the decade and a half after he left the military, Washington was first and last what he had decided to be: a planter. As hard as he worked to embellish his house and the grounds around it, he worked even harder to turn Mount Vernon into a productive, profitable agricultural enterprise. Nor did his efforts go unrewarded. In the end he did make the place pay, at least to a limited extent, an achievement that testified to both his perseverance and his skills as a manager. But success came in ways very different from those he imagined when he began.

Believing that knowledge was essential if he was to prevail, he had not been settled at home a month when he ordered Thomas Hale's four-volume *Compleat Body of Husbandry*, one of many works on agriculture he acquired—and read—over the years.[62] All of them taught the importance of system, order, and attention to detail, a lesson he had already learned in the military, and as nearly as possible he ran his plantation as he had his regiment, keeping meticulous records of everything, experimenting constantly with new methods, and personally overseeing the repair of buildings, the slaughter of hogs, the curing of pork, and the sowing and harvesting of crops each year.

That first summer, in order to "find out . . . the true bounds of my Mount Vernon tract of land," he resurveyed the original grant made to his great-grandfather and Nicholas Spencer, identifying the landmarks of that "ancient" past.[63] He also began acquiring adjoining tracts of land. Between 1760 and 1772 he made thirteen such purchases, ranging from six to eighteen hundred acres. The total came to more than thirty-seven hundred acres, which, with the land he had inherited and two small pieces he had added earlier, brought his holdings to just over sixty-five hundred acres. Mount Vernon by then included almost all the land between Dogue Creek and the broad bend in the Potomac to the east.[64] And more land to cultivate meant that more slaves were needed to do the work. In the twelve years from 1760 to 1772 the number of slaves over age sixteen at Mount Vernon rose from forty-three to ninety-five. Some of the increase came through natural reproduction, but Washington also regularly bought slaves during these years, financing his purchases for the most part as he financed his purchases of land, with drafts on Robert Cary and Co. in London.[65]

The purpose of all this, at least initially, was to produce more and better tobacco, the crop that had been Virginia's mainstay for well over a century. In that endeavor Washington was to be sorely disappointed, however. Despite his close, careful management and his high hopes at the beginning of each growing season, his estimates of the earnings his tobacco would yield were invariably too optimistic. Each year seemed to bring drought or heavy rains, either of which could ruin the crop and which, occurring in succession, washed the thin layer of topsoil into the Potomac, leaving behind a hard, clay surface cut by deep gullies.[66] One of Washington's experiments consisted of dredging the river, then growing seeds in soil mixed with varying proportions of Potomac mud and carefully recording the results in his diary. They were not encouraging.[67] The plain fact was the soil of Mount Vernon would never be rich enough to produce satisfactory yields of the kind of tobacco that commanded top prices in European markets. Washington also suspected that Cary did an indifferent job of selling the tobacco sent to him. Other planters received better prices for their tobacco of "the same kind exactly."[68] Yet even if his suspicions about Cary were incorrect, it remained true that Washington had little control over the marketing of his tobacco, a situation that made him acutely uncomfortable, as such things always did.[69]

Worse still, he was running into debt, and year by year the negative balance in his accounts with Cary grew larger. Adding to it, of course, were those interminable orders for London finery, not to mention his heavy purchases of land and slaves, all of which were supposed to be financed out of sales of tobacco. At first Washington had seen the situation as temporary, the result of that year's poor harvest or of Cary's failure to get a better price for the crop. But as the negative balance grew, it began to seem that something more fundamental might be wrong. By the spring of 1764 the debt had reached £1,811, and Cary was becoming concerned.[70]

To Cary's suggestion that Washington might consider reducing the balance, he replied testily that he was surprised someone "so steady, & constant as I have provd" would be reminded "how necessary it was for him to be expedious in his payments." He did not mind being charged interest on the debt, but it was not in his power, at least "in a manner convenient and agreeable to myself," to make payments "faster than my Crops . . . will furnish me with the means." He did concede that he hoped to see the situation resolved, even if he was unable to suggest how it might be done, because, as he remarked to Cary, "it is but an irksome thing to a free mind to be any ways hampered in Debt."[71]

Being in debt was irksome to "a free mind"—reason enough to avoid negative balances. Though in Washington's case it was already too late for that, at least he could try to keep his debt to Cary from becoming any larger, and if the cause of the problem was tobacco, he could stop growing it and concentrate on other crops instead, which is what he proceeded to do. As early as the autumn of 1766 he was writing that he had decided to discontinue "the business of Tobacco making . . . totally on this River."[72] Only at the Custis holdings on the York River, where the soil was better and the yields had been consistently good, would he continue to grow Virginia's traditional staple.

As replacements for tobacco he experimented with hemp, alfalfa, buckwheat, corn, and flax. His principal crop, however, became wheat, a choice that many Chesapeake planters were to make during these years, though Washington made it earlier than most. Wheat was less labor-intensive than tobacco, and he could grind the grain in his own mill and arrange for its sale locally. To add to the market that had long existed in the West Indies, a burgeoning population and years of poor harvests were creating a rising demand for American wheat in Europe, and the new port of Alexandria—only a few miles from Mount Vernon—offered easy access to both markets.[73]

Washington also found that a profitable business could be made of setting his slaves to fish in the Potomac. Curing and packing the catch, he used it at first to feed "the family" at Mount Vernon, but in 1769 he sent a small shipment to Antigua, which earned a good profit.[74] Thereafter he expanded his fishing operations steadily. Also, at the same time that he was developing new sources of income, he was searching for ways to cut expenses. Month by month he worked to make Mount Vernon as self-sufficient as possible. When his slaves fished, they did so in a schooner crafted by Washington's carpenters. A new mill was built, and both the flour it ground and the fish caught on the river were packed and shipped in barrels made "at home." Increasingly, too, the clothes worn by Mount Vernon's slaves were made of materials raised and processed on the plantation by slave spinners, weavers, seamstresses, and shoemakers.[75]

The Washingtons' orders to Cary reflected these changes. Luxury goods there still were, but fewer in proportion to items that would free Mount Vernon from dependence on the London market: coopers' tools, millstones, fishing nets, wheat sieves, looms, a book on weaving.[76] And if the debt to Cary persisted, at least it stopped growing at the rate it had been earlier. Though hardly a complete victory, this was a start, suggesting that with continued planning and hard work the negative balance might be reduced, even eliminated altogether.

Meanwhile, events elsewhere had taken a singularly portentous turn. As Washington struggled to make Mount Vernon pay, Parliament in England voted—for the first time—to tax His Majesty's North American subjects to raise revenue. With the legislative session in Williamsburg nearly over, Washington was probably already at Mount Vernon when news reached Virginia that the Stamp Act had finally passed, after months of rumor. If so, he missed Patrick Henry's impassioned attack on the measure. Nor would he have seen the end of the drama, with the boldest of Henry's resolutions first passed, then expunged the next day. Apparently some of Henry's fellow burgesses considered his utterances treasonous. Washington left no record of his opinion, but in two letters written later that year he did make clear what he thought of the Stamp Act.

Both letters went to England, one to Robert Cary and the other to Francis Dandridge, an uncle of Martha's. Essentially the letters repeated one another, but Cary was first treated to a long series of complaints about his handling of Washington's affairs. Washington chose to revisit this familiar ground, he announced pointedly, so he would "stand acquitted of the Imputation of fickleness if I am at last forced to a discontinuance of my corrispondance with your House." As for the Stamp Act, he noted that it was much discussed by what he called "the speculative part of the Colonists," who saw it as unconstitutional and "a direful attack on their Liberties." The language seemed to suggest that those were not Washington's own opinions, and in fact the most he said in criticism of the new tax was that it was "ill Judgd."[77] On the other hand, the reasons he gave for thinking so amounted to an intriguing and highly revealing mixture of theory, prediction, and conclusions drawn from his own personal situation.

He began by observing that "the whole produce of our labor," by which he meant the profits earned on American exports to England, already went to the mother country to pay for manufactured goods. Necessarily, therefore, any tax would reduce sales of British goods, since Americans would have that much less money to pay for them. As harmful as this would be to British interests in the short run, if it continued, it could have only one result: the growing—and finally complete—economic independence of America. "The Eyes of our People (already beginning to open) will perceive, that many of the Luxuries which we have heretofore lavished our Substance to Great Britain for can be well dispensed with whilst the Necessaries of Life are to be procured (for the most part) within ourselves. This consequently will introduce frugality, and be a necessary stimulation to Industry. Great Britain may then load her Exports with as Heavy Taxes as She pleases but where will the consumption be?"[78]

Where indeed! Patrick Henry might talk of rights and liberties; for Washington the quarrel over the Stamp Act had a different face. If England persisted in trying to tax Americans, Americans would do what he himself had already begun to do, given the difficulties he labored under as a planter dependent on the British market: one by one they would cut those ties that bound them, as producers and consumers, to England; they would wage, in fact, an economic revolution.

As the conflict with England deepened in the years ahead, Washington's sense of what was at stake took on a variety of dimensions, but at bottom his response would remain, as it was in this pair of letters, rooted in his personal experience. When his countrymen spoke of dark conspiracies to rob them of their liberties—using the paradigm they borrowed from English "Country Party" opposition ideology—he had only to think of Lord Loudoun, or Captain John Dagworthy at Fort Cumberland, or Robert Cary in London. As early as 1765, too, his experience had led him to contemplate, with no apparent anxiety, the prospect of at least one kind of American independence.[79]

The next round of attempted imperial reform and colonial protest found him even more forthcoming. When Parliament followed repeal of the Stamp Act by approving the so-called Townshend duties taxing paint, lead, glass, paper, and tea, the House of Burgesses once again protested. Yet many people, including Washington, thought stiffer measures were needed. "At a time when our lordly Masters in Great Britain will be satisfied with nothing less than the deprivation of American freedom," he wrote George Mason in the spring of 1769, "something shou'd be done to avert the stroke and maintain the liberty which we have derived from our Ancestors." No man ought to hesitate "a moment to use a[r]ms in defence of so valuable a blessing," Washington believed, but that should be done only as a last resort. Several of the northern colonies were planning to boycott British imports; he thought "this scheme" was a good one and hoped Virginia would follow suit.[80]

Washington also felt that a boycott would have certain "private, as well as public advantages," and here again his personal experience came to the fore. Many families in Virginia were overburdened with debt, he noted, yet found it almost impossible to curtail expenses because they were "ashamed to do it" and because any marked change in the way they lived might "create suspicions of a decay in . . . fortune, & such a thought the world must not harbour." With a boycott in place, however, those people would finally be able to economize because they would be "furnished with a pretext to live within bounds. "[81]

As it happened, Mason himself favored a boycott and was already working on a plan for one, which Washington carried with him to the next session of the burgesses, and which a majority of the members, meeting in Raleigh Tavern after Governor Botetourt had summarily dissolved the House, accepted with only minor changes. Signatures, including Washington's, were then affixed to formal Articles of Association, copies of which the burgesses took back home and urged their neighbors to sign. Washington's letter to Cary that summer also made clear his intention to comply. "If there are any Articles contain in either of the respective Invoices (Paper only excepted) which are Taxd by Act of Parliament for the purpose of Raising a Revenue in America, it is my express desire and request that they may not be sent, as I have very heartily enterd into an Association . . . [and] . . . am fully determined to adhere religiously to it."[82]

In 1770, the second and final year of the Virginia Association's existence, more than four hundred people in Washington's district pledged to abide by its terms. Even though the Townshend Acts, as a revenue-raising measure, did little more than attach a few pennies in duties to a very short list of luxury goods, taxes were taxes, and the average Virginian was fully capable of understanding that no one in the colony had given any kind of consent to these taxes, or had even been consulted about them. For men like Mason and Washington and the other burgesses, however, the issue did not end there, for the Townshend Acts did more than just raise revenue; they also specified how that revenue was to be spent. A new, centrally controlled customs system was to be funded by the duties, along with the salaries of governors, judges, and other royal officials. Thus was the power of the purse to be wrested from colonial assemblies, and even if the long-term consequences did not turn out to be the utter destruction of liberty that Patrick Henry had predicted, the consequences in the short run were likely to be grave enough. From time immemorial royal governors had had to dicker with the legislature for their salaries as well as every other expense of government in America, and their chief bargaining chips had always been the favors—the offices, the contracts, the land grants—it was uniquely in their power to distribute. Years before, William Byrd had described the system as accurately and succinctly as anybody ever did when he wrote: "Our government is so happily constituted that a governor must first outwit us before he can oppress us, and if he ever squeeze money out of us, he must first take care to deserve it."[83]

It is easy to imagine Washington nodding knowingly at these words, because just then he happened to be in the midst of a complex, protracted, and, from his standpoint, vitally important venture that depended absolutely on the goodwill and cooperation of Virginia's governor. Various proclamations issued during the late war had promised land to colonial troops as compensation for their services, and Washington had taken the lead in seeing that those promises were fulfilled. The stakes were high. The land would be in the West, and tens of thousands of acres were involved, the precise location of which had to be worked out in detail. Over a period of several years Washington met repeatedly with two successive governors, arguing step by step for what he took to be the most advantageous arrangement for his former troops, and, of course, for himself. At any point in the process, the governor could have ended the negotiations or so loaded them with obstacles that they became interminably protracted. But in more than a decade in the House of Burgesses, Washington, in his quiet way, had become someone it was important not to alienate. In the end he won most of what he wanted, and a rich prize it was. By 1773 the colony had distributed two hundred thousand acres of bounty land to veterans, of which Washington himself had received more than thirty thousand acres, all prime land in the valleys of the Ohio and the Great and Little Kanawha Rivers.[84]

Would the result have been the same if the king's ministers had carried the day over the issue of colonial taxation? In the spring of 1770, thanks to American resistance and protests from British merchants, Parliament had voted to repeal all of the Townshend duties except the one on tea. Yet the fact that the tax on tea remained in force—and for the purpose of raising revenue—proved that the British had not entirely abandoned their larger goal. So Washington could consider himself fortunate to have persuaded the governor to act when he did in the matter of the bounty lands. Who could tell what the future would bring if the British continued their assault on American rights?

Apart from that stubbornly persistent cloud on the horizon, however, Washington's affairs appeared to be moving forward more or less on track. He still owed Cary a great

Portrait of George Washington painted by Charles Willson Peale, 1772. Courtesy of The Washington/Custis/Lee Collection, Washington and Lee University, Lexington, Virginia.

deal of money, but the prospect of leasing his new western lands seemed to promise relief in that quarter, and the changes he had made at Mount Vernon were beginning to yield significant results. In 1771 his second grist mill went into operation, making it possible for him to process not only his own wheat but his neighbors' as well. As a mark of his faith in Mount Vernon's new staple, he would soon be registering his "G. Washington" brand of flour.[85] The spring of 1771 also saw an enormous catch of fish on the Potomac, from which Washington sold almost seven hundred thousand herring at 3s per hundred.[86] The plantation's other industries, too, were doing well, with cotton, wool, even silk cloth all being made "at home." At the end of 1771 Washington found that he had £371 in cash on hand at Mount Vernon, nearly enough to take care of the family's needs for an entire year.[87]

Of changes in and around the house there were relatively few, at least for the present. In May 1772 Charles Willson Peale painted Washington looking quietly self-confident in his Virginia Regiment uniform. Together with miniatures of Martha and the two young Custises done at the same time, the finished portrait would hang in the west parlor.[88] And early in 1773 the grounds acquired a new gardener, ending a search that Washington had begun two years before.[89]

———

With Mount Vernon approaching financial solvency, an important milestone had been reached. But the relative calm of the opening years of the decade was not to last. The second half of 1773, the year that had begun quietly enough with the arrival of the new gardener, saw the beginning of a rumbling succession of events that would do more to alter life at Mount Vernon than all the changes that had occurred up to then.

By midsummer the Washingtons had suffered two grievous losses. Early in July George William Fairfax and his wife, Sally, departed for England—permanently, it turned out—and the month before, Martha's daughter Patsy had died at the age of sixteen. Financial affairs that required their attention and poor health were the reasons given for the Fairfaxes' leaving, but undoubtedly the troubled state of relations between the colonies and England was also a factor. At first the question of whether they would return was left open, but within a year the decision had been made.[90] To Washington their going must have seemed particularly poignant. From the earliest days of his marriage to Martha, the two couples had been the best of friends, and then there were all the memories that stretched back even farther. He owed the Fairfaxes a great deal: their support had done much to launch him in life. Yet the world of patronage and influence they represented was the same one that had denied him a royal commission. Nor was he particularly indebted to them for his current standing. Since leaving the army he had made his own way, and as a result his friendship with the Fairfaxes had become more nearly one between equals. Ironically, with Belvoir empty, the Washingtons of Mount Vernon would now be the leading family in the neighborhood.

Patsy Custis had been suffering from seizures for several years. On the afternoon of June 19 she suddenly lost consciousness and within a matter of minutes died. A loving mother, Martha Washington was devastated by the loss.[91] But along with the pain it caused, Patsy's death promised to have certain other consequences, for her portion of the Custis inheritance would be divided between her next of kin—her mother and her brother. Martha's share would come to more than £8,000, and the first thing Washington proposed to do with it was pay off his debt to Cary. Cary raised questions about the legality of the transaction, however, so technically the negative balance remained, but in Washington's mind the matter had been fully and fairly resolved.[92]

Even with the payment to Cary, too, there would be more money to spend than there had been for years, and that very summer a decision was made that would claim at least part of the surplus. At the end of July, two weeks after the family's usual order had gone off to England, an addendum followed. The pretext Washington gave was the need for garden seeds, but he also "recollected . . . some other articles" that he wanted—one hundred panes of the "best" window glass, trowels for bricklayers and plasterers, and a long list of carpenters' tools, including measuring and drawing instruments and tools for fashioning window sash and interior woodwork detail.[93]

Clearly preparations of some sort were under way. During much of the summer Washington remained at home with Martha, except for a brief trip to Maryland. Meanwhile other supplies were being gathered together. August saw the purchase of pine plank, including more than two thousand feet of flooring, as well as a large quantity of oyster shells, presumably for making mortar and plaster.[94] Then, early in October, a third order went off to Cary, and this time Washington was more forthcoming about his plans. "I am almost ashamed to trouble you in the same year with such frequent orders for Goods," he wrote, "but . . . I am under a necessity of making some Repairs to, and alterations in my House." In addition to another hundred panes of window glass, he wanted paint, hinges, locks, brads and nails, sash line and lead for window weights, glue, and plaster of paris.[95]

Perhaps out of eagerness to impress Cary with his prudence, Washington had described his plans for Mount Vernon in distinctly modest terms, but in fact what he had in mind was anything but modest. His only surviving drawing of the exterior of the house almost certainly dates from that summer, and it shows a completely transformed west front, with a projecting central pediment added to the roof, a cupola rising above it, and additions to both the north and south ends of the building that effectively doubled it in size.[96] There were to be other changes as well: two new pairs of outbuildings flanking the lengthened house and connected to it by curved arcades; a soaring piazza facing the river; and on the inside, a new study and a bedchamber for the Washingtons to the south, and a very large room with an imposing "Venetian" window to the north.

Presumably all of these elements were fixed in Washington's mind sometime before the end of 1773, but there is no indication when they first occurred to him, or how and when a mass of separate details coalesced into a single plan. Nor is there much informa-

Drawing by George Washington of the west front of Mount Vernon, 1773. In the drawing, Washington corrects the asymmetry of the facade, which in reality could not be done. Courtesy of the Mount Vernon Ladies' Association.

tion on another, even more basic point. Washington had already rebuilt Mount Vernon once, scarcely more than a decade earlier, and it had not been easy. Why, then, had he decided to begin the entire process all over again?

In his note to Cary he had described the work on the house as a matter of "necessity," and certainly a case could be made for that view. The recent changes that had done so much to alter operations at Mount Vernon had clear implications for the physical fabric of the place. A more diversified set of economic activities required a more diversified range of facilities: spaces in which to process and store a variety of crops, to spin, weave, and sew, to make and repair equipment of all kinds. Growth and diversity also called for rethinking the relations between buildings with special functions and the main house. Where should they be placed to operate most efficiently yet still not interfere with the social life of the plantation's hub, and what arrangement of spaces would seem most orderly, most pleasing—and most impressive?

As important as such issues were, however, virtually all of them could have been taken care of by improving and repositioning the plantation's outbuildings, a process that was already under way in 1773 and would continue for years afterward. Old structures were torn down, new ones were built, the uses of existing buildings were changed, alterations were made: this was routine work for the plantation's slave carpenters and need not have involved any changes in the main house at all.

Yet the centerpiece of this latest version of Mount Vernon was to be a renovated and expanded "Mansion House." A moderately large and imposing house was to be made bigger and more imposing, and it was to acquire several unusual spaces, including a very large room obviously meant for entertaining, and the more private configuration of rooms for the Washingtons' own use at the other end of the building. Up to a point, too, the altered economy of Mount Vernon probably did influence these changes. Managing a mixed collection of enterprises demanded more thought and concentration than managing a single one. It also required more elaborate systems of recordkeeping. The new study would provide space for both.

Similarly, every year brought scores of visitors to Mount Vernon, but whereas once most of them had been relatives or old friends, now they were as likely to be business or political associates of Washington's. Though it was still imperative that they be shown every courtesy, more privacy for the mistress of the house at certain times during the day would surely have seemed appealing. Hence the Washingtons' new bedchamber, or "Mrs. Washington's room," as it was invariably called.

But here too it is easy enough to imagine how the needs of both Washingtons could have been met without a full-scale rebuilding of the main house. Patsy was gone, and earlier that year Jackie Custis had entered King's College in New York. He was also engaged to be married. As a result there would be more free space at Mount Vernon than there had been at any time since the Washingtons' marriage, and in that situation simply changing the uses of a few rooms might have worked well enough. Yet if Washington ever considered that possibility, clearly he rejected it. Again, the question is why.

One obvious answer could have been the endlessly shifting tides of fashion. The years since Washington's first rebuilding of the house had brought no letup in the rate at which tastes changed, as he had good reason to know. Earlier in 1773 he had spent a month traveling to New York to take Jackie Custis to college, stopping along the way in Philadelphia, among other places. As always on such trips there were new buildings—and new building styles—to see. Recently, too, the Washingtons had begun crossing the Potomac two or three times a year to visit a growing circle of friends in and around Annapolis, where there was also much to see and learn.

A prosperous port as well as Maryland's capital, Annapolis was a lively place. Washington especially liked attending the races there each fall, which were celebrated with a nonstop round of social festivities. In 1772 he had stayed at Governor Robert Eden's for the occasion, and over a period of six days went to the theater four times; attended a ball at Assembly House and at least two late evening supper parties; dined the first day with the Jockey Club at the Coffee House, another day at the governor's, and at a different private house on each of the remaining four days. Meanwhile he lost £1.6 at the races, a small enough price to pay for what appears to have been a thoroughly enjoyable time.[97]

Annapolis was also a place that wore its wealth on its sleeve, and during those years it was undergoing a building boom of major proportions, at least among the rich. Virtually all the people the Washingtons regularly saw when they visited the city had either built houses within the past few years or were in the midst of doing so. Of Washington's five dinner hosts when he was there for the races in 1772, Daniel Jenifer, John Ridout, and Governor Eden himself had all recently completed houses in or near Annapolis, and Edward Lloyd was just overseeing the finishing touches on a new, three-story town house that he confidently expected would be the grandest private residence in the city.

Like the great houses of the Virginia tidewater, those in Annapolis were built of brick, but the Virginia houses tended to be thirty or forty years older. They also owed much to local vernacular building traditions, and since 1750 American builders had come to rely more and more instead on British pattern books. With their crisply engraved designs—all done in "correct" classical taste—of doorways, chimneypieces, cornices, pediments, and every other type of architectural detail, the pattern books provided surefire access to the latest styles. Some even included plans for entire buildings. Though American houses were rarely copied in toto from books, skillful builders working with the designs for individual details could produce impressive results. At their best, such houses exuded an engaging sophistication that gave them considerable appeal, and nowhere in America could one have seen pattern books used to better effect than in Annapolis.[98]

As it happened, much of the credit for the high quality of the city's stylish new houses belonged to a single individual—William Buckland—whom Washington almost certainly knew. Trained in England as a carpenter, Buckland had come to America eighteen years earlier as an indentured servant to design and execute the woodwork at Gunston Hall, the new house then being built by Washington's neighbor George Mason. After that he worked for a time in Richmond County before shifting operations to Annapolis in 1772. In addition to doing interior and exterior woodwork, he acted as an undertaker supervising general construction and provided architectural plans for an unknown number of houses. In 1773 he was finishing work on Edward Lloyd's house and was about to begin one for Matthias Hammond. The Hammond house, for which he served as architect in the full modern sense, was to be his finest achievement but also one of his last, for he died suddenly in 1774.[99]

The Harwood–Hammond House, Annapolis, Maryland, William Buckland, architect.
Photograph by William H. Pierson.

Buckland's great gift as both an artisan and an architect was his talent for adaptation. The inventory of his estate listed a large collection of pattern books, and from them came all the elements of his work. His contribution was to select, combine, and blend those elements, which he did with consummate finesse. He was also adept at adjusting what he found in the pattern books to local conditions and materials. Together those abilities made him perhaps the most accomplished American architect of his day.

But even though Washington was regularly in Annapolis during the years Buckland was doing his most important work and undoubtedly knew him, nothing indicates that he ever worked on Mount Vernon. This seems all the more surprising because so many of the prominent features of Buckland's houses were to find counterparts there, including the pediment on the redesigned west front, the Venetian window at the north end of the house, and the basic, five-part composition that linked the main house to the flanking outbuildings. Evidently, however, Washington was satisfied that such details could be incorporated in his plans without additional architectural expertise—that, guided by what he had seen, and borrowing liberally from the pattern books (as Buckland himself had), he and his builders could give Mount Vernon everything it needed of style and beauty.

This was the system he had followed the first time he rebuilt the house. It was also the way a great many other buildings in Virginia had been built, and recently he had seen it used with notable success at Pohick Church, which he had helped plan as a member of the Truro Parish Vestry. There had been no "architect" in that case either. The vestry,

Pohick Church. Courtesy of the Mount Vernon Ladies' Association.

which also included George Mason and George William Fairfax, made the major design decisions, presumably in consultation with Daniel French, the undertaker. Later, when French died, Mason volunteered to see the project through to completion.[100] The result was a handsome two-story brick building with graceful arched windows and elegantly worked limestone doorways (taken from Batty Langley's *Treasury of Designs*) that Washington was proud to show off to visiting friends and relatives.[101]

At Pohick Church he also found two of the artisans he would need for the work at Mount Vernon: Going Lanphier, who agreed to serve as undertaker, and William B. Sears, a gifted woodcarver who had worked under Buckland at Gunston Hall and later in Richmond County. No doubt before hiring them he explained his plans at length, and certainly much of what he wanted done would have seemed familiar to the two men. Balanced, symmetrical facades, pediments, Venetian windows, and elaborate cornices and chimneypieces were their stock-in-trade. Mount Airy, one of the houses in Richmond County that Sears had worked on with Buckland, was laid out almost exactly as Mount Vernon would be, with a central block connected to flanking outbuildings by curved, quadrant arms, in the best neo-Palladian manner.

But some aspects of Washington's plans must have surprised Lanphier and Sears, for in the end the rebuilt Mount Vernon would be more than simply a pastiche of borrowed details—it would include elements that owed little or nothing to the fashionable taste of the day. At crucial points Washington had chosen to strike out on his own in his plans for the house. The open design of the quadrant arcades (or "covered ways," as he called them), the cupola used as a flourish on a private house, and the great piazza fronting the river were all features that ignored the dictates of fashion. And with them, Mount Vernon succeeded in being something that none of Buckland's creations, for all their finesse, were: it succeeded in being original. In that respect, too, the house would hint at yet another reason for its rebuilding—perhaps the most compelling one of all.

Fifteen years earlier Washington had remade Mount Vernon in the image of the houses lived in by those privileged souls who stood at the top of Virginia's social order. Now he too was part of that charmed circle and could afford to be less concerned about the opinions of other people. But before 1773 all of his accomplishments had been clouded by debt, a situation Patsy Custis's death had changed. To be burdened with debt, he had told Cary, was "irksome . . . to a free mind," and to George Mason at the time of the Virginia Association he had written movingly of the constant anxiety people in debt felt about the judgment of "the world." To be out of debt, then, was to be free of such fears—free too of the sense that his life was lived at the sufferance of others—and what better way for him to mark those freedoms than to enlarge and embellish a house that did not need further enlarging or embellishment, simply because he wanted to? Viewed in this light, the rebuilding of Mount Vernon becomes a gesture, a celebration, an affirmation. Through it Washington would proclaim himself once again a free man, and do so with a house that was indisputably his own creation.

Given the timing of the decision, too, another obvious source of that impulse suggests itself. For the moment relations with England remained calm, but nothing had been done to resolve the fundamental disagreement dividing the colonies and the king's ministers. Until that changed there could be no security, no real peace. Nor was there any reliable guarantee of American liberty beyond the determination of those who sensed the danger to stay the course they had chosen, wherever it might lead. In time Washington would offer formal, public pledges on that score, but through all the vicissitudes of the years ahead, he also would continue rebuilding his house—his personal declaration of independence.

By October 1773 Going Lanphier had drawn up a "Bill of Scantling" for framing the new construction.[102] After that there was nothing left to do but collect the necessary building materials, wait for shipments from England, and hope that the weather would turn early the following spring. Finally, toward the end of April, Lanphier arrived, ready to start the addition to the south end of the house. The process of building had begun again, and for the moment Washington was free to be sure that everything took shape as he had planned it would.[103] Before turning to that process, however, it will be useful to look more closely at what preceded it—at how, exactly, Washington functioned in his role as architect of Mount Vernon.

CHAPTER 4

"Things Not Quite Orthodox": George Washington, Architect

PLANNING BUILDINGS combined two of Washington's great enthusiasms: his surveyor's passion for imposing order on space and his lifelong love of the theater, coupled with his sense of life itself as a series of theatrical performances. A well-conceived building was one that both satisfied the mind and set the stage for purposeful, dramatic action. But as important as architecture was to Washington, he never had much to say about it in general terms. Happily, however, his silence was not absolute, for in a series of letters written toward the end of his life, he did hazard several singularly revealing remarks on the subject.

The letters resulted from his decision to build a pair of rental houses in "the Federal City," as he continued to call the place that would soon become the nation's capital and bear his name. Half investment and half patriotic gesture, the project turned out to be more troublesome than he had expected, but it did have one pleasant consequence: it enabled him to pursue his acquaintance with Dr. William Thornton, who generously offered to supervise construction of the houses. Washington had first encountered Thornton through a design he had done for the national capitol, which would eventually house Congress. The deadline in the competition for the project had already passed when John Trumbull sent Thornton's plans to Washington, but liking what he saw, Washington sent the design on to the judges, who eventually chose it as the best of those submitted. Born in Tortola, Thornton had earned his medical degree in Scotland and, in addition to busying himself as an amateur architect, was an inveterate tinkerer as well as a gifted painter and writer. In accepting his help, Washington wanted no misunderstanding about his own architectural abilities: he knew what he liked and nothing more. What he neglected to add was that in his own mind such knowledge counted for a good deal.[1]

By the time Thornton became involved in the project, Washington had already drawn up in neat, workmanlike fashion a ground-floor plan for the two houses. They were to be joined in a single structure, with their principal doorways side by side in the center. Apparently there were no elevation drawings, but in a letter to Thornton, Washington did propose placing a pediment in the center of the roof, with a dormer window on either side of it. In Philadelphia he had seen double houses with pediments, which, as he said, "pleased me."[2] But Thornton did not like the idea of a pediment, arguing that it would not add "any beauty" and taking it to be, as he wrote, "a Desideratum in Architecture to hide as much as possible the Roof." In London, parapets often served that purpose, and that was the solution he recommended.[3]

In framing his reply, Washington seemed a bit stung by Thornton's reaction to the pediment scheme (after all, Mount Vernon had a pediment!) and in a roundabout way tried to justify his original suggestion. He knew that "rules of Architecture" existed "to give Symmetry, and just proportion to all the Orders, and parts of building in order to please the eye," and being ignorant of those rules, he had probably violated them. Still, he felt that "small departures" would be noticed "only by the skilful Architects, or by the eye of criticism." The great majority of people could just as easily be pleased "with things not quite orthodox," which, presumably, "would be the case relative to a Pediment in the Roof over the *doors* of my houses in the City."[4]

But evidently having asked Thornton's advice, Washington felt obliged to take it. The houses went up without a pediment. The debate need not have ended there, however, for Washington was by no means alone in his willingness to depart from the "rules of Architecture." William Hogarth in his *Analysis of Beauty* had rejected all such dogmatic and, as he described them, "pompous terms of art."[5] And no less an authority than David Hume in *Of the Standard of Taste* had declared flatly that "beauty and deformity . . . belong entirely to the sentiment. . . . Each mind perceives a different beauty."[6] Yet for all the support they lent his views, it is unlikely that Washington ever heard of the works

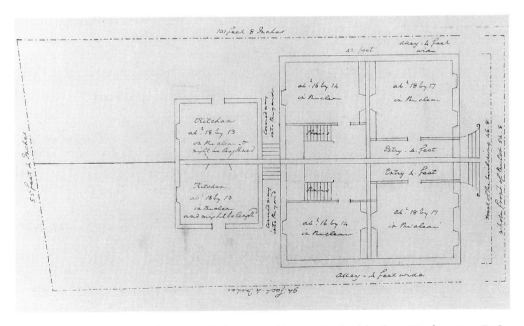

Drawing by George Washington of the pair of houses he had built in Washington, D.C. Courtesy of Albert H. Small, Washington, D.C.

in question. As he made clear in his remarks to Thornton, he approached architecture first and last through personal experience; there was scant room in that process for treatises on taste.

In deciding how and what to build, Washington also tended to focus on specific problems and solutions. If theory did not enter into it, neither was there much sense of the building as a total composition. No wonder he was surprised by Thornton's advice. The younger man recommended hiding the roof for the sake of the beauty of the building as a whole. He also knew that the usual function of a pediment was to call attention to a centrally placed main entrance. Such a flourish was bound to sit oddly on a double house with two main entrances.

In thinking in these terms, Thornton was approaching the subject very much as architects today do, albeit in ways that were still somewhat novel at the time. That architects design buildings seems axiomatic, but the very word "design" implies any number of things that are by no means essential if the only issue is how to erect a particular structure. A design is something in which all of the separate parts are related to one another and, more important, to a fundamental aesthetic. In addition, if the building is an important one, its design must be original—noticeably different from the designs of other buildings. Understood this way architectural design becomes, in fact, one of the fine arts, which is also basic to our sense of what architects do.

Yet all of these ideas, including the notion of architecture as art, took firm hold in England only in the early years of the eighteenth century, and in America the change came even more slowly. Near the end of his life, while he was working in Annapolis, William Buckland's portrait was painted by his friend Charles Willson Peale. It shows him seated at a table, wearing a handsome brown suit, with a set of drafting tools and a pile of books at his elbow and the ground-floor plan of the Hammond house lying before him. What we see, in short, is a confident, learned, professional gentleman, but in reality Buckland's profession barely existed in America at the time. Most colonial buildings owed their shape to the artisans who built them, or their owners, or some sort of collaboration between the two.[7]

Still, projects of any size or complexity had always required builders and owners to make choices—many of them—and Mount Vernon was no exception. Moreover, "planning," the word Washington himself used to describe what preceded construction, was apt enough: if the desired result was not designed, it was at least carefully planned, and "the Plan" was invariably in hand before the first shovelful of earth was removed. It might be a drawing or simply a set of instructions, but regardless of the form it took, it remained a crucial part of the building process, and at Mount Vernon Washington provided the plans. Moreover, as time passed he tended increasingly to rely on his own instincts: to please himself, as he said to Thornton, rather than following either the fashionable taste of the day, or what he called the "rules of Architecture."

But in the beginning the conventional sources were crucial, and Washington never abandoned them entirely. Since, too, he had no opportunity to see English or European buildings *in situ*, the most authoritative guide remained the pattern books. The Venetian

Portrait of William Buckland by Charles Willson Peale. Courtesy, Yale University Art Gallery, Mabel Brady Garvan Collection.

window at the north end of Mount Vernon, the central doorway, the oval window in the pediment, and much of the interior woodwork all came from one pattern book or another, with Batty Langley's *City and Country Builder's and Workman's Treasury of Designs* being the chief source.[8]

Yet it is also possible to exaggerate the influence of pattern books at Mount Vernon. Like the frosting on a cake, the details from them tended to spread over the surfaces of the building without ever really engaging its structure. The Venetian window, for example, lacks the entire bottom portion of Langley's design, including its principal supporting elements, and hence is left to float, unanchored, against the rusticated weatherboarding around it. And the pediment fares little better, clamped down as it is on a facade originally planned with no notion that one day it would have to bear the added visual weight of so grand an accessory.

Nor, for all the use he made of them, did Washington seem particularly interested in owning pattern books. His orders for English goods never mentioned them, and the inventory of his estate listed only a handful of titles having anything to do with building. Useful largely for practical information, there was Francis Price's *The British Carpenter*. Langley was represented only by his book on gardening. A small volume by W. Watts,

Left: *Design for a Venetian window from Batty Langley's* City and Country Builder's and Workman's Treasury of Designs *(London, 1750). Courtesy of the Mount Vernon Ladies' Association.*

Right: *The Venetian window, Mount Vernon. Courtesy of the Mount Vernon Ladies' Association.*

titled *The Seats of the Nobility and Gentry*, contained a collection of views, largely picturesque, that revealed little about design. The only other relevant title was "Middleton's Architecture," which presumably referred to Charles Middleton's *Picturesque and Architectural Views for Cottages, Farm Houses, and Country Villas.* Part pattern book and part architectural treatise, this was an important publication, in full folio, which presented designs for houses modest in size but still quite modishly detailed. However, it was not published until 1793 — long after it could have had any impact on the several rebuildings of Mount Vernon.[9]

Since Washington owned none of the major published sources used in planning the changes at Mount Vernon, he must have borrowed them, which would have been easy enough to do. Several of the artisans who came to work on the house doubtless carried a pattern book or two in their gear. Another likely source was John Mercer, the family lawyer, whose large library at Marlborough included a number of important works on architecture.[10] Judging from the results, too, pattern books must have been much in evidence when the members of the Truro Parish vestry met to plan projects such as Pohick Church.[11]

But wherever Washington found the pattern books he used at Mount Vernon, he took from them only specific details. The basic, five-part configuration of the main house and its attatched dependencies was pictured in dozens of architectural publications, but the precise layout and proportions of Mount Vernon came from no known British design source, though several architectural historians have diligently attempted to prove otherwise.

The most ambitious such attempt is the case Thomas Waterman presents in *The Mansions of Virginia, 1706–1776.* Waterman argues that an architect named John Ariss was responsible for planning most of the changes made at Mount Vernon over the years, and that he took his designs from William Adam's *Vitruvius Scotius.*[12] Neither of these contentions stands up to scrutiny. "John Oriss" did advertise his services as an architect in the *Maryland Gazette* in 1751, mentioning that he used "Gibbs' Architect" in his work. And a John Ariss rented land from Washington at one point. Yet there is no evidence in Washington's papers that Ariss, or Oriss, ever worked on Mount Vernon, and the various elevations of the house bear no resemblance to any of the plates in *Vitruvius Scotius.*[13]

The truth is that Washington's most important borrowings at Mount Vernon were not from published sources at all, but from American buildings he knew firsthand. The great houses of tidewater Virginia and others that he saw and admired on his travels across the Potomac to Maryland and northward to Philadelphia and New York and on beyond to New England: those were his chief architectural models.

However, to say this and nothing more would be to ignore the fact that the American models Washington followed at Mount Vernon also tended to be distinctly British in conception and detail. The idea of covering the main house with beveled, sand-painted boards to imitate dressed stone, for example, probably came from Peter Harrison's work in Newport and Boston, but Harrison owed a large debt to British sources. The same was true of William Buckland, whose Annapolis houses seem to have contributed so much to Washington's second rebuilding of Mount Vernon.[14] In the broadest sense, too, virtually all the buildings he saw were products of a culture still fundamentally British, and if anything, the influence of British taste on American houses and house furnishing had grown stronger as the eighteenth century progressed. Twenty years after the Declaration of Independence, William Thornton could still hope to convince Washington to use a parapet on his rental houses by citing English precedent, and whatever he thought of the argument, Washington accepted the suggestion.

Ultimately there is no way to banish the specter of British influence at Mount Vernon because Washington himself could not have done so even if he had wanted to, and at least during the early years he seems to have been comfortable with that fact. Examples of English taste are everywhere at Mount Vernon. The taste in question also bears the indelible stamp of that most English of institutions—the aristocratic country house. In this case, too, the connection goes much deeper than just the occasional detail, for the way Washington planned the changes at Mount Vernon was remarkably similar to the process that shaped hundreds of smaller country houses across Great Britain. Few of the structures in question qualify as great monuments of architectural history. Often built, like Mount Vernon, piecemeal over many years, they reveal their histories plainly enough. Yet at any given moment even the most modest of them tended to follow as closely as possible the fashions set at grander establishments.

With singular insight, architectural historian Mark Girouard has described English country houses, in his book on the subject, as "power houses."[15] His point is not just that such houses were lived in by powerful people, but that the houses were actually part of the process by which power was acquired and maintained. From the end of the sixteenth century on, no Englishman lacking a suitable country seat could hope to win a place in the nation's ruling class. The typical country house thus became, in another of Girouard's apt phrases, "an image-maker."[16] It displayed the owner's credentials as well as his or her aspirations, and the key component of the display was style, which, like power, moved through the hierarchy from the top down. But unlike power, which was jealously guarded, style could be appropriated through the simple device of imitation.

When power depended mainly on military force, fashion and necessity together favored houses that looked like the armed fortresses they often were. Thick stone walls punctuated by towers topped with battlements, courtyards surrounded by lodgings for retainers, and, invariably, the great hall in which the whole household gathered for meals: these were standard features of a house type duplicated in versions of every size. Yet by the eighteenth century the taste for such dwellings had long since passed, and in its place reigned classicism—that harkening back to the architecture of ancient Greece and Rome that was one of Renaissance Italy's principal gifts to the world.[17]

The earliest wholly classical English buildings were designed by Inigo Jones in the second decade of the seventeenth century, but the new style was slow to take hold at first. Based on his own observations of Italian architecture, and in particular the work of Andrea Palladio, Jones's designs must have seemed startlingly novel to his countrymen. They also had to compete with a vigorous native style that blended Renaissance elements with a rich array of traditional decorative details.[18]

In the end, however, the appeal of classicism proved irresistible. As a style it was ideally suited to the changing character of Britain's ruling class. With military prowess at a discount, power had come to depend on other qualities, and chief among those were the talents and graces associated with life at court. Education and the knowledge and polish it brought became valuable tools for anyone wishing to rise. Turning a neat couplet—or being able to recognize the proper turning of a Corinthian column—were more than just pleasant diversions: such things stood as the mark of a well-bred person, and having an architecturally "correct" house made the point with particular clarity.[19]

Classical architecture also greatly enhanced the altered patterns of upper-class life. The elaborate symmetries of exteriors bristling with pediments, columns, and arcades were more than skin deep. Inside the house, rooms were generally arrayed in mirror image of one another on either side of a central axis running from front to rear, beginning with an imposing entrance hall and a great room beyond it. A noble staircase was also an essential part of the ensemble, for here, at the center, was where the building made its grandest gestures; from this point one moved on to lesser spaces, in a carefully controlled progression leading from larger rooms to smaller, more intimate ones. Nothing was left to chance; everywhere system, order, and formality ruled. The same principles applied to the rest of the structure as well. Typically, its central core was set aside for the owners and their guests. Service functions and functionaries were relegated to the periphery, to distant kitchen and stable wings and to separate servants' quarters. In Vir-

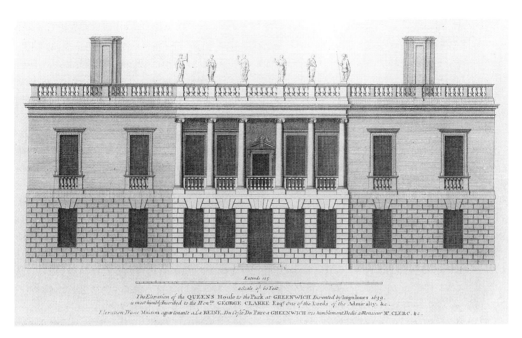

*The Queen's House, Greenwich, England, Inigo Jones architect, as shown in Colin
Campbell's* Vitruvius Britannicus *(London, 1715) . Authors' collection.*

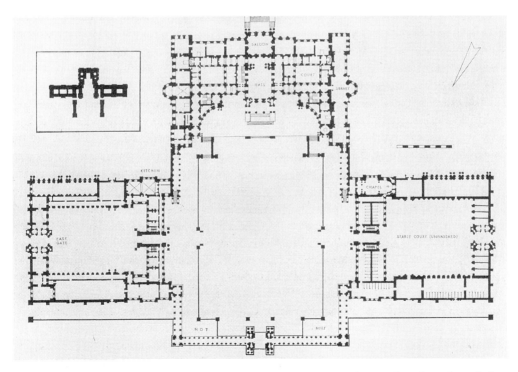

*Blenheim Palace, Woodstock, England, ground-floor plan, John Vanbrugh and Nicholas
Hawksmoor, architects. Courtesy of the Williams College Art Department.*

ginia the characteristic pattern appeared early on, and Washington followed it scrupulously at Mount Vernon.

The world of the classical style house was thus thoroughly compartmentalized, which in turn reflected the way life was meant to be lived in such houses. Architectural formality went hand in hand with social formality, and both stemmed from a vision of human relationships that saw society itself organized according to precise gradations of status and rank. In the earlier, fortress-style house, rank was also important, but it was expressed differently. When presiding in the hall, the head of the house sat in a throne-like chair, often on a raised dais. Without the actual, physical presence of someone at the apex of the pyramid, the confused jumble of the medieval hall had little visible meaning. In contrast, in a classical-style house the meaning—that vision of hierarchy—was made palpable in the very fabric of the building, becoming thereby both less personal and more permanent, truly part of an immutable "order of things." At a time when traditional categories like family, clan, and community were giving way steadily before more abstract forms of social organization, that amounted to a shift of major significance. Ahead lay the growing importance of class as a structural element in modern life; quite literally classical architecture set the stage for that change.

Also crucial in bringing about the triumph of classicism was the increasing emphasis on privacy in architecture as well as in society. Being powerful had always meant living surrounded by dependents, and that was still important; but increasingly, too, so was the opportunity to spend time away from the crowd, and the higher one's rank, the more elaborately protected his or her privacy would be. In large houses there was usually at least one state suite, consisting of an antechamber, a "withdrawing" chamber, a bedchamber, and finally a cabinet—the most private space of all—with access granted to fewer and fewer people as the sequence unfolded. Thus not only was the status of the suite's occupant affirmed, but also the status of others could be fixed by the depth of penetration they were permitted.[20]

To be sure, only in the grandest households were such intricate dramas of power and place routinely enacted. Farther down the hierarchy, life was less formally arranged, and so were houses. Yet that by no means weakened the grip of classicism, for one of its appealing features was the ease with which it could be adapted to different kinds of building projects. New houses of every size could be built in classical style, and it was equally useful to owners planning to alter existing structures.[21] Windows and doors could be replaced, facades could be redesigned, outbuildings could be added. Or an entire run of new rooms could be built, parallel to and adjoining existing ones, thereby creating a "double pile" configuration and effectively doubling the size of the house. With means enough, the owner and his builder might even add a fully developed temple front, complete with freestanding classical columns. But if that proved too expensive, the mass and dignity of a temple could still be suggested by projecting the central portion of the building forward and topping it with a pediment. Or, as Washington did at Mount Vernon, a pediment alone might be used. And at the very least a symmetrical arrangement of windows and doors would make any house look more classically correct.

For the most part, it was in such relatively modest guises that architectural classicism made its way across Britain and ultimately to America. If few of the buildings Washington saw in Virginia or later, on his travels to places like New York, Newport, Annapolis, and Philadelphia, would have satisfied London standards, that was equally true of dozens of country houses, confidently embellished with eye-catching details in "the latest taste," in every county in England. All the while, too, the standards themselves continued to change, so the ambitious provincial or colonial builder aimed at what amounted to a constantly moving target, with predictable results: direct hits were rare.

In the early eighteenth century the single most pronounced shift in English architectural taste—and one that touched Mount Vernon more than a little—was the rise of that curious phenomenon, neo-Palladianism. Less a distinct style than a refinement of the prevailing classical idiom, neo-Palladianism drew its inspiration in part from Inigo Jones's early "pure" classicism, but even more important was the work of the man Jones had so much admired, Andrea Palladio. The initial practitioner and leading publicist of the new mode was Colin Campbell, the author of *Vitruvius Britannicus*. Its central figure, however, was Richard Boyle, the vastly rich third earl of Burlington, who, having employed Campbell on various projects, eventually took up architecture himself in collaboration with his versatile protégé, William Kent.[22]

With Palladio and Jones as their heroes, the neo-Palladians rejected out of hand almost all of recent British architecture. Far too many "Absurd Novelties" was Campbell's verdict.[23] Yet the distinctions involved could be very subtle. Like the houses Campbell criticized, those he designed tended to be boldly palatial, with massive central blocks, symmetrical floor plans, and attached dependencies. The difference was evident in details like flatter, plainer wall surfaces, more widely spaced windows and hence fewer of them, and, on the exterior at least, a more sparing use of classical ornament.

Such was Campbell's homage to Palladio's "Antique Simplicity": an architecture defined as much by what it left out as by what it included. It was also an architecture deeply committed to formal, immutable "rules" of the sort Washington referred to in his correspondence with Thornton. But that was still only part of the story, for in the political battles of the day the neo-Palladians were ardent adherents of the Whig side, especially as it involved opposition to Stuart "tyranny" and support for the Hanoverian succession.

The link between Whiggery and Palladio's architecture was no accident. He himself had pointed the way in his *I Quattro Libri dell' Architettura*, the first full English translation of which appeared in 1716, by embedding his work in a rich framework of meanings, including a lyrical celebration of rural life. In the country a gentleman, "fatigued by the agitations of the city," could be "restored and comforted" through farming, recreation, and "studies of letters and contemplation." That was the ideal Palladio held out to his readers, and to help them achieve it he provided plans for a series of country houses or "villas," as he called them, designed to accommodate in a single structure every aspect of gentlemanly rural life. The goal was to create, in his phrase, "a little city," complete and all-sufficing, where the gentleman could be truly his own master, truly free.[24]

Whatever the appropriateness of such houses—part palatial residence, part philosopher's retreat, part barn—to the actual situation of England's upper classes, Palladio's linking of personal independence and country life was full of significance for his Whig

*Design for a villa after Palladio, from Edward Hoppus and Benjamin
Cole,* Andrea Palladio's Architecture *(London, 1736). This was one of
the earlier publications presenting Palladio's work to the British public.
Though the engravings took substantial liberties with Palladio's designs,
the book went through at least two editions. Authors' collection.*

devotees. In British political culture at the time, "court" and "country" were ever at odds. The one stood for the arena of corrupt power and privilege at the center, the other for principled opposition by liberty-loving individuals on the periphery. Through much of the middle half of the eighteenth century, the Tories had a better claim than the Whigs to being "country," but in the beginning when the Whigs were solidifying their power under Sir Robert Walpole—England's first "prime minister"—they remained eager to reserve that distinction for themselves. What Palladian architecture gave them was a way of translating the abstract symbols of political rhetoric into the solid stuff of houses and horse stalls.[25] Significantly, with the enormous profits he made from office, Walpole built a lavish country house designed by Colin Campbell.

In time there even came to be a way of treating the land that neatly fit the Whig vision. Sweeping aside countless geometrically precise allées, canals, and parterres done in the "French taste," Lancelot "Capability" Brown and other landscape architects brought the lawn directly up to the house and created around it a terrain of rolling fields relieved by seemingly random drifts of trees, meandering streams, and irregularly shaped ponds and lakes. The point, as Batty Langley and other popularizers of the new style noted, was to have everything appear as unartificial as possible, thereby laying claim to all those special virtues that were presumed to reside in the "natural" world.[26] Invariably, too, the effect was to soften the visual impact of the house, making it, as architectural historian John Summerson has observed, "less a command than a statement . . . an object not controlling the landscape but seen within it."[27] Thus could the independent Whig gentleman, having built a house that he surely hoped would awe his neighbors, turn around and pay his respects to *their* independence by inviting them to appreciate his taste instead of his power.

Yet for most country house builders such niceties were probably of negligible consequence. Nature versus art, country versus court, "the Ancients versus the Moderns," the battle of categories, the many meanings that could be translated into architecture or discovered there: these may have been vitally important to some people, as they are to some scholars still. But the stylistic vocabulary favored by the neo-Palladians could be adopted just as easily as other versions of classicism—adopted, too, without the heavy freight of political and philosophical ideals that so preoccupied Lord Burlington and his circle. From an intellectual standpoint the result might have left something to be desired, but in other ways it was likely to work well enough.

A case in point is Saltram, a substantial country house in Devonshire much embellished in the latter half of the eighteenth century by an ambitious family named Parker. Unlike Walpole's Houghton Hall—a monumental residence, built for someone at the pinnacle of national power, from plans provided by a leading architect—Saltram seldom receives more than the briefest of mentions in architectural histories of the period, but the facts of its construction are revealing. There are also some surprising similarities between Saltram and Mount Vernon.[28]

As Washington did, the Parkers started with an existing house and over a period of several decades radically altered it. Working outward from a Tudor core onto which had been grafted a large, three-story block at the end of the seventeenth century, the family's original architect, whose name is unknown, developed the east, south, and west facades of the building and added a line of rooms behind each. Two of the facades were wholly new, and the third consisted of the seventeenth-century block augmented by a pair of low wings leading to taller pavilions. At the time, some of the added rooms were probably left unfinished, for ten years later Robert Adam was called in to design a series of interiors, including a "great room," or "saloon," on the south side of the house. And as that work neared completion, the grounds were extensively relandscaped in the Capability Brown manner.

Standing in its remade setting with its walls smoothly stuccoed and painted, the transformed Saltram made a fetching picture, as many a visitor testified. Everything had been done in the latest taste. The symmetry of the new facades was flawless, and their careful detailing emphatically bespoke Palladian influence, as did the house's lavish interiors. Yet for all its appeal, Saltram in the end fails, at least as a total composition. On close examination, the three new facades bear little relation to one another and none at all to the basic structure of the building. As the author of the National Trust guidebook for Saltram remarks: "Evidently it was beyond the architect-builder to integrate the new work in three dimensions; viewed from the angles, all three facades of Saltram begin to look like elevations cut from a pattern book and wrapped around the Tudor building like a sash."[29]

Did it matter to the Parkers that their architect had failed them in this respect? Possibly, but chances are it did not. At least two designs survive for far more grandiose, more aesthetically satisfying remodelings of the house, but evidently the family preferred to limit the scope of the project. Indeed, the "architect-builder" in question may well have been Lady Catherine Parker herself, who seems to have commissioned the work. As the daughter of the first earl of Poulett, she doubtless had a well-developed sense of what it took for a family to rise in the England of her day. Insofar as houses mattered—and plainly she thought they did—they ought to be fashionable and imposing, but it would have been foolish to overburden the family financially in laying that particular wager. The point was to avoid both undue scrimping and unnecessary extravagance, and apparently Catherine Parker's calculations came close enough to the mark, because in 1785 her son, John Parker, was created Baron Bovingdon, and a generation later his son, another John Parker, became the first earl of Morely.

So Saltram, along with whatever else the Parkers brought to the table, served its purpose. A charming and comfortable house, it was also a credible country seat for an earl. If it was not a particularly good example of architectural style, the Parkers themselves did not always fulfill the idealized picture of country life sketched by Palladio and the Burlingtonians. At one point the duchess of Devonshire wrote with affection of finding her friend John Parker, the one who later became Baron Bovingdon, "as dirty, as comical and talking as bad English as ever."[30] Yet the same John Parker had the good sense to hire Robert Adam to decorate his rooms and to let Sir Joshua Reynolds, whom he counted among his close personal friends, choose the pictures for Saltram's walls. Like the several facades of his house, Parker's personal qualities may have sat oddly together, but in the great game the family was playing, the purer forms of style were not required. Taste was enough.

Saltram House, Devon, England, west front, showing the Parker family's additions with bits of the orginial Tudor building peeking out from behind. Courtesy of the National Trust Library, London, England.

As for comparing Saltram to Mount Vernon, there are at least three ways in which the two houses resemble one another. Both mix construction from different periods, both work hard at incorporating the high tide of Georgian fashion in architecture and decoration, and both succeed finally more in detail than as integrated wholes. At the root of these similarities, too, one senses the same kinds of complex calculations being made: the same determination to impress, balanced by the same careful adjustment of means to ends. At both Saltram and Mount Vernon, for example, the desired effect would have been easier to achieve had the existing buildings been removed from the site, but that would have raised costs as well.

Judicious economizing also had its limits at both houses, however. Where they produce their grandest flourishes, they do so without stinting, and in each case on the interior the grandest flourish comes in the form of a single, large room—the one at the north end of Mount Vernon and Saltram's "Saloon." The two rooms even have certain features in common. Both are a full two stories high with deep cove ceilings; both are rectangular in shape with outsized Venetian windows centered on one long wall and fireplaces on the other; and in both, the ceilings, walls, and woodwork are decorated in the same way:

Saltram House, the saloon, Robert Adam, architect. Courtesy of the National Trust Library, London, England.

Mount Vernon, the room at the north end of the house. Courtesy of the Mount Vernon Ladies' Association.

with geometric shapes, swags, and garlands, molded in low relief in plaster, in the manner made popular by Robert Adam.

The difference was that the Parkers could commission Adam himself to create their room and to provide, in the bargain, designs for the carpet, the looking glasses, and even such minutiae as door handles. For Washington such an arrangement was clearly out of the question, and while the north room at Mount Vernon is at least a tasteful example of the style he chose for it, the saloon at Saltram is still sometimes described as one of the most beautiful rooms in England. In the end it came to simple arithmetic. As provincials eager to appropriate metropolitan taste, Washington and the Parkers shared a common goal, but the Parkers were closer to London by several thousand miles, and that made an enormous difference in how they played the game.

Yet the game in question was also the only one the Parkers were interested in playing, and therein lies a far more significant difference between the two houses. When Brian Fairfax described Mount Vernon as an "uncommon" place, he knew whereof he spoke.[31] There is nothing at Saltram analogous to Mount Vernon's cupola or its piazza. Both were marked departures from the standard taste of the day, which was something the Parkers chose not to risk. Relentlessly, uncompromisingly correct, Saltram follows the approved rules to the letter; Mount Vernon definitely does not.

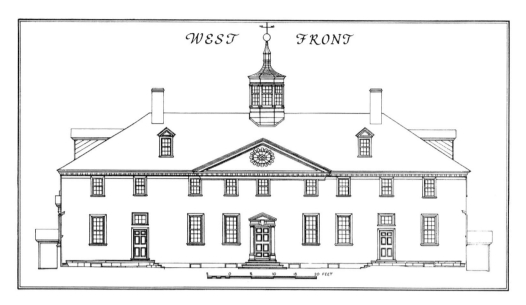

Measured drawing of the west front of Mount Vernon. Courtesy of the Mount Vernon Ladies' Association.

What led Washington to stray when he did from the path of architectural correctness? Certainly he knew enough to stick to the rules if he had wanted to. The same pattern books from which he copied windows and chimneypieces contained a variety of standard roof designs without cupolas, and the east front of Mount Vernon, minus the piazza, was a reasonably acceptable example of a classically composed facade. If the rules were broken at Mount Vernon it was because Washington made a conscious decision to break them.

Invariably, too, it is possible to imagine a variety of reasons why he made the choices he did. Several of the "things not quite orthodox" he added to the house improved its appearance considerably. For example, extending the main structure to the north and south during the second rebuilding tended to make it look too long relative to its rather modest height. The piazza and the cupola provided a pair of strong vertical thrusts that helped counter that effect. The cupola also drew attention away from the asymmetry of the west front. And together the piazza and the cupola worked to combat the heat of Virginia summers—the one by shielding the east front from the noonday sun, and the other by providing a means of ventilating the upper story of the building.

Unorthodoxy had other uses as well. Much of what Washington did to Mount Vernon was calculated to distinguish more precisely, in fairly conventional ways, between the public and private spaces of the house. In adding a full second story in the first rebuilding, he doubled the amount of private space and set it off crisply from the public rooms below. In the second rebuilding, by adding both a large space for entertaining and a separate set of rooms solely for his and Martha's use, he granted strict parity to the two sides of the public/private division. At other points, however, the changes he made had the effect of blurring, if not eliminating altogether, that same division. And again the piazza provides

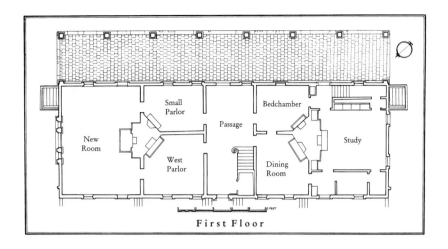

First Floor

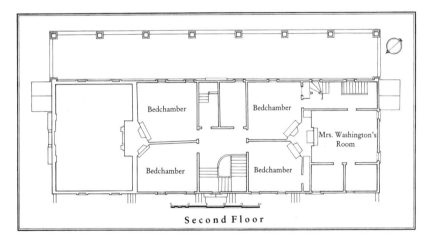

Second Floor

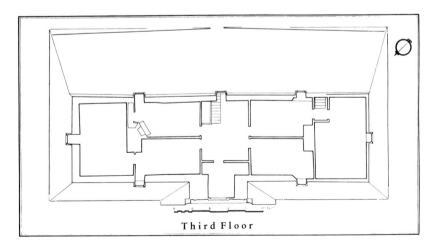

Third Floor

Mount Vernon, first-, second-, and third-floor plans. Courtesy of the Mount Vernon Ladies' Association.

the most striking example, for it connected the spaces within the house in ways that were very different from the tightly controlled patterns of access in the typical classical-style house. Here there were no prescribed paths of circulation. People were free to come and go from outdoors or from inside the house, through any one of three different doors.

When Washington added the piazza, porches—front, rear, and side (but invariably called "piazzas")—had just begun to appear in America. By 1770 he could have seen them on vernacular as well as high-style houses, particularly in the middle colonies, and there may even have been an earlier, smaller version of one at Mount Vernon.[32] No doubt, too, he had seen porches used in Barbados during the time he spent there with his brother Lawrence. But porches had yet to make their way into the pattern books, and none of these examples would have had the dimensions of Mount Vernon's new piazza — its great, airy height or its broad sweep across the entire length of the building. In that sense Washington's creation was truly original.

Ultimately, however, the piazza was more than just a departure from orthodox classical taste; it was directly at odds with that taste. Its primary function was to provide a sheltered space from which to enjoy the magnificent view of the Potomac that was Mount Vernon's greatest single asset. It was no classically inspired, columned portico framing a grand entrance. In their simplicity, the pillars echoed the Tuscan order, but the proportions Washington chose for them stretched far beyond those mandated in the pattern books. The standard proportions would have produced much thicker, heavier pillars, thereby impeding the view.[33] Similarly, in using quadrant arms to connect the main house and the outbuildings on either side of it—a standard Palladian device—Washington boldly broke with established practice by not closing them in. The effect was lighter

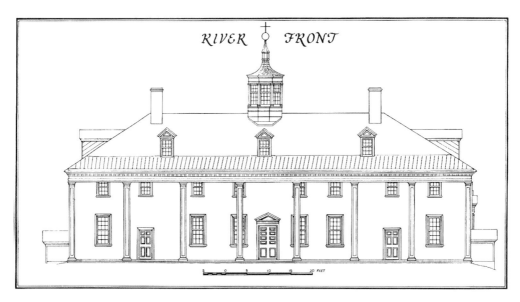

Measured drawing of the river front of Mount Vernon. Courtesy of the Mount Vernon Ladies' Association.

and gave visitors arriving at the west front a tantalizing hint of the delights that lay in store for them on the other side of the house.

In a word, pleasure: that seems to have been the standard Washington followed in such instances. Moreover, in making it his standard, he was opposing head-on the architectural paradigm—the "rules"—that through much of the century had controlled the tangible representation of social and political power in aristocratic country houses.

Yet, in the end, the case was more complicated than this, for Washington's first rebuilding of Mount Vernon was not particularly original, and in the second he added any number of conventional details along with the piazza and the open colonnades. So the resulting house mixed innovation and orthodoxy—combined pleasure and power—in a way that makes it difficult to characterize. In that respect, too, it is interesting to compare Mount Vernon with two other familiar, albeit very different, monuments of eighteenth-century Virginia architecture: the Governor's Palace in Williamsburg and Thomas Jefferson's Monticello.

Built over a period of years beginning in 1706, the Governor's Palace proclaims unambiguously not only the status and dignity of its principal occupant but also the might of the entire system of imperial authority he represented. Standing alone, at the end of a broad avenue leading from Duke of Gloucester Street, Williamsburg's main thoroughfare, the high, brick structure with its symmetrically arranged windows, imposing roof, and tall cupola dominates the scene completely. To the end of the colonial period it remained one of the two or three grandest official residences in British America, if not the grandest.[34]

Here also was the prototype of so many houses built by the Virginia gentry over the next fifty years, and in what would become a familiar pattern, the Palace was more than just a single structure. Two smaller brick buildings stood at right angles to it in front, linked by brick walls pierced at the center by an iron gate emblazoned with the king's arms. The walls created a fortresslike air, an impression strengthened on the interior, just beyond the central doorway in the great hall, by an extraordinary display of score upon score of muskets, pistols, and swords arranged in great swirling, decorative patterns across the walls and ceiling. As one scholar has remarked, the result was an awesomely "compelling symbol of political power and social order."[35] And from there, the twin themes of power and order marched step by step through the rest of the ground floor, up the elaborate stairway, and on into the second-floor audience chamber, where important guests were received and entertained.

Moving through this succession of spaces, what one encountered was in fact a scaled-down version of the state rooms in any one of half a dozen royal residences in England. Kensington Palace comes to mind, as do innumerable Renaissance palaces in Italy, and in each case the purpose of the arrangement was the same: to create a setting that dramatically elevated a particular individual above the rest of humanity. By the time the Governor's Palace was built, the basic elements in this union of architecture and power had long since been established; it was simply a matter of giving them palpable form in Williamsburg.

The arms display in the hall of the Governor's Palace in Williamsburg. Courtesy of the Colonial Williamsburg Foundation.

Necessarily, too, in the gentry houses that took so much from the Palace, some of the more obvious symbols of power were omitted. Displays of arms and second-floor audience chambers may have been appropriate for the king's personal representative in Virginia, but the gentry's power was rooted in the countryside, and one of its most important functions was mediating between local and imperial interests. Similarly, the richly embellished staircases that became *de rigueur* in gentry houses were associated with different rituals than those staged in the Governor's Palace. Instead of receiving guests on the second floor, the master and his lady descended to greet them, or, as another mark of respect, lit their way upstairs at night. Such courtesies still spoke the language of power, but they did so in gentler, less insistent tones.[36]

Yet in all these respects Thomas Jefferson's Monticello departed, both from the example of the Governor's Palace and from the houses of other prominent Virginians. Unerringly mirroring its creator's mind, it was a place that followed no rules except its own.

Like Washington, Jefferson built an initial, fairly conventional version of his house, then later drastically altered it. Even before starting the first version, however, he made a decision that offered a preview of the direction in which he eventually moved. The Governor's Palace was built in the colony's capital; Mount Vernon, like almost every other gentry house, was built on a river. Monticello, in contrast, would stand in isolated splendor on Jefferson's "Little Mountain."[37]

The logistics involved in building on a mountaintop several miles from the nearest river were formidable. Still, Jefferson was determined to have his way. The view was glorious, and he had loved the spot from childhood. Philosophically, too, it had great appeal. To live apart from the bustling world below, apart even from any easy means of communication with it, made the point about one's personal independence in particularly dramatic terms. Palladio, whose *I Quattro Libri dell' Architettura* Jefferson knew well, could be read as having just such a thing in mind.[38]

Yet even Palladio did not rule absolutely at Monticello. He had envisioned the gentleman's villa incorporating visibly, as part of its design, the work spaces necessary for supporting both the household and substantial agricultural activity. Instead, Jefferson chose to keep such facilities almost entirely out of sight. Barns and other agricultural structures were located partway down the mountain. The stables, wine cellar, kitchen,

Monticello, the garden front, Thomas Jefferson architect. Photograph by William H. Pierson.

and food storage areas were attached to the house but built belowground, so that from any distance away one saw only the main structure and two small pavilions on either side of it.

The house alone—Jefferson alone: that is the illusion all this seems calculated to create, and much else about Monticello reinforces it. Axial in plan, the main house has the usual grand, central entrance space, but instead of furnishing it in the typical way with matching chairs arranged against the walls, Jefferson crammed in an extraordinary assortment of objects: knickknacks, gadgets, artifacts from a dozen different cultures, and natural specimens of all kinds—everything from a giant, eight-day clock, built to his own specifications, to the mastodon bones given him by Lewis and Clark after their expedition to the West. Guests were thus immediately confronted with a stunning, if somewhat jumbled, sampling of their host's interests and enthusiasms. In England it was not uncommon for gentlemen to assemble such collections as "cabinets of curiosities." Sometimes the "cabinet" even became a separate building, but the word itself implied the essentially private nature of the space. At Monticello one entered the house by passing directly through this preserve, thereby encountering Jefferson at once, not only in all his complexity, but also in highly intimate terms.[39]

Much of the rest of the ground floor was also taken up by the rooms set aside for Jefferson's own use—his bedchamber, his study, his library, and his greenhouse. Significantly, too, the other spaces on the ground floor, including the drawing room and dining room, were arranged to minimize the intrusion of servants. The wine was transported from the cellar to the dining room on a dumbwaiter tucked into the chimneypiece, for example, and the food appeared on shelves fixed to a revolving panel in the wall. Again, Jefferson alone, unbothered by the mundane details of life.

But most striking of all, perhaps, was the complete absence at Monticello of that all-important feature of other Virginia gentry houses—the grand staircase. In its place, located out of public view in narrow service passages, were two twisting runs of stairs, each, as one visitor accurately commented, no more than "a little ladder of a staircase, about two feet wide, and very steep."[40] The inconvenience for the entire household must have been substantial, but evidently the consequences in other respects more than made up for the difficulties. For with the grand staircase gone, the rituals focusing on it, with all their subtle and not so subtle intimations of power, could also be eliminated, leaving guests free to experience the house and its pleasures as equals. In this way, too, access to Jefferson was made to seem all the more immediate and direct. And again, it was Jefferson alone one discovered at the center of this web of impressions, for along with the grand staircase and its rituals, most obvious architectural ties to his family had been eliminated. Where were their rooms? How did they get there?

Some of this can be put down to a kind of playfulness that Jefferson plainly delighted in. Moreover, for those clever enough, part of the pleasure Monticello offered was the opportunity to see through the various ruses built into the house. Also, in altering standard classical design, Jefferson was working very much in the spirit of the neoclassicism he had encountered in France during the time he spent there as American minister during the 1780s.[41] Yet in the ways it broke the classical mold, Monticello was more than simply fun or stylish. In his *Notes on the State of Virginia*, Jefferson referred to the pub-

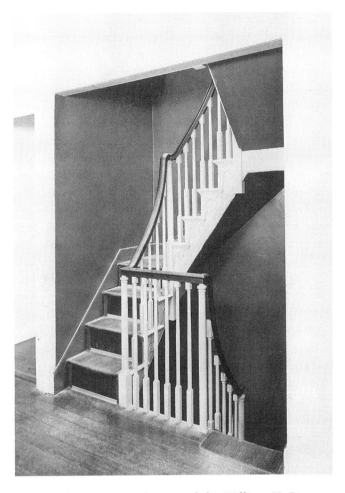

Monticello, stairway. Photograph by William H. Pierson.

lic buildings of Williamsburg as "rude, mis-shapen piles, which, but they have roofs, would be taken for brick-kilns."[42] At Monticello he assaulted the basic *raison d'être* for such structures: the use of architecture to objectify traditional notions of power and social order. By doing away with the more obvious symbols of hierarchy, by centering the house on a single individual rather than the ordered ranks of family members, retainers, and servants that made up the typical aristocratic household—and, yes, by building a house that was meant to be fun—he offered an appealing lesson in something approaching democracy. On the other hand, this may have been the greatest ruse of all, for the master of Monticello was hardly, at least in any ordinary sense, a man of the people.

If George Washington ever saw Thomas Jefferson's home, no record of his impressions survives. Also, he could only have seen an early, unfinished version of the house, since he had long since died by the time it assumed its final form. Still, it is interesting to speculate on what he might have made of Jefferson's creation had he seen it in its finished state.

Surely he would have admired the house's grace, as well as the ingenuity of such things as the clock in the passage and the dining room serving devices. Yet it is hard to imagine him liking some of the more eccentric features of the place—the entrance passage full of curiosities, for example, or the peculiar stairways. Would he have understood the point they were meant to make? Perhaps, but it was not a point he himself would have been comfortable making. A place so palpably focused on his own person would have embarrassed Washington. He was also too conscious of the courtesy due other people to burden them with notably odd domestic arrangements. And while he could not but have been charmed by the view, the site of Monticello would probably have bothered him. As someone much in public life, Jefferson had an obligation to make himself accessible to those he served, or so Washington would have thought. The mountaintop location, too, would have struck him as foolishly impractical for agricultural purposes.

In sum, for Washington's taste, Monticello would have seemed too completely centered on its creator and his pleasure. By temperament he was too moderate, too measured in all things, to travel where Jefferson did in his loftier flights. In the piazza, Mount Vernon made its own bow to pleasure-seeking, but ultimately what Washington hoped to achieve—what he must have hoped he had achieved—was some sort of balance between contradictory ideals and imperatives, between pleasure and power.

Such a balance, after all, was the stuff of which virtue was made, at least as he understood it. And in 1774, the year that began the rebuilding of Mount Vernon that would include the piazza, virtue had become a singularly important concept. In its name Washington and scores of other colonial leaders were seeking to define the ground on which they stood in their continuing quarrel with Great Britain. Their goal, they said, was simply to preserve rights and liberties Americans had enjoyed since the earliest days of settlement. This they were doing, moreover, not for any selfish reason of their own, but for all Americans confronting the exactions of a government locked in the hands of corrupt, overbearing officials. Disinterestedness and restraint: those were the hallmarks of true patriotism. For Washington to have planned, against that background, a house as frankly self-indulgent as the one Thomas Jefferson designed twenty years later would have been surprising indeed.

Balance, then—pleasure and power, freedom and restraint—that is how Washington seems to have seen Mount Vernon as he planned his second major rebuilding of the house. If his vision was less tidy than Jefferson's, or the vision of the men who had planned the Governor's Palace, it was every bit as purposeful and carefully considered as theirs. Surely, too, the work begun at Mount Vernon in 1774 represented a pledge to a future beyond resistance—beyond America's deepening conflict with Great Britain. For there the house would stand, greeting the world with its formal, highly Anglicized west front, while on the river side, with the piazza, it became something totally different: open, informal, bare of unnecessary ornament, its soaring structure reduced to a minimum, thanks to Washington's ingenious design. Two worlds, with a clear progression laid out from one to the other: an American political primer in wood.

*Mount Vernon's cupola. Courtesy of the Mount
Vernon Ladies' Association.*

There as well, presiding over it all, would be that cupola—unfashionable but also
intriguingly evocative; for of the houses with cupolas that Washington knew, the most
familiar one, unquestionably, was the Governor's Palace, and finding himself in conflict
with the authority that structure represented, what could have been more logical than to
appropriate its details for his own use? A single, imperial source of power was unacceptable in America; a cupola was simply a bit of decoration anyone could have who wanted
one. To be sure, none of this may have been on Washington's mind, but he was a person
who hardly ever acted without reflection. He also had a superb feel for gesture.

In the crowded years ahead that same feeling for gesture would be revealed time and
again, and through all those years Washington would remain committed to independence—and to building. He may never have read Palladio, but his own experience had
taught him that architecture could be more than simply a matter of aping the fashionable
taste of the day. If buildings set the stage for human action, they could also, in their shape
and substance, be made to express the highest human ideals. Like everything else connected with Washington's life, however, his plans for Mount Vernon were about to be
overtaken by events—events that would create new ideals, fresh imperatives of their own.

CHAPTER 5

The Third Edition —
with Revisions — 1774–1787

THE FIRST TIME Washington rebuilt Mount Vernon almost all the work was done while he was away at the front. Sixteen years later, in 1774, he was at least there to watch Going Lanphier's frame for the addition to the south end of the house take shape—to watch and to satisfy himself that the joints were tight and that the corners of the building would stand straight and true. Always inclined to move, sometimes doggedly, in incremental steps to achieve what he wanted, he plainly enjoyed his role. To Bryan Fairfax, George William's half brother, who had chosen to remain in America, he remarked that summer: "I am very much engaged in raising one of the additions to my house, which I think (perhaps it is fancy) goes on better whilst I am present, than in my absence from the workmen."[1]

But even then events were moving to cut short Washington's time at home. The previous December the act of protest that would be remembered as the Boston Tea Party had raised American resistance to British taxation policies to new heights. While Washington was not particularly sympathetic to an approach that he suspected would agitate tempers needlessly, the response of the British government, when it came, shocked him to the core. The closing of the port of Boston, coupled with the abrogation of the colony's charter in the Government of Massachusetts Act, clearly called for strong action in return.

When the burgesses congregated in Williamsburg for the spring session, the decision was made to act on routine business before responding to the latest parliamentary initiatives in case Governor Dunmore was provoked into dissolving the body, as had happened several years earlier. Thus three weeks passed before the members voted overwhelmingly to set a fast day on June 1 in support of Massachusetts. Predictably, Dunmore dismissed the assembly, causing the burgesses to adjourn once again to Raleigh Tavern, where resolutions were approved denouncing the Boston Port Act, prohibiting the use of East India tea as long as it was taxed, and calling for a meeting of delegates from all the American colonies. Though not an active participant in the discussion, Washington fully supported the resolutions. On the other hand, he could still compartmentalize the situation. The day the burgesses voted the fast he dined with Dunmore, and two days later he attended a ball given by the burgesses in honor of the governor's wife.[2]

By the time Washington returned to Mount Vernon, he had been absent for six weeks. Work on the house had continued without him, but there were supplies to be ordered and workmen to be paid. The owner of a quarry received £19 for eight hundred feet of stone, some of it faced, which presumably was used to augment the foundation of the main house. The ledger also shows payments in cash and corn to Lanphier, and on one occasion rum to Caleb Stone, who was probably already working on the new dependencies. Nails for lathing and large batches of oyster shells were purchased so the interior walls of the additions could be plastered. More window glass, pine plank, and locks and hinges for doors arrived.[3]

Yet even at home, politics continued to claim a substantial amount of Washington's time and energy. There were new elections of burgesses, and the voters of Alexandria met, adopted resolutions, and appointed a committee, chaired by Washington, to oversee future protest activities. Then at the end of July it was time to leave again for Williamsburg and a convention where seven delegates were picked to attend a "General Congress" of colonial representatives, scheduled to convene in Philadelphia on September 5. Washington received the third highest number of votes. Hurrying back to Mount Vernon, he did what he could to ensure that work on the house would go smoothly for the rest of the building season, even though he was unlikely to be there. In the middle of August he faced the sad task of organizing the sale of the Fairfaxes' furniture at Belvoir. With the prospect of a larger house to furnish, Washington himself spent liberally, buying a dozen chairs, a sideboard, a mahogany chest, a gilt-framed mirror, and more.[4]

There were also people who had to be convinced that the political turmoil of the past several months was appropriate—in fact imperative—and one of them was Bryan Fairfax. In a letter written on August 24, Washington did his best to explain how he felt to his old friend. It was "an Innate Spirit of freedom" that had first told him that the policies of the ministry in England were "repugnant to every principle of natural justice." Now he believed that a "Crisis" had been reached: either the colonists would assert their rights "or Submit to every Imposition that can be heap'd upon us" until they became "as tame, & abject Slaves, as the Blacks we Rule over with such arbitrary Sway."[5]

Freedom or slavery: that was the choice Washington saw. He was also convinced that the recent acts of Parliament were "the result of deliberation" and that "a regular Systematick Plan" had been formed to enforce them. As for remedies, he saw only one. "Nothing but Unanimity in the Colonies (a stroke they did not expect) and firmness" could prevent the British from working their will.[6] Within a week of so declaring himself he was off to attend the first Continental Congress in Philadelphia in the company of Edmund Pendleton and Patrick Henry.

In essence, the Congress adopted the stance Washington hoped it would: further restrictions on commerce, no mention of compromise, and a stated determination to unite in meeting force with force, if necessary. Characteristically, he did not play an active role in the deliberations but led a full social life outside the sessions, often spending his evenings with other delegates. For all of them it was a chance to become acquainted. Washington was also much entertained by the local notables. In the two months that he was away, he dined in thirty-one different private houses.[7]

Back at home later that fall there were miscellaneous business affairs to attend to, including a second sale at Belvoir. But wherever he went, Washington was called on to advise and inspect the independent companies of militia now becoming active in the counties, and in March at a convention in Richmond he was chosen as one of the Virginia delegates to the second Continental Congress, due to meet in Philadelphia in May. To his brother Jack he wrote that he fully intended "to devote my Life & Fortune in the cause we are engagd in, if need be."[8] Still, as deliberate as his approach was, he remained cautious. When it became known that Governor Dunmore had secretly removed a supply of gunpowder from the magazine in Williamsburg where it was stored, Washington was one of those who urged restraint rather than military retaliation.[9]

Then at the end of April word reached Virginia of the events that had occurred earlier that month at Lexington and Concord, in Massachusetts. American citizens defending their homes and families had been killed by British troops. There had been no declaration of what Washington was calling "independency," or of war, yet both seemed distinctly more possible than they had a month earlier, and Washington was too much of a realist not to set his course accordingly. War against the greatest naval and military power on earth—war that was bound to turn into civil war, tearing communities and families apart—was certainly not something he wanted. It was the British who seemed determined to fight. As always, however, the chance of war brought with it the chance for glory, and together the risks and opportunities must have multiplied endlessly in Washington's imagination as he made his way, for the second time in less than a year, from Mount Vernon to Philadelphia. In his luggage he carried his Virginia military uniform, which he regularly wore to the sessions of Congress in the Pennsylvania State House.[10]

With surprisingly little dissent, the delegates agreed to hold to the line that had been laid down the year before. The British had turned to force; it was imperative that the colonies unite to prevent the final destruction of American liberty. What this meant in practical terms was that the resistance that had taken shape around Boston had to be turned into a broader effort, supported and organized by the Philadelphia Congress itself. Above all, a commander had to be appointed by Congress to take charge of the volunteers camped at Cambridge and Charlestown and mold them into an effective fighting force. On June 15 the delegates offered the post to Washington. No other name had been placed in nomination; the vote was unanimous. The following day—protesting his inadequacy and declaring that he would serve without pay beyond whatever was necessary to cover his expenses—he accepted.[11]

Given the urgency of the situation, even a brief trip home to Mount Vernon was out of the question. Washington remained in Philadelphia for little more than a week while Congress completed its preliminary organization of his army, then hurried northward, to Massachusetts. Several days earlier he had written Martha a long letter explaining the intense anxiety he felt in his new position. He had not sought it; he did not want it. But he had seen no way to refuse "without exposing my Character to such censures as would have reflected dishonor upon myself, and given pain to my friends." He hoped she would understand and make whatever arrangements she wished until he returned in the fall. His affairs, he assured her, were in good order.[12]

Nowhere in his letter to Martha, however, did Washington suggest that the work on Mount Vernon should stop or be slowed in any way. On the contrary, he fully expected it to continue, as he made clear in repeated inquiries and instructions in his letters to Lund Washington, the distant relative who had been serving as his manager at Mount Vernon for the past decade and who would stay on for the duration of the Revolution. "I wish you would quicken Lamphire & Sears about the Dining Room Chimney Piece (to be executed as mentioned in one of my last Letters) as I could wish to have that end of the House compleatly finished before I return," he wrote in August.[13]

Considering the appalling difficulties he faced in his new command, Washington's concern about a dining room chimneypiece spoke volumes about just how much the work at Mount Vernon meant to him. Clearly this was no ordinary building project, but then it never had been.

Writing from the front in the summer of 1775, Washington confidently predicted he would be home by fall. Altogether six years were to pass before he saw Mount Vernon again and another two before he finally came back to stay. At that point the house was still unfinished, but the amount of work that had been done, under the circumstances, was extraordinary. For that Washington could thank his own determination to see the project through, and even more Lund Washington's stalwart dedication to fulfilling his employer's wishes. In letters between the two, their shared feelings of urgency emerge clearly, tempered a bit by Lund's understandable doubts about the wisdom of spending so much time, energy, and money rebuilding a house that might at any minute be destroyed.

Before leaving, Washington had stressed to Lund the need for regular communication: Lund was to write frequently, and Washington would answer at least once a week. But the postal services were uncertain, and Washington also came to suspect their letters were subject to prying eyes. "Such is the infernal curiosity of some of the Scoundrel Postmasters that I am distressed exceedingly in my business, not being able to get any directions home," he wrote his brother that September.[14] It was obvious to Lund when he received letters from headquarters that some had already been opened. Others took many weeks to arrive; one, written at the end of that first August, finally reached Mount Vernon on October 4. Necessarily, questions and instructions passing back and forth between the two men were repeated. "I believe you have generally mention'd in more Letters than one, what it was you desire'd to have done," Lund wrote, as if to reassure them both.[15]

Added to the difficulties of communication was the menacing situation at home. Governor Dunmore had a number of ships under his command, and fear was rampant that they would sail up the rivers, ravaging the countryside while Continental forces were concentrated far to the north. There were even rumors that Mount Vernon would be attacked and Martha Washington kidnapped in a retaliatory strike by the British. Washington was skeptical, however. "If these disputes continue another year — I can hardly think that Lord Dunmore can act so low & unmanly a part, as to think of siezing Mrs. Washington by way of revenge," he wrote Lund.[16] Martha herself was not at all fazed by the danger. In October, when Washington wrote that she could join him at camp for the winter, she went with no apparent thought of the risk of traveling up the coast to Cambridge. Nevertheless, at Lund's urging, she packed her husband's papers and accounts in a trunk that could easily be moved to safety, and left the key with Lund.

In Alexandria, Lund promoted the idea of a blockade downriver, but it seemed too impractical and expensive, so an armed defense would be their only recourse. Fifty men, he calculated, could protect Mount Vernon from an attack below its banks. As the weeks passed, however, the situation grew more threatening. "The common people are most Hellishly freightned," he wrote, adding that he did not think they could be counted on to defend the Potomac plantations.[17] That winter the city of Norfolk was reduced to ashes, and women and children were evacuated from Alexandria in panic. The local militia, with few arms and little powder, was kept on constant alert.

There was also the vexing problem of runaways, for whom the enemy now provided a ready refuge, Dunmore having issued a proclamation promising freedom to all indentured servants and slaves joining his ranks. In September an indentured painter whom Washington had loaned to his brother-in-law, Fielding Lewis, escaped, evidently in response to the proclamation. "If he comes up here and indeavours to Land at mt. Vernon Raising the rest, I will shoot him," Lund wrote. "That will be some Satisfaction."[18] At one point during the fall of 1775 William Sears, the carpenter working on the dining room chimneypiece, told Lund that he thought all the slaves would leave "if they believe'd they coud make there Escape" and that only one of the indentured servants was certain to stay.[19] Ironically, that person did run off later, with another of Washington's workers.

Finally there was the weather. It had started to rain in the middle of August, and the rains continued through September and October. Fields became so drenched they could not be plowed or seeded. Bricklayers had to stop work, stalling construction outdoors for weeks. The damp and chill also brought on sickness. Sears was at home unable to work for more than a month.

But in spite of all the difficulties the work continued, though often at a maddeningly slow pace. At the time of Washington's departure for the Second Continental Congress, the south addition to the main house had been raised and closed in, but its interiors were still unfinished. In the existing core of the house, the dining room was awaiting Sears's new chimneypiece as well as a new ceiling. Earlier that spring Washington had spent two nights with his sister and her husband, the Lewises, in Fredericksburg, and met the "stucco man" his brother-in-law had hired to apply decorative plasterwork to their ceilings. Since Washington had a talented painter and both the Lewises' house and Mount Vernon were undergoing renovations, an exchange seemed natural. The plasterer would come to Mount Vernon to work on the dining room ceiling and possibly the rooms in the south addition, and Washington's painter (the one who eventually escaped and joined the British army) would go to the Lewises to coat their refurbished rooms.[20]

Washington had chosen a design for the new dining room chimneypiece from the same pattern book, Abraham Swan's *British Architect*, that had been used for the chim-

Left: *Design selected by Washington from Abraham Swan's* British Architect *(London, 1745) for the dining-room chimneypiece at Mount Vernon. Courtesy of the Mount Vernon Ladies' Association.*

Right: *The dining-room chimneypiece at Mount Vernon as completed in 1775. The paint shown in the photograph is lighter than the finish currently used in the room, but the lighter tone shows the details of the carving more clearly. Courtesy of the Mount Vernon Ladies' Association.*

neypiece in the west parlor sixteen years earlier.[21] At the time the carver had simplified and flattened the design; now Sears was told to do an exact copy. With all the embellishments included, however, it took a great deal of time to execute. "Sears is Still here about the Chimney piece," wrote Lund almost six weeks after Washington's instructions to hurry the process along. "I suppose he will finish it next week you no doubt think him long about it, so do I, but I can assure you he is Constantly at worck."[22] To Lund the result also began to seem too elaborate—in fact much too elaborate. "I think you never Intended such a one & must have been mistaken in the look of the Draught."[23] But to Washington it probably had been a sore point all those years that the parlor chimney-piece was a modification. If so, he would not be disappointed now, though Sears's illness delayed completion of the work until November. The new dining room ceiling came next. Fielding Lewis—still in the midst of his own renovation, with his great room yet to be done—sent the plasterer on as promised, and Sears provided a design. Carving plaster was easier than carving wood; even so, the work took time. "God knows when he will get done," Lund wrote at one point, and later: "The man is still at it, & will be for a fortnight."[24] At length the ceiling was finished, however, and the artisan and Lund agreed that it was a "Hansomer one than any of Colo. Lewises, although not half the worck."[25]

Handsome it may have been, but Martha Washington had scant patience when it came to elaborate plasterwork. Her chief concern was moving into the new addition, not its decoration. When the "stucco man" was finally ready to start on her bedroom, she gave orders that it was to be "quite plain," with none of the decorative motifs used downstairs. Whatever Washington might have thought, the room was done as she wished.[26]

The plasterer finally returned to the Lewises in December 1775. By then the south

The kitchen at Mount Vernon. Courtesy of the Mount Vernon Ladies' Association.

addition was complete except for the chimney serving the study, which was letting smoke into the room and discoloring the walls so badly that additional coats of paint were necessary once the problem was solved. In the absence of the painter who had run off, Sears did the work, finishing everything by Christmas.

Meanwhile, work of a different sort continued outdoors. As Washington struggled to gain control of his ragtag army, Caleb Stone and the Mount Vernon carpenters had begun the four new outbuildings to go in front of the main house. After the existing structures were removed and the materials carefully saved for reuse later, a new kitchen was raised off the southwest corner of the main house and completed during the summer. Next to it, but leaving room for carriages and carts to pass up and down the south lane, went a new storehouse, finished in the fall. The third building to be erected occupied a position on the north side of the house corresponding to the kitchen on the south side. Both Lund and Martha assumed it was to be a new laundry house, and Martha had its chimneys built specifically for that purpose. But Washington had a different plan in mind. The laundry house was to be placed along one of the side lanes, and the new outbuilding would be a "Servant's Hall," used to provide accommodations for a resident manager or visiting servants. Unfortunately, by the time Washington made his wishes known, the building had been framed with two front doors (to facilitate the flow of laundry?) and therefore would not match the kitchen across the way. This bothered Lund, and he repeatedly questioned it in letters to Washington. Eventually the anomaly was corrected, though the building was almost finished before instructions came to change it.[27]

The use of the last of the four new outbuildings seems to have been unclear to everyone, including Washington, but its decorative function was obvious. It was to match the storehouse across the way, completing the ensemble. Washington had also supposed that all four of the outbuildings would be finished with rusticated boards to harmonize with the main house. Although those at home had not known this, his wishes were eventually carried out. He also directed that the chimneytops of the outbuildings, some of which had already been finished plain, should be smartly edged with stone.[28]

By the beginning of 1776 it was clear that the conflict with Britain would not end easily or quickly. In March, General Howe and his troops abandoned Boston, eventually reaching New York, and Washington followed.[29] At home, meanwhile, workmen were more scarce than ever. Many townspeople in Alexandria moved inland, seeking shelter in the back country rather than remaining on the more exposed banks of the Potomac, and others joined the army. Supplies were hard to come by as well. Yet Washington was determined to continue building. In the face of all the difficulties and risks, he decided that spring to proceed with the north addition to the main house. Plank had been purchased earlier and set aside, and Lanphier agreed to do the work.[30]

But as always, progress on the new addition was excruciatingly slow. The frame that both Washington and Lund had hoped would be up and covered in by the end of the summer was still lying on the ground in pieces at the end of August. There were no nails to be found anywhere, according to Lund.[31] And the old chimney that would serve the north wing had not been rebuilt. The day before the Battle of Long Island—the Continental Army's first pitched battle and a resounding defeat for the American forces—Washington wrote Lund urging him to do whatever he could to hurry the work along. "I wish most ardently you could get the North end of the House covered in this fall, if you should be obliged to send all over Virginia, Maryland, & Pennsylvania for Nails to do it with." It was equally important that the chimney be completed. And all this Lund was told to do even if it meant hiring "many Workmen of different kinds to accomplish it."[32] But what workmen? Where were they to be found?

Winter weather would have spoiled the new frame, but Washington was eager to have that part of the house finished for another reason. Before he left for Philadelphia plans had already been made to extend the garden walls on either side of the drive, and that project was under way. Now he decided he also wanted to put in groves of trees at each end of the house, and the sooner the better. The week before the British landed on Long Island he had sent detailed instructions describing what he wanted, instructions that at the best of times would have been optimistic. The groves were to stretch a considerable distance from the house, with the trees, as he said,

> to be Planted without any order or regularity (but pretty thick, as they can at any time be thin'd) and to consist that at the North end, of locusts altogether. & that at the South, of all the clever kind of Trees (especially flowering ones) that can be got, such as Crab apple, Poplar, Dogwood, Sasafras, Lawrel, Willow (especially yellow & Weeping Willow, twigs of which may be got from Philadelphia) and many others which I do not recollect at present—these to be interspersed here and there with ever greens such as Holly, Pine, and Cedar, also Ivy—to these may be added the Wild flowering Shrubs of the larger kind, such as the fringe Tree & several other kinds that might be mentioned.

In other words, the trees were to be "naturally" placed in long, irregular sweeps. But before that could be done the construction at the north end of the house had to be finished. "Otherwise," wrote Washington, "it will be labour lost as [the trees] will get broke down, defaced and spoil'd."[33]

In the fall, with New York City lost, the Continental Army retreated across the Hudson, down through New Jersey, and then across the Delaware into Pennsylvania. Subsequently Washington recrossed the Delaware twice, staging successful raids at Trenton and Princeton. Otherwise he and his troops fared badly, and he felt himself all but completely hamstrung by Congress's willingness to rely on local militia units and regular enlistments for very short periods to fill up the ranks. "I see the impossibility of serving with reputation, or doing any essential service to the cause by continuing in command," he had written Lund in September 1776 before leaving New York, "yet I am told that if I quit the command inevitable ruin will follow. . . . I never was in such an unhappy, divided state since I was born."[34] In December Congress moved from Philadelphia to the comparative safety of Baltimore, and the following summer Philadelphia itself was occupied by the enemy.

But despite the sorry aspect of affairs, the construction at Mount Vernon slogged on. The chimney at the north end of the house was rebuilt as directed. A new door was installed leading from the west parlor into the large room in the addition, the wainscoting was redone to accommodate the door, and the parlor was repainted. One way or another the addition itself was also raised and closed in. Washington's instructions about it and the room it was to contain were emphatic: "The chimney in the new room should be exactly in the middle of it," he had written Lund in the same letter in which he described his wretched "divided" state of mind, "the doors and every thing else to be exactly answerable and uniform—in short I would have the whole executed in a masterly manner."[35]

Not for the first time—or the last—Mount Vernon had plainly come to provide Washington with a much-needed way of dealing with his frustrations. As mastery of his troops, of Congress, of the larger military situation continued to elude him, he had created in his mind a world at home wholly amenable to his control, one where his every wish would be followed to the letter. To Robert Morris he complained early in 1777 that very few letters sent from home reached him and declared that this was "mortifying," since it deprived him "of the consolation of hearing from home, on domestick matters."[36] But the truth was that the news from home was seldom consoling. It was writing *to* home and seeing it in his mind's eye transformed precisely as he intended that mattered. And for their part, those at Mount Vernon did their best to sustain the illusion. "The Trees shall all be planted agreeable to your Wishes," Lund wrote at one point after receiving a typically ambitious—and largely unworkable—plan for transplanting still more trees.[37]

But little by little, things did get done. Probably it was in 1777, during the low point of the war, that Mount Vernon acquired its two most striking additions: the cupola giving the house a strong, upward thrust, and the piazza bringing its airy magic to the east front. It was early the following spring that Bryan Fairfax stopped by to take a look and afterward wrote: "I like the House because it is uncommon."[38] By then the army had survived the winter at Valley Forge, and the Conway Cabal—aimed at replacing Washington as commander—had been quashed.

Lanphier was persuaded only with difficulty to return to work in 1778. "He said money would not purchase the necessarys of Life and that he must endeavour to make them," wrote Lund.[39] With currency worthless and prices hopelessly inflated, Lanphier was undoubtedly right, but Lund was reluctant to offer more pay to someone so slow and unreliable. On the other hand, no one else could be found to do the work, so he finally agreed to make Lanphier "a present"—over and above his regular wages and wages for his man—of "40WF. of Wool and next Fall 30 Barrels of Corn," provided he stuck to his work and finished it.[40]

By this time the pediment had been added to the roof on the west side of the house, but its window was still not finished, and the covered ways that would link the house and the flanking outbuildings had not even been started. For weeks, while Lund waited for Lanphier to begin work, he could only stare helplessly at the scaffolding mounted on the front of the house to reach the pediment. In addition to its sorry appearance, it blocked the front door, where new steps were waiting to be put in place. The windowless state of the pediment also stalled work on the interior of the attic. Eventually Lanphier did appear, but at the end of the season the covered ways and "other jobs" were still unfinished. Lund wanted to withhold the thirty barrels of corn agreed upon earlier, but Washington thought it best not to do so. However, he did advise doling the corn out a "little at a time," and only if the work continued.[41]

Presumably it did, but for two full years—starting in 1779—the narrative thread tracing the rebuilding of the house disappears from the correspondence between Washington and Lund. There are few such letters in any case, suggesting that some may have been destroyed, possibly by Lund's widow at his instruction. But the letters that do survive say nothing at all about work on the house. One simple explanation is that by the beginning of 1779 the project was in large part finished, or at least had reached the point where little more could be done without Washington there to make decisions and give directions.

Another explanation is that by the end of 1778 the fortunes of war had begun to change. In April word arrived that France had recognized the independence of the United States; the next logical step was an alliance. At the same time, von Steuben was performing wonders with his endless drilling of Washington's troops. In June the British abandoned Philadelphia, and a month later a French fleet appeared off the American coast with four thousand marines. At Monmouth, New Jersey, meanwhile, the Continental forces had acquitted themselves respectably in a major engagement with the British. None of these events brought instant relief for the worst of Washington's problems; cooperation with the French proved difficult, and the Battle of Monmouth was by no means an unqualified victory. But at least he could begin to believe that the task he faced was not utterly beyond him. In that frame of mind he may well have felt less need to build castles in the air, or on paper in anxious letters home.[42]

Finally, at the end of March 1781, he wrote repeating the familiar questions, but in a notably more relaxed tone. "Is your covered ways done?" Lund was asked, "What are you going about next? Have you any prospect of getting paint and Oyl? are you going to repair the Pavement of the piazza? . . . An account of these things would be satisfactory to me, and infinitely amusing in the recital, as I have these kind of improvements very much at heart."[43] A few months later Washington had a chance to satisfy his curiosity personally on such points. While French and American troops were maneuvering into position to attack the British at Yorktown, he made a brief visit home to entertain the commanders of the French forces, Rochambeau and Chastellux. He left no record of his impressions of his much-altered house, but Jonathan Trumbull, Jr., who was with him, did. "An elegant seat and situation, great appearance of opulence and real exhibitions of hospitality and princely entertainment" was his verdict.[44]

Following the great triumph at Yorktown, Washington was back at Mount Vernon for a week, but it was a sad time, for Jackie Custis had died. Not until April 18, 1783, would the army's general orders announce "the cessation of hostilities between the United States of America and the King of Great Britain," and even then, Washington felt obliged to stay at his post as long as British troops remained on American soil. As the months passed, however, he began to sound more and more like someone who was about to return to civilian life. In letters home he urged Lund to collect long-overdue rents and draw up the annual accounts, which by then were three years in arrears, enumerating Mount Vernon's livestock, crops, and sales. There were instructions, too, about acquiring another piece of land "for the gratification of a mere fancy, (for it is no more) of putting the whole neck under one fence."[45] A letter to a Philadelphia merchant complaining about a shipment of paint and oil read strikingly like those Washington had sent Cary & Co. in the old days.[46] A letter also went off to George William Fairfax urging him to come home and rebuild Belvoir, which had accidentally burned to the ground that summer.[47]

The Fairfaxes never did return to America, but the new tablecloths and napkins Washington had ordered from Philadelphia and the pieces of French silver plate he asked Lafayette to buy for him eventually found their way to Mount Vernon[48]—a Mount Vernon transformed in spite of long years of war, standing serenely on its bluff, flanked by stands of sturdy young trees sweeping down toward the river below.

On December 4, 1783, with the British at last gone from New York City, Washington was finally able to begin his slow, celebratory progress south to Philadelphia, Wilmington, Baltimore, Annapolis, Georgetown, Alexandria, and finally home. Everywhere along the way he was eulogized as the figure upon whom everything had depended as well as the embodiment of hope for the welfare of the new nation. For what now seemed crucial to many people faced with the task of securing the liberty won at such cost was the exemplary character of the men who would lead. Washington disagreed. He believed institutions were at least as important as men, and he thought that the Articles of Confederation had very nearly doomed the nation to defeat during the war. In private, he spoke of the need for a convention to revise or replace the Articles altogether, yet publicly he said nothing of such a plan, hoping that time would recommend it to his countrymen. About his own future he was more forthcoming. His work was finished; he would not be one of those responsible for leading the new nation. He had seen to it that all his papers were meticulously copied, put in order, packed, and sent to Mount Vernon by the safest possible route. Posterity could judge his reputation; he was bound for home—and retirement.

In the months ahead, talking of his new life, Washington liked to picture himself, metaphorically, sitting in the shade of his own "Vine and Fig Tree," a phrase he would return to again and again.[49] Biblical in origin, it follows the words of the prophet Micah about men beating "their swords into plowshares," after which each would sit "under his vine and under his fig tree," where "no one shall make them afraid." Peace, home, and freedom from fear: the vine and fig tree connoted each of these. But for Washington it symbolized, above all, the life he led in retirement. Thus, in a particularly memorable use of the phrase, he wrote Lafayette early in 1784:

> At length my Dear Marquis I am become a private citizen . . . & under the shadow of my own Vine & my own Figtree free from the bustle of a camp & the busy scenes of public life, I am solacing myself with those tranquil enjoyments, of which the Soldier who is ever in pursuit of fame—the Statesman whose watchful days & sleepless nights are spent in devising schemes to promote the welfare of his own—perhaps the ruin of other countries, as if this Globe was insufficient for us all—& the Courtier who is always watching the countenance of his Prince, in hopes of catching a gracious smile, can have very little con-

ception. I am not only retired from all public employments, but I am retireing within myself; & shall be able to view the solitary walk, & tread the paths of private life with heartfelt satisfaction—Envious of none, I am determined to be pleased with all. & this my dear friend, being the order for my march, I will move gently down the stream of life, until I sleep with my Fathers.[50]

Before the Revolution the great issue had been freedom from control by others; now it was freedom from the burdens—and even more, the temptations—of power that mattered. The republican ideology that had played so large a part in the struggle with Great Britain permitted no equivocation: power could never be sought for its own sake, nor could it ever be more than a temporary possession. All of Washington's public actions were calculated to conform to these precepts, and none more so than those moments when he voluntarily laid aside power to return to private life. For Washington, retirement would remain the quintessential republican act.[51]

Retiring to "the paths of private life" meant, of course, retiring to Mount Vernon. It was to be his vine and fig tree, the tangible embodiment of his independence, just as it always had been. Yet it was also a place that had been made and remade by generations of proud, ambitious Virginia planters, himself included. Just ten years earlier he had formulated a plan for rebuilding and substantially enlarging the house. How appropriate would those changes seem now, given his altered circumstances? Though it would have been unlike Washington to pose such a question explicitly, something like it does seem to have been on his mind, for before long he began to modify that earlier design in significant ways.

There was another, even more serious issue that had to be faced, too. Early in the war, referring to his "Negroes" in a letter to Lund, Washington had put in parentheses afterward "whom I every day long more & more to get clear of."[52] He offered no explanation for his feelings, but they were to grow stronger year by year. The problems involved in "getting clear of" slavery were enormous, however. At one point he and Lund had written back and forth about the possibility of selling slaves to raise cash, but Washington made it clear that he would not sell them if it involved separating wives from husbands, or children from their parents.[53] So nothing was done. Similarly, when Lafayette wrote after the war proposing a scheme for emancipation, Washington warmly endorsed the goal but evidently found his friend's plan, for the present, impracticable.[54] As much as he had come to dislike slavery, life at Mount Vernon as he knew it would have been unimaginable without slaves. In short, the problem was insoluble.

Fortunately, others were not. The work that remained to be done on the house could begin forthwith. In Philadelphia on his way home at the end of 1783, Washington had talked with several men in the throes of building projects of their own. William Hamilton was experimenting with a cement that could be variegated to look like flagstone or flooring tile, and he told Washington of a skilled workman he had found.[55] Samuel Vaughan, a London merchant who had recently settled in Philadelphia with his family, lent him a book on preparing cement for tiling and stuccoing. Evidently they talked of both the piazza, which needed flooring, and the large room at the north end of the house. Describing some of the latest English fashions in interior decoration, Vaughan generously offered the loan of his own workman to execute any carpentry "the General" might want done.[56]

A few days later Washington was back at Mount Vernon, having arrived on Christmas Eve. At first most of his time was spent dealing with correspondence, visitors, and petitions from veterans needing help. Also, the plantation's records were in complete disarray, so often had they been shoved into trunks to be carried to safety. Money due Washington from England before the war was still unpaid, and crops had been poor for several seasons. Given the number of people to be fed and cared for at Mount Vernon, it was essential to have the farms properly managed, the accounts put in order, and the rents collected regularly.

With everything else there was to do, little progress was made on the house and grounds that first year, and in at least one instance Washington must have been sorely disappointed. The new roof leaked, and badly. Even before coming home he had written Lund in high dudgeon on the subject:

> I am truly unfortunate that after all the expence I have been at about my House I am to encounter the third Editien, with the trouble & inconvenience of another cover to it, after my return.—that there can have been little attention, or judgment exercised heretofore in covering it is a fact that cannot admit a doubt; for he must be a miserable artizan or a very great rascal indeed who, after one experimt. could not tell what kind of shingles were necessary to prevent a common roof from leaking, or him to place them as they ought to be. . . . besides ruining the Plaister within, I shall have the furniture all spoiled; & remain in a scene of continual vexation & trouble till it is done.[57]

Before the roof could be replaced, however, both the necessary materials and competent workmen had to be found, which was true of everything that had to be done to the house—including finishing the north room.

Of all the changes made at Mount Vernon over the years, none took longer to complete than the north room. Meant to be the most imposing space in the house, it remained an empty shell on Washington's return, yet oddly enough he seemed reluctant to begin work on it. Declining Samuel Vaughan's offer of the services of his carpenter, he noted, "I found my new room . . . so far advanced in the wooden part of it—the Doors, Windows & floors being done, as to render it unnecessary to remove your workman with his Tools (the distance being great) to finish the other parts; especially as I incline to do it in s[t]ucco, (which, if I understood you right, is the present taste in England)."[58] In reality, the room was far from finished, even "in the wooden part of it." The floor had not yet been laid, the Venetian window, missing its glass panes, had been covered with planking to keep it from rotting, and the walls were still unlathed. As for getting the stuccowork done, for the moment Washington confined himself to gathering information. If it was fashionable to have stuccoed walls instead of paneled ones, he asked Vaughan, should they be stuccoed below the chair rail as well as above it? And should the walls be painted or left the natural color of the stucco?[59]

On other points there was less confusion, and slowly the search for skilled workmen began to yield results. Before returning home, Washington had applied to Clement Biddle, the merchant in Philadelphia with whom he now did business, for a house joiner and a bricklayer, should any arrive on ships from overseas.[60] He also wrote Tench Tilghman, a former aide who had set up a mercantile business in Baltimore, and John Rumney, a merchant in Whitehaven, England, with whom he was negotiating for flagstone for the piazza floor.[61] In June Tilghman found a carpenter and hired him for Washington for a three-year term, and the following winter Rumney arranged to send Matthew Baldridge, a joiner, to Mount Vernon. Meanwhile, Samuel Vaughan had decided to make Washington a present of a marble mantelpiece for the north room, explaining (truthfully or not) that he had purchased it some years earlier in England and now had no use for it.[62] It arrived in Alexandria in February 1785, just as the ice was setting in. As soon as the river was passable, all ten cases were shipped to Mount Vernon, and Edward Vidler, an undertaker from Annapolis, was engaged to unpack them. While he was at Mount Vernon, Washington asked if he could take on the plastering of the north room, but Vidler refused, saying that he could not get the workers he would need.[63]

In writing Vaughan to tell him that the chimneypiece had arrived in Alexandria, Washington observed that judging from the number of cases, it was probably "too elegant & costly by far . . . for my own room, and republican stile of living."[64] Though obviously meant in jest, the remark may have explained some of the anxiety Washington seemed to feel about finishing the new room. As originally conceived, it was to be used for entertaining on a grand scale; it had no other imaginable function. Yet what possible need could the hero of the American Revolution, living in peaceful retirement, have for such a thing? Hence, perhaps, Washington's initial reluctance to get on with the project. Hence too, perhaps, the fact that neither he nor Martha would ever refer to the room as anything other than simply "the New Room."

Yet something had to be done with the space, and whatever was done had to be well done, so the search for the right artisan continued. Just two days after Vidler had declined the job, William Fitzhugh, a family friend of long standing, came for dinner and spent the night. Evidently the problem of the plasterwork was discussed, and Fitzhugh recommended Richard Boulton, someone he himself had once employed. After returning home, however, Fitzhugh wrote that he had had problems with Boulton, who drank, and had actually fired him. In Boulton's defense, he added that there had been a wife and daughter who "liked company" too well, and since then the wife had died and the daughter had married. Apparently persuaded, Washington did strike a bargain with Boulton several weeks later. With luck the project could still be finished before winter.[65] But soon after agreeing to come to Mount Vernon, Boulton went to Maryland to arrange his affairs and from there penned an abject note saying that he could not come after all because of various debts he owed. "I have heard of several Rits being out against me, which I expect dailey to be served, the consiquence of which will be that I must Inavoidable goe to Joal."[66] Whether this was true or not, another season had been lost.

The search for a master workman finally ended in August, when John Rawlins wrote Washington that he might be available. Originally from England, Rawlins worked for a time in Annapolis but had recently moved to Baltimore.[67] Washington replied at once, describing the new room and adding "it is my intention to do it in a plain neat style; which, independantly of its being the present taste, (as I am inform'd) is my choice."[68] At

*Marble chimneypiece in the new room at Mount Vernon,
given to Washington by Samuel Vaughan. Courtesy of
the Mount Vernon Ladies' Association.*

the same time he wrote Tench Tilghman, asking him to check on the quality of Rawlins's
work and find out whether his terms were reasonable.[69] Early in the fall, Rawlins came to
Mount Vernon and agreed to produce designs for the ceiling, a deep cove under it, the
cornice, the doorways, and the Palladian window. Washington also wanted an estimate of
the cost, and when neither it nor the designs materialized on schedule he became anxious.[70] If Rawlins did not come, he wrote Tilghman, there was a second solution. Sir
Edward Newenham of Dublin had written him mentioning a stucco worker by the name
of "Mr. Tharpe," whom he would be bringing along when he visited in the spring.[71] But
that winter an agreement was reached with Rawlins, who promised to send plans so the
house joiners could prepare for his arrival in April. It had taken two years to get this far.[72]

In the meantime, other projects were moving ahead more swiftly, especially outdoors.
Washington had admired Robert Morris's ice house and wanted his own altered and
improved. Also, in the summer of 1784, work had begun on a "Green House," where

exotic plant and tree specimens could be protected during the colder months of the year. Graced by a central pediment, a handsome brick building (to which wings were later added for housing slaves) was finally competed in 1787. Cool drinks and fresh meat in the middle of summer, lemons and oranges in the dead of winter: Washington meant to have them all. Such things bespoke control—the power to defy the natural progression of the seasons, to countermand the march of time itself.[73] On other fronts, however, Washington seemed to be striving for a different effect.

In the midst of the Revolution he had ordered great drifts of randomly spaced trees planted at either end of the house. Now he had come to envision a whole series of similar plantings that would completely transform the approach to the house and the grounds around it. On an unusually mild day in January 1785, he noted in his diary that he had spent his time "laying out my Serpentine road & Shrubberies adjoining."[74] Together that "road"—which was actually a pair of drives or walks—and the "Shrubberies" were to be the focal point of the new arrangement. Beginning several hundred feet from the house, between the garden walls, the drives would move toward it in a series of undulating curves. Each drive would be closely bordered by trees and shrubs,

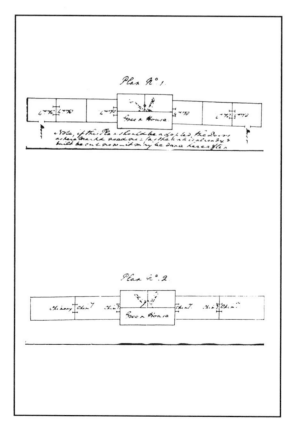

Washington's plans for Mount Vernon's greenhouse showing two versions of the adjoining slave quarters. Courtesy of the Mount Vernon Ladies' Association.

and in the center would be a large, open bowling green. Meanwhile, the existing drive, which Washington had laid out twenty years earlier to run straight through the middle of the area, would be eliminated. Curved lines in place of straight ones; informal plantings after the manner of "nature" itself: Batty Langley would have approved.[75]

With the larger design set, Washington threw himself into the project with gusto. Making detailed notes in his diary of the species of trees he found on his daily circuit of the plantation's farms, he had likely candidates marked for transplanting around the house.[76] "Road to my Mill Swamp, where my Dogue run hands were at work & to other places in search of the sort of Trees I shall want for my walks, groves, & Wildernesses," ran another diary entry in January 1785.[77] On paper he painstakingly diagramed where the many species of trees were to be placed, and outside, on the ground, he marked the places for each of the transplants and had holes dug, sometimes in temperatures close to freezing. Locations were carefully chosen for George Mason's Persian jasmine and guelder rose and the linden trees sent by Governor George Clinton of New York, but most of the plantings were of familiar native species found on the plantation itself: alternating weeping and yellow willows along the fences that stretched down the north and south lanes; fringe trees, locusts, hawthornes, and black gum trees for the decorative "Shrubberies." A pine grove on the south side of the house toward the river was also cleaned out and "vistoes" were cut through it. Trees were shaped and pruned.

The weather constantly posed problems. In the winter, even when there was no snow, wind and rain often interrupted the work. The ground froze and thawed in turn, changing the soil into a miry, slippery morass and filling the open holes dotted about waiting for transplants with half-frozen slush. At one point, anxious that the project not be deferred another day, Washington had his laborers remove the snow from the areas where he wanted them to work. In March 1785, after the serpentine drives were finished and most of the trees along them planted, a heavy frost coated the young saplings in ice, which bent them to the ground, causing some to snap apart and uprooting others.[78]

The following summer there was a drought. By mid-July most of the locusts, the black gum trees, the poplars, the mulberries, and all of the pines (the species chosen to line the serpentine drives) were dead or dying. The grass underfoot was burned to a crisp. Then, when it looked as if the drought might be over, the bricklayer's assistant and two slaves from the plantation began the slow, tedious job of creating the bowling green between the serpentine drives. Dividing the area into sections, they started by the house and moved outward from there, spading, leveling, seeding with grass, and finally rolling and rerolling each section as they went. But after a month, a series of heavy rains washed the seed "into heaps" and the whole process had to be begun again. By the end of October only a little more than half the area had been leveled and seeded.[79]

Of course even with all the work finished, it would be several years before the plantings took hold. Still, what Washington had in mind was eventually accomplished, and the change must have struck those who had known Mount Vernon before as startling. Where once the house and its outbuildings had stood out starkly against the surrounding landscape, now the outbuildings were all but completely hidden from view, and the main house—tucked among the trees—slipped in and out of view as one moved toward it. The whole effect was much softer. Gone was the surveyor's relentless insistence on straight

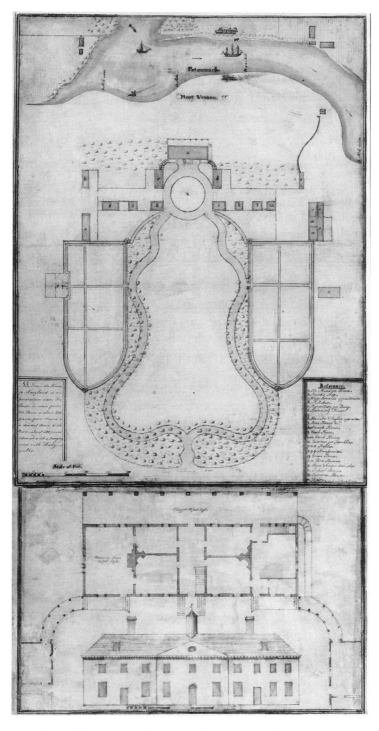

Mount Vernon, plan of the mansion house and the approach to it as redesigned by Washington in the 1780s. The drawing was done by Samuel Vaughan in 1787. Courtesy of the Mount Vernon Ladies' Association.

lines and right angles. Instead the visitor was invited to experience Washington's home through its relation to nature, to come upon it nestled in a leafy bower, sparkling with dappled sunlight and glimpses of distant vistas.

All of which, in 1785, was the height of fashion. But it would have been just as fashionable twenty years earlier, as Langley's book indicates. At the time, intent on making Mount Vernon seem as grand as possible, Washington had ignored Langley's advice. Now he chose naturalistic landscaping effects that also made the house appear distinctly less grand, less imposing. If he was concerned about adapting Mount Vernon to a postrevolutionary world, here was one way of doing it.

In addition to the relandscaping, several other projects were carried out in 1785. The piazza acquired a new ceiling in September, and later the same month John Saunders, an undertaker from Alexandria, spent part of a day at Mount Vernon advising Washington on reshingling the roof and using copper to line the wooden gutters and the areas around the pediment and dormers. Saunders also promised to return in a few days and direct the plantation's carpenters in the work. Scaffolding was put up on the west side of the house, and the old shingles were removed, but Saunders failed to reappear, so the Mount Vernon crew continued without him.[80]

Then came the day—with the leveling and seeding going on out in front and the work on the roof proceeding above—when Washington sat while his face was brushed with fresh plaster the consistency of thick cream by the renowned sculptor Jean Antoine Houdon. Having postponed a commission to do Catherine the Great, Houdon had come from France to do a life mask for a statue of Washington commissioned by the General Assembly of Virginia. He had appeared at Mount Vernon with three assistants and an interpreter on October 2. During the first part of his stay, he had struggled to find a pose he liked. According to legend, he was watching Washington ask a farmer the price of a pair of oxen, and Washington's indignant reaction when he heard the figure was just what Houdon had been looking for—an unsubstantiated story, but believable all the same. In spite of all the distractions inside as well as outside of the house, too, Washington still found time to take careful notes on the steps involved in preparing the plaster. Then he sat encased.[81]

Though Saunders never did return to supervise work on the roof, the shingling on the west side of the house was finished later that month. By the end of the year most of the dead trees and bushes along the new serpentine drives had been replaced, and the early months of 1786 saw still more work done on the grounds. At the beginning of February, two of the garden houses were moved to the far ends of the garden walls, which had been extended during the war. In March additional willows were planted along the drives and at the base of the bowling green, where the earth had been mounded up to form a "natural" barrier.[82] And about the same time the willows were being planted, work on the "New Room" finally began in earnest.

As a first step, Rawlins stopped by briefly one day with directions for Washington's joiners and carpenters. A pattern was needed for the curved studs of a cove that was to extend almost two feet downward from the ceiling to the walls. Particularly complicated

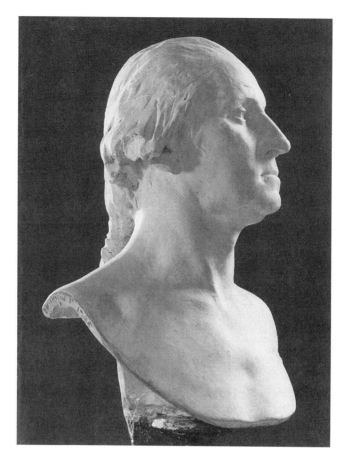

*Bust of Washington by the French sculptor Jean
Antoine Houdon. Courtesy of the Mount Vernon
Ladies' Association.*

would be the part of the cove interrupted by the arch of the Venetian window. A chair
rail and trim for the doors and windows also had to be put in place before the stuccoing
could begin, and to further complicate matters, when the carpenters took the planking
off the Venetian window, it became apparent that the passage of time had not been kind.
The sill, the ends of the posts, and the studs under the window had rotted inside the
"protective" covering and had to be replaced.[83]

Nevertheless, by the middle of April the room was sufficiently ready for the first of
Rawlins's workmen, who came by packet from Baltimore, to begin covering the walls
with lath provided by Washington's workers. The day after the lathing began, Rawlins
himself arrived in the company of Richard Tharpe, the stucco artisan from Ireland Sir
Edward Newenham had recommended earlier.[84] But when it became clear that Rawlins
intended to return to Baltimore once the work was begun, leaving Tharpe in charge,
Washington objected. He was paying Rawlins's "exorbitant" price for Rawlins's work.

In the end Rawlins did agree to come back later "prepared to attend to it himself,"[85] but whether he actually returned before the end of the summer, when he presented his bill, is unclear. Tharpe may well have done most of the decorative work called for in the plan. In the meantime, the flagstones ordered from John Rumney for the piazza floor had arrived from England. So while the Baltimore artisans worked in the new room, the new flagstones were laid in rows across the east front of the house.[86]

Rawlins's men remained at Mount Vernon until the middle of August. During that time the ceiling was finished and the walls were stuccoed above the chair rail.[87] Washington had also commissioned Tharpe to plaster several other rooms in the house, but the results were unsatisfactory, as he complained later to Rawlins. "The Stucco work in the Parlour is much cracked and Stained . . . and in every other part of the house, is in fact but little better than the plaster which was pulled down."[88] Rawlins promised that the stains would be taken care of the following year, and he agreed to send further enhancements for the new room, including plaster ornaments for the pilasters of the Venetian window and friezes to go over the doorways. Matthew Baldridge, one of the Mount Vernon carpenters, could put these up, and someone would come in the spring to help him.[89]

That fall Washington discovered to his great annoyance that two thirds of the pine plank set aside earlier for the floor of the new room had been stolen. Such occurrences were common enough, but this instance was especially irksome because the wood had been purchased so long ago that the remaining supply could not be matched. And since Washington wanted boards "all of a colour, and entirely free from Knots & sap," finding more took time. It was May before the new plank was delivered.[90]

As 1786 ended, there was still more than enough to do on the new room. Each span of chair rail and cornice and every door panel were to be embellished with decoration. In March Rawlins sent the additional ornaments he had promised, and by April Matthew Baldridge was applying them to the friezes that had been placed over the doorways as well as to the pilasters flanking the Venetian window. Some of the ornaments were missing from the packages that had arrived from Baltimore, so the delays continued, but that summer Thomas Hammond, one of Rawlins's workmen, came with the remaining decorations. By the third week in July, the scaffolding was set up so Hammond could wash the lingering stains from the plaster. Before the end of the month the work was finally finished — the last of the ornaments were in place, and Hammond could leave.[91]

Was the result worth all the trouble and expense it had cost? Rawlins, who died that summer, clearly knew his business. The work was skillfully executed, and his design was both deft and nicely calculated to appeal to Washington. Perhaps taking his cue from the delicately carved pastoral scenes on Samuel Vaughan's chimneypiece, he had chosen agricultural symbols for the friezes over the doorways and the four main panels of the ornamental plasterwork of the ceiling. The decorative detail in the cove below the ceiling and around the windows was more conventional, but still notable for its dignified restraint. If the "New Room" remained something of an embarrassment to Washington, Rawlins had perhaps done as much as anyone could have to reconcile it to his republican consciousness — and conscience.

Detail of the plasterwork over the doorways of the new room at Mount Vernon. Courtesy of the Mount Vernon Ladies' Association.

Unfortunately, Washington was not there to witness the end of the work. In May 1787 he had ridden off to Philadelphia as one of the Virginia delegates to a convention called to alter the Articles of Confederation. It was an enterprise he heartily endorsed in theory, but whether he himself ought to attend was another matter. He had actually become ill agonizing over the issue. Friends told him that if he did not go, the deliberations would have insufficient weight in the eyes of the people. But what if he went and the convention proved to be a failure? What would become of his reputation? And what of his promise to retire from public life? How could going to Philadelphia not be seen as a violation of that pledge?[92]

Nevertheless, he went and even agreed to serve as the convention's presiding officer. Nor, when the sessions had finally ended, would he have any major fault to find with the delegates' handiwork. Afterward he labored long and hard to see the Constitution ratified, despite the fact that a growing chorus of opinion had begun to predict yet another new role for him: president of the United States in the new government.

In the summer of 1787, however, he could still think of the time spent in Philadelphia as an interlude in life under his vine and fig tree. Come fall he would be back at Mount Vernon, and with that in mind he directed homeward a steady stream of instructions and requests. On a rare evening spent alone in his lodgings in May, he wrote asking for measurements so he could order hinges for the doors of the new room. In June he asked for the dimensions of the room's fireplace to have iron castings made for its back and sides while he was in Philadelphia. Next, he wanted the dining room windows measured so he could buy one of the new Venetian blinds, which could then be copied for some of the other windows by the Mount Vernon carpenters. For the new room, he sent window glass and locks, and he asked for the dimensions of the other fireplaces in the house as well.[93]

As the summer days grew shorter, a painter was employed to coat the wood trim in the new room in "buff inclining to white," but very carefully, using small brushes, so as not to obscure the intricate decoration with too much paint. Bright green wallpaper would be added later, as well as fine paper borders depicting architectural elements, outlining the moldings around the doors and windows. Still, with the painting of the new room finished, the larger plan for the house, after more than fourteen years, was essentially complete—except for one last flourish.

During a recess in the convention's proceedings that summer, Washington went off for a few days' fishing in the countryside near Valley Forge. Early the first morning he rode over to the site where he and his troops had been quartered during the winter of 1777 and 1778. Almost ten years had passed since then. As he picked out the ghostly lines of the encampment, reconstructing it according to landmarks recalled in the August haze, did he think of the terrible cost that had been paid and of the blessings that peace had brought since then? As a general he had helped win that peace—he and the bleeding, freezing, half-starved men who had camped there.

Were there other ghosts as well? His father, Gus, his brother, Lawrence, whose portrait still hung at Mount Vernon, the Fairfaxes? Would his ancestors have recognized the land above the Potomac that they had ventured to acquire all those years before? Belvoir was abandoned, a burned-out shell, in its own way a poignant casualty of the conflict with Britain. But Mount Vernon had survived and grown. It now stretched for two and a half miles along the Potomac, and at its heart stood the mansion house, three times rebuilt, an uncommon place, as Bryan Fairfax had said. All of this too was safeguarded by peace.

After an absence of more than four months, Washington finally reached home on September 22, 1787. As he rode through the new front gate, past the freshly planted saplings of many varieties—far younger and smaller than the woody, virgin forests of Gus's day—surely he must have looked up at the roofline of the house ahead to see if his instructions had been followed. For outlined against the evening sky, he would have expected to find that final touch he had planned for the house. In July he had ordered a weather vane for the cupola, giving its maker, Joseph Rakestraw, detailed instructions. On top of an iron spire was to be "a bird"—its wings spread, and in its mouth an olive branch.[94]

The dove of peace. Rakestraw had correctly read his meaning, and there was the proof, flying aloft the cupola—that bold assertion of Washington's personal freedom. Peace and independence: that was the message with which Mount Vernon, at last, was to be crowned.

But did it also occur to Washington that peace could have more than one meaning in this case? Was it peace in the world, peace in the nation, or peace at home that most concerned him? For the moment, the first two seemed secure. What of the third, however? As calm and serene as life under Washington's vine and fig tree was meant to be, in reality the transformation of the house just completed—in its human, as opposed to its phys-

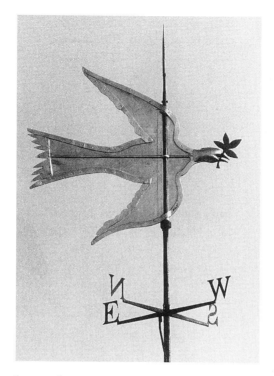

The weathervane on the cupola at Mount Vernon. Courtesy of the Mount Vernon Ladies' Association.

ical dimensions—had been anything but peaceful. Over the years a large and constantly changing cast of characters had been involved in the project. Some were slaves, some were bonded servants, some were independent artisans or workers. A few benefited significantly from the experience of working on Mount Vernon, but no one got rich as a result, and at least one person lost his life.

What comes through the records most clearly, however, is that Washington was a demanding master and employer, and most of those working for him did not meet his standards. One or two individuals may have shared his commitment to making the outcome everything he dreamed it could be, but that was all. The rest worked because he paid them to, or because he ordered them to—or because in some cases, surely, they were physically coerced, or knew that they would be if they refused. Ultimately his goals and theirs were not the same, and they were just as determined as he was to have their way. Thus the years of building had also been a time of conflict, a time when peace proved at best an elusive condition at Mount Vernon, thanks to the stoutly defended independence of its builders. In the long run, too, that situation may have done more to determine Mount Vernon's future than anything else.

PART II

Toward Democracy

Planceer of ye 2^d Type

A Hexangular Pulpit.

Plate CXIV.

Type

Plan of the Pulpit

B

C

D

E

A

1 Feet

Feet

Batty Langley Invent and Delin. 1739.

Thos Langley Sculp

THE BUILDERS

BUILDING AND REBUILDING Mount Vernon taxed Washington in many ways, but finding, holding, and managing an adequate labor force was surely the stiffest challenge he faced. In some respects his military experience had prepared him for the task, but war was different from normal, day-to-day existence. Building, by contrast, was the stuff of which most of his workers made their lives.

Also, unlike the shifting fortunes of war, certain things about building never changed. The hardest, dirtiest, least pleasant work—the deepest digging, the longest hauling, the heaviest lifting—was done by slaves, always. Some slaves had acquired skills at trades like carpentry and brick masonry, and their lot was slightly easier, but all slaves, skilled or not, had to be supervised. And invariably building involved skills that no member of the Mount Vernon "family" possessed, so additional workers were needed. As a rule they served under contract for greater or lesser amounts of time, but finding them in the first place was never easy.

When fully assembled, the building crews at Mount Vernon thus had a polyglot character. Indeed, they came close to replicating, in miniature, the larger Virginia society from which they were drawn. They also displayed, sometimes dramatically, the pressures and tensions that eddied through that society. On any given day Washington was probably more aware of the problems he faced with particular individuals, but the broader issues posed by his complex and sometimes troubled relations with his workers were never far beneath the surface, as his growing unease on the subject of slavery demonstrated. Over time, too, those issues pressed increasingly to the fore.

CHAPTER 6

Slaves and Overseers

EARLY IN FEBRUARY 1760, "passing by" his slave carpenters, Washington was surprised to discover that, together, four of them had managed to hew only 120 feet of poplar logs the day before. Curious as to why more had not been done, he sat down, pocket watch in hand, to observe two of the crew work and later recorded what he saw in his diary:

> Tom and Mike in a less space than 30 Minutes cleard the Bushes from abt. a Poplar Stock-lind it 10 Foot long and hughd each their side 12 Inches deep.
>
> Then, letting them proceed their own way—they spent 25 Minutes more in getting the cross cut saw standing to consider what to do—sawing the Stock of [sic] in two places—putting it on the Blocks for hughing it square lining it &ca. and from this time till they had finishd the Stock entirely; requird 20 Minutes more, so that in the Spaces of one hour and a quarter they each of them from the Stump finishd 20 Feet of hughing: from hence it appears very clear that allowing they work only from Sun to Sun and require two hour's at Breakfast they ought to yield each his 125 feet while the days are at their present length and more in proportion as they Increase.[1]

In short, when Washington was there to check on them, his slave carpenters worked at four times the speed they did when he was not there. Or so he concluded.

But if building was truly a performance, the role the still relatively inexperienced master of Mount Vernon assigned himself that day was quite unlike the one he would be playing in years to come. Time and motion studies of slaves at work may have proved something in abstract terms, but the demonstration was just that: an abstraction, unrelated to the day-to-day transactions between master and slave that made up the reality of the relationship.

From his slaves Washington wanted efficiently executed work of high quality. Their objectives were more varied. Near the top of the list would have been the opportunity to maintain personal bonds with other slaves and the achievement of the greatest measure of well-being for themselves and the people they cared about, as well as the chance to move from place to place in pursuit of those objectives. Some slaves were also eager to acquire skills as a way of improving their lot; others were interested in doing as little work as possible; and still others wanted more than anything else to escape. Washington hoped his slaves would work docilely and productively. They dreamed of living their lives as free men and women.

Logically, of course, those goals were mutually exclusive, but in reality it was possible to reach at least provisional accommodations. Recalcitrant slaves could be beaten or sold, but that would not get the work done any faster or better. For their part, the slaves could and did employ any number of strategies to thwart their managers' wishes, but beyond a certain point such tactics netted them little. Ultimately rewards were likely to accomplish at least as much as punishments, just as compliance was likely to earn a better reward than its opposite. Recognizing this, both sides generally found ways of compromising, but for each of them the implicit threat of less pacific behavior—occasionally acted out—remained a powerful element in the negotiations.[2]

None of the four slaves whose work Washington observed that day—Tom, Mike, George, and Billy—had African names, so they probably had been born in the colonies, with parents or grandparents who had survived the middle passage. There are some other clues as to who they might have been, but identifying slaves from the written records often involves considerable uncertainty. Tom could have come to Washington from his brother Lawrence, who owned at least one slave of that name, though more likely he and Mike were the "Tom" and "Michael" listed in Martha Washington's share of her first husband's estate. Lawrence Washington also owned a slave named George, who had been young enough six years earlier to have his height registered instead of his worth in pounds sterling, a common practice when slaves had not yet entered the workforce. And Billy too might have been Lawrence's property, or he could have been the child Washington had purchased along with his mother just the year before.[3]

New slaves had begun appearing at Mount Vernon as soon as Washington leased the property. By 1760 the number above age sixteen had reached 43, and a decade later it stood at 81. By 1774 it had climbed to 119, and in 1786 the total number of all slaves at Mount Vernon was almost twice that figure, including 92 children and 6 adults designated as "old" or "past labour." The year Washington died he owned or rented 317 slaves at Mount Vernon, of whom 132 were either too young or too old to work.[4]

Part of the increase was natural, and part of it was due to Martha's inheritance. But slaves also came to Mount Vernon as the result of purchases at public auction, as well as from Washington's brothers, from Anne Fairfax Washington Lee, from the owners of neighboring plantations, and from merchants dealing in the slave trade. In 1772 a group of West Indian slaves—generally thought to be preferable to Africans since they were already familiar with plantation ways—came in exchange for a cargo of wheat and flour.[5] Typically Washington's directives regarding new slaves were plain-spoken. "Let there be two thirds of them Males, the other third Females," he wrote at one point, "The former not exceeding (at any rate) 20 yrs of age—the latter 16—All of them to be strait Limb'd & in every respect strong & likely, with good Teeth & good Countenances—to be sufficiently provided with cloaths."[6]

Though increases predominated, subtractions from Mount Vernon's slave population were also frequent. Slave children died more often than whites of the same ages. Eighteenth-century plantation records indicate that one quarter of the babies born to slaves died within their first year and almost as many more died before age fifteen.[7] At Mount Vernon the rates may well have been comparable. Overseers often reported that "Our Negroes" were "Sickly" with "fevers & Agues." The swampy areas of the plantation bred mosquitoes, and hence malaria, freely, and various respiratory illnesses took their toll, particularly in the colder months.[8] Although Washington tried to minimize the number of cases of prolonged illness or death by employing doctors to come whenever necessary, he felt that his overseers tended to neglect sick slaves:

It is foremost in my thoughts, to desire you will be particularly attentive to my Negros in their sickness; and to order every Overseer *positively* to be so likewise; for I am sorry to observe that the generality of them, view these poor creatures in scarcely any other light than they do a draught horse or Ox; neglecting them as much as when they are unable to work; instead of comforting and nursing them when they lye on a sick bed. . . . If their disorders are not common, and the mode of treating them plain, simple and well understood, send for Doctr. Craik in time.[9]

Occasionally, too, there were tragic accidents, such as occurred in August 1778, when Cooper James, who had been sent to help the millworkers ditch a swamp, finished his dinner earlier than the rest and went wading in the millrace. Evidently he walked into a deep spot and, because he could not swim, drowned before his companions could save him.[10]

Most of the plantation's slaves fared better than Cooper James, but not all of them remained at Mount Vernon. At least nine were sold at different times to raise cash to pay taxes.[11] When another was executed by the commonwealth of Virginia for an unspecified crime in 1781, Washington appealed for and was granted a tax credit equal to the slave's market value plus the allowed three years of interest, which amounted to £138.[12] The same year seventeen slaves were taken by the British when the sloop *Savage* docked at Mount Vernon's landing. Among them were an overseer, a brickmaker, a weaver, a "Horseler," and a cooper. Eight of their number were recovered later, most of them in Philadelphia.[13]

Other slaves left on their own initiative, often at the earliest possible opportunity. Boson ran away in 1760, only to be recovered five days later,[14] yet he seems to have tried again and succeeded, for the same year his name was subtracted from the list of tithables. Or perhaps Washington simply decided to sell him. Soon after that, four slaves disappeared from one of his other landholdings "without the least Suspicion, Provocation, or Difference with any body or the least angry Word or Abuse from their Overseers."[15] Tom, a field hand, ran away so often that, as an example to his fellows, arrangements were made to sell him to the West Indies. The captain of the ship taking him was warned to "keep him handcuffd till you get to Sea—or in the Bay."[16]

If Tom failed to make good his escape, other Mount Vernon slaves were more successful. Philadelphia, with its large population of freedmen and the relative ease with which slaves could find refuge there, cost Washington at least two of his most valuable slaves. Martha's personal maid ran off while the family was living there during Washington's presidency, and even more irksome, Hercules, the cook, followed suit two years later.[17] After months of hunting for him, Washington wrote an agent in Philadelphia from Mount Vernon:

> We have never heard of Herculas our Cook since he left this; but little doubt remains in my mind of his having gone to Philadelphia, and may yet be found there, if proper measures were employed to discover (unsuspectedly, so as not to alarm him) where his haunts are. . . . I neither have, nor can get a good Cook to hire . . . if Herculas was to get the least hint of the design he would elude all your vigilance.[18]

Apparently he did just that, for his name does not appear on the roster of slaves drawn up in 1799.

Unquestionably there would have been more runaways had it not been for the family ties that bound many slaves to Mount Vernon. Those ties also led them to resist being sold or sent away. The tactics varied, but surprisingly often they succeeded. In 1773 it was decided not to send a newly purchased slave to another landholding "As the Negro Fellow I bought In Alexandria will by no means consent to leave this Neighbourhood."[19] When Washington's mother asked to have one of his female slaves, Priscilla, sent to her in Fredericksburg in 1778, Lund Washington demurred. "They appear to live comfortable together," he wrote of Priscilla and her husband, one of the Mount Vernon coopers. Two weeks later the issue was still unresolved. "Am very sorry to part her from Jack. He Cryes and Begs, sayg. he had rather be Hang'd than seperated." The plan was given up, and Priscilla stayed.[20] When "Phillip," another female slave, was offered for sale to a man in Maryland, she too found ways of resisting. "She was so alarmed at the thought of being sold that the man cou'd not get her to utter a Word of English, therefore we believed she cou'd not speak. The man was to come two days after. When he came she was Sick & has been ever Since. . . ."[21]

As Mount Vernon's acreage and slave population continued to grow, both required increasingly complex systems of organization. More than a half hour's walk between the slave quarters and the fields was commonly seen as a waste of time and energy, and Washington's concern on this point is clear in his frequent orders not to move gangs of slaves about without good reason. "Besides loosing much time in marching and counter-marching, it weakens the exertion," he wrote.[22] The solution, as at other large plantations, was to divide the property into separate units or "farms," each with its own gang of resident hands. In addition to the Home or "Mansion House" Farm, the final configuration at Mount Vernon included four others: Muddy Hole, Dogue Run, Union Farm,

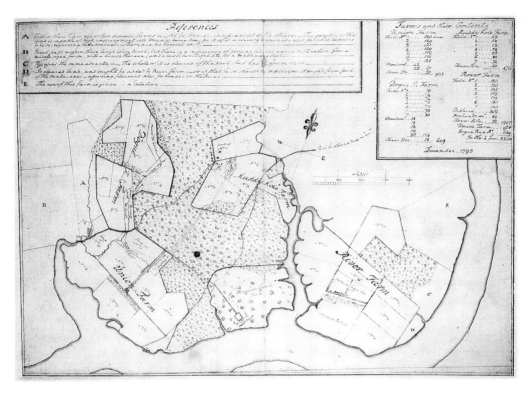

Map of the five farms at Mount Vernon drawn by Washington. Reproduced by permission of The Huntington Library, San Marino, California.

and River Farm.[23] The divisions represented Washington's view of how the plantation's agricultural enterprise could be run most profitably, and within that framework the slaves were meant to conduct their lives as best they could.

For efficiency's sake most of the slaves lived and worked on the outlying farms, yet Washington was also aware of the importance—to him—of keeping morale up and "night-walking" to a minimum, so at least some effort was made to group family members together on individual farms. Young children almost always lived with their mothers, for example. But invariably a slave's occupation was the primary factor dictating where he or she lived, and husbands and wives were in fact separated more often than not. Of the married men, including those in one of the trades or employed inside the mansion house, more than half lived away from their families. Women's chances of bringing up their children while also living with their husbands were even slimmer. In 1799 at Mount Vernon only eighteen women lived with their husbands. Thirty-two women lived apart from their husbands, and another twelve were unmarried mothers or widows with children, making a total of forty-four families with no resident husband or father. At Union Farm there were no nuclear family units. Of the five adult men living there, four were single and one was married to a slave on another plantation; of the eleven women, three were single and two were married to husbands on neighboring plantations, two had husbands who were assigned to the mansion house, and four had no husbands but were bringing up children by themselves. Aside from the overseer and his wife (who were slaves), at Muddy Hole there was only one nuclear family present: Will, a self-ordained minister; Kate, his wife, who practiced midwifery; three of their children; and two grandchildren.[24]

With three generations all living on the same farm, the family of Kate and Will at Muddy Hole was doubly anomalous, but the records point to at least a few other instances in which extended families—whether aunts, uncles, and cousins or grandparents and grandchildren—were brought together in the same place. There was also a fair degree of stability in living arrangements. Of the young children listed at Muddy Hole in 1786, all but two were there thirteen years later, suggesting that individuals did tend to remain on the same farm. Moreover, six of the adult slaves at Muddy Hole had siblings living there, and three of the women had grandchildren with them. Almost certainly, too, there were instances of extended family members living together that do not show up in the records. In general, with so few nuclear families living undivided in the same place, alternative family structures of all kinds would have been important, particularly when young children were involved.[25]

For the same reason, the hours after work was finished for the day were much taken up with visits. A certain amount of night-walking was permitted—or just plain ignored—but at times there was more involved than simply treading along well-worn pathways under cover of darkness. On several occasions Washington complained of horses being taken from the barns and used without permission, and some visits, particularly those off the plantation altogether, could extend well beyond a single night.[26] Short of mounting a full-scale search, not much could be done in such cases. In the 1790s, when a hired slave working at Union Farm was reported missing, Washington wrote:

> I think it not unlikely that French's Will is in Maryland: when he was guilty of these tricks formerly (before I had him) his walks, and harbouring place was, as I have been informed, somewhere within the circle of Broad Creek, Bladensburgh and upper Marlborough: the precise spot I do not know, nor is it worth while (except for the sake of example, nor for that, if it stops with him) to be at *much* trouble, or at *any* expence over a trifle, to hunt him up.[27]

Structuring their relationships in flexible, innovative ways, refusing to be sold or sent away, using whatever means they could to be assigned places near one another, and traveling miles at night to be together, Mount Vernon's slave families could and did remain united. Other personal ties, too, bound individuals together. And though such relationships are less evident in plantation records, one enduring memorial to the sturdy network of ties of all kinds that linked individual slaves is the frequent repetition of certain names given to children generation after generation—names such as Will, George, Ben, Nat, Suckey, Peg, Hannah, Kate, and Darcus. Not only did shared names acknowledge the existence of a relationship, they also perpetuated it through time, giving it permanence.[28]

In comparison with slaves on many other plantations, those at Mount Vernon were generally well housed, well fed, and well clothed; visitors often remarked on the fact, and Washington's instructions on the point were clear.[29] Well-cared-for slaves were more productive. From the slaves' perspective, however, what they were given was altogether inadequate, and they worked tirelessly and often with great ingenuity to make up the deficit. Some of their efforts were encouraged, others were at least tolerated, and still others crossed the line into overt disobedience. If caught, the miscreants were punished, but more often than not, as individuals, they eluded detection, leaving their managers to choose between punishing entire groups of slaves or simply letting the matter drop.

On the outlying farms the slaves lived in one- or two-room huts, clustered close together near the overseer's house, so they could be supervised at night and easily assembled at daybreak for work. Made of logs daubed with clay, the huts were simple enough to build. They had dirt floors, unglazed windows, and wooden chimneys and roofs. One foreign visitor found them "more miserable than the poorest of the cottages of our peasants," yet he noted seeing in them "beds, a little kitchen furniture," and items such as teakettles and cups.[30] The slaves were also allowed small garden plots near their huts, as well as space to grow fruit trees and raise chickens.

Mount Vernon, slave quarter in one of the greenhouse wings as currently furnished. Courtesy of the Mount Vernon Ladies' Association.

House servants and slaves who worked at other specialized tasks generally lived either close to the main house or near their work if it was any distance away. Thus the coopers, distillers, and millers lived at the mill. Cooks lived over the kitchen, and smiths over the blacksmith shop. North of the main house there was also a large quarter—rebuilt at least once—that provided housing for slaves, and later the two wings of the greenhouse were used for the same purpose, with the slaves sleeping together in a few large rooms on berths. In these ways the multitude of ditchers, gardeners, seamstresses, spinners, knitters, the shoemaker, the milkmaid, the postilions, the bricklayers, and the carpenters took their places in the larger scheme of things.[31] But if work determined the structure, it fell to the slaves to animate it with other impulses, which by all accounts they did readily enough. Visitors to Mount Vernon wrote of the lively social life in the quarters, of teams playing at "prisoner's base" and of "jumps and gambols as if they had rested all week."[32]

The preparation and eating of food, often done communally, was also an important social activity. Typically on Virginia plantations, slaves were allowed two periods a day for eating, and the diet consisted primarily of corn and cornmeal flavored with a small amount of pork. At Mount Vernon the provisions were more ample: adult slaves were given eleven pounds of corn, two pounds of fish, and one-half pound each of pork, milk, and fat every week, plus half the allowance of rum allowed to hired whites. To this allotment, however, the slaves themselves added a rich variety of items. In addition to what they raised in their own gardens, they hunted at night for squirrels, raccoons, opossum, quail, ducks, geese, and rabbits. They also caught delicacies like catfish in the river.[33] And though they were strictly forbidden to do so, some of their number regularly helped themselves to additional meat from the plantation's meathouse as well as to livestock, including lambs, pigs, and cattle. In the same manner they acquired barrels of flour, fruit ripening in the orchards, and wheat, if it was not harvested, threshed, and put under lock and key as soon as it was ripe.[34]

Against such incursions Washington repeatedly urged vigilance. "The greatest attention is to be paid to the stocks of all kinds on the farms; . . . They are to be counted regularly, that no false reports may be made; and missing ones, if any, hunted for until found."[35] From time to time he also offered tips as to who the guilty parties might be. "I wish you could find out the thief who robbed the Meat house at Mount Vernon and bring him to punishment," he wrote at one point, "Nathan has been suspected, if not detected, in an attempt of this sort formerly; and as likely as any one to be guilty of it now. Postilion Joe has been caught in similar practices; and Sam, I am sure would not be restrain[ed] by any qualms of conscience, if he saw an opening to do the like."[36] But suspicions were not the same as proof, and generally the offenders went unapprehended—and unpunished—regardless of Washington's strictures.

Catching the guilty parties would have been easier if they had held on to their booty, but any telltale surpluses were quickly bartered away for other desirable items. Indeed, hints of informal networks of exchange occasionally surface in the plantation's records. Male slaves were annually allotted shirts and trousers of coarse cloth, as well as shoes and stockings, and women were provided with shifts, shoes, and stockings. Eventually the slaves themselves made all such clothing, yet despite close supervision by Martha

Artifacts uncovered during a recent archaeological dig in the basement of the "House for Families," a large slave quarter, no longer standing, built near the greenhouse at Mount Vernon. Such objects provide invaluable evidence about the lifestyle and diet of Washington's slaves. Courtesy of the Mount Vernon Ladies' Association.

Washington herself, the seamstresses seemed to be forever cutting out patterns with no regard to the material wasted. "Wasted" material, on the other hand, could easily have served as a valuable trade commodity: a piece of cloth too small to make a man's shirt could be used for a child's shirt or shift not allowed for in the annual allotments of clothes.[37]

Still another item Washington's slaves were inclined to appropriate for their own use was space, and here the most persistent offenders may have been the children. One of his managers, on arriving at Mount Vernon with his family, was particularly disconcerted by what he found in this respect and wrote Washington, "I thought I saw a great many at your mansion house,"[38] to which the reply came back promptly:

> There are a great number of Negro children at the Quarters belonging to the house people; but they have Always been forbid (except two or 3 young ones belonging to the Cook, and the Mulatto fellow Frank in the house, her husband; both of whom live in The Kitchen) from coming within the Gates of the Inclosures of the Yards, Gardens, &ct; that they may not be breaking the Shrubs, and doing other mischief; but I believe they are often in there

notwithstanding; but if they could be broke of the practice it would be very agreeable to me, as they have no business within; having their wood, Water, &ct at their own doors without.[39]

The slave children were not to use the area around the main house as a playground: Washington's wishes were clear on that point, just as it was clear that he suspected his wishes were regularly ignored. But if the new manager was astute enough to pick it up, another point could be gleaned from the reply. Washington did not want to give the order directly to the slaves, and that feeling ran, like a leitmotif, through much of what he wrote his managers. He knew that the rules he wanted enforced were perpetually broken, he knew of the liberties the slaves constantly took with his property, his stores, his livestock, his orchards, his gardens, his tools, but against all reason he never stopped hoping that somehow someone would put a stop to it all. The truth was, of course, that if anything was to be done, he stood a much better chance of succeeding than anyone else. But for whatever reason, he chose not to try. Nor is it likely that any of this was lost on the slaves.

At night the slaves had more opportunity to circumvent the rules than they did during the day, which was supposed to be devoted to work—work that was closely supervised and often done by groups of slaves acting together. Even then, however, things seldom went as smoothly as intended.

Each of the four outlying farms had its own overseer, who was sometimes a slave, sometimes a hired white. The hands they supervised worked six days a week, from sunup to sundown, clearing land, preparing fields by removing stumps and roots, plowing, tending fields, harvesting crops, and mending fences. Monitoring their work was always problematic, but in time a system was devised whereby the overseers submitted regular accounts, recording each hand for each day as one unit and totaling units and calculating the productivity every week.[40] Infants went to the fields with their mothers, and children were put to work at about age eleven. "A small boy or girl for the purpose of fetching wood or water, tending a child, or such like things, I do not object to; but so soon as they are able to work out I expect to reap the benefit of their labour myself," Washington instructed his overseers.[41]

Working closer to the main house, "the home house gang"—also field hands—cultivated lawns as well as fields, in addition to pulling out stumps and weeds, building fences, and occasionally assisting at the other farms. There was also a crew of ditchers who not only dug all the irrigation and drainage ditches in the fields but also made and kept up roadways, loaded and unloaded boats, and sometimes dug clay for brickmaking. Then there were all the slaves who did not work on the land (except perhaps at harvest-times, when extra hands were needed). The jobs they did were manifold, but many involved specialized skills, sometimes of a high order. In this category fell those slaves who were regularly mobilized to work on major building projects, most notably brickmakers and carpenters.

For many years Washington hired brickmakers and masons, both slave and free, from the outside. But in 1774 "Gunner" was purchased at age thirty-seven, and whether he did so initially, by 1781 he was recorded as making brick.[42] He continued to work until at least 1792. Will, Sam, and Tom Davis also worked at brickmaking at different times, but of the three, only Tom Davis was listed as a brickmaker in the Mount Vernon records in 1799 — Tom Davis and his younger coworker Muclus.[43]

It was possible to rely on hired brickmakers for specific projects because their skills were not regularly required. Carpenters were a different matter. As early as the 1750s Washington kept a corps of slave carpenters at Mount Vernon, and by 1759 it included seven adult slaves with a boy to help.[44] Working under a skilled white overseer, they repaired outbuildings, moved houses, and made and mended carts and wheels. They also repaired tobacco sheds and at one point built a new quarter at Muddy Hole to replace one that had burned down. When necessary they were detailed to other jobs on the plantation, including plowing, reaping, and helping at the mill, and when there was no work for them at Mount Vernon they were hired out to neighbors, building a kitchen for one and a barn floor for another.[45]

With the addition of James, a slave Washington hired from outside for a three-year period,[46] the crew of carpenters listed in 1759 was probably already in place when the main house was rebuilt in 1758. For that project, they searched the surrounding woods for framing timbers, which according to Washington's specification were to be white oak, ". . . which made it a bundance the Teadiousr to get," Humphrey Knight, his manager, remarked. The slave carpenters also did a "vast deal of Sawing work besides a vast Deal of other work." Taking care to remove the nails so they could be reused, they pulled down the "old works," including the shingles and clapboarding. They hewed the trees cut in the woods and hauled them to the saw pit and sawed them into plank. They carted, lugged, and stacked timbers for the joiners to work on, and they helped lift the heavy beams, girders, sills, plates, and posts into place. They built the scaffolding, made the laths, and probably nailed in the studs and laths for the walls and roofing under the direction of the master carpenter. "Mr. Pattason Tells me he will see it is well Dun, and hurry em about it we Shall keep no more about it then Needful I have taken [hired out] other work for em to Do when that is Dun . . ." Knight wrote, anxiously watching the slow progress of the work.[47]

The carpenter crew remained fairly stable in the years after the first rebuilding of the house. Michael and George (assuming they were the same Mike and George whom Washington sat down to observe in 1760) were still listed as carpenters in 1774.[48] To their ranks had been added Isaac, bought from Lund Washington's brother in 1773.[49] Anthony — bought at public vendue the year before and at the outset assigned to the home plantation — might have worked with them also, since he was listed as a tradesman in 1774.[50] Before the second rebuilding was completed, Sambo, a young African, became one of the carpenters,[51] as did Tom Nokes, the two of them taking the places of George and Michael. When Sambo ran away with the British in 1781, the Mount Vernon overseers had to do without his skills until he was recovered in Philadelphia sometime later.[52]

During the second rebuilding of the house and its flanking outbuildings, the carpenters played a role similar to the one they had played during the first rebuilding. They pulled weatherboarding off the north and south ends of the main house, and they pulled down the existing outbuildings on the west front. They hewed timber, and hauled it to the building site. They made laths and nailed them in place. They were probably also skilled enough to do simple joinery, and in the 1780s one of their number, Isaac, was singled out from the rest to do bench carpentry in the shop.[53]

When tradesmen—including carpenters—were drawn from the ranks of the slaves, they were likely to come from the home farm, which was also true of house servants. Between 1760 and 1774 five of the slaves picked to work in the main house came from outlying farms, but almost double that number came from the home farm. During the same period, of the eight slaves chosen for the trades, six came from the home farm.[54] The chief reason was probably familiarity. Slaves on the home farm worked near the main house and therefore would have been better known. Often, too, they were the children of artisans or house servants and had been brought up to understand the house and the ways of its occupants.[55] Slaves freed from vital agricultural activity had to be both willing and able to learn, and they had to be trustworthy, since they worked more autonomously than other slaves. And still another criterion may have come into play. One of Washington's visitors noted that a high proportion of Mount Vernon's house servants were mulattoes.[56] The same could well have been true of the skilled slave labor force.

That work in the trades was considered more desirable than life as a field hand is clear from the fact that the threat of being reassigned to the fields was a potent means of compelling improved performance. "Tell Muclus, as from me," Washington wrote his manager at one point, "that if his pride is not a sufficient stimulus to excite him in industry, and admonition has no effect upon him, that I have directed you to have him severely punished and placed under one of the Overseers as a common hoe negro."[57] Muclus, the brickmaker, had a wife living on a neighboring plantation, and evidently his night-walking was affecting his "industry" during daylight hours. In the fourteen-year period 1760–74, several of the carpenters were subtracted from the rolls because of death or retirement, but few were actually transferred to fieldwork, and of those who were, one was placed back in the ranks within a year. Another was reassigned to Dogue Run as overseer.[58]

As a rule, the slave carpenters at Mount Vernon worked under a hired white carpenter, but their work carried them all over the plantation, out of sight of the main house. Up to a point, they set their own work pace, though to Washington their progress often seemed infuriatingly slow. In the spirit of his initial time-and-motion study of wood-hewing, he came to require detailed reports of what the crew accomplished each week, including precise measurements of the amount of wood they prepared. Yet "the slothfulness of my Carpenters"[59] remained a perennial problem, causing him to remark on one occasion, "there is not to be found so idle a set of Rascals."[60] Perhaps most galling of all was contrast between his carpenters and those he saw working elsewhere. "It appears to me, that to make even a chicken coob [sic], would employ them all a week; buildings that are run up here [Philadelphia] in two or three days (with not more hands) employ them a month, or more."[61] If Washington's carpenters performed so badly, what did that say about his performance as their master?

It was easy to suspect, too, that the slave carpenters were implicated in the constant disappearance of valuable lumber as well as the gutting of unused buildings left standing. "That house as has been the fate of all the rest, under similar circumstances, will be lost;

as my negros dismantle them as their occasions require, without leave, and without scruple," wrote Washington.[62] Dismantling houses took a certain amount of skill, and more than likely the carpenters were involved, just as they probably took advantage of the opportunities that came their way to help themselves to building materials. How, Washington once asked, could they possibly have used six thousand nails to build a single cornhouse?[63]

Then there were the "accidents." James, one of the carpenters and according to Washington a "very worthless fellow," cut himself suspiciously often, earning long recovery periods away from his work.[64] Yet the true master of mischance may well have been Isaac, the most talented of Washington's slave carpenters.

Since he fetched a top price of £90,[65] Isaac had undoubtedly already acquired his woodworking skills, which may have included joinery, when he was purchased in 1773. At Mount Vernon he served as part of the general carpentry crew at first, but by the 1780s he was working more or less on his own. His particular domain, the shop, called for both turning skills and bench carpentry. He made spokes for wheels; axletrees for carts; handles for chisels; and fingers for cradling. He made and repaired plows; repaired locks; and prepared sills, plates, posts, and rafters for building frames. His weekly reports were more precise and detailed than those of the white overseers, noting (to Washington's delight, no doubt) such minutia as the number of augur holes bored in a given piece of dressed timber.[66] By the 1790s Isaac was directing the other carpenters in making simple buildings, and on one occasion, when the overseer needed to be told where to put a "Necessary" for a new quarter, Washington wrote: "Isaac knows where it is to be placed."[67]

Along with his various responsibilities, Isaac enjoyed several significant perks. He was doled out the same amount of rum as the black overseers.[68] He lived near the main house and married another skilled worker, a spinner named Kitty. He was luckier than most other husbands, too, because he lived with his family. In the late 1790s he and his wife shared their quarters with nine daughters and four grandchildren.[69] Isaac also kept bees and sold honey and chickens to Washington for cash.[70]

Yet if Isaac's situation at Mount Vernon was relatively autonomous and comfortable, he still was not free. There were, to be sure, subtle ways of registering his feeling about that fact. "The Ploughs made by Isaac must be badly executed, or vastly abused at the Farms, from the continual employment he has in making them," Washington observed wryly after scanning one set of weekly reports.[71] But there were also more dramatic forms of protest. On a December day in 1792 the carpentry shop, along with all the tools and lumber in it, burned to the ground. Was it a willful act of sabotage? The evidence was inconclusive: a fire left burning in a fireplace with no one there to watch it. So whatever Washington's suspicions, his hands were tied. In the end he put the loss down to carelessness, remarking: "If Isaac had his deserts, he wd. receive a severe punishment."[72] Yet perhaps Isaac did get his "deserts," for if anyone controlled the situation in this case, he had.

Isaac's experience was unusual, however. Most slaves at Mount Vernon labored under the control of an overseer. "I . . . has whipt them when I could see a fault," Humphrey

Knight, the general overseer of that time, wrote of the slave carpenters working on the rebuilding of the main house in 1758.[73] Simple and direct, it was an approach based on assumptions firmly locked in place: from Knight's perspective slaves had to be driven to get them to work.

Up to a point, certainly, Washington, would have agreed, but he also knew that however hard slaves were driven, they had to be supervised as well. Like foot soldiers in the army, they needed captains, and captains did more than just command their troops: they taught them skills, planned and organized their efforts, and rallied them to the task at hand through a combination of inspiring exhortation and personal example. They recognized, too, that the energy of their troops was the primary resource at their disposal and took pains not to squander it. Soon after resigning from his regiment in 1759 Washington noted in his diary, "Wrote to Lieutt. Smith to try if possible to get me a Careful Man to Overlook my Carpenters."[74] Presumably a "Careful Man" was one who would not merely whip his charges.

In the years that followed there was invariably at Mount Vernon a skilled white artisan whose duties, unlike Humphrey Knight's, were limited to overseeing the plantation's slave carpenters. In detail Washington's hopes for the arrangement were reflected in the contracts he drew up each year for the overseer of his carpenters to sign. The agreement with John Askew in 1759 obliged him not only "to work true and faithfully at his trade as a joiner" but also to "use his best endeavour's to instruct in the art of his trade" any slaves working with him.[75] In 1771 the emphasis was on the overseer's managerial responsibilities and the authority needed to fulfill them. Thus he was "to use his utmost endeavours to hurry and drive [the slaves] on to the performance of so much work as they ought to render and for the purpose he . . . is hereby invested with sufficient power and authority which he is to make use of and to exercise with prudence and discretion."[76] The power granted was impressive, but it was by no means absolute; "prudence and discretion" were to temper its use. And a few years later the contract again stressed the overseer's role as teacher, stipulating that Caleb Stone, a new recruit, should "to the best of his knowledge and skill, instruct [the slaves] in the Art and Mistery of the trade of a Carpenter."[77]

In return for carrying out the multiple duties assigned him, the carpenters' overseer lived rent-free in a house on the place if he had a family, or in rooms above one of the dependencies if he was single. He also received food from the plantation's stores plus a salary paid at the end of twelve months' work. For a time, Washington experimented with paying on a commission basis, giving a percentage of the value of work done to the overseer instead of a salary. Since the carpenters were sometimes hired out to do specific jobs at other plantations, after which their work was evaluated and Washington was recompensed, the system was a familiar one that should have both provided good incentives and worked to Washington's advantage.[78] Apparently, however, he felt that he lost too much money as a result and reverted to hiring overseers at an annual salary.

In general, the terms of employment were strict and confining. Carpenters' overseers were expected to work themselves "allowing proper time only for Eating" throughout the day, and any day taken off "either by negligence, Sickness or private business" had to be made up before they received their annual pay and a new contract was signed.[79]

Still, an overseer living frugally might hope to save money and eventually even set up a business of his own. That was what Caleb Stone did, but Stone was exceptional. The other carpenters' overseers chose to behave in ways that netted them little material benefit, and in the bargain often infuriated Washington. Certainly that was true of John Askew, and for Thomas Green, who came along after Stone, life at Mount Vernon seems to have been even less rewarding.

Askew's problem was that he failed to appear at work almost as often as he showed up and, as a result, dug himself hopelessly into debt. By the end of his first year, he had taken off so much time that it would have required another five months to work off his contract. Also on the debit side of the balance were a series of cash advances, several charges at the smith's, and a steep charge for payments due on his tools, which, all told, amounted to almost double his annual salary of £25 Virginia currency. In an attempt to balance the books, Washington drew up an indenture, writing off £38 of the debt in exchange for possession of the "sundry joiner's tools" that he had imported for Askew the year before. In effect Askew was pawning his tools to stay afloat.[80]

As an overseer Askew was also wholly unsatisfactory. He missed far too many days to manage, let alone instruct, the slaves in his charge. Within months of his hiring, Washington was looking for a replacement,[81] and before the year was out Turner Crump had started overseeing the Mount Vernon carpenters.[82] Askew was kept on the following year, however, working alone, on a per diem basis at £4 a month less rent.[83] Perhaps Washington hoped he would eventually pay his debt, and at one point he did make up some of it by working for John Carlyle,[84] but when he was hired out to Belvoir the results were less happy. "That he went to work at your House, was not only with my knowledge but by my express desire, and had he stayd there 'till this time it woud have been perfectly agreable to me; but as you know when he left your Work, so I can assure you that he never came to mine," Washington wrote George William Fairfax.[85]

Apparently Askew, finding himself out of reach between the two plantations, took the opportunity to do nothing, and what he had left undone was an even greater offense in Washington's eyes. Before leaving for Williamsburg he urged Askew "in the strongest manner I coud" to fix a particular gate, yet Askew failed to do so, and as a consequence sheep ran loose in a ten-acre field of peas. "I then asked him if he did not think himself one of the most worthless and ungrateful fellows that lived for his treatment of me," Washington exclaimed. "I have once or twice redeemed him and lent him money to Cloath & [buy] necessaries for his Family." If only he would finish the gate, repay the seven days of work due, and repay the money he owed Washington, he could leave. "I never desire to see his Face again."[86] Yet five years later Askew was still at Mount Vernon. Perhaps in addition to his determination to be paid back, Washington sympathized with Askew's distressed family. In any case, he was allowed to work on a per diem basis throughout 1764 and 1765, and the next year he was back on an annual contract. His salary was only £35 minus £10.10. for rent—less than he had received the first year he worked—but in 1767 he signed yet another contract. By April of that year he was gone, however, and whether he died or simply left, the records do not indicate.[87]

Seven years later, just as Washington was about to begin rebuilding his house a second time, Caleb Stone signed on as overseer of the Mount Vernon carpenters. The terms were notably generous: food, lodging, and pasturage for his horse, plus a salary of £40 a year.[88] Yet if ever a workman was worth the cost of his hire, it was Stone. Among other things he directed the dismantling of the older outbuildings flanking the main house and the construction of the new ones.[89] While he was at Mount Vernon not a word was written by anyone, including Washington, about the carelessness or slothfulness of the carpenters—a familiar theme both before and after his time. During the war, Lund Washington had to weigh carefully the advisability of keeping hired hands on or letting them go. Crop yields had been disappointingly low, and cash supplies were limited. But the recommendation in Stone's case was emphatic: "You woud not shuse to part with him, (he is a good hireling)."[90]

Unlike Askew, Stone also seems to have been prudent in his spending habits. During the four years he was at Mount Vernon, he took small advances, bought corn and bran, and had a waistcoat and coat made up by Washington's tailor, possibly with wool he bought from the plantation's weaver. When the final settlement was made he had cleared over a year's wages, which was enough to build a modest house or buy a complete set of carpenter's tools with money to spare.[91]

Stone had probably learned his trade from his father, William, who not only farmed for a living but also practiced carpentry and made shoes as a sideline. He owned one hundred thirty acres in Henrico County, but at some point the family moved to an eight-hundred-acre tract in the new county of Fluvanna. By the time he died, William Stone had sixteen slaves to divide among his seven children and his wife, Frances, and two plantations, one of them well stocked with hogs and sheep. He left an ample supply of carpentry tools; in fact, his assessors found more molding planes among his effects than they did dishes for the table. The inventory also listed farm tools and livestock, but little in the way of consumption goods. Clearly it was a household centered on work rather than leisurely occupations.[92]

Circumstances at home may well have precipitated Caleb Stone's departure from Mount Vernon. In September 1777 he witnessed his father's will, and in less than a year's time he and his siblings came into their inheritance. The farms and livestock went to two of his brothers, and the slaves were divided among them all, bringing him a woman, Bilsey, and her son Simon. Presumably the tools also went to Caleb, since they did not appear in the inventory made at the time of William Stone's widow's death in 1791. That year also saw the final distribution of the proceeds from the estate to Caleb and his brothers.[93] By then he had a large family of his own. The census taker for the county had recorded him as owning two dwellings (one probably a slave quarter) and four outbuildings.[94] And a generation later, "Caleb Stone & Sons" was taxed for four males over sixteen, six adult slaves and two slave children between nine and twelve, seven horses and mules, eight cows, and a house assessed at $700.[95]

At his own death, Caleb Stone's estate also exemplified a lifetime of hard work and careful stewardship. He left his wife and children nineteen slaves, and a home plantation of more than eleven thousand acres, plus additional tracts of land for each child. His furniture was walnut—not mahogany—but the total value of his estate came to almost $6,000.[96]

By all accounts, Stone's employment at Mount Vernon worked well for both parties.

During a period when Washington was mostly away from home, he had a reliable over-seer for his carpenters and did not have to worry about whether they were working sat-isfactorily. It was an unsettled time when carpenters were scarce and could easily be enticed away from previous commitments. Yet Stone stuck to his obligations, saved his money, and significantly bettered his lot in life.

In all these ways Thomas Green was Stone's antithesis. While Green was the overseer of the carpenters, the greenhouse with its wings for housing slaves and an innovative six-teen-sided barn for threshing and storing wheat were built. Evidently he was a skilled workman who knew enough about building to execute the carpentry for such structures, and for that reason Washington needed him.[97] But his unexcused absences and his habit of "flying" from one project to the other without finishing anything were constant sources of irritation, and his idleness and drinking badly impaired his performance.[98] His weekly reports were "stuffed with nothing but trifling jobs that turn to no acct"—if indeed they appeared at all. "Supply Green . . . with paper that [he] may have no excuse," Washington once wrote in exasperation.[99]

Yet year after year Green signed contracts pledging to be sober and honest, to execute his work faithfully, and not to absent himself except when necessary.[100] In his third year there was an additional indenture, stipulating that if he was found to be negligent in his work and did not abide by the terms set, he could be summarily dismissed with no legal recourse.[101] Green put his signature to this document like all the others and promised to do better. But time and again he had to be rebuked for disappearing on drunken binges, and on at least one occasion he was driven to composing a direct appeal to Washington, begging him to overlook the escapade:

> I left work a Monday Night a took a little Grog and I found it hurt me the next day so that
> I was not fit to do any thing the next day and for Mohonys [sic] part [an indentured ser-
> vant doing joinery at Mount Vernon] he was worse then my self so we took a [walk?] as
> far as Colo. [?] house and then was fool a nough to be perswaded by Mahony [sic] to go
> up to town which he promised me that he should not stop, half a hour and when we got
> to town I never Cold git site of him any more untill about Nine or ten OClock yesterday
> when I beged of him to Come home. . . .

The tale went on. Mahoney had promised to come along if they stayed a little while longer and had eventually gone "all most to the turnpike and then turned back again and I have not seen him since." Unfortunately the records do not contain Mahoney's version of these events, but Green, as always, was abjectly contrite. "You never shall have any a thing to find fort with me again for I will not ever be perswaded by any person like him again Sr I am Yours. . . ."[102]

As Washington prepared to leave Mount Vernon to assume the presidency in 1789, he took the time to write Green a letter painstakingly covering all the old ground. First, there was the matter of the contract he had signed. If contracts were not binding on the parties involved they were "of no use at all." If one of the parties contracted to give his labor and did not or if he "trifles away that time for which he is paid" that amounted to robbery—"a robbery of the worst kind, because it is not only a fraud but a dishonorable, unmanly and a deceitful fraud." Then there was Green's drinking. "The other matter which I advise you to keep always in remembrance is the good name . . . necessary for every workman who wishes to pass thro' life with reputation." Green was known to be a drinker, and Washington considered drinking "the source of all evil, and the ruin of half the workmen in this Country." Green had a family to support as well, and too much money went to his drinking habits. Thus he had every reason to stop. "Reputation the care and support of a growing family and society which this family affords within your own doors which may not be the case with some of the idle (to say nothing worse of them) characters who may lead you into temptation." In addition, of course, drinking interfered with work. "An aching head and trembling limbs which are the inevitable effects of drinking disincline the hands from work; hence begins sloth and that Listlessness which ends in idleness."[103]

In spite of the constant admonition, however, Green's drinking and moving from project to project continued, and the weekly reports for the carpenters remained a travesty. But from Washington's standpoint, Green's greatest transgression was his failure to provide adequate supervision for the slaves under his command. Instead of working together on duly assigned tasks, they seemed to do whatever they pleased, and the source of the problem, Washington believed, was that Green did not sufficiently distance himself from his charges to be a credible leader. "Although authority is given to him, he is too much upon a level with the Negroes to exert it from which cause, if no other every one works, or not, as they please and carve out such jobs as they like."[104] Green was a commander who could not—or would not—command, because he was "too much upon a level with the Negroes."

The solution, obviously, was to fire him, yet as often as Washington considered doing so, he could not. When pressed for an explanation, he was inclined to point out that however bad Green was, he was better than nothing. "If the work in hand cannot be carried on without a head to execute it, and no other presents in whom confidence can be placed, there is no alternative but to keep him."[105] Of course, a diligent search might have produced another "head," but that did not happen either.

The truth was that Green was kept on for reasons that had nothing to do with his performance as overseer of the carpenters. Either before or after arriving at Mount Vernon he had married Sally Bishop, the daughter of Thomas Bishop, who had come to America with Braddock's troops twenty-five years before and subsequently served as Washington's personal servant. Though Bishop was retired, Washington was not about to send his daughter and her children out into the world with no more support than Green was likely to provide. "I am so well satisfied of Thomas Greens unfitness to look after my Carpenters, that nothing but the helpless situation in which you find his family, has prevailed on me to retain him," wrote Washington.[106] So Green stayed on.

But that did not stop the steady outpouring of criticism, which finally rose to a kind of crescendo at the end of 1793. Washington had left Mount Vernon to return to Philadelphia eight weeks earlier and apparently the carpenters had done little or nothing in the interim. To repair his own house, Green also had taken the masons off two projects they were hurrying to finish, as ordered, before the frost set in. "I know full well, that to speak to you is of no more avail, than to speak to a bird that is flying over one's head," sputtered Washington. He could only conclude that Green was "lost to all sense of shame, and to every feeling that ought to govern an honest man, who sets any store by his character." It was also apparent that he was utterly unable to supervise the slaves assigned to him. "You have no more command of the people over whom you are placed, than I have over the beasts of the forists [sic]."[107]

And so it might have continued indefinitely, had not Green himself finally taken the initiative early in 1794 and quit both his position and Mount Vernon, leaving Washington to care for his family. Since their house had to go to Green's successor, Washington offered to help them once they found a new place. Sally decided she wanted to live in Alexandria, explaining that she could take in washing and sewing and set up a small shop. Though he was dubious about the plan and suspected that stolen goods from Mount Vernon would make up a large part of the shop's stock, Washington let her go ahead, gave her provisions, and paid her rent.[108] Later, too, in his will, he left her an annuity of £100.[109]

As for Green, considering his sorry experience at Mount Vernon it would be pleasant to discover that he met with better luck after leaving Washington's employ. He was still a relatively young man and had at least proven himself to be a skilled craftsman, but within four years he was dead, leaving an estate that consisted of little more than a modest collection of carpenter's tools.[110]

⁂

Perhaps, as Washington claimed, Thomas Green's character was fatally flawed. Even so, the situation at Mount Vernon could have emphasized personality traits and behaviors that under other circumstances would have receded into the background. Working for Washington—in any capacity—was not easy. He insisted on results of high quality; he wanted things done as quickly and efficiently as possible. He abhorred waste, and parting with money invariably made him unhappy. He also had a horror of being taken advantage of and tended to see it happening even when it was not. All of these qualities were a problem for his overseers, as they were for his workmen generally, but in addition the overseers had to contend with his views on how best to manage their crews, and the particular model of leadership he favored, for some temperaments, at least, was highly problematic. In finding Green "too much upon a level with the Negroes," Washington was signaling that he considered distance a vital component of the relationship between overseers and slaves. Being too close, too familiar, too accessible could only dilute one's authority. A studied aloofness was the proper face of command.

In the hierarchy of command, too, that quality was meant to be manifest at every level. Washington was just as insistent that the individual serving as manager of the entire plantation maintain his distance from the overseers he supervised as he was that the overseers stand above and apart from the slaves. "To treat them civilly is no more than what all men are entitled to, but my advice to you is, to keep them at a proper distance; for they will grow upon familiarity, in proportion as you will sink in authority, if you do not," he once wrote a new manager.[111]

Nor were such views lightly held, as Washington's own public demeanor made clear.

From an early age he had borne himself in a manner that discouraged casual familiarity. Courteous, even affable he could be; indeed, he liked nothing better than sitting by the hour talking and drinking at dinner with his fellow officers. Still, over the years the stories of his aloofness would become legion. There was a barrier he erected between himself and the rest of the world that was not to be breached, even by those who knew him well. Obviously, too, he was both comfortable with this persona and used it to great effect.

For someone less self-confident than Washington, however, or more at ease within a sustaining circle of close, human relationships, the distance he saw as essential to effective leadership might well have seemed singularly unappealing. Isolated from those both below and above them in the hierarchy, the overseers were meant to inhabit a kind of vacuum, untouched by the people they lived and worked with day in and day out. Not surprisingly, it was more than some of them could manage. So they chose to escape—by absenting themselves from work, by establishing something like normal human ties to their coworkers, by drinking too much too often.

All of which made Washington even angrier, but the overseers may also have seen something he missed. For whatever his public persona, Washington's own relations with his slaves were by no means uniformly cool and aloof. The compassion he showed in refusing to sell them against their will, his willingness to tolerate a certain amount of night-walking, and his refusal to give orders personally to prevent slave children from playing around the mansion house all bespoke feelings of concern at odds with the model of distanced, dispassionate authority set forth for the overseers to follow. Then, too, there was his forbearance in instances such as the burning of the carpentry shop. In effect he was asking his overseers to pay attention to what he said but ignore what he did.

Of course, Washington was the master; he could give whatever orders he chose, and surely the easiest thing to do was to take him at his word, as Caleb Stone apparently did. Work hard, save money, and hope to move on to a better life: it could be done. Yet some people chose not to follow that path. What were their rewards? Washington's records are silent on the point, but for all the criticism he heaped on such individuals it was a fact that he proved no more willing to discipline them than he was someone like Isaac. When Thomas Green left Mount Vernon he did so freely, of his own accord.

Thus did the paradoxes of plantation life multiply and ramify year by year. From the slaves in the fields, to their counterparts in the trades, and finally to the overseers placed in authority over them, Washington seemed surrounded by people bent on breaking his commandments. But while he went to great lengths to make both his wishes and his displeasure clear, the bite that should have accompanied his bark was often withheld. In retrospect, it is easy to see him playing the role of the stern but forgiving parent to the offenders, yet that was not at all the role he wanted to play. He dreamed of something quite different from patriarchy—he dreamed of a rational, orderly system that motivated workers to work efficiently and rewarded managers for seeing that they did. But giving substance to that dream was something else again.

Ultimately, too, the source of the problem was slavery itself. As an institution it simply could not be made to deliver what Washington wanted from it, and its failure from the standpoint of efficiency was only part of the deficit. For in addition to everything else, Washington also wanted and needed to think of himself as a good man. Efficiency bespoke control, control promised independence, and with independence ought to have come virtue. Yet slavery confounded the equation. At Mount Vernon, control did not conduce to virtue; the two remained fundamentally at odds with one another.

As time passed, Washington himself came to see this, at first only fleetingly and then in the years after the Revolution, with increasing clarity, but between understanding the problem and solving it lay a vast, uncharted gulf that no amount of hope or goodwill seemed likely to conquer anytime soon.

CHAPTER 7

Artisans

IN ALL OF WASHINGTON'S building projects, slaves and their overseers played a vital role, but some of the changes he made at Mount Vernon called for skills they did not possess. Isaac in his shop crafted wheels and plows, and the outside carpenters built kitchens, washhouses, and barns, but for a finely carved chimneypiece in the dining room of the main house, or ceilings decorated with ornamental plasterwork, or properly cultivated specimens of rare plants, Washington did what other planter-builders did: he brought in artisans with specialized training. Some were indentured servants working to pay off the cost of their passage to America; others were independent members of fledgling artisan communities precariously planted in the New World. But whatever their circumstances, finding qualified artisans was no easy matter in Virginia, and managing their work could turn out to be every bit as difficult as managing the labor of slaves and overseers.

In the seventeenth and eighteenth centuries an estimated 350,000 "servants" immigrated to the colonies, first from England, and later from Ireland, Scotland, and Germany as well.[1] Most of those who settled in the southern colonies were farm laborers, but about 20 percent professed to be trained in the "Art and Mistery" of a trade.[2] Such "tradesmen," if they spoke the truth, were products of what remained of the medieval guild system. As apprentices they had served under a master for seven years. If the work was satisfactory they became journeymen and were free to travel and practice. As a final step, journeymen were admitted to the guilds as masters themselves.[3]

In England by the eighteenth century, guilds had lost much of their power, including the ability to limit entry into the trades and maintain standards of workmanship. Nor in America did artisans' associations ever become true guilds, but some still achieved considerable power. Among them was the Carpenters' Company of the City and County of Philadelphia. At any given time only a minority of carpenters in Philadelphia belonged to it, but its members were active in government, and the company had a near monopoly in measuring and setting prices for carpentry work done in the city. The group's power and solidarity were manifest in its handsome headquarters, built in 1768, which served as the meeting place of the first Continental Congress.[4]

In the South, artisans' associations were notably weaker than in the North. The population was more dispersed, the movement of people was at least as fluid, and life expectancy was shorter. Many of the white servants brought over in the seventeenth century did not survive the "seasoning" of the first year, and those who lived beyond it could not expect to live past age forty. With only a short time in which to marry, have children, and provide for their families, tradesmen were regularly diverted into farming. Land was cheap, and tobacco brought quick returns.[5]

The shortage of ready money was also a problem, but the major factor limiting the number of artisans in the South—and organization among them—was the lack of towns and cities where they could market their skills and purchase the necessities of life. In 1725, apart from Williamsburg, Annapolis, Yorktown, and Norfolk, only three small tobacco ports in the Chesapeake boasted more than fifty inhabitants.[6] In areas like the Northern Neck, where settlement was dispersed on farms and large plantations, tradesmen had to farm simply to eat. "For want of Towns, Markets, and Money, there is but little Encouragement for Tradesmen and Articers," wrote one observer. "A tradesman having no Opportunity of a Market where he can buy Meat, Milk, Corn, and all other things, must either make corn, keep Cows, and raise Stocks, himself, or must ride about the Country to buy Meat and Corn where he can find it."[7] Still, some artisans did manage to establish themselves in the more settled parts of the region, often by bartering their services for needed provisions.[8] Later in the eighteenth century, too, more towns were established. Within reach of Mount Vernon, both Fredericksburg and Alexandria were sufficiently developed by 1760 to have modest-sized artisan populations.

Initially developed as a tobacco port, Alexandria was laid out in 1749, and to encourage early development buyers were given a maximum of two years to build houses "of brick, stone or wood, well framed, of the dimensions of twenty feet square and nine feet pitch at the least."[9] The legislature also permitted two annual fairs for the exchange of "cattle, goods, wares, and merchandizes,"[10] but Alexandria's rapid growth did not begin until the 1760s, when crop failures in Europe stimulated the wheat trade. Washington himself used the town for wheat shipments and also had a small house built there. By 1770 the town's population stood at one thousand.[11]

One of the first lots sold in Alexandria went to William Munday, a carpenter and joiner. In 1752 William Waite, a tradesman working at Mount Vernon in Lawrence's time and again in the later 1750s, signed a petition to the legislature asking that court sessions be held in town.[12] The master carpenters who served as undertakers for both of Washington's major rebuildings of Mount Vernon were living in Alexandria as early as the mid-1750s.[13] Moreover, efforts were continually made to persuade tradesmen to settle in town. In 1774 three leading merchants wrote their legislative representatives urging expansion of the town's boundaries specifically for that reason. "Not longer than a few days ago a Shop Joiner and Cabinet Maker, a Man well known to many in this place to be of reputation and wou'd have introduced three or four workmen to carry on his business, was obliged to return because he cou'd not get a house to fix in; this is a real loss to the community."[14] Of Alexandria's 2,750 residents in 1790, two fifths of the adult males were in the trades or worked in taverns.[15]

Though the guild system was no more developed in Alexandria than elsewhere in America, apprentices were still trained in the traditional way, and by 1774 the Carpenters' and Joiners' Society of Alexandria had been founded.[16] A notice in the *Alexandria Gazette* in 1797 chastising a local carpenter for underbidding his fellow tradesmen indicates there was at least some agreement on pricing, which evidently grew stronger in time.[17] By the early nineteenth century the Carpenters' and Joiners' Society was publishing rates for everything from floors to elegantly finished staircases.[18] In a different vein, a pair of pattern books—one by Batty Langley and the other by William Pain—discovered in the 1930s on the floor of an old warehouse slated for demolition, points to the stylistic lineage of the many fine doorways, cornices, and chimneypieces found in houses and taverns dating from the town's early years.[19]

For the artisans who settled there, Alexandria offered palpable advantages. Not only was there work to do in building the town, it also functioned as a base of operations, making it possible to undertake projects in the surrounding countryside while leaving families at home, often to earn additional income working in one or another of the trades themselves. Alexandria provided, too, the fellowship and support of a growing community of artisans with shared interests. One consequence of all this was a distinct independence of spirit among the town's tradespeople. These were individuals who meant to do things their own way and in their own good time, as William Munday—that pioneer carpenter and joiner—demonstrated when he had to be ordered not once but twice by the town trustees (a body that included both George William Fairfax and George Washington) "to put his chimneys in safe order, as they are too low and dangerous."[20]

Still, as a working city, Alexandria never offered the opportunities that Williamsburg or Annapolis did, let alone those available in places like Philadelphia or New York. Judging from Washington's experience, competent workmen remained scarce in the area, often leaving him no choice but to search farther afield, which usually meant turning to bound laborers—individuals committing their services for a specific number of years in exchange for passage to America and a new start in life.

Bound service was an established practice in England long before it was used to supply labor for the colonies. In the skilled trades, apprenticeships amounted to bound labor. Young boys were also commonly bound out as agricultural laborers for a year at a time before marrying and setting themselves up on their own farms. But to cover the cost of transporting workers to America, the system was modified. Terms of service could be as long as seven years. Yet the opportunity to migrate to the "plantations" was attractive to a home population laden with surplus workers, and the trade in indentures was a lucrative one for merchants.[21]

Most bound workers had already come from the countryside to the larger towns and cities in England and Ireland in search of jobs. "Whereas there are many idle Persons who are under the Age of one and twenty Years lurking about in divers parts of London, and elsewhere, who want Employment," a Parliamentary Act in 1717 declared, it would be legal for merchants to contract with any "inclined to be transported."[22] Advertisements for indentured workers appeared in the newspapers, in handbills, and on marketplace walls. Merchants used agents who frequented public houses and other places where they were likely to find willing candidates. Not all agents were honest: unsuspecting boys were sometimes enticed into the holds of ships and held there until they were at sea. An estimated 10 percent of all bound servants, too, were convicted criminals sentenced to be transported for a period of years.[23]

Individuals selling their services had to swear that they would serve "well" and "truely" for a specific length of time. In return, the merchant or ship captain buying the indenture agreed to provide passage and provisions.[24] Some bound servants, including many Germans emigrating with their families, paid at least part of their own passage, thus becoming "redemptioners." After arriving in the colonies, they were given a short time to raise the rest of the cost. Failing that, they were sold into service for the amount still owed.[25]

The voyage usually took about two months. Bound servants were bunked in the cargo area between decks, giving them headroom of only four and a half to five feet. The space was airless, damp, crowded, and unsanitary. The food provided was barely adequate, if that.[26] Most ships embarked in the winter or early spring, giving their captains sufficient time in port to unload, refit, reload, and return before winter set in again. Any unnecessary storage of servants cut into profits. It was also important to avoid ports that had recently had shipments of servants, and to schedule the sale when planters' attention was not taken up with other matters. Spring or early summer, before the July harvest, were best.[27]

As soon as a ship arrived, the date of the sale, the number of servants to be sold, and any trades represented among them were advertised. At the appointed hour, "the goods"—men in one place and women in another—were lined up on deck for inspection. Convicts were mixed in with voluntary recruits; apparently buyers did not always distinguish between the two groups. Most servants were sold off while still on board; typically the rest were bought by jobbers and marched into the back country by "soul drivers," to be sold there.[28] In some respects the transportation and selling of bound servants was not unlike the traffic in African slaves.

One major difference, however, was that servants who arrived with demonstrable skills found almost at once that they were in a position to bargain over the terms of their contracts. Master builders and merchants acting as agents for plantation owners like Washington competed with one another for skilled artisans, and since ship captains commonly allowed servants to choose their masters, the length of service was sometimes considerably shortened in the negotiations. In the competition for workers, too, planters were at a disadvantage because of the relative isolation of their establishments. "You may suppose few or none of such as you want, ever go out of this Town, but upon such terms as I have mentioned—Indeed there is something so alluring in a Town to people of that Class, that they would generally prefer it . . . to the Country," wrote one of Washington's agents from Baltimore.[29]

But regardless of the specific terms of the arrangement, all indentures included certain common features. The servant's labor was pledged to the buyer for a specific period of time, and in return the buyer was obligated to provide food, clothing, shelter, and good treatment during the term of service, plus a final bonus or "freedom dues" at the end. A servant could sue for nonpayment of the bonus; an owner could get a term extended if a servant disobeyed by marrying or running off. And it was easy enough for white servants to run away, change their names, and reappear somewhere else in a new guise. To deal with the problem, all travelers were required to carry passes.[30] Even so, purchasers of indentures took significant risks, and Washington was among the many who occasionally lost all or part of their investment.

In 1774, just as he was about to begin his second major rebuilding of the main house and its dependencies, he bought the indentures of four artisans: two joiners, Thomas Spears and John Broad; a stonemason, Henry Young; and a brickmaker, William Webster.[31] Henry Young's name never reappears in the records. Presumably he died, and the following spring, Spears and Webster escaped downriver in a small yawl. Washington advertised rewards and warned masters of vessels against taking them on board. In the event, the adventure was cut short: both men were quickly apprehended and returned.[32] With John Broad the problem was a tragic accident. During his second Christmas at Mount Vernon, while playing at fencing with one of the slaves, he was grazed on the thigh with the rusty blade of his companion's sword, a wound that festered and resulted in a lingering death months later.[33]

Washington had particularly bad luck with indentured painters. When he bought John Winter, a convict servant from England, he acquired a "very compleat" painter,

Advertisement, placed by Washington in the Virginia Gazette, *for a pair of runaway servants. Courtesy of the Chapin Library of Rare Books, Williams College.*

highly skilled at imitating mahogany and marble and adept at making floor cloths "as neat as any imported from Britain." However, it was Winter who in 1759 escaped, taking most of the paint and oil that was left, just as he was finishing Washington's newly enlarged house.[34] Then there was the painter who ran off late in 1775 while on his way to work for Washington's brother-in-law, Fielding Lewis. Worse still, the man chose to join the British army, though four months later he was unlucky enough to be captured at Hampton and confined in the Williamsburg jail. As a punishment, Lund Washington arranged to have him publicly whipped, then taken to the back country, where his indenture was to be sold.[35]

To be sure, not everyone ran away. Most of Washington's indentured servants stayed their terms, and some even served beyond that. John Knowles, an indentured mason who built the chimneys for the principal outbuildings during the 1770s, married one of the plantation's weavers and continued working at Mount Vernon after his contract was up, receiving wages intermittently for the next sixteen years.[36] In August 1784 two ships, the *Angelica* and the *Washington,* arrived in port from Cork, and John Fitzgerald, an Alexandria wheat merchant, sold off twenty-four servants the day the boats landed. Washington bought two of them: Thomas Mahoney, a joiner, and Cornelius McDermott, a mason. Thomas Green's sometime-drinking companion in Alexandria, Mahoney worked on several outbuildings at Mount Vernon. In 1788, after working a term for pay, he wrote saying that he would be "willing to Engage" for an added year, provided he received a small raise. He was promptly turned down, but 24 hours later he signed a contract at the old wage and remained at Mount Vernon until 1792.[37]

Cornelius McDermott was eventually joined by two brothers, Edward and Tim, and also continued to work at Mount Vernon after serving out his indenture, though only for occasional jobs. He raised stone, planed shingles with Mahoney, and made bricks and lime. As late as 1791 he was still being paid for work, though eventually he resettled in the new federal city. Apparently Washington remembered him favorably. After returning to Mount Vernon from his two terms as president he wrote his secretary, Tobias Lear, wondering whether McDermott—"my old Servant"—could be engaged to make some much-needed repairs. "I should be disposed to give him a preference; first because I am acquainted with his temper and industry; and 2ndly because I foresee many other things in his line that must be done."[38]

Johann Ehlers was another longtime workman at Mount Vernon who began as a bound servant. His trade was gardening. Keenly interested in the seeds and plants friends sent him, Washington wanted someone who understood both greenhouse culture and the propagation and tending of exotic plants. In 1788 he wrote a ship captain sailing for Holland, asking him to look out for a German redemptioner with such knowledge. "I should prefer a single man, but have no objection to one who is married provided his wife understands spinning &c. . . . A middle aged man will suit me best, as the necessary services cannot be expected from, or performed by, one advanced in years."[39] Head gardeners abroad generally directed other workers who did the actual labor, but at Mount Vernon everyone, no matter how highly trained or skilled, was expected to do a full day's work.

In response to Washington's request, Johann Christian Ehlers arrived from Hamburg, Germany, with a document—wrapped in gold brocade—in his trunk certifying him as a graduate apprentice trained in the "Worthy, Free Craft of Gardening" at the Royal Garden in Montbrillant. He also came armed with more than twenty years' experience as a landscape gardener on King George II's Hanoverarian properties.[40] Although Ehlers did not speak or understand English, after interviewing him in New York, Washington arranged to send him on to Virginia.[41] At the same time he wrote a friend whose greenhouse and plants he had admired, asking if she would send along some of her rare specimens, as he now had a gardener "who professes a knowledge in the culture of rare plants and care of a Green-House."[42]

Typically, Ehlers would have signed a three-year contract obliging him to perform "faithfully and industriously . . . every part of his duty—to the best of his knowledge and abilities." There was probably also a clause pledging him not to "at any time, suffer himself to be disguised with liquor, except on the times hereafter mentioned." If Washington could not forbid drinking, he could at least try to control it. Provisions for the previous gardener had included cash for Christmas "for which he may be drunk 4 days and 4 nights," as well as funds for two-day binges at Easter and Whitsuntide. Other than that he was allowed a dram in the morning and a drink of grog at dinner.[43]

Strict as the terms were, however, care was also taken to see that Ehlers would be comfortable in his new life in Virginia. Washington purchased an English–German dictionary from Clement Biddle in Philadelphia and on at least one occasion bought a German newspaper for Ehlers to read.[44] When Ehlers's initial contract was up, his wife was permitted to join him at Mount Vernon, and they were provided with larger accommodations.[45] Washington also hired a second, younger, German gardener to assist Ehlers and, as a friendly gesture, gave Ehlers a pitcher that had been sent to Mount Vernon as a gift.[46] He even let Ehlers set up a small nursery and sell plants, allowing him to keep a share of the profits.[47]

For his part, Ehlers used his training to the Washingtons' advantage, raising specimen plants from the seeds forwarded to him, including lima bean and artichoke seeds sent by Martha, who had a particular fondness for fresh vegetables. He also supervised the tending of the exotica in the greenhouse, the flowers in the upper garden, the fruit trees in the orchard, and the vegetable patches in the lower garden.[48] "I shall expect an abundance of every thing," was Washington's typical request before visiting home.[49] But Ehlers's personal passion seems to have been cultivating parterres—ornamental gardens with knots and squares formed of precisely trimmed boxwood. If Washington cherished the trees and shrubs he had planted informally around the grounds, Ehlers took great pride in the parterres, the designs for which he no doubt copied from books brought over from Germany in his trunk. Aesthetically speaking, the two men were at odds. Also, in English gardens parterres had long since gone out of fashion, yet Washington—perhaps to indulge Ehlers—kept his. The reactions of his guests were not always kind. "For the first time again since I left Germany I saw here a *parterre,* clipped and trimmed with infinite care into the form of a richly flourished *Fleur-de-Lis:* The expiring groans I hope of our Grandfather's pedantry," architect Benjamin Latrobe commented caustically in his journal when he visited Mount Vernon in 1796.[50]

The greenhouse at Mount Vernon and a modern version of the parterres on which Johann Ehlers lavished so much attention. Courtesy of the Mount Vernon Ladies' Association

Yet for all the latitude he was allowed, everything was not well with Ehlers, at least according to the tales passed down in successive generations of his family. When he first arrived at Mount Vernon, he was shocked not to be housed in the mansion, as someone of his station would have been in Germany. He did not speak English, and he was "unacquainted with the country" and separated from his wife. He also found Washington's manner autocratic. Sensitive, lonely, and depressed, he later remembered drinking grog and reading his Bible by candlelight on cold winter nights. Alone in his room, he imagined demons on his bedpost, chiding him for being a mere dirt gardener, and threw his Bible at them to make them go away. He thought of himself as an artist, but Washington had hired him as a practical gardener, insisting that he work alongside the slaves he supervised.[51]

Nor, for his part, was Washington wholly satisfied with his temperamental head gardener. As he scanned the weekly reports from home, he concluded that not only Thomas Green's work, but Ehlers's as well, was going more slowly than it should have. So at the same time he admonished Green, he wrote to Ehlers, "in hopes to impress them with the necessity, and to stimulate them to the practice of proper exertions."[52] Ehlers was also prone to saying he could not take on new tasks because he already had too much to do, which infuriated Washington. Evidently Ehlers was not organizing the work properly. "If it is found," he wrote on one occasion, "that the hands with the Gardener are not usefully (I mean industriously) employed, I shall withdraw them; as I did not give them to him for *parade,* to be *idle,* or to keep him in *idleness.*"[53] To make matters worse, he suspected that Ehlers drank more than he should have. Concerned for the work but also for him, Washington sent a long letter (at the same time that he sent a similar one to Green) urging him to abstain. Drinking "will prove your ruin," he declared. "Consider how little a drunken Man differs from a beast . . . and . . . acts like a brute; annoying, and disturbing everyone around him. . . . Don't let this be your case. Shew yourself more of a man, and a Christian, than to yield to so intolerable a vice."[54]

But Ehlers's drinking may have been caused by his unhappiness. He had mentioned leaving Mount Vernon, which came as a surprise to Washington, who finally persuaded him to stay with a small raise. "He, like so many others, I presume has golden dreams, which nothing but experience can demonstrate to be the vision only of an uninformed, or indigested imagination," wrote Washington, who predicted that if Ehlers went he would be leaving behind "a safe and easy birth to embark on a troubled Ocean, where, soon, he may find no rest."[55] In Ehlers's view, however, the berth Washington described as safe and easy was a trap: the longer he stayed, the lower he would sink, and the harder it would be to embark on that ocean at all.

And four years later Ehlers did leave. Yet he came back later to lay his adopted baby daughter in his former employer's lap, and after Washington died, Ehlers actually returned to work at Mount Vernon. In time the infant he placed in Washington's lap was married on the lawn, and her wedding breakfast took place inside the mansion house, in the new room. Long afterward, too, visitors to Mount Vernon remembered an elderly gardener with a German accent who had showed them around the grounds and talked about the place in Washington's day. The box-trimmed parterres remained, and the pitcher Washington once had given his troubled gardener was carefully passed down in the family from one generation to the next.[56]

What had it all come to in the end? No doubt Washington was right about the likelihood that a man like Ehlers would ever fulfill his "golden dreams." America was a far cry from Hanover, but surely for most bound servants that was precisely the point. Someone like William Buckland, a joiner who lived to become an architect and sit for his portrait surrounded by the symbols of his profession, proved that indentured artisans willing to take the chance and venture out on their own could, with enough skill and luck, succeed in the New World. Yet Washington's view of what best served their interests was hard work, diligence, and sobriety: cultivating the virtues he prescribed, laboring at the tasks he assigned. If his servants met that standard, they would have ensured their own good reputations—something slaves had no opportunity to do—and thereafter they could look forward to remaining at Mount Vernon, in the "safe and easy" berths they had won.

Ultimately, however, almost none of Washington's bound servants saw it his way. Sooner or later they all left, and not necessarily because he was a bad master. He was difficult to please and demanded a day's work for a day's pay, but he was not unfair, or even unkind, as some of his workmen discovered. Still, one after another they continued to choose the "troubled Ocean," as he called it. After all, it was what they had come for: they too dreamed of freedom.

Although bound servants predominated among the tradesmen who worked on Mount Vernon over the years, the labor force also included a certain number of independent artisans. Essentially free agents, they contracted in most cases to do specific jobs at a mutually agreed-upon price. Before hiring them, Washington often had the opportunity to see and judge examples of their work, but there were drawbacks as well. In an environment where their skills were a scarce commodity, independent artisans had the most control over their lives. They could be, and sometimes were, the least tractable of workers. A case in point was the Triplett brothers.

In the beginning, Washington looked for artisans close to home or not far from it. Friends and family members regularly recommended tradesmen to one another in the spirit of sharing useful information. On a number of occasions Washington asked his military aides to look for willing workers among the soldiers serving under him.[57] He also received information from his brother-in-law, Fielding Lewis, in Fredericksburg, and John Carlyle, in Alexandria.[58] At times he shared carpenters with his neighbors the Masons and the Fairfaxes. It was only natural, then, that when he needed brickwork done on the foundations of the house he was enlarging in the late 1750s, his sights extended no farther than William and Thomas Triplett.

Like Washington, the Tripletts belonged to a family long established in the Northern Neck and fell within the circle of kin and easy hospitality. Just as their father and Gus Washington had probably cantered across the frozen fields of their adjoining farms chasing foxes, so the brothers were regular hunting companions of Washington's during the winter and spring months.[59] Nor was that all they had in common. Their great-grandfather Francis Triplett had arrived in Virginia just three years after John Washington and had settled in the same neighborhood in Westmoreland County. Like John Washington, he accumulated land by bringing over servants, which eventually netted him 10,500 acres.[60] Also, Francis Triplett's attorney was Nathaniel Pope, John Washington's brother-in-law. And Originall Browne—another neighbor of the Washingtons, Popes, and Tripletts—appointed Lawrence Washington guardian of his young daughter, Mary, who grew up to link all three families by marriage. One of her brothers-in-law was a Pope; one of her nieces, Jane Butler, was Gus Washington's first wife; and she herself married one of Francis Triplett's sons. A son of theirs, in turn, would become the father of William and Thomas Triplett.[61]

By the early 1730s both the Washingtons and the Tripletts had moved to the rougher, less settled Northern Neck. Thomas Triplett, the brothers' father, had arrived as a twenty-one-year-old bachelor and soon afterward married Sarah Harrison, whose family had been settled in the area since 1700. In due course Sarah inherited half of her father's land on Dogue Creek, and there, at "Round Hill" plantation, she raised her family.[62]

For all the Tripletts and Washingtons had in common, however, there remained significant differences between them. John Washington, "the immigrant," served in the House of Burgesses and was an intimate of Governor William Berkeley's. His sons, grandsons, and great-grandsons were educated as gentlemen in England. Francis Triplett, on the other hand, came to the colonies as a cooper, and future generations of Tripletts continued to make their way as tradesmen. In his will, Originall Browne had stated that he wanted his only son to be apprenticed to a shipwright, and failing that, to a carpenter, a millwright, or a joiner.[63] In the next generation his daughter, Mary Browne Triplett, apprenticed one of her sons, the Triplett brothers' uncle, to a shipmaster. Just before his term was up he jumped ship "still so ignorant in his business," his stepfather argued later in court, "that he was forced to turn bricklayer, to get a livelihood."[64] No doubt Mary Browne Triplett's other sons were also apprenticed to tradesmen, and it may well have been through the sixteen-year-old runaway that brickmasonry became a family pursuit, handed down through subsequent generations.

Growing up at Round Hill as George Washington's contemporaries, William and Thomas Triplett lost their father, as he did, while still quite young.[65] Whatever education they received would have come from itinerant tutors, since the area was still too sparsely settled to support a grammar school. The family did not own many slaves, so the boys must have done their share of farmwork—and on marginal soil, if it was no better than Mount Vernon's, emphasizing the wisdom of carrying on a varied set of enterprises.

Amid the comings and goings in the neighborhood, the brothers would surely have met George Washington on one of his visits to Mount Vernon, if they had not become acquainted earlier, when Gus's family lived there. But any friendship between the Tripletts and Washington would have had distinct if subtle limits. They would not have been invited, as he was, to Westover for the Christmas holidays, and they lacked the Fairfax patronage that George had access to through his brother. Moreover, if George, as a young man, found himself using a variety of strategies to improve his lot in life just as the Tripletts did, the stakes in the game he was playing were of a very different sort.

By his early twenties (as Washington moved upward through the ranks of military command) William Triplett, the older of the two brothers, was taking on jobs involving brickmasonry and plastering. Whether he did the work himself or merely provided a crew and supervision—which would not have been unusual for someone of his standing—is unclear. What is clear is that rather than depending on a single employer, he juggled his jobs among many of them, parceling out his time as he chose.[66] Sometimes he bartered his services, sometimes he received cash. In return for the work he did on Mount Vernon's foundations in 1758, Washington's carpenters built him a log stable. Later, in partial payment for other work, he had Mount Vernon's blacksmith shoe his horses. He also used Washington's weavers.[67]

But however they were paid, as workers the Tripletts were less than wholly satisfactory. The source of the difficulty was not the quality of their work; it was getting them to do it in the first place that frayed tempers at Mount Vernon. During Washington's first rebuilding of the house, both John Patterson and George William Fairfax complained repeatedly about the problem. "Triplet has certainly used you ill," wrote Fairfax when the interior plastering was not finished in a timely fashion. Yet Triplett had work to do for other neighbors.[68] His energies were also increasingly focused on activities other than building.

Earlier in the decade he had married Sarah Peake, a woman from the same circle of neighboring planter families. They remained at Round Hill, producing seven children, five of whom reached adulthood, and as his family grew, so did Triplett's enterprises. He bought 392 acres on Marble Hill for the stone quarries on the property. He sold timber and stone from other holdings, and he began participating in trading ventures with Alexandria merchants. When Pohick Church was built, he bought a pew located near the front of the church, but on the side, behind the Washingtons' and Fairfaxes' pews. Also, in 1776, Triplett was elected to the Pohick vestry.[69]

By then, too, he had found another way of marking his place in the world. In 1772, two years before Washington began his second rebuilding of Mount Vernon, Triplett carried out a major building project of his own at Round Hill, adding two wings to the house. Placed symmetrically at either end of the existing structure, they extended its length to eighty-seven feet, and as would be true at Mount Vernon, the added space was equally divided between public and private uses, with one wing becoming a dining room and the other a bedchamber. At the same time, the old dining room in the basement was made into a servants' hall, and the spaces under the wings were fitted out for storing wine and food.[70]

Guests invited to Round Hill dined at a mahogany table, drank their wine from glass goblets, and ate with silver-plated knives and forks. When William Triplett was at leisure, he could sit in his easy chair equipped with a fan (Washington owned a similar one) and read from his small library of classics.[71] Yet he seems to have been more a man of action than someone given to reading or writing. In Washington's vast correspondence there is not a single letter from William Triplett, and there are only two to him.[72]

As it happens, both letters concerned land, a subject that often resulted in dealings between the two men, though again not always to Washington's satisfaction. Triplett owned several pieces necessary to round out Mount Vernon, and he continued to add to

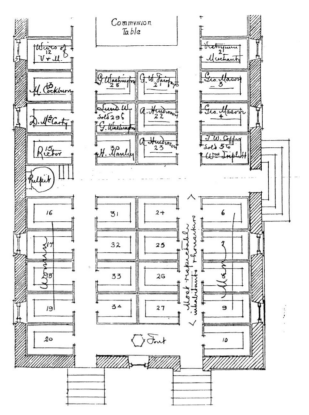

Seating plan, Pohick Church. Philip Slaughter, The History of Truro Parish in Virginia *(Philadelphia, 1908).*

his holdings. When his aunt, Sybil Harrison West, decided to sell a 107-acre tract adjoining Round Hill, she offered it to him and he bought it. But the land also abutted Washington's mill, and when he heard of the sale he was extremely annoyed.[73] Writing home from the front during the war, he asked Lund to intervene and propose a trade, but in typically independent fashion Triplett turned down the offer, and he and Washington did not reach an agreement until after the war.[74] The brothers' mother, Sarah Triplett, also owned a piece of property Washington coveted, though he never managed to talk her into selling. Only after she died did he finally negotiate successfully for it.[75]

While Washington and others were off fighting, William Triplett spent much of the Revolution closer to home. Although he later served as a lieutenant, he refused to enlist in the army at first because it appeared he would not receive a commission.[76] When the war ended, he owned fourteen slaves, and an agent employed by a British mercantile firm to identify prewar debts that might still be collected listed him as "well able to pay."[77] By 1785 there were fifteen outbuildings at Round Hill, and William Triplett had sufficient business in Alexandria to own a warehouse there.[78]

Meanwhile, William's younger brother, Thomas Triplett, seems to have attached himself wholeheartedly to the patriot cause. Almost the same age as Washington, he had fought in the French and Indian War as a member of the militia, and while still in his twenties he served briefly as undersheriff, then deputy sheriff, of the county. In the 1760s he and Sarah Dade married and settled on a small plantation near Pohick Church, where they raised six children. In addition to planting, Thomas shared in his brother's enterprises and did well. He too owned a pew in Pohick Church and served on the vestry. It was as a solidly established citizen of the community, then, that he signed the Fairfax Resolves in 1774. He also acted as a member of the Committee of Safety, and his service to the cause seems to have earned Washington's good opinion.[79] According to his diary, "Mr. Thos. Triplet" dined at Mount Vernon with George Mason, Edmund Pendleton, and Patrick Henry the evening before Washington, Pendleton, and Henry set off for the First Continental Congress.[80] Pendleton later remembered Martha Washington's "spirit" on that occasion and the words she spoke to her son: "I hope you will stand firm, I know George will."[81]

When hostilities began, Thomas Triplett received a commission as a captain in the Continental Army and served with Washington until a prolonged bout of bronchitis at Valley Forge forced him—on the advice of Dr. James Craik, Washington's personal physician—to return to Virginia. Not long after he reached home, he volunteered to escort Martha Washington back to camp, but he resigned that spring because of worsening health and died back in Virginia in 1780. Though he left no will, his estate included twenty slaves, and the same agent who had declared his brother as "well able to pay" labeled him "rich."[82] His only son, Thomas, who eventually trained to be a doctor, marched in Washington's funeral procession.[83]

William Triplett lived on for more than twenty years after his brother. He left thirty-one slaves and a house full of imported furniture, books, and china: luxurious accoutrements of gracious living. He also left in his outbuildings evidence of hard work and an enterprising life: plank, beehives, tubs, iron wedges, shovels, tongs, steelyards, knives, grindstones, millstones, and iron. In addition there was a parcel of wooden brick molds, eventually purchased from the estate by his son George in a filial act perhaps practical, perhaps only symbolic of a trade passed down from one generation of his family to the next.[84]

From the start, as a tradesman William Triplett had made it clear that he intended to work where and when he chose, and ultimately that attitude ended his employment at Mount Vernon. Impatient to continue his improvements—and on his own schedule—Washington increasingly used slaves and bound servants as brickmasons after the early 1760s. Yet both Tripletts seem to have managed quite well without the extra work. By varying their activities and holding on to their independence, they rose in life. To be sure, they never became Washington's equals, but William Triplett still could refuse to join the army without a commission or trade land that he wanted to keep, whoever asked the favor. And if his younger brother, Thomas, was prepared to extend himself in the patriot cause, it was only appropriate to invite him to dinner. Indeed, Martha Washington's words to Jackie Custis that evening—"stand firm," she had said—could well have been the brothers' motto.

With their deep roots and established position in the neighborhood, the Tripletts remained unusual among the independent artisans who worked at Mount Vernon. As a rule, Washington hired comparatively recent arrivals in America, and in that respect William Bernard Sears, or Sayres, was typical. In another way he stood out, however, for of the many artisans who contributed to the building of Mount Vernon, he was the most talented.

In all likelihood he left England in 1752 as a convicted felon: the "Barnard Sears, carver," who received a seven-year sentence for transportation to the colonies for steal-ing "one cloth waistcoat, one worsted waistcoat, one cloth coat, one pair of cloath breeches, four linnen shifts, two linnen shirts, twelve linnen aprons, and one guinea"—perhaps in the act of running away from his master.[85] He was just twenty years old. In Virginia, his indenture was bought by Washington's neighbor George Mason, who soon afterward began building his new house. Though relatively modest in size, Gunston Hall was meant to be one of the finest houses in Virginia, and it was to design and execute its interiors that Mason purchased William Buckland's indenture as well as Sears's. The result was a dazzling array of ornamental woodwork that took more than five years to complete and testified not only to Buckland's skills but also to Sears's talent and dexter-ity as a carver.

According to family tradition Mason, a knowledgeable student of architectural style and taste, particularly encouraged Sears in his art. However it came about, he was given the opportunity to work on the principal ground-floor rooms, using his chisels and gouges to produce fretwork and garlands of stemmed flowers and ruffled, veined leaves to set in the spandrels of arches; to dress chimneypieces, stair brackets, the tops of newel posts, and the keystones on drawing room cupboards; and even to adorn furniture carved to harmonize with the decorative details of the rooms. The project gave enormous rein to a skilled carver, and Sears proved more than equal to the task. Especially note-worthy were the delicacy and liveliness of the effects he achieved through angular under-cutting of foliage and using several different sizes of gouges to give finer definition to the leaves and petals he was modeling, all very much in keeping with the latest rococo style. His technique, indeed, amounted to a signature that makes it possible to trace work to his hands and no other.[86]

As Gunston Hall was nearing completion, Washington began his first rebuilding of Mount Vernon. His own plans were distinctly more modest than Mason's, but seeing his friend's house, he could not but have admired the quality of Sears's work. The two would meet again in 1772 at Pohick Church.

Meanwhile, even before finishing the work at Gunston Hall, Sears had made an inde-pendent arrangement with William Buckland,[87] who by then was taking commissions on his own: a glebe house for Truro Parish; a house for Mason's brother-in-law, Major Sel-don; and another, overlooking Occoguin Falls, for John Ballendine. In 1761 Buckland set up shop in Richmond County and probably soon afterward began working on John Tay-loe's Mount Airy.[88] Traces of Sears's hand can be seen in pieces of molding salvaged from the fire that destroyed the interior of the house in the nineteenth century. Sears also worked at Buckland's shop, where commonplace staples like coffins were produced, as well as venetian blinds, chimneypieces, and furniture modeled on such sources as Chippendale's *Gentleman's & Cabinet Makers' Guide* (which Buckland had in his collection). A Chippendale-style sideboard still belonging to the Tayloe family clearly bears Sears's "signature" in the distinctive undercutting on the edges of leaves and the high ridges on details like bellflower petals.[89]

When Buckland shifted operations to Annapolis in the early 1770s, Sears stayed behind in Virginia, probably because of his family, thereby establishing his independence. In 1769 he had married Elizabeth Whaley, and their second child was due early in 1772.[90] By the middle of that year he was working on Pohick Church, where he remained until the winter of 1774. For part if not all of that time he boarded with James Hardwick Lane (who also sold oyster shells to the parish for the project).[91] Though he did some work on the exterior of the church—cutting glass for the windows and installing them, for example—the woodwork on the interior was his major contribution, one remembered in the neighborhood long afterward.[92]

By prescription, the interiors of Anglican churches provided opportunities for woodwork well beyond the usual trim for building interiors. Altarpieces were adorned with the Lord's Prayer, the Apostles' Creed, and the Ten Commandments. Pulpits, rising in two, sometimes three stages, usually backpaneled, and always canopied, were meant to be dominant features. Every church also had a reading desk; a communion table; and a chest, often elaborately carved, to hold vestments and other accoutrements.[93]

Hardly anything remains today of the original interior of Pohick Church, which was abandoned after the Revolution and ransacked during the Civil War, yet given the vestry's specifications and work done at other churches nearby, a clear picture of the principal features emerges. The vestry stipulated that the altarpiece was to be twenty by fifteen feet and finished "after the Ionic Order."[94] At Falls Church, which was built just before Pohick and closely resembles it, the Lord's Prayer, the Apostles' Creed, and the Ten Commandments, done in black letters, were set inside crossetted frames, a detail appearing in Batty Langley's *Treasury of Designs*. The Pohick builders also used Langley for their pulpit design.[95]

It is possible to be more specific about the pulpit because of a sketch done by Benson J. Lossing before the Civil War. It shows a traditional hexagonal top, rising from a fluted Ionic column, resting on a hexagonal base. A sunburst framed by a palm branch and drapery was prominently carved on the front panel, and perched on top of the pulpit, as if it were about to take flight, was a dove.[96] The dove was included in Langley's design, but evidently the vestrymen (presumably with Washington among them) had not noticed it and felt Sears's price for carving it was too high. He is supposed to have replied, "Well, Gentlemen, if you refuse to pay my price, I will take it down, put breath in it, and set the bird to singing."[97] *Singing*? Did Sears mean tattling—telling on them? "Sing" was in fact a slave expression having that meaning.[98] In any case the vestry agreed to pay, and the dove remained on its perch. Moreover, such was the power of Sears's work that people would remember its creator's name and honor it for years to come. In *Memories of a Plain Family, 1836–1936*, Susan Annie Plaskett wrote movingly of her mother's experience in that regard. "The Church had been practically abandoned for some years and was in a bad state of dilapidation, but the beautiful carved work that had been done by William Bernard Sears, soon after the church was

Design for a pulpit from Batty Langley's City and Country Builder's and Workman's Treasury of Designs *(London, 1750). This was the design, complete with the bird, used at Pohick Church. Courtesy of the Mount Vernon Ladies' Association.*

The remains of the bird William B. Sears carved for the top of the pulpit at Pohick Church. Photograph by R.F. Dalzell, Jr.

built, had not then been molested. My mother used to sit in the church and read the Lord's Prayer and Ten Commandments over the Chancel, and admire the gilded dove that Mr. Sears had placed high over the Pulpit."[99] Later still, when the church was vandalized by Union troops during the Civil War, Sears's reputation ensured that what was left of the bird ended up in the hands of a family member, whose descendants have since returned it to Pohick.

Susan Plasket's mother had a keen eye. With gold leaf supplied by Washington and George William Fairfax, Sears had gilded the letters and the carved ornaments on the altarpiece, the palm branch and drapery on the pulpit, and the dove, which still shows traces of gilt today. The vestry also commissioned him to design the pulpit cushion and the cloth for the communion table and "furnish Colo. Washington with proper Patterns" for the same.[100]

In the spring of 1774, at about the time Going Lanphier began to raise the new addition to the south end of Mount Vernon, Sears finished his work at Pohick. By the following fall he was at Mount Vernon, executing the design from Abraham Swan's *British Architect* that Washington had selected for the dining room chimneypiece. Despite Lund Washington's misgivings, the result was a masterpiece.[101] Acanthus leaves rose from shells, twisting around pendants of flowers and scrolls of richly articulated foliage surrounded by egg-and-dart, rope, and ribbon-on-reel moldings, all executed with extraordinary deftness. It was a pattern book copy, but Sears's personal techniques and skill brought it brilliantly to life. He also recommended a design for the stucco decoration on

Detail of dining-room chimneypiece at Mount Vernon carved by William B. Sears. Courtesy of the Mount Vernon Ladies' Association.

the ceiling that would complement the chimneypiece, and he painted the dining room, as well as the rooms in the new south addition, and made a picture frame for Martha Washington.[102]

While working at Mount Vernon, Sears boarded there for a number of weeks, presumably with the other workers.[103] During that time, Lund Washington was particularly anxious that the indentured servants and slaves might leave in response to Dunmore's proclamation offering them freedom. It was Sears to whom he confided his fears and Sears who predicted—from his own position as an independent artisan—that all of them, with a single possible exception, would leave if they thought they could get away with it.[104]

Freedom was important to the man who arrived in Virginia under sentence for theft and went on to become a respected craftsman. Indeed, just how deeply Sears felt about his independence was signaled by the names he gave his three oldest sons: Charles Lee, Horatio Gates, and between those two, born in 1777, George Washington—all three heroes of the American Revolution. Only after the war would two younger sons be named for their father and grandfather.[105] Sears would also remain loyal to the Federalist Party in later years.[106]

Though the Mount Vernon ledgers contain no record of Sears working there after 1775, according to the reminiscences of one of the slave carpenters, Sambo Anderson, William "Barney" Sears was a continuing presence. Anderson, who joined the slave carpenter force during the Revolution (and who ran away with the British in 1781, only to be recovered later in Philadelphia), remembered Sears as being "a great favorite" with

Washington, coming by "the most of his time" to "lay out" work. Anderson also talked of how he learned carpentry from "one of the best mechanic [sic] in the land," and claimed Sears "could make anything" out of wood.[107]

When Sears died in 1818, his obituary described him as a man of "astonishing mechanical talents."[108] By then he had lived for more than forty years after completing his last documented work at Mount Vernon. According to family records he built "many public and private edifices" during that time.[109] Yet none of his later work has been identified, and the reason may have been foreshadowed as early as the time he was working on the dining room chimneypiece at Mount Vernon. As he shaped the hard walnut with his chisels and gouges, the stucco man working alongside him carved plaster ornaments for the entire ceiling in far less time. When the new room was finished a decade later, its walls and woodwork as well as its ceiling were even more efficiently decorated with pre-molded plaster ornaments, and there was no bold, deeply articulated carving of the sort Sears had done in the dining room. In the intervening years, the taste for such work had passed, and lighter, flatter plaster ornamentation had become fashionable. Washington himself was clear on the point in 1797, when the buildings for the new federal city were being planned. In a letter to the commissioners, he wrote, "I am informed that Mr. Hadfield is enquiring in this City, for Carvers. I earnestly recommend, that all carving not *absolutely necessary* to preserve consistency, may be avoided; as well to save time and expence, as because I believe it is not so much the taste now as formerly."[110]

When the fashion for what Sears did best—his intricately executed rococo carving in wood—ended, what was most memorable about his work disappeared with it. Doubtless his later projects were as skillfully done, but there was nothing to stamp them as his own, no signature, only an anonymous sameness. Most artisans working at Mount Vernon, however, left no distinctive mark at all. Sears did, in a chimneypiece that is unquestionably the finest piece of work in the house.

Appropriately enough, Sears's obituary celebrated him as one of those men "who, leaving the oppressions of feudal Europe, have planted scions in this land of liberty, where every man can sit under the shadow of his own vine and fig tree and can say there is none to hurt us."[111] He had come to America as a convicted criminal and had achieved his independence as an artisan. He had named three sons after patriot heroes. He also lived to see another son, James Whaley Sears, carry on his trade in Alexandria, and one of his daughters, Elizabeth, marry a practitioner of the same craft, Robert Goin Lanphier. From the start he had earned a reputation for producing work of the highest quality, and though tastes changed, the work itself remained, striking someone sitting in Pohick Church seventy-five years later as "beautiful"—someone who still, after all that time, knew his name.

No doubt if pressed to explain the anonymity that overtook Sears's work, Washington would have had recourse to something like the "troubled Ocean" he predicted awaited Johann Ehlers if he chose to pursue his "golden dreams." And in truth changes in fashion were like waves, surging across the deep. If carving was "not so much the taste now as formerly," it was to be avoided unless "*absolutely necessary.*"

Yet making such changes could have other consequences as well. In turning from Sears's work to the decorative system used in the new room at Mount Vernon, Washington also entered into a decidedly novel relationship with John Rawlins, the man he engaged to do the work. Always before, the artisans plying their trades at Mount Vernon had worked on the premises, under the watchful eye of Washington or someone he chose to act as supervisor. Inevitably, under those circumstances, the relationship took on a personal character, a kind of intimacy that shaped the parties' behavior, even when relations were not particularly smooth or cordial.[112] But Rawlins proposed to do nothing more at Mount Vernon than take measurements and check the work when it was finished. Headquartered in Baltimore, he would create the design as well as the decorative plasterwork in his workshop, and someone else would be sent to do what needed to be done at Mount Vernon.

Reluctantly Washington agreed to Rawlins's terms, yet he continued to grumble about the arrangement, and what the grumbling revealed was that he simply did not like the position in which he found himself. He wanted to see the work taking shape before his eyes; he wanted to feel that he knew the people who were doing it. That was the way it had always been. Like any theatrical performance, building required a supporting cast, yet in this instance the key supporting player remained offstage. Building had always provided, too, a forum in which Washington could offer useful instruction—could hope to mold his workers' behavior in ways beneficial to them as well as to himself—but here there was no one to instruct, no one to coax along the paths of righteousness.

Instead there was a highly efficient, thoroughly modern means of getting a difficult job done. Rawlins's system of production took the dictates of fashion and wedded them to the imperatives of the marketplace with a precision every bit as crisp and sharp as the plaster garlands he made to adorn the new room's woodwork. He could create, by the yard, on demand, entire, fully decorated rooms and send them anywhere they were wanted. By the same token, his relations with his customers could be put on a simple and straightforward basis. He set his prices, and if people wanted his work, they paid the prices he asked, though in Washington's case it turned out to be more complicated than that. By mistake, Rawlins was actually paid more than he was owed for the work he did at Mount Vernon. When Washington found out, he wrote, asking to be reimbursed, but Rawlins died before the matter could be resolved, so the only recourse Washington had, if he wanted his money back, was legal action against Rawlins's estate.

Yet what was this if not a thoroughly modern ending to the entire saga? Certainly it is impossible to imagine John Rawlins bringing his infant daughter, as Johann Ehlers did, to place in Washington's lap. Ehlers's struggle to achieve his independence, like the independence that came with the Tripletts' established position in society or Sears's extraordinary skill, was real enough, but this was different. Rawlins's relationship with the master of Mount Vernon was strictly a matter of business, nothing more and nothing less. Truly they were all afloat on the "troubled Ocean"—and no one more so than Washington himself.

CHAPTER 8

Undertakers and Managers

AT THE TOP of the hierarchy of Mount Vernon's builders stood the undertakers and managers. The equivalent of modern-day contractors, undertakers were figures of consequence in Virginia, who in addition to plying their own trades, assumed responsibility for organizing and supervising entire projects. If Mount Vernon had been built of brick, its undertakers would have been masons; as it was, Washington hired house carpenters. Each of them came with small crews of their own, but they were also at liberty to draw on the plantation's labor force if necessary.[1]

Still farther up the ladder of command, managers were responsible for overseeing all plantation activities, though that charge did not necessarily include a major role in the building process. When construction began at Mount Vernon in the spring of 1774, Washington implied that he himself would superintend the work, noting that it seemed to go better "whilst I am present."[2] Yet he was to miss almost all of the second rebuilding of the house, just as he had missed almost all of the first. In 1758 George William Fairfax, as a personal favor, had taken over for him. Fifteen years later the job fell to Lund Washington, Mount Vernon's regular manager.

Ultimately, Washington's prolonged absences from home increased the responsibilities of his undertakers and his managers alike. Acting in unison, they were to stand in his stead: to make the choices he would have made; to anticipate and solve problems he had not foreseen; to stretch often scarce materials and labor in the most efficient ways possible; in sum, to do everything as he would have done it himself. It was a tall order. In that world, however, long-standing traditions of deference and dependency were taken for granted. To submerge one's own point of view in another consciousness was the duty of every good servant, and Washington expected nothing less. The higher the level of service, too, the more complete the union was meant to be—at least in theory.

In practice it did not always work out that way. Washington was well served by one of his undertakers and badly served by the other. On balance Lund Washington proved to be an excellent manager, but even he was prone to maddening lapses. The result, in short, was a draw. But the issues were more complex than this suggests, for together time and events were creating a new social landscape across America, one that left scant room for traditional notions of service.

———

In many respects John Patterson could have served as a model for the way the traditional system was meant to function. A young house carpenter and joiner already working as overseer of Mount Vernon's slave carpenters, he was the person Washington chose as undertaker for his first rebuilding of the house. Since he knew that he would be away much of the time, he must have taken pains to impress on Patterson the importance of doing the job well, of managing funds carefully, and of staying in regular touch. For his part, Patterson saw his new role as a great opportunity and was eager to do whatever was required. "[I] shall allways make it my study to please & serve a Gent. that has done me such a singular peice of Service," he declared.[3] Many of Washington's workers would say such things over the years, but Patterson meant what he said.

Though he would be plying his trade as a house carpenter,[4] Patterson's primary responsibility as Washington's undertaker would be organizing the work: seeing to it that materials were on hand when they were needed; that the workers performed their tasks efficiently; that everything went forward on schedule. And fortunately for his sake he was no stranger to large-scale building projects. His introduction to Mount Vernon had probably come through the Washingtons' lawyer, John Mercer, who had recently completed his own house, Marlborough, and who described Patterson—in the only clue we have regarding his origins—as a young Irish apprentice who had worked on its interior.[5]

Mercer was tied both personally and professionally to several families in Fairfax County. He had married Catherine Mason, and as legal guardian to young George Mason, his nephew, he visited the neighborhood regularly. He was Lawrence Washington's lawyer, and three of his sons held commissions under George Washington during the French and Indian War. He was also a passionate reader, with one of the largest personal libraries in the colony, which included a number of important architectural publications: not only Langley's *City and Country Builder* but Palladio's *I Quattro Libri dell'Architettura* and Salmon's *Palladio Londinensis*.[6]

Nothing remains of Marlborough other than traces of brick walls, but based on recent archaeological excavations, it was no ordinary house. For inspiration, Mercer seems to have turned to Palladio's villas, designing an elegant structure incorporating the arched loggias that were also a common feature of Virginia courthouse architecture. He recruited his chief builders with care: David Minitree (who later built Carter's Grove) from Williamsburg for the exterior, and William Bromley for the interior. Records of payments to Bromley and his workers still exist, and they suggest that Marlborough's interior finish was opulent.[7] Indeed, Mercer's plans were probably ambitious to a fault, for he died deeply in debt, with his affairs in shambles. Nevertheless, for an aspiring young carpenter like John Patterson the work at Marlborough must have served as a useful training ground.

Patterson next emerges from obscurity on a March day in 1754, when he walked into Ramsay & Dixon's store in Alexandria to purchase a small file. The ledger lists him as a joiner good for credit living in town.[8] Alexandria was just beginning to grow, and

William Munday, another of the carpenters who worked at Marlborough, had already bought one of the original lots for 11 pistoles.[9] But there may have been an added attraction for Patterson in Alexandria. The same day he bought the file at Ramsay & Dixon's, he picked up four yards of silk (enough for a wedding dress?) to be charged to the account of Susannah Lanphier, who soon afterward became his wife.[10]

In 1755 Patterson started to work for Washington at Mount Vernon.[11] In later years the overseers of the slave carpenters were required to live with them, but the arrangement with Patterson seems to have been flexible enough to allow him to maintain a base in town. And it was as "John Patterson, House carpenter & Joyner of Alexandria" that he acquired the services of an apprentice, William Page, in 1757.[12] While his regular wages at Mount Vernon might not have sustained such an arrangement, he could have been receiving additional money from Susannah, who was a skilled weaver. In any case, he appears to have been optimistic about his prospects, and his optimism was justified. In April 1758, when the rebuilding of Mount Vernon was in its early stages, he was paid £40 in addition to the £20 he had received at the end of the previous year.[13] Before the house was finished, he took on a second apprentice.[14] By then he and Susannah had at least one child, William, and perhaps their second, Betty.

Along with his other duties at Mount Vernon, Patterson acted as paymaster, passing along Washington's funds to others. Thus he was given money to buy plank, and in order to cover the cost of building materials ordered at Carlyle & Dalton, Washington placed a sizable money order on account in Patterson's name. Patterson also was given £75 for Washington's brother Jack Washington, who was managing the plantation in his absence, and a smaller amount for Humphrey Knight, the overseer.[15]

Except for matters over which he had no control, such as Triplett's refusal to do more than initially agreed to and the delivery of the window glass to the wrong river, Patterson's management of the building project at Mount Vernon was more than satisfactory. He worked well with George William Fairfax, who acted as Washington's eyes and ears on the job. John Carlyle also saw Patterson regularly when he came to pick up supplies or post letters to Washington and reported very favorably on him, writing at one point, "Jno. Pattinson has your Interest At heart as much As If it Was his own."[16] Patterson kept his word about staying in touch with Washington, too. "As you are pleas'd to desire hereing how your building goes on, I think its a sadisfaction more than otherwise," he wrote at the beginning of September 1758, with obvious pride.[17]

How much of the finished carpentry on the inside of the house Patterson did himself is unclear, but at a minimum he supervised whatever work he did not do, and the results are impressive. While the overall effect may seem somewhat crowded, the wall paneling, the pediments over the doorways, the pilasters supporting them in the west parlor, and the large-scale modillions running along the cornice and beam in the passage are all well executed, with a bold, monumental quality that Patterson might well have imagined would appeal to his employer. Much the same is true of the carved details—the Greek key frieze in the stairwell; the scrollwork, leaves, and flowers on the west parlor chimneypiece; and the fish-scale patterning on the consoles supporting the mantel. If they lack the virtuosity of Sears's later work in the dining room, in their straightforward way they are handsome enough.[18] The chimneypiece in the study, which has identical fish scale patterning on the consoles, was probably also done at this time, initially for the dining room and then moved later to make room for Sears's work.

Perhaps most effective of all is the design Patterson arrived at for the stairway in the passage. Because the space between the dining-room door and the west wall was so limited, the supporting girder above was set forward to accomodate the main flight of stairs, and the line of the stairwell was curved to create the necessary headroom at the top. It was an imaginative and graceful solution to a difficult problem.

On September 15, 1759, John Patterson received his final payment for supervising the rebuilding of Mount Vernon.[19] He had finished his work, and Washington's "singular peice of service" had enabled him to buy the thing he most needed to put his family's life on solid footing: land. Washington himself may have had a hand in the matter, for the land Patterson bought the following January for £150 was Lawrence Washington's pair of adjoining lots in Alexandria.[20] They were conveniently located just south of the town center near the waterfront, at the corner of Fairfax and King Streets. William Fairfax owned the lot immediately to the south, and John Carlyle's house and business were across the street to the north. Also, Patterson's brother-in-law, Going Lanphier, lived just a block away on property he had bought five years before.

Having established himself in Alexandria, Patterson seems to have had little difficulty finding work. He was paid almost £100 by the town trustees for building a schoolhouse in 1760. Two years later he received an additional amount for the same purpose.[21] He repaired the courthouse as well that year.[22] He was also commissioned by the vestrymen of Truro Parish to build a coffin for one of the parishioners.[23] And he made furniture: an unfinished chest with five drawers was later listed in the inventory of his estate. As is true of most eighteenth-century craftsmen, his personal records have not survived, and his private commissions, other than those he did for Mercer and Washington, are unknown, but the presence of servants and slaves in the Patterson household suggests that a significant amount of work came his way. Susannah also seems to have been in business, carding, spinning, and weaving, with a female servant and several slaves to help her.[24]

The household was evidently a busy one, but indications are that it was not trouble-free. In 1758 one of Patterson's servants, a man by the name of Murphy, was sentenced to serve extra time for running away, and three years later Patterson had to advertise in the *Maryland Gazette* after he disappeared again. James Jackson, another of Patterson's servants, was sentenced to serve extra time that year.[25] Susannah too seems to have had trouble with her workers. Because of Penelope Mandervaell's complaints against the household, the court ruled in 1765 that "for the future" Patterson should not "immoderately correct her." He was to provide her with better clothes as well.[26]

But 1765 also brought tidings of a happier sort: a letter to Going and Venus Lanphier and their sister, Susannah Patterson, from their uncle, William Lanphier, in Cork, informing them that they had inherited an estate "at home" in Ireland worth £1,200 and urging that one of them come to Cork to claim the property.[27] As the only male of the three siblings, Going Lanphier would have been the logical person to go. But instead it was John Patterson who made the necessary preparations for the trip, including sitting down one October day to write out his will. As long as she was a widow, Susannah Patterson was to receive "everything I am Possessed of," including the two Alexandria lots and the buildings on them. As executrix of the estate, she was to provide a "suitable gen-

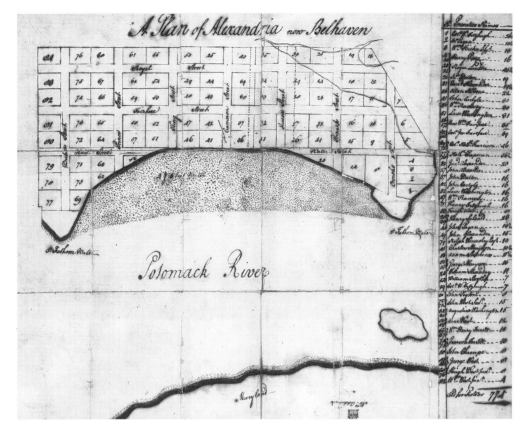

Map of Alexandria drawn by George Washington. Library of Congress.

tle" education for their children, William, Betty, and Thomas. If Patterson was not able to purchase a Negro girl for Betty before leaving for Ireland, Susannah was to do it. If Susannah remarried, the estate would be divided among the three children. The will was witnessed by Susannah's brother, Going.[28] A few months later, Patterson left on a ship owned by Stephen West, another Alexandria resident.[29]

Sadly, he never reached Ireland. Months went by while the family waited, with no word. Finally Susannah, who could not read, must have heard the news, either from her brother or one of the merchants in town: Stephen West's ship had gone down, and all aboard were lost at sea.[30] Another two years passed before she took Patterson's will to be recorded at court, and it was two years more before the inventory of the estate was completed. Long before then, however, she would have taken possession of the two lots; the buildings; the two cows; the calf; the two yearlings; the six "old" books; the three female slaves (two of them girls); the services of the woman servant and the male servant, James Jackson, who still had fifteen months left on his contract; the typical furnishings of a small house; and John Patterson's joiner's tools, which she sold for seventeen pounds.[31]

Though not insignificant, the estate was modest, but there remained the inheritance that Patterson had gone to Ireland to collect, which Susannah proved more aggressive in trying to claim than her brother, Going. When their sister, Venus Lanphier, died in 1769, the matter was no nearer resolution, and she left her share of the hoped-for money to Susannah's three children, pointedly bequeathing only five shillings in Irish currency to her brother, Going.[32] Susannah herself could not undertake the voyage to Ireland; nor did she succeed in prevailing on her brother to go. Yet after her sister died, she did dictate a letter to her uncle, sending him documents that she hoped would suffice.[33] Two years earlier Harry Piper, an Alexandria merchant, had written a Mr. Dixon, a business associate in White Haven, England, about the Lanphiers' situation, asking him to write to William Lanphier in Cork "as he is the only Person that can probably see them righted."[34] Now Susannah enlisted Piper's aid again. She even offered to pay him half of whatever he recovered,[35] but Going refused to pay such a high percentage. "I have spoken to Mrs. Patterson [about] the Lanphier affair. . . . I have not seen Going, but she says he is averse to giving one half, and she can't do anything without him."[36] Attempts to secure the claim went on intermittently until August 1771, but in the end Susannah's efforts to enlist her brother's help failed. The pot of gold at the end of the rainbow that had cost John Patterson his life was gone.

No doubt it must have seemed an uncharacteristic impulse that led Patterson to venture back home in the first place. His work at Mount Vernon revealed him to be steady, conscientious, and thorough, and he had established a life that might well have gone on in that vein, bringing him to a comfortable old age surrounded by a large family. Yet at a critical point he did what Washington himself was to do more than once in his own life: he risked everything on an uncertain gamble. Had he not lost that gamble, too, he might well have returned to oversee the next major rebuilding of Mount Vernon. As it was, the task fell to his brother-in-law, Going Lanphier, a very different sort of person.

Going Lanphier's on-and-off association with Mount Vernon lasted almost three decades. In that time he proved to be a disappointing worker, serving Washington grudgingly and producing work of indifferent quality. Or so Washington thought. But Lanphier can also be seen another way: as a stubborn, argumentative, independent craftsman, equipped with a heritage that combined a tradition in the trades with fiercely held beliefs and a strong sense of self, someone who came to, and left, Mount Vernon very much his own man.

To begin with, there was his name. Over the years both the first and last parts of it had assumed innumerable forms as they were translated by British ears and pens: Guin, Goin, Guion, Goan, Goulin, Gawen, Gaven, Gowen, and Going; and just as variously, Lampriere, Lampier, Lamphiere, Lamprie, Lampere, Lauphier, Lamhire, Lamphier, Lanphier, Lanphire, Langphier, and Langhir. Sometimes several versions were recorded in the same document, and the Mount Vernon ledgers vary from Lanphier's own spelling. Yet the name was emblematic of his origins; to him, it must have served as a constant reminder, if he needed one, of a particular past.

When his father, Thomas Lanphier, decided to immigrate to America with his family in 1732, he was thirty-three years old and Going was five. With the prospect of a new life ahead, the senior Lanphier might have told his son about the times other Lanphiers had uprooted themselves. Twice before the family had gone to new countries, and just as the stories came down through Going's children and grandchildren, so too those stories must have come to him, if not at the time of the move to America, then later.[37]

Before Ireland there had been England, and before that, France, where the Lanphiers were Huguenots, French Protestants at odds with both the established church and the state. Though they never amounted to more than 8 percent of the French population, what the Huguenots lacked in numbers they made up for in strength of conviction and organization. The movement drew from the artisan classes, especially metal- and cloth-workers, and the *petit bourgeoisie,* including teachers, notaries, and lawyers. It also attracted half the members of the French nobility, along with their armies. The Lanphiers were from Languedoc, a Huguenot stronghold, and were probably among the many clothworkers there who embraced the faith.[38]

Eventually the movement became too powerful in the eyes of the French crown, and on St. Bartholomew's Day, 1572, the Paris militia took action, slaughtering three thousand people. The butchery spread to the countryside until more than ten thousand Protestants had been killed: "wholesale murder," later generations of Lanphiers would say. Unwilling to change their beliefs and possessing portable livelihoods, thousands of Huguenot artisans, including the Lanphiers, fled along routes organized by the church and escaped to England, where Elizabeth I offered them protection.

For three generations the family remained in Wiltshire County, England, their religious rights guaranteed and their livelihood assured—assuming they followed the cloth trade, which was the economic mainstay of the area.[39] Then, during James I's reign, a series of acts was passed denying the Huguenots some of the privileges they had enjoyed up to then.[40] At the same time, the woolen industry was depressed. But Cromwell's assault on Ireland brought fresh opportunities, which at least one of the Lanphiers embraced.

With the force of twenty thousand men whom Cromwell assembled in 1649 in Dublin, he proposed to extend England's revolution to Ireland and "liberate" the country from Catholicism. Subjugating stronghold after stronghold, he pressed on until virtually all Catholics were dispossessed of their lands, which he distributed to his soldiers as payment in arrears.[41] During the winter and spring of 1649–50 he was headquartered in County Cork, in the port of Youghal, and in all likelihood it was there that the Lanphier who had joined the army decided to settle. At some point, too, he married into another Huguenot family, the Goins (or Guins). According to stories told later to Going Lanphier, they seem to have been a fierce tribe. One of them served as a colonel of the cavalry under William of Orange, and there was a tale that once, dreaming he was fighting, he woke himself by pounding his feet against the wall.

The chief industry in County Cork was the manufacture and dyeing of linen and sail-cloth. Still, whatever opportunities the area afforded do not seem to have been strong enough to hold Thomas Lanphier there.[42] Nor in later years, for all the family lore associated with Ireland, did his son Going ever show the least interest in returning. The trip that took the family to the town of Cobh, where ships embarked for America, was to be his last view of his native country.[43]

The Lanphiers arrived in Princess Anne County, Virginia, in May 1732, and family legend has Thomas quarreling with the captain who brought them over. After settling briefly in Occomac, they moved to Port Tobacco on the Maryland side of the Potomac, where Thomas became a partner in a brewery. He died in 1748, leaving three children: Going, and two daughters, Venus and Susannah. Two inventories taken of his estate list possessions valued at just over £53.[44]

The earliest evidence of the family's presence in the vicinity of Alexandria dates from four years later, when Going Lanphier was credited with £2.6.8 in the Mount Vernon ledgers for making slave clothing, shortly before Lawrence Washington's death.[45] Over the next two years, he bought goods at Ramsay and Dixon's store, paying for them in part with tobacco. The items included bolts of rough "slave" cloth, cotton, linen, figured plush, silk, plus hooks, thread, needles, and scissors. The account also lists hinges, brass nails, a compass, a two-foot rule, and twenty-five handsaw files, suggesting that Going was doing carpentry work as well.[46] In 1755 he bought a lot in Alexandria on the corner of Duke and Fairfax Streets from John and Martha West for £10.15.[47] Four years after that he appeared again in the Mount Vernon ledgers when he made the balusters for Washington's new staircase.[48] Two years later he served on a jury for the county,[49] and sometime between 1766 and 1777 he made the staircase balusters for a tavern that John Carlyle and one of his partners were enlarging.[50]

During the 1760s and 1770s Lanphier also made and mended tools for Mount Vernon, including plow handles and axletrees, as well as items linked to spinning and weaving—linen wheels, woolen wheel whorls, spools, and flyers—suggesting again the tradition of textile work in the family.[51] He seems to have owned a slave named Joe and employed at least two carpenters, James Tasker and Wentworth Aldon.[52] In 1764 he had a sawyer, Robert Boggess, or Hoggess (who sawed the plank for six benches at Pohick Church), in his employ. Later Boggess and Lanphier were codefendants in a suit as a result of which they had to pay Robert and William Brent the sum of £6.10 plus the interest that had accumulated. During the same court session Lanphier was ordered to pay £3 and costs to William Allason. As it happened, Washington was one of the five presiding justices at the session.[53]

By the end of the decade, the saga of the Lanphier family's Irish inheritance had played itself out. Going's uncle, William Lanphier, his sister Susannah, and Harry Piper all urged him to go to Ireland and claim the estate, but he refused. "Indeed he is such a person there's no knowing what to make of him—I believe he will never go home himself," Piper wrote in 1770.[54] And since Lanphier also refused to pay someone else to retrieve a portion of the estate, the matter was dropped.[55] Did he feel any guilt because his inaction had not only cost the family what might have been a significant windfall but also left Susannah a widow with three children to support? Possibly. In later years some of his payments from Mount Vernon went to his sister and her family,[56] and he may have trained one of her sons as a carpenter. As for why he did not go, perhaps it was no coincidence that the year the issue of the Irish inheritance was finally put to rest he started the first of the two commissions for which he remains best known: Pohick Church.

Because Pohick was walled in brick, Lanphier and his crew concentrated on the balconies, the railings, the pews, the paneled doors, the window and door surrounds, and the pulpit. They worked in good company. In addition to William Bernard Sears, there was William Copein, who did the stonework—including the baptismal font—and who had also worked on John Mercer's Marlborough.[57] Shortly before the church was finished, Lanphier asked Copein to deliver a letter to Washington describing adjustments in the bill of scantling for the additions to Mount Vernon.[58]

At Mount Vernon, Lanphier and Lund Washington got on poorly from the start. Lund found Lanphier's frequent absences infuriating, and the two did not communicate well. When Lund asked Lanphier about the proportions for the columns for the covered ways, for example, the reply left him completely baffled. "I have once or twice talk'd to Lanphier about it but he mouths & talks in such a way that I do not understand him," he wrote Washington in the fall of 1775.[59]

There is some evidence that the problem may have been exacerbated by politics. Lund stood wholeheartedly behind the patriot cause, but according to Lanphier family legend, Going was a Tory. After all, many of his ancestors had fought for England, and presumably the tales of their bravery in battle had not been lost on a young boy's ears. Yet in those wars the issue had been religion. For Lanphier in this war the issue might have been simpler: just what did he have to gain from a patriot victory?

Meanwhile—whatever his politics—he carried on a war of his own at Mount Vernon, making his independence clear by coming to work when he chose and completing projects in his own good time. If he appeared at all, that is. When Lund needed him to work in 1778 he refused to come until he was promised payment in produce instead of cash,[60] and when wheels were sent to him to mend, he apparently felt no compunction at all about leaving the work undone.[61] Finally, in 1779 he seems to have left Mount Vernon for good. By then the basic construction of the mansion house was complete, but the interior finish of the new room and the paving of the piazza had yet to be started.

Also, time would reveal that Lanphier's skills could have been better employed at Mount Vernon than they were. Unlike Patterson, he was not responsible for the fine carpentry in the additions he built; his primary task was to be sure that the structure itself was sound. Yet when Washington returned home, he found the sill under the north end of the house rotted and the roof leaking where it had been altered to accommodate the cupola and the pediment on the west front.[62] Still, at his uncompromising insistence and in spite of all the difficulties involved in carrying on a major building project in time of war, the work had been done, and for that he owed his troublesome undertaker more than a little.

After leaving Mount Vernon, Lanphier continued to ply his trade, although not much is known about him between that time and his death in 1813. He arranged to rent several properties on the north and south sides of Princess Street in Alexandria in 1785, and on one of them he agreed to build a dwelling for the owners, Hannah and David Griffith.[63] He is also said to have built his own house on Shooter's Hill in Alexandria, near where the Masonic Temple now stands.[64]

A bit more is known about the four children he and his wife, Elizabeth, raised. The most successful of them seems to have been Robert Goin. The eldest child, he was born the same year that Going Lanphier and Sears were working on the south addition at Mount Vernon, and appropriately enough the two artisan families were to be formally linked when Robert grew up to marry Elizabeth Sears, William Bernard's daughter. The couple stayed in Alexandria near their parents and had eight children (one of whom was named for Going, and another of whom was christened William Bernard Lanphier).[65] Robert spent part of his time involved in various land transactions. In 1797 he offered ten lots for sale on Alexandria's waterfront.[66] He also sold yard goods and worked as a dyer, and in 1806 his wife was advertising "a handsome assortment of materials for Millenery" at her establishment on King Street.[67] By then, too, he had sold a lot on St. Asaph Street that he received from his father, which had on it a smokehouse and a two-story, four-room dwelling probably built either by Going or by the two Lanphiers together.[68] For in addition to everything else, Robert was carrying on his father's trade as a carpenter, having given notice in 1806 that "The subscriber wishing to engage in business for the ensuing season, will do any Carpenters' work, and receive in payment wet or dry goods for one half the amount of work contracted for."[69]

But for Robert Goin Lanphier knowledge of carpentry was only a first step. He reportedly designed the box enclosed in the cornerstone of the masonic temple in Washington, D.C., as well as the seals for the U.S. Senate and the House of Representatives.[70] He also dreamed of being an architect, and in one particularly notable instance he acted on that dream. In 1792, at Washington's instigation, a competition was held for an architectural design for the new capitol in the federal city. The commissioners asked for ground plans and elevations and an estimate of how many bricks the building would require. The winner would receive a $500 stipend plus a lot in the new federal city. Robert Goin Lanphier was among the sixteen people who entered the competition.

His elevations and ground plans show a certain talent at drafting and a vigorous imagination. The commissioners had stipulated that they wanted a flat, balustraded roof; a dome; columns; and a colonnade. All are present in Lanphier's design, a dizzying medley of pattern-book flourishes spread across a building twenty-one bays wide and six stories high. In the approved Palladian manner, the main mass of the structure is broken into three parts, with symmetrical blocks on either side of a curved central section that features a portico supported by freestanding columns. The dominant feature of the design, however, is the massive dome. Soaring to a height equal to that of the block beneath it and as wide as it is high, it completely overwhelms the structure. At the same time it has no visible means of support apart from the walls below it.[71]

Despite its flaws, Robert Lanphier's design did survive the first cut in the competition, but then William Thornton's plan was submitted and carried the day (with Washington's strong endorsement). So in the end Going Lanphier's son did not design the nation's capitol. Yet interestingly enough he tried, and for all its naiveté, his design shows considerable flair. There is also about it an air of optimism stemming, perhaps, from faith in the new republic itself and in the opportunities it offered those willing to strive for better, fuller lives. At the time he entered the competition, Lanphier was just seventeen years old.

No likeness of Going Lanphier exists, nor, for that matter, is there one of his brother-in-law, John Patterson, or of his son's father-in-law, William Bernard Sears. But Robert Goin Lanphier did have his portrait painted. It reveals a sensitive, stylish, well-dressed man with dark hair and eyes.[72] It is fitting that his portrait survives, too, for on top of everything else, he was to be the storyteller for later generations of Lanphiers—passing on verbally the family's past in France, England, Ireland, and finally America.

Yet on one point those stories would remain silent. They speak of the family's many migrations and tell of the lost Irish inheritance, but there is not a word in them about George Washington or the building of Mount Vernon. One senses that this was Going Lanphier's doing, that in later years, when his son was old enough to remember what he said, he simply did not talk of his experiences at Mount Vernon. Evidently his pride in who and what he was counted for more than whatever he owed the Washingtons. The same conviction had made him hard to bargain with and even harder to understand, but in the end it left him free to be himself—as his fabled ancestors had been.

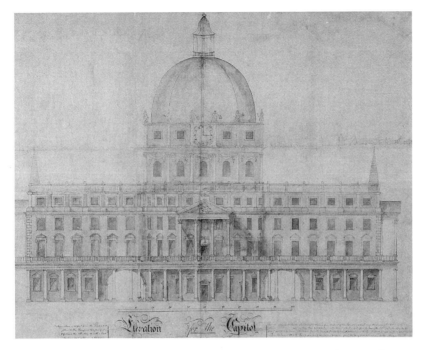

Robert Goin Lanphier's design for the front facade of the Capitol in Washington, D.C. Courtesy of the Maryland Historical Society, Baltimore, Maryland.

If Going Lanphier preferred to downplay the importance of Mount Vernon in his life, for twenty years Mount Vernon *was* Lund Washington's life, and despite some awkward moments, he appeared content with that fact. His loyalty to Washington was rock-solid. He firmly believed that his distant cousin, friend, and employer was a great man. His own role, as he saw it, was to serve, and serve he did, from the time Washington hired him as manager of Mount Vernon to the day in 1785 when he finally left.

The responsibilities of a plantation manager were manifold. Of primary importance to any owner—and Washington was no exception—were successful crop yields. It was also important to know about millwork, keeping livestock, slaughtering, fishing, salting, and pickling to ensure that the people doing those things worked efficiently. "Keep every one in their places, and to their duty; relaxation from, or neglect in small matters, lead to like attempts in matters of greater magnitude," Washington wrote at one point.[73] Added to a plantation manager's responsibilities, too, was the need to be a "complete clerk." He was in charge of provisions, clothes, and tools. He was the keeper of the keys to the smokehouse, the barns, and the plantation store, where every handsaw and file was meticulously signed out. All financial transactions had to be recorded in the plantation ledgers, along with counts of supplies of every kind to curb stealing or neglect.[74]

Hiring Lund was not the first or the last time that Washington would draw on his extended family to handle these duties. He had already employed one of his brothers as manager, and later the job would go to a favorite nephew.[75] A descendent of John ("the immigrant") Washington's brother, Lund had grown up in the Chotank neighborhood of the Potomac where that branch of the family had settled. As a child Washington had visited his cousins there, and he and Lund almost certainly became acquainted then.[76] Although Lund's family had some means, he had no property of his own, and in that sense he was well placed for Washington's purposes. He would be grateful for the employment and the chance it brought to add to his assets. Presumably, too, as a kinsman he was someone Washington could trust.

Before coming to Mount Vernon, Lund had managed large plantations for both the Beverley family and Henry Fitzhugh, and he had supervised a mill for William Fitzhugh at Chatham, just outside Fredericksburg.[77] In demeanor he was sociable, good-natured, uncomplaining, and not given to excessive drinking.[78] From the outset Washington treated him as much like a friend as an employee. Evidently he lived in the house, and he and Washington regularly rode off together on winter days to hunt with the Triplett brothers.[79] When the Washingtons went to Berkeley Springs with the Fairfaxes, Martha entrusted her children to Lund's care.[80] When Washington bought up land patents from veterans of the French and Indian War, for appearances sake he had two thousand acres put in Lund's name, a practice he repeated with one of his brothers.[81] At times Lund was also asked to act as a coconspirator in family matters. When Washington decided that Martha's son, Jackie, who was away at school, should be inoculated for smallpox, he was afraid she would be opposed. So without her knowledge, he wrote Jackie's schoolmaster, asking him to go ahead with the plan and adding that all letters on the subject should be sent to him "under cover to Lund Washington, & in a hand not your own."[82] For Sunday services at Pohick Church, Lund sat in the pew just behind the Washingtons.[83] He often signed his letters to Washington, "Your affectionate humble servant" or simply "Your affectionate servant," thereby deftly combining the concepts of friend and employee. In turn, Washington signed his letters to Lund as "Your affectionate friend."[84]

In more peaceful times, Lund might not have remained as long as he did at Mount Vernon. He had already been there for ten years when war broke out in 1775, but if he had any plans to leave, he put them aside and stayed on for another decade, receiving as compensation the use of a farm and a share of the crops.[85] Having owned slaves of his own before coming to Mount Vernon, he acquired more during his years there.[86] He also had his clothes made by the plantation's tailor: in 1775 he ordered a pair of gaiters, six coats, seven pairs of breeches, and five waistcoats. Another waistcoat was altered, suggesting that he was getting heavier as time passed.[87]

During Washington's long absence at the front, Lund's job became considerably more complex. It was now he who had to be sure that Mount Vernon was supplied with provisions and that the crops were sold at good prices. He had to collect rents from Washington's tenants, and he had to bargain with neighboring plantation owners over hiring extra labor. When servants or slaves ran away, he had to advertise for their recovery. It was his responsibility to watch over their health and to summon doctors if necessary. He also meted out reprimands and punishments. In sum, he was responsible for everything but owned none of it himself; furthermore, he was overseeing slaves and hired laborers who were fully aware of that fact.

To add to his problems, there was a run of very poor crop yields. Wet weather hampered plowing during the fall of 1775, and the following winter was cold and raw without snow, resulting in a miserable wheat crop. Then for the next three years the wheat was almost totally destroyed by an infestation of the weevil, and because trade with the West Indies had virtually stopped, Washington's mill stood idle most of the time. Wartime shortages made matters even worse. There was a lack of salt for putting up herring. If Lund envisioned growing tobacco as a substitute for weevil-infested wheat, he despaired of finding the materials to build sheds for drying the crop. Meanwhile, the value of all currencies fluctuated wildly, and in the middle of the war the rate of inflation soared to 500 percent.[88]

Anxiously, Lund experimented with pressing corn stalks for molasses, which did not work. But he was proud of another innovation: to make up for the shortage of salt, he had the brine used for putting up bacon recycled for preserving fish. Also, in his search for markets other than the British West Indies, he tried both the French Caribbean islands and New England and finally managed to sell some flour in Boston. Unfortunately, it had soured in storage and had to be tossed repeatedly to get rid of the moisture, a problem he eventually solved by using the new room to stockpile goods for market.[89]

When rumors of an invasion circulated in the neighborhood, Lund packed up china and glassware and had them moved out of range, but he fretted about whether he should have moved more, and he worried especially about Washington's papers. Martha had so much company, he wrote, and had left for camp in such haste, that she might not have taken everything she should have, yet Lund's scruples prevented him from unlocking and searching Washington's desk in his absence.[90]

He also worried about provisions for "the family" and for the guests, who came in an endless stream whenever Martha was home.[91] "It is seldom that this House is without Company," he wrote.[92] Company usually meant extra horses and servants to feed, too, but things were almost as bad during the long months Martha spent with Washington in camp, for then the housekeeping chores fell to Lund. "I am by no means fit for a House keeper, I am affraid I shall consume more than ever, for I am not a judge how much shoud be given out every Day."[93]

Then there were all the debts that Washington adamantly insisted had to be paid, even when there was nothing to pay them with. "Some of these people must go without money for I cannot tell where to find it," Lund wrote at one point.[94] Nor did lack of cash deter Washington from trying to expand Mount Vernon's boundaries even farther, so Lund was repeatedly sent out to negotiate for various tracts of land that looked as if they might become available.[95] Poor crops and disrupted markets also cut into income, as did Lund's reluctance to dun Washington's tenants for rent. Most of them were suffering hardships of their own, and most, too, probably sensed a soft heart in Lund. He explained the shortfall by claiming that he could not find an adequate list of tenants and said that he felt compelled to stay close to home, especially after Dunmore's proclamation offering freedom to all slaves and servants who joined his forces.[96]

And further complicating everything, of course, was the rebuilding of the house, which Washington insisted go forward no matter what. If Lund worried about his shrinking labor force, Washington seemed oblivious to the problem. If Lund fretted about finding provisions for the workers, Washington continued to demand that the work be done as quickly as possible. If nails or oil and paint were hard to come by, Washington wrote that even if it meant searching for hundreds of miles, they had to be found. Once, on hearing discouraging news from the front, Lund commented frankly: "From the Ac[coun]ts . . . we are dayly haveing here—it looks like lost labour to keep on with our Building—for shoud they get Burnt it will be provoking."[97] Washington's only reply was to suggest that something might be done to block ships from coming up the river.[98]

Lund's problems with building were also augmented by his limited knowledge of the subject. A farm manager he was; an architect or builder he was not. He knew that Washington wanted the south addition finished much sooner than it was, and he worried about the time Sears and "the Stucco man" were taking, but he did not know how to move things along more quickly. He also worried about the look of the work—was it too fussy and elaborate?—and he was relieved when it was finally finished.[99] He understood the importance of symmetry: the double doors of the servants' hall opposite the single door of the kitchen bothered him, until finally Washington ordered one of the doors eliminated.[100] However, he could not understand Washington's insistence that the chimneys be redone so that they could be capped with stone. "I think the Kitchen Chimneys look very well finish'd as they are," he wrote.[101] Nor had it occurred to him that Washington might want the outbuildings dressed up with rusticated weatherboarding to match the main house, and when it came time to build the covered ways, he had trouble envisioning the result. Unfortunately Washington had not provided a plan or left detailed instructions, and talking to Lanphier was no help at all.[102]

Indeed, everything about Lanphier was problematic. Lund found it infuriating to deal with a worker who was so obstinate in his demands, and it was only for lack of an alternative that he kept him on after the addition to the south end of the house was completed. But the truth was, Lanphier had the upper hand. Lund had no choice but to bargain with him, and to make matters worse, Lanphier continually broke his promises. When Lund exploded, "of all the worthless men live G. Lanphier is the greatest," no doubt he meant every word he wrote.[103]

Finally—and perhaps at times almost as annoying—there were Washington's endless instructions for the continuing beautification of the grounds, often sent with no regard for the difficulties involved. In November 1775, when a particularly daunting list arrived calling for transplanting cherry trees, replanting the vineyard, and clearing the underbrush at "Hell hole," Lund questioned the wisdom of transplanting trees at that time of year and wondered who could be spared to do the work. "We have a Fence to make intirely Round the pasture the present one being quite Rotten, Flax to break, Swingle, & Heckle, Earth to turn up for Brick makeg next Summer, Stone to Raise at an immense deal of Labour for makeg Chimney Tops & and many other things to do, that is not worth mentiong."[104] Still, the tree-planting did take place, though, as Lund predicted, the trees did not survive the winter.

For Washington, on the other hand, Lund's letters could be a source of irritation, and occasionally he grew quite impatient with what he saw as his kinsman's indecisiveness and inertia. When Lund asked for more precise directives regarding work on the house and grounds, Washington did not always feel he was in a position to give them. Lund would have to do the best he could.[105] But on other matters the way should have been clear. Rents due from tenants had to be collected, whatever it cost in added effort. "You seem to have had an unconquerable aversion to going from home; one consequence of which, is, I expect I shall lose all my rents," commented Washington at one point.[106]

Even more serious was the issue of Lund's "long promised" farm accounts detailing crop production and livestock holdings. As the time grew near for Washington's return, he became increasingly anxious about the accounts, and when Lund offered the excuse of his "aversion to writing" for not sending them, Washington did not even try to conceal his anger. "You do not seem to have considered the force and tendency of the words of yr. letter," he began. "These are but other words for saying, 'as I am not fond of writing . . . it is *quite* immaterial whether you have any knowledge or information of your private concerns or whether the accts. are kept properly or not.'" By his own lights Washington had been patient, but now his patience had run out. "Delicacy hitherto, and a hope that you long ago would have seen into the propriety of the measure, without a hint of it from me, has restrained me from telling you that annual Accts . . . ought to have been sent to me as regularly as the year came about. It is not to be supposed, that all the avocations of my public duties, great and laborious as they have been, could render me totally insensible to the *only means* by which myself and family; and the character I am to maintain in life hereafter, is to be supported."[107]

Also, of course, there was Lund's mistakenly courteous behavior to the enemy when the *Savage* appeared in the Potomac in the spring of 1781. Yet even when he was most vexed, Washington took care to repeat again and again the faith he had in Lund's integrity. The trust he placed in his kinsman was unique; it could never have been given to a "common" manager.[108] He confided in Lund in personal matters too—for example, his increasing desire "to get clear of" slavery[109]—and he freely expressed opinions to Lund that he would never have aired in public. From Boston, at the beginning of the war, he wrote in scathing terms about the people he met: the officers struck him as "the most indifferent kind of People I ever saw" and the common soldiers seemed hardly any better—"an exceeding dirty & nasty people."[110] And later when military prospects looked particularly bleak, he let Lund know the full measure of his despair: "Such is my situation that if I were to wish the bitterest curse to an enemy on this side of the grave, I should put him in my stead."[111]

Washington also worried constantly about whether Lund was being fairly compensated. During the first year that he was away he wrote several times about wages, proposing an amount based on the highest crop yields since Lund came to Mount Vernon. "I offer it in consideration of the great charge you have upon your hands, and my entire dependance upon your Fidility and Industry." It was the least he could do for "a person in whose Integrity I have not a doubt."[112] Lund replied that he was pleased to have Washington's trust, adding, "If I ever injured anyone it was my self. I believe I have Neglected my own Business but never yours or any man who I have serve'd."[113] Still, he did not feel entitled to the extra pay and even seemed a bit hurt by Washington's offer. "I shoud be sorry that you shoud believe that i wou'd exact more of you now than when you live'd at Home," he wrote. He was content with things as they were; his needs were modest. "I never expect to be Rich, my only Wish, or ambition has been to save so much out of my wages . . . as woud be sufficient to purchase a small Farm in some part of the Country where the produce of it wou'd enable me to live, and give a Neighbour Beef, & Toddy."[114]

In time Lund would get his "only Wish," and by then he also had a congenial partner with whom to share his new life. On a trip home in the summer of 1779, stopping to visit his brother's family, he encountered Betsy Foote, a pious woman with whom he was probably already acquainted, since she was not only his brother's wife's sister but also the niece of his uncle's wife. Whatever sparked the romance, the two were married shortly afterward and took up residence together at Mount Vernon.[115] "I do think there is not one other man scarce to be found that would have suited me so well as my dear Mr. W," Betsy confided to her journal five years later.[116] In 1782 Lund started building their house on a farm he named Hayfield, and three years after that, Washington deeded them the property.[117]

Yet there were also disappointments. The couple lost two infant daughters, leaving them childless. "Give me patience O'Lord to submit to Thy Will as I ought," Betsy wrote in her journal after one of the deaths.[118] In 1789, when George and Martha Washington were about to leave for New York where he was to assume the presidency, it occurred to Martha to leave their two wards, Jackie Custis's younger children, behind with the Lund Washingtons as a way of comforting them. No sooner had she reached New York, however, than letters began to arrive from the children, complaining about the long stretches of time they were made to spend on their knees in prayer. Finally, the Washingtons grew concerned enough to send for them.[119]

Lacking children of her own to lead in religious devotions, Betsy turned to her slaves. "But they do not seem fond of it," she admitted. She also tried to teach them to read. Still, she felt uncomfortable with her slaves and found it impossible to discipline them. "Few would put up with their servants doing so little as mine . . . I can not get them to do more without scolding & whipping & I can not do either."[120] Neither, apparently, could Lund.

Despite the trials Betsy met, however, she remained completely content with her marriage. "Nothing but perfect peace & harmony reigns in our habitation." Lund even seemed to adopt her rather stern moral convictions. "There can be no one who dispises drinking more than he does . . . he hates to see any one tippling at the grog or toddy through the day."[121] But happy marriages cannot solve every problem. Soon after retiring from Mount Vernon, Lund's sight began to fail, and for the last seven years of his life, he slowly went blind. "My poor dear Mr. Washington for near a year has been extremely afflicted," commented Betsy in 1792, adding "I doubt anyone else would strive to walk alone, but himself."[122] Finally, in July 1797, Lund's struggles came to an end. "Thou my gracious Lord has thought fit to take the dear partner and companion of my life from me—after being seven years in the furnace of affliction," wrote his grieving wife.[123]

Characteristically, Lund never complained about his plight. In the same spirit during the war he had shouldered in Washington's behalf a great deal more than a "common" manager would have taken on. In return, despite the occasional bursts of temper, he had earned Washington's deepest gratitude. "Nothing but that entire confidence which I reposed, could have enabled me . . . to have given not only my time but my whole attention to the public concerns of this country," his "affectionate friend" had written at one point.[124] But for Lund there never seemed to be any question about the path he would follow when Washington left for Cambridge in 1775. He would serve.

Like Washington, too, he realized that the world he knew had changed as a result of the Revolution, and on one point in particular he was determined to acknowledge the change. Washington had written of his desire "to get clear" of his slaves; Lund meant to do exactly that. In his will, he stipulated that all his slaves should be freed.[125]

———

John Patterson, Going Lanphier, and Lund Washington: three men, each of whom played a large role in the making of George Washington's Mount Vernon. Two of them, John Patterson and Lund Washington, served him well, leaving Going Lanphier the odd man out, the gritty individual who insisted on putting his own interests before his employer's. Yet the calculus that arranges the three stories this way almost certainly misses the point.

Lanphier's intransigence can be explained in a variety of ways. Stubborn by nature, he was the product of a family tradition of independence. He also lived in a world that was itself undergoing a violent revolt against established authority. Even if he was a Tory, loyalty to the crown could hardly have screened out all the social and intellectual ferment of those years. George Washington was commander of the revolutionary forces; he was as well an aloof and demanding employer, and he was rich. Could political opposition and social grievance have combined with family tradition in Lanphier's mind to fix him in the posture Lund found so infuriating? Possibly.

In contrast, it is easy to see Lund himself and John Patterson fitting comfortably into the traditional mold of deference and dependence. There, too, qualifications are in order, however. For all his diligence and reliability, Patterson was ready enough to break out of the ordered regularity of his life when the chance for something better offered itself. Too ready, it turned out.

Lund's case was even more shot through with contradictions. He served Washington with an almost spiritual selflessness, but when it came to exercising authority over others, he balked. He could not hound Washington's tenants for rent. At Hayfield, he and Betsy found themselves unable to discipline their slaves. Finally, at the end of his life, by freeing those same slaves, he cut through the chain of interlocking dependencies in the most dramatic way imaginable. Here, truly, was a revolutionary act of the first order.[126]

Going Lanphier, then, was not the only rebel among the three individuals on whom Washington had most relied to carry out his plans for Mount Vernon. Taking them in chronological order, too, there was a steadily escalating force to their assaults on the traditional order of things. And with each step, climaxing with Lund's bold gesture, the process moved closer to Washington himself. That the world had changed and was continuing to change, he well knew. What his own responsibilities were in that situation may have been less clear, but Lund's decision to free his slaves posed the question with stunning clarity.

THE USES OF
A GREAT HOUSE

MOUNT VERNON was built to be used. As its builders labored to give substance to Washington's plans, that fact probably seemed so elementary that it went unmentioned, even by Washington himself. On the other hand, asking exactly how the rebuilt house and its altered grounds were to be used would have produced no single, clear-cut answer, for Mount Vernon had multiple uses, always.

One of its primary functions was to provide an appropriate setting for Washington's encounters with the endless parade of people who found their way to his doorstep, and in that sense his "home" had a decidedly public character. Yet layered in with its public uses were others, in their own way just as important. For forty years, with some significant interruptions, Mount Vernon was where George and Martha Washington lived together as husband and wife. Also, through all that time, it was never out of Washington's mind. Even when he was away, visions of it proliferated constantly in his thoughts. All too often the reality belied his imaginings, but thinking about the house and the land, planning improvements in them, and putting his thoughts and plans on paper were clearly things he enjoyed doing, at times needed to do.

A public place, a private place, and a vital part of George Washington's inner life: Mount Vernon was all of these. And all three were altered forever by the fame he earned beyond Mount Vernon as well as by the events that brought him that fame. They also continued to change in new and unforeseen ways as he moved from retirement back to public life as president, then home again for the last time.

Of all the twists and turns, however, none would be more surprising than the course he charted in the summer of 1799, when he sat down to write out his last will and testament. Most wills are about transmission, perpetuation; Washington's was designed—finally and irrevocably—to mark endings.

CHAPTER 9

At Home and Away, 1788–1799

In February 1787, in the midst of considering whether to attend the constitutional convention called for later that year in Philadelphia, Washington wrote his mother a longish letter about her future. Relations between the two had never been smooth. Mary Washington continued to live in Fredericksburg but managed her affairs badly and now was suffering from cancer. Over the years Washington had done what he could, often with thinly veiled impatience, to help keep her domestic establishment afloat. Eventually he had persuaded her to move to a smaller house in town, yet given the state of her health he had come to feel even that might be too much. Enclosing fifteen guineas—which he claimed was all the cash he had on hand—and recounting at length his past generosity to her, he urged her to consider renting out her property, including her slaves, to bring in steady income. After that, he believed, she ought to "break up housekeeping" and go live with one of her children. He then went on to offer her a home at Mount Vernon but simultaneously explained why such an arrangement could not possibly work.

> My House is at your service, & [I] would press you most sincerely & most devoutly to accept it, but I am sure, and candour requires me to say it will never answer your purposes in any shape whatsoever—for in truth it may be compared to a well resorted tavern, as scarcely any strangers who are going from north to south, or from south to north do not spend a day or two at it.[1]

Whatever Mary Washington thought of her son's advice, she did not descend on Mount Vernon to live, nor on any of her other children's houses. She died two years later in Fredericksburg, in her own bed. And certainly she would not have been comfortable at Mount Vernon: Washington was right about that. In the years after the Revolution, the house was perpetually full of company—it was no place for an ill, elderly woman apparently none too concerned about her personal appearance or cleanliness.

Yet Washington's words could equally well have described Mount Vernon at any point in its history. For like all gentry houses in Virginia, it was in some ways a very public place, which in turn is likely to seem odd to a modern consciousness. In our experience, houses have become private preserves devoted to family life. By the same token, any entertaining done "at home" is most often an intimate affair, with few if any public connotations. In eighteenth-century Virginia, however, houses were places of business as well as centers of family life, and that included the houses of the gentry, since the business of getting, keeping, and exercising power went on constantly at home. When Washington welcomed visitors to his home, he was welcoming fellow burgesses, fellow justices of the county court, fellow vestrymen, voters in local elections, influential citizens from other colonies, people bringing information he needed, people who owed him money, and people to whom he owed money. As a rule they were social equals, but even if they were not, it behooved him to treat them as such. So his door was always open, and his table was always full—even before he became a great and famous man.[2]

It has been estimated that during the seven years between 1768 and 1775 roughly two thousand people were entertained at Mount Vernon, many of whom stayed for days on end and visited repeatedly.[3] In April 1774, a typical month, an average of four to five guests joined the Washingtons every time they sat down to dinner. Guests were present all but five days of the month. Twice the couple dined at other houses in the neighborhood, which reduced to three the number of times they were, as Washington noted in his diary, "At home all day alone." Two thirds of the people who came to dinner also spent at least one night in the house, and thus had to be given tea and breakfast as well. The largest number of people at a single dinner was eleven, all of whom stayed the night.[4]

A majority of the month's guests fell, in roughly equal proportions, into one of three categories: family members, neighbors and friends, and business associates of Washington's. Martha's sister, Anna Maria Dandridge Bassett, and her family visited for fourteen days in the middle of the month and were part of that large dinner party of eleven. So was Washington's brother, John Augustine, who stayed at Mount Vernon afterward for two nights, on the second of which the company was joined by Warner Washington, a cousin who had married a Fairfax. The friends and neighbors were mostly local landowners and hunting companions but also included George Mason, a close political ally of Washington's. Among the business associates were several merchants from Alexandria active in the wheat trade and at least two others from as far away as Philadelphia, one of whom, William Milnor, bought fish from Washington and was renting a new fish house that had just been built at Mount Vernon.

The shad were running on the river that month, and on several occasions Washington took his guests to the fish landings to watch the catch being hauled in. There were also trips to Pohick Church and Alexandria, and in the middle of the month Washington spent a day hunting. Compared with these rather modest amusements, dinner must often have been the most interesting event of the day, a fact underscored by Washington's careful enumeration in his diary of those present. And making a house party of it, with the guests spending the night, would have provided yet another way of varying the daily routine.

In a physical sense, the patterns of public life at Mount Vernon were set when Washington planned his first rebuilding of the house. The passage, the west parlor, and the din-

Table set for tea in the west parlor of Mount Vernon. Courtesy of the Mount Vernon Ladies' Association.

ing room remained "best" rooms, spaces set aside for receiving and entertaining company as long as he lived. To complement their richly expressed, academically correct classical decoration, they contained the best, most expensive furniture: mahogany chairs in the passage; a carpet, a couch, mahogany chairs, and a tea table in the west parlor; a mahogany dining table, side tables, and chairs in the dining room. The evidence also indicates that the Washingtons replaced a fair amount of this furniture through the years, presumably with newer, more stylish pieces. The colors of the rooms, too, were changed, becoming generally darker and richer over time.[5]

The most important function of the passage was receiving visitors as they entered the house. Often this would be done by servants, who would either ask people to wait or show them to another room, depending on who they were and what their business was. In Virginia, passages also served as informal entertaining areas, especially in the summer, when the breeze blowing through them offered welcome relief from the heat. Dancing was another activity passages could accommodate, and if necessary additional tables could be set up in them for dining.[6]

Of the three rooms—passage, west parlor, and dining room—the parlor was the most lavishly finished and decorated. Here company would gather at appropriate times during the day, and here occurred that most vital social ritual: the serving and drinking of tea in the late afternoon. With family portraits lining the walls and the Washington coat of arms topping the chimneypiece, the room was, in effect, a shrine of family honor and prestige. Present in paint on canvas and wood, if not in the flesh, were the Washingtons as they meant to appear to the world at large—gracious and sociable but also formal and correct and very much in control of their surroundings, as indeed Washington looks in the 1772 Peale portrait that hung in the room to the end of his life.[7]

As it emerged from Washington's first rebuilding of the house, the dining room was more plainly finished than either the passage or the west parlor, but the new chimneypiece and ceiling added during the second rebuilding changed that. Dining rooms had just begun to appear in Virginia houses of the grander sort during Washington's boyhood, and their spread indicates how important the daily formal serving of meals became in gentry households. Guests were invariably present as well as family members, and to break up days that began and ended early, dinner was served in midafternoon. The timing of the meal also made it possible for those who lived nearby to get home before dark, though doing justice to the occasion could take several hours, as course followed course. The display of such abundance was an important part of the ritual, with fully prepared food often placed in the center of the table and around the room for purely decorative purposes.[8] One visitor recalled the menu at Mount Vernon as follows:

> Leg [of] boil[ed] pork, top [*head of the table*]; goose, bot [*at the foot of the table*]; roast beef, round cold boil[ed] beef, mutton chops, hommony, cabbage, potatoes, pickles, fried tripe, onions, etc. Table cloth wiped [*crumbs brushed off*] mince pies, tarts, cheese. . . nuts apples, raisins.[9]

In addition, of course, there would have been an abundance of liquid refreshment. (One is reminded of the outrageously expensive case with its sixteen large glass bottles that Robert Cary sent from England on Washington's orders.)

With Washington's second rebuilding of the house, the piazza and the new room joined the existing ground-floor rooms as settings for both formal and informal entertaining. Weather permitting, tea was regularly served on the piazza, and the new room was obviously planned with dining and dancing in mind. In England large "saloons" or "great rooms" had become a common feature of aristocratic houses by 1750, though not always with happy results, as Isaac Ware noted in his *Complete Body of Architecture,* published in 1756:

> In houses which have been some time built, and which have not an out of proportion room the common practice is to build one to them: this always hangs from one end, or sticks to one side, of the house, and shews to the most careless eye, that, though fastened to the walls, it does not belong to the building.[10]

Whatever their aesthetic failings, such rooms represented a definite loosening of the bonds of strict formality in the social realm. Designed for large-scale social gatherings—

The Washington family and Lafayette at Mount Vernon, by Thomas Pritchard and Louis R. Mignot. This mid-nineteenth-century depiction of the great men and the Washington family relaxing on the piazza is not without Victorian touches; still, it represents fairly accurately the informal social life made possible by the piazza. Courtesy of the Metropolitan Museum of Art, bequest of William Nelson.

what Ware called "routs"—they were meant to hold many more people at once than would have been entertained in the state rooms of earlier classical-style houses. Routs were by no means completely democratic, but they did betoken a drift in that direction, and in relatively short order the fashion spread to America.[11] In the 1750s the Governor's Palace in Williamsburg acquired both a ballroom and a large supper room that no doubt served as progenitors for Mount Vernon's new room. But unlike those rooms, which lay at the rear of the Palace and had to be entered through the hall and central passage, Washington's new room was located at one end of the house, where it could be entered directly from the outside.[12] (It was also better integrated into the structure than the rooms Ware described so unflatteringly.)

When meals were served in the new room, boards were set up on saw horses to serve as tables. Except at those times, the furniture, including the chairs, would have been lined up against the walls. No doubt this was the arrangement in the other ground-floor, public spaces as well, for even in highly specialized rooms, a certain amount of flexibility remained desirable. Most furniture was relatively light, so it could be moved from place to place within rooms as the need arose, a sensible practice at a time when central heating and cheap, clean sources of artificial illumination were undreamed-of luxuries.

After the Revolution, the constant coming and going of visitors at Mount Vernon resumed almost immediately. There were differences, however. Before the war Washington had chosen his guests; now they came whether he invited them or not, and often the group around the table at dinner included people he had never met before. Some arrived on specific errands, others made their way up the drive out of pure curiosity; many were individuals who themselves cut a large figure in the world. But high or low, famous or not, they all had to be received with appropriate courtesy.

In time, too, as the numerous surviving accounts of visits to Mount Vernon indicate, Washington developed a system for handling guests. Rising at five in the morning, he worked in his study until seven. At that point he joined his visitors and the rest of the household for breakfast, then went off alone on horseback to oversee work on one or more of the outlying farms. While he was away, it fell either to aides or to younger family members to amuse visitors. Most often they were given tours of the house and grounds, which seem to have been accompanied by a more or less standard running commentary, for the same facts appear again and again in the accounts—a few details about the history of the house, the dimensions of the new room and the piazza, the size of the estate, the number of slaves, something about their treatment, lists of plant species and livestock, the number of acres owned elsewhere by Washington. At two in the afternoon Washington returned and changed for dinner, which was at three. Tea was at six, and usually no supper at all was served. After bidding their guests good night, the Washingtons retired at nine.[13]

On the standard tour, some parts of the house were bypassed completely. Not one of the visitors who left accounts mentioned having seen the Washingtons' bedchamber, for example. So it was possible to maintain a certain level of privacy. Similarly, Washington continued to be able to limit access to himself, either by retreating to his study or by riding off on plantation business. Most visitors, in fact, saw him only at meals and, if he chose, for brief periods afterward. Conversation at the table could be lively or slow, depending on his mood and, one suspects, his interest in the company present. The topic that seemed to appeal to him most was farming. Occasionally he would reminisce about the past. Contemporary politics were not discussed.

In all of this one senses a great deal of careful management. Thanks to his routine, Washington succeeded in preserving at least half of each day for his own purposes, even when visitors were present. Without undue awkwardness, some parts of the house remained off-limits to the curious. Keeping his innermost thoughts to himself, too, was a skill Washington had long since elevated to a minor art form. In each of these ways he could and did control the extent to which visitors impinged on his life and on the life of the rest of the household. On the essential point there was little if anything he could do, however. People had to be shown what they had come to see: the great hero of the Revolution, retired at last from his labors, with nothing more pressing on his mind than the business of everyday life.

Yet in reality Washington's situation was hardly that simple. If he was obliged to transform his private life into a perpetual performance for the touring public, surely the performance itself was a public act. Where, then, did the boundary lie? What was public and what was not, or had the two simply flowed together in a formless muddle? And this in the house that Washington had twice rebuilt as a palpable expression of his personal independence, his freedom. Yet plainly he felt that nothing less was demanded of him. By retiring to Mount Vernon he had proved that great power, assumed in the service of the people, could be relinquished when the need for it had passed.[14] Now it fell to him to demonstrate that he could be content amid the quiet delights of life at home, and for that there had to be witnesses to observe him and to describe what they had seen. Hence the general welcome extended to the world at large. And on top of everything else, Washington was required to compose the entire performance from scratch. Others might talk of Cincinnatus; he never did. Even less could he pattern his days on the gossamer stuff of classical allusion. Here too, as in so much else, he was first, without predecessor or peer, on the stage of history.

Such was life under Washington's vine and fig tree. Was he happy with it? The question is not one he was likely to have asked himself. Most visitors found him good-humored, if rather reserved. The pleasures Mount Vernon afforded were real enough, and if his existence there was interpreted as he hoped it would be, he could see it as a genuine service to the nation. He was also able to continue work on the house and grounds and had the satisfaction of seeing his plans for them come to fruition. At times there were signs of darker moods, but only rarely did anything resembling frustration or impatience disturb his outward calm, as when at one point he testily referred to "the expensive manner in which I am as it were involuntarily compelled to live."[15]

And certainly expense was an issue. Many people who arrived at Mount Vernon may have expected to find in Washington the consummate model of republican restraint, but most of them probably hoped for something more expansive when it came to the arrangements for guests. They were not disappointed. The Washingtons had always entertained amply, and that continued, though Washington did worry constantly about money. By the end of the war his income had dropped to virtually nothing, and the first few years of peace brought little improvement. In 1787, in the same letter in which he told his mother she ought not to plan to live at Mount Vernon, he claimed to have "made no Crops" for the past two years. "In the first I was obliged to buy Corn and this year have none to sell, and my wheat is so bad I can neither eat it myself nor sell it to others, and Tobaca I make none." In other quarters, too, he found himself equally hard pressed. "Those who owe me money cannot or will not pay it without Suits." He was trying to sell some of his land but refused to do so if it meant "taking much less than the lands I have offered for sale are worth."[16]

The truth was, of course, that Washington was still a very rich man. What he lacked was cash, but for entertaining guests at Mount Vernon not much of that was needed. Most of the food was grown on the plantation, even though certain choice items, such as butter, had a way of suddenly disappearing, despite the fact that Washington owned more than a hundred cows.[17] He suspected the slaves were at fault. Yet Mount Vernon's slaves also made an absolutely essential contribution to the hospitality he dispensed so open-handedly: they did the work, and again minimal amounts of cash were involved.

So for all his grumbling, Washington was in no danger of being bankrupted by his guests. However, those same guests did serve to deepen even further his dependence on slavery, which amounted to a cost of a different sort, and one that must have seemed hardly less disturbing.

—

As hedged with complexity as it was, the public character of Mount Vernon had little in common, at least at first glance, with its private side. Full of guests or not, the house was the center of the Washingtons' life together. Over the years they lived in many different places but called no other home.

Mount Vernon was also where two generations of Custis children grew to maturity. After Jackie Custis died, cutting off the first generation, the Washingtons adopted his two youngest children, George Washington Parke Custis ("Wash") and Eleanor Parke Custis ("Nelly"). As a result, except for the years just before the Revolution, there were always young children in the house. Yet the children were not Washington's. How the couple dealt, together and separately, with the fact that their marriage was barren can only be imagined. For Washington the sense of deprivation, and quite possibly failure, must have been acute. As kind and thoughtful as she seems to have been, Martha would surely have done whatever she could to ease his pain, but she also devoted herself to nurturing her children and grandchildren with a passion that sometimes seemed to leave room for little else. She made them, if not the center of her life, the focus of unending worry and concern, and she indulged them with something approaching abandon.[18]

Washington responded very differently to his responsibilities as a stepparent and stepgrandparent. He managed the children's financial affairs (being careful to transfer to his own account whatever was due him for their expenses). He spent considerable time overseeing the boys' education, choosing their schools and eventually their colleges. He also tried to impose a certain amount of discipline on them, though with no great success. Jackie Custis seems to have been especially adept at eluding control. One of his teachers claimed never to have known anyone "so exceedingly indolent or so surprizingly voluptuous: one wd suppose Nature had intended Him for some Asiatic Prince."[19]

In all of this Washington can be seen as playing the role of traditional paterfamilias. It was the role he had watched his own father play, sending his sons off to England to be educated even before they reached their teenage years. Nor were Washington's relations with his mother such as to demonstrate the value of a more intimate approach to parenthood. Mary Washington professed to care deeply about her children, but she was demanding, difficult, and overprotective. Of course, Washington could have followed Martha's example, which as it happened had much in common with newer, less restrictive methods of childrearing being practiced by many of Virginia's leading families.[20] Yet clearly he chose not to do so. Neither did he seem interested in endowing the young Custises imaginatively with his own paternity. They were not his children, and he would not (or could not) pretend otherwise.

Washington's inability to share Martha's feelings for her children meant that their marriage lacked one of the bonds that customarily unites couples, but through the years the two formed other, equally strong ties. Good-natured and unpretentious, she was an accomplished hostess who quickly put people at ease, creating a more relaxed social

Jackie and Patsy Custis, Martha Washington's children. Courtesy of The Washington/ Custis/Lee Collection, Washington and Lee University, Lexington, Virginia.

atmosphere around him than he could achieve himself. While he was president it was an open secret that he preferred her teas to his own notoriously stiff "levées."[21] At Mount Vernon, because he was so often away from the house supervising work being done elsewhere on the plantation, it frequently fell to Martha to entertain guests, and she did the honors with a cheerful graciousness regularly noted in letters and diaries. The architect Benjamin Latrobe wrote of her "good humored free manner that was extremely pleasing and flattering."[22] "She has something very charming about her," commented Polish Army officer Julian Niemcewicz, who mentioned as well her "gay manner" and "bright eyes."[23] And of all he found at Mount Vernon, Joshua Brookes, a young Englishman, wrote, "Mrs. Washington and Miss Custis pleased me most, especially the former."[24]

If Martha Washington brought to the couple's public activities the warmth and intimacy of private life, Washington in return gave her a public life full of interest and significance. He also helped her fashion, as he had himself, a persona suitable for that life. On meeting her, Abigail Adams commented: "She received me with great ease and polite-

Miniature of Martha Washington late in life, painted by James Peale. Courtesy of the Mount Vernon Ladies' Association.

ness. She is plain in her dress, but that plainness is the best of every article. . . . Her hair is white, her teeth beautiful. . . . Her manners are modest and unassuming, dignified and feminine, not a tincture of hauteur about her."[25] And later: "Mrs. Washington is one of those unassuming characters which create love and esteem. . . . I found myself much more deeply impressed than I ever did before their Majesties of Britain."[26] However, the same woman who so impressed Abigail Adams never really mastered English grammar and spelling, at least on paper. The letters she wrote friends and relatives are lively and engaging, but in some circles her usual epistolary performance was likely to prove embarrassing. The solution, which seems to have been perfectly agreeable to her, was to have Washington draft those letters intended for people of consequence in the larger world (including Abigail Adams), after which Martha carefully copied his words in her own hand.[27]

The letters produced in this way were more or less free of error, and not surprisingly, they also tended to express sentiments Washington himself repeatedly uttered. Thus Mercy Otis Warren—the wife of the hero of the Battle of Bunker Hill and a woman with a keen sense of what it meant to stand before the bar of history—was told soon after Martha took up her duties as First Lady of her strong "predilictions for privet life," a point on which "the generals feelings" and her own were "perfectly in unison." It seemed unfortunate, therefore, the letter continued, "that I, who had much rather be at home should occupy a place with which a great many younger and gayer women would be prodigiously pleased. . . . I [know] too much of the vanity of human affairs to expect felicity from the splendid scenes of public life." Nonetheless she described herself as "determined to be cheerful and to be happy in whatever situation I may be."[28]

With such phrases was Martha Washington transformed into a model republican matron. Did they in fact express her feelings? Perhaps. But she could also declare, and not for public consumption, "vegetable [sic] is the best part of our living in the country."[29] No doubt the remark was intended as a joke, but it is the sort of joke one would expect from a sophisticated urbanite. Before she married George Washington, Martha Custis owned a house in Williamsburg as well as a plantation nearby and thus had lived very much at the center of things in Virginia. Privately, too, during those first few months as First Lady, she complained not of being away from Mount Vernon, but of being unable to go about New York as she wished. "I live a very dull life hear and know nothing that passes in the town—I never goe to the publick place—indeed I think I am more like a state prisoner than anything else, there is certain bounds set for me which I must not depart from."[30]

In later life Martha Washington read several newspapers a day, and the spirited charge Edmund Pendleton remembered her giving her son as Washington was about to set out for the First Continental Congress, suggests that she was fully conversant with public affairs. And this may well have been the closest bond of all between the two. Washington had few close friends with whom he could share his thoughts, but he had a wife who was sympathetic, understanding, and discreet. It would be surprising if he had not confided in her. Moreover, the way he configured the spaces in his second rebuilding of Mount Vernon seems to point to just such a relationship. Each of the Washingtons had a separate room at the south end of the house, his study below and "Mrs. Washington's" chamber above. But there was also easy communication between the two rooms via the small stairway in the adjacent passage, a stairway visible from nowhere else in the house.

Another clue to the Washingtons' relationship is the fate of their correspondence. After his death Martha burned all but two of their letters to each other. Whether she took the step on her own initiative or because he had asked her to is unclear. It has been suggested that she did so in what amounted to a fit of pique—"a possessive reaction to having been forced to share her husband so extensively with the public."[31] This seems unlikely. Martha Washington was not a vindictive person. The letters she and Washington had written to one another were part of the life they had shared away from public scrutiny. One imagines she destroyed them, if not at his request, knowing that it would have been his preference as much as it was hers. More than likely, too, in addition to being intimate and personal, the letters contained candid remarks about public events and personalities. And if they did, might they not also have cast the Washingtons in a rather different light from the one they took such care to train on themselves most of the time? If Martha Washington, longing for the forbidden delights of New York City, could joke in a letter to a friend about being a state prisoner, what feelings did she confide to Washington and he to her? Did she really miss Mount Vernon all that much when she was away? Did he? They both claimed to, certainly, but when duty called they left, time and again.

The Washingtons' bedchamber, Mount Vernon. Courtesy of the Mount Vernon Ladies' Association.

They also returned when duty required it, and in retirement Washington needed Martha every bit as much as he did in the larger world. Yet without children and the constant demands they made on her time and energy, there was less for her to do at Mount Vernon than away from it. In that sense, the death of Jackie Custis made it possible for her to establish, just as she was returning after the Revolution, a second family at Mount Vernon by bringing to it two of his children. At various times, too, the circle was enlarged even further with the addition of one or more of Washington's young nephews.

For Washington, however, nothing had changed. The children who played on the lawns at Mount Vernon and learned their lessons from the tutors he hired, who rode the ponies he bought for them and dined at his table when their manners were good enough to pass muster, were not his own. He remained a thoughtful, conscientious stepgrandfather and uncle, but in the end he could not fill his days, or his heart, as Martha did with the pleasures of childrearing. He needed something else.

And what filled the void was Mount Vernon itself. Growing and changing over the years at his direction, it was never far from the center of his consciousness. He dreamed of owning the entire point of land around it, and in time, piece by piece, he acquired it. He imagined different houses—initially a grander one, then something more emblematic of the particular virtues to which he aspired—and he transformed the modest dwelling that had come to him from his forebears into those houses. He envisioned fresh landscapes—quite formal at first, then softer, more natural—and the earth itself and the trees on it were made to conform to his visions. Through it all, too, his involvement was direct, immediate, and personal. It even extended to the people who worked for and with him on his creation. He had dreams for them as well and tried to direct their lives as he thought best. In that respect his efforts met with only limited success, but he never stopped trying.

Nor was Washington's passionate involvement with Mount Vernon something he and Martha shared, or so the evidence suggests. In some areas her influence was obvious. She had opinions about the colors and fabrics used inside the house; she took an interest in the china and glassware ordered for the dining room. She superintended the making of slaves' clothing, a task that became considerably more complicated once it was decided to use as little imported cloth as possible. She may have had some interest in the gardens, and she oversaw the day-to-day running of the house, its cleaning, and the preparation of meals, though eventually with a housekeeper working under her. For the rest, she seems to have been content to leave things in Washington's hands, even to the point of not discussing with him major changes he was planning on the house. When she gave directions to have their bedchamber finished "plain," for example, the inconvenience of waiting longer for the room to be completed was apparently uppermost in her mind; he might have made a different choice. Similarly, when the new outbuildings were going up in 1776, not knowing what uses he planned for them, she assumed—incorrectly, as it turned out—that the one immediately to the north was to be a laundry house instead of the "Servants Hall" he had in mind.[32]

Of such accommodations was the Washingtons' marriage constructed. She had not been the great love of his youth; Sally Fairfax was. He had needed money, and she was rich; she had been a widow with two small children to raise, and he was an eligible bachelor. Still, for forty years they lived together contentedly, and through a maelstrom of events that left their world totally transformed, in no small part through his agency.

In the midst of it all, however, one question remained for which there was no ready answer: what was to become of Mount Vernon after the Washingtons died? It might have seemed logical to leave it to the Custis grandchildren, but they were already well off, and their wealth would increase on Martha's death. Also, they were not, by blood, members of the family that had owned the property for four generations.

If consanguinity became the criterion, there was at least a large cohort of nieces and nephews to choose from, and two who seemed to have particularly strong claims. Washington's first manager at Mount Vernon had been his younger brother Jack (John Augustine Washington), and at the time it was understood between them that if Washington did not survive the French and Indian War, Jack would inherit Mount Vernon. Afterward the two brothers remained close, and though Jack died in 1787, his oldest son, Bushrod, was much admired by Washington and later became a close political ally.[33]

An even likelier candidate to inherit Mount Vernon was another nephew, George Augustine, the oldest son of Washington's brother Charles. Not only had he served with distinction in the Continental Army, he also had taken over Lund Washington's duties as manager of Mount Vernon in 1785. That year, too, he married Martha's niece, Frances (Fanny) Bassett, duplicating the Washington–Dandridge ties represented in the Washingtons' own union. And to his credit, George Augustine proved to be an unusually able manager.³⁴

But if Washington were to single out one of his nephews as his heir, how would it strike the rest of the Washington clan, not to mention the Custises? Also, by the time he left to assume the presidency there were already signs of the tragedy that would eventually overtake George Augustine, for he was suffering from tuberculosis. As in Lawrence Washington's case, the progress of the disease would be relatively slow, but no less inexorable. The end finally came in 1793. Thus the question of Mount Vernon's long-term future remained unresolved, even as the ever-changing picture of all he hoped to see it become continued to fill Washington's mind.

In the darkest days of the Revolution, that mental picture of Mount Vernon had provided Washington with a much-needed source of relief, a refuge from the trials that seemed to multiply around him constantly. It was to perform exactly the same function through the eight long years of his presidency. If the pressures and tensions of that time were different from those he had encountered as a commander in the field, in their own way they were just as harrowing.

Characteristically, Washington had agonized over whether to accept the presidency, but with entreaties pouring in from every side and his political friends arguing in unison that the survival of the republic depended on his acceptance, he prepared to leave Mount Vernon and take up this latest burden. On April 14, 1789, when he received formal notification of his election in a brief ceremony in the new room, all the necessary arrangements had already been made. Two days later he set out for New York, and Martha left the following month. By the time they were reunited, the inauguration was behind him, and he had become, however reluctantly, president of the United States.

In most respects Washington's life as president differed dramatically from the one he had been leading for the past five years, but there were some similarities. As always he remained vitally interested in his material surroundings, in the stage on which he was to perform his duties, to use the theatrical imagery he so often did himself. The Cherry Street house that had been engaged as his official residence he found disappointingly small and not particularly handsome. By the beginning of the new year he had arranged to move to another, larger house on Broadway, and much time was spent visiting his new quarters, rearranging the furniture, improving the lighting, and ordering items such as a large carpet with a "Pea Green ground."³⁵

In general, in the arrangements he made for the several houses he occupied during his two terms as president, Washington self-consciously strove for a grander, more formal style than he used at Mount Vernon. In Philadelphia, for example, he had seen the Morrises and Binghams decorate the center of their dining tables with mirrored platforms instead of the dishes of meat traditionally placed there, and in New York the French and Spanish ministers followed the same fashion. The president ought to do likewise, Washington concluded, and he instructed Tobias Lear, his secretary, to write Clement Biddle in Philadelphia and ask about "those waiters, salvers or whatever they are called."³⁶ Biddle apparently knew what was wanted but could not find anything of the right size. The next

The "plateaux" ordered by Washington for his official residence as president, shown here with one of the porcelain figurines purchased at the same time to adorn it. Courtesy of the Mount Vernon Ladies' Association.

person to be approached, and with better success, was Gouverneur Morris, who was then in France on private business.[37] On Washington's behalf Morris purchased a set of "plateaux" (the proper term) complete with appropriate porcelain ornaments to place on them.[38] Washington was delighted. In thanking Morris he described the entire ensemble as "very elegant" and "much admired," which, after all, was the point.[39] But seven years later, when he was leaving office and tried to sell the plateaux, he found no buyers. Since they had been purchased with government funds, it was difficult to know what to do. Finally, Washington gave orders to have them packed up and shipped to Mount Vernon, where they languished in the attic.[40]

Meanwhile, there were more serious matters to be attended to during Washington's early months in office. An entire government had to be organized; people had to be chosen to fill positions in it; policies and procedures of all kinds had to be settled on. In retrospect it seems that much of this was well done. From the beginning, some people thought otherwise, however, and over time they became more outspoken, developing ultimately into a full-fledged opposition. In public Washington deplored the burgeoning "spirit of party"; privately he was saddened and felt betrayed by not a few of the opposition leaders. Still, he did his best to remain above the fray, even as his supporters organized their own forces to do battle with those proud Virginians and former protégés of Washington's, Thomas Jefferson and James Madison.[41]

There were and are many ways to explain the split between the Federalists and the Republicans. Conflicting personal ambitions played a part. Not all of the extraordinarily talented individuals conducting the new government could be equally influential, and only one of them could succeed Washington as president. Questions of foreign policy also became increasingly divisive as hostilities ricocheting outward from the French Revolution transformed the globe into a vast theater of war. With long-standing domestic issues unresolved as well, it sometimes seemed as if an unbridgeable gulf had opened in American life between "The Friends of Liberty" (or "Liscence," depending on one's point of view) and "The Friends of Order" (or "Tyranny"), a division that was as much cultural as political, as the terms themselves suggested.

In the beginning, however, it was specific questions of domestic policy that divided the governing circle, and what most bothered the administration's critics was the shape the new government seemed to be assuming in the hands of Washington's secretary of the treasury, Alexander Hamilton. For the instruments of government Hamilton favored were only too familiar: a large and more or less permanent national debt; a national bank; the vigorous promotion of manufactures by the national government; and a substantial military establishment, all to be paid for through a system of duties, collected in every port in the land, on goods imported from abroad. In time there would also be excise taxes on items like whiskey.

Examining the list, what Madison and others thought they saw was nothing less than the hated system Sir Robert Walpole had created seventy years earlier in England, and which more recently had been directed with such ruthless single-mindedness at crushing American liberties. In the spring of 1792, while Washington was making up his mind whether to serve a second term, he received a letter from Jefferson detailing in more than twenty numbered paragraphs his objections to the "system of policy" the federal government had thus far pursued. The size of the debt, the burdens imposed by taxes "and tax gathering," the banking system with its paper money and the "barren and useless" speculation it fostered, "the corruption of the legislature" by a growing "squadron of paper dealers," and the conviction that what these portended, finally, was "a change, from the present republican form of government to that of a monarchy; of which the British Constitution is to be the model." Such was the litany of grievances that Jefferson was already identifying as "republican."[42]

Copying Jefferson's paragraphs almost verbatim in his own hand, Washington sent them off without disclosing their source to Hamilton, requesting a response. By Hamilton's own admission, "some severity" crept into his reply, but he was adamant. "The project, from its absurdity refutes itself," he wrote of the charge that a plot was afoot to transform the national government into a monarchy, adding: "The truth unquestionably is, that the only path to subversion of the republican system of the country is by flattering the prejudices of the people, and exciting their jealousies and apprehensions, to throw affairs into confusion, and bring on civil commotion"—which, he implied, was exactly what Jefferson and his allies were doing.[43]

Determined to bring about some sort of reconciliation, Washington wrote both Jefferson and Hamilton later that summer from Mount Vernon expressing his "earnest wish and . . . fondest hope . . . that instead of wounding suspicions and irritable charges, there may be liberal allowances, mutual forbearances and temporising yieldings on *all sides*."[44] But it was not to be. Early in 1794 Jefferson left the government. By then party strife had escalated to the point where Washington himself was being openly attacked in the Republican press. Also, later that year it became necessary to send troops to western Pennsylvania to deal with violent resistance to the whiskey excise that had developed there.[45] On the diplomatic front, too, difficulties mounted. Having adopted a policy of neutrality in the war between France and its enemies, the administration found itself under increasing pressure, both from the combatants themselves and from the Republicans, whose sympathies lay strongly with the French. Then came the highly problematic treaty John Jay negotiated with Great Britain in the closing weeks of 1794. Instructed by Washington to address a wide range of issues, Jay ended by putting his signature to an agreement that conceded substantially more to the British than it gained in return.[46] When the terms were finally made public, a whirlwind of Republican protest ripped across the country. "[The treaty] has, in my opinion completely demolished the monarchical party here," declared Jefferson with obvious satisfaction.[47] The Senate had already ratified the treaty by the time its terms were released, however, and as little as he liked it himself, Washington concurred.

Eventually many Americans came to think better of Jay's handiwork, but for Washington the wounds inflicted by the conflicts of those years were too severe ever to heal fully. To read of the "royal pomp and parade" of his levées; to find himself described as the leader of the "monarchical party," or worse, to be accused of being little better than a traitor bent on delivering the republic into the hands of the British; to have his motives, his character, his honor, and his patriotism impugned day after day in publications like Philip Freneau's *National Gazette* and Benjamin Franklin Bache's *Aurora* was almost more than he could bear.[48] In his view, the Republican indictment was patently false, and anyone with any sense ought to recognize that fact. He had supported Hamilton's policies because they seemed likely to salvage the nation's credit and put its finances on solid footing—not to subvert the republic. He was no monarchist, and he certainly had no great fondness for the British. He honestly believed a strict and fair neutrality was the best foreign policy for the United States. In short, his opponents were wrong on every count.

Even with all the charges refuted, however, might there not still be buried in the mountain of error a kernel of truth? It is hard to imagine Washington not asking that question. His own sense of politics was too much shaped by the same fears reverberating through the Republican indictment for him to dismiss out of hand all his opponents said. Even if they were wrong about him and wrong about his motives, what about the consequences of his actions? Perhaps the new government did contain within it the seeds of tyranny. Most of the time Washington was more conscious of its weakness than its strength, but the future might tell a different story.

And along with the future, there was the past to think of—his own past. How had it happened that men with whom he had once been in absolute accord on political questions now appeared in the ranks of the opposition? He had counted as one of the early triumphs of his presidency Jefferson's willingness to serve as secretary of state, but by the time Jefferson left the government, relations between them were decidedly cool. Even more disheartening was the loss of George Mason's support. The two had been the closest of allies before the Revolution. Mason died in the autumn of 1792, but not before making his disapproval of the administration's course abundantly clear. While Jefferson's conduct could be put down to personal ambition, Mason had not the slightest interest in power or office. If ever someone's politics were disinterested, his were. How had he and Washington moved so far apart?[49]

One answer to that question was simply that Mason was wrong, just as Jefferson and the others were. Old and infirm, he did not see that a great deal had changed since the days of the Virginia Association, when the path of principled action—of virtue—had seemed so straight and true. But that amounted to saying virtue itself had changed, and how could that be? Virtue was permanent, unmovable, unchanging. For Washington and his opponents alike it remained the ultimate guide in public life. Had he, however unwittingly, sacrificed virtue to the demands of the moment, or worse still, to some personal need of his own? That was the judgment implicit in Mason's defection.

Yet given the choices Washington had made, there was no way to turn back, nor was he inclined to do so. Hamilton's policies had in fact rescued the nation's credit. The wisdom of neutrality was demonstrated daily by the reckless folly of those who opposed it. The basic direction of Washington's administration still seemed correct. And for any stubborn doubts that lingered he found, if not a remedy, at least a ready source of solace, when week after week he sat down to spin out on paper his visions of Mount Vernon, of home.

The routine hardly ever varied. Having told his managers and overseers to report weekly, Washington set aside several hours each Sunday for writing his replies and sending fresh instructions. The detail of the letters is extraordinary. In his printed works they regularly run to five or more pages. The only breaks in the torrent of requests, commands, admonitions, and advice came when he was actually at Mount Vernon. Otherwise the river of words rushed on, regardless of whatever matters of state may have been competing for his attention.

Thus in the autumn of 1792, in the midst of trying to heal the breach between Jefferson and Hamilton, Washington was writing Anthony Whiting, who had recently taken over as manager at Mount Vernon, about spreading gravel on the garden walks, planting trees, planting ivy around the icehouse, clearing fields, putting up pork, cutting "Vistoes" through the trees, getting in a supply of oyster shells for the following spring's building projects, keeping track of tools, and caring for sick slaves.[50] On the eve of his second inauguration, he sent instructions home about brickmaking; dealing with Thomas Green's drinking; repairing gates; clearing yet another "Visto" through the trees; and punishing "Matildas Ben," a young slave who had committed various unspecified "offenses."[51]

The following year, falling victim to the same fate that had overtaken George Augustine Washington, Anthony Whiting died of tuberculosis and was replaced by William Pearce, who proved to be the ablest of all Washington's managers. Still, week in and week out, the letters continued. On June 7, 1795, the day before the Jay Treaty went to the Senate, Pearce was asked to specify the precise dimensions of any plank or shingles he ordered; to inform Washington whether the slave cabins had been removed from two of the farms, as he had instructed; and to identify, if he could, and punish the slave who had been stealing from the meathouse. Pearce was also told to pay particular attention always to the way things looked. "I shall begrudge no reasonable expence that will contribute to the improvement and neatness of my Farms," Washington wrote, adding: "nothing pleases me more than to see them in good order, and every thing trim, handsome and thriving about them; nor nothing hurts me more than to find them otherwise."[52]

Coping with a never-ending barrage of such dicta must have been daunting. Read carefully, however, the letters do exhibit certain patterns. Over and over Washington stressed the importance of planning work carefully, of having the proper tools and materials on hand, of carrying projects through to completion before going on to something else. "In a word, let whatever you do, be well done," he wrote in January 1794. "Much labor and much time is saved by this means."[53] Accurately calculating the proper number of hands needed to do a particular job was also vital. Nor should workers be moved constantly from job to job. "More work will be done in the *sametime* when people are kept steadily at it, than when they are taken from, and return to it again." The point was to think as far ahead as possible. "If a person only sees, or directs from day to day what is to be done, business can never go on methodically or well."[54]

"System to all things is the soul of business."[55] If there was a single, overriding principle that Washington wished to see embodied in everything done at Mount Vernon, that was it. He was also fond of repeating two other maxims: "Many mickels make a muckel" and "A penny saved is a penny got."[56] The first was a warning to avoid small errors or compromises in quality because they had a way of multiplying; the second referred to the gains that resulted from not spending time, energy, or money that could have been saved under more careful systems of management.

All of which made Washington sound very like a modern corporate executive. When he quipped about muckels and pennies got, he was talking about quality control and cost-cutting. And when he urged William Pearce, in his initial letter of instructions, "to correct the abuses which have crept into all parts of my business, to arrange it properly and to reduce things to system,"[57] what he hoped to achieve was greater efficiency.

But modern business managers work to cut costs and maximize efficiency in order to maximize profits, and Washington well knew that Mount Vernon would never make him any richer than he was. Rather it was in the moral realm that efficiency assumed, for him, its greatest force. He abhorred waste and disorder; laziness and slovenliness cut to the very core of his being. Had he been in the habit of using words such as "evil" or "sin," these were the transgressions to which he would surely have applied them. When he spoke of "good rules" and "a regular system" as "the soul of every business," he meant exactly what he said. He was talking about salvation, or something very like it. To be efficient was to be good, to be virtuous.

During Washington's years as president he dreamed with particular intensity of two outward manifestations of efficiency that he wished to see at Mount Vernon. Both represented novel solutions to long-standing problems. One of them eventually appeared; the other never did.

In 1792 the crews began gathering materials for a large barn for threshing and storing wheat, to be built of wood on brick foundations at Dogue Run Farm. The plans, which survive in Washington's hand, show a highly innovative, sixteen-sided structure of two stories, fifty-two feet in diameter, with a central octagonal core and an inclined runway leading to the second story wide enough to accommodate teams of horses or oxen. The floor at that level was formed of heavy boards, spaced a fraction of an inch apart from one another. At threshing time wheat would be spread on the floor, and horses would be driven at a trot over the stalks, separating the grain, which would then sift through the spaces between the boards to the floor below, where it could be collected and stored.[58]

Visitors who saw Washington's "round barn" marveled at it. From his standpoint one of its chief advantages was the added security it would provide for Mount Vernon's principal cash crop. While construction was under way in the winter of 1793, he continually urged that it be pushed forward as quickly as possible, declaring at one point that "no building was ever more wanting, both for convenience, and to prevent the loss which I am sure is sustained by theft from the grain in the open yards."[59]

But even more important was the time Washington hoped his ingenious new barn would shave off the threshing process, and he had similar hopes for his other great agricultural enthusiasm of those years. In England, farmers had been relying on hedges for

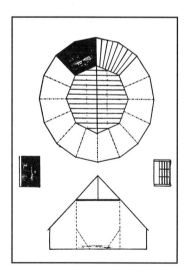 

Left: *Washington's design for the innovative, sixteen-sided "round" barn at Mount Vernon. Library of Congress.*

Right: *Mount Vernon's round barn photographed in a state of near-collapse about 1870. The building was demolished several years later. A reconstruction of it was completed in 1996. Courtesy of the Mount Vernon Ladies' Association.*

generations to fence their fields and meadows, and this was the system Washington now proposed to institute. The complicated crop rotation schedule he had adopted from the writings of British agricultural reformers required a great deal of fencing, and the amount of time his slaves spent building fences had always annoyed him, especially since the results were so inferior: shoddy constructions of posts "a strong man would break across his knee" and rails so thin as to be "unable to bear the weight of a Child."[60] Here was a solution. Instead of fences made of "dead" wood, mile upon mile of luxuriant English "live fences" would spread across Mount Vernon's broad acres.

The sense of urgency Washington brought to the subject was truly amazing. "Let me . . . in the strongest terms possible, call your attention to this business," he wrote Anthony Whiting at one point, "nothing is nearer, both to my interest and wishes; first, because it is indispensably necessary to save timber and labour; and secondly, because it is ornamental to the Farm and reputable to the Farmer."[61] And a month later: "I can never too often nor too strongly impress upon you [the need] to begin and make a business of rearing hedges, without the loss of a single season; for really there is no time to lose."[62] And two weeks after that: "As I have often, and often declared, this business of hedging must not be considered in the light of a secondary, or trifling, or an occasional thing; but on the contrary, as one of the first magnitude."[63]

Willows, honey locusts, and cedars were the plants Washington favored for live fences. Seedlings were to be set out in spring and fall, in shallow trenches specially dug for the purpose. As the young plants grew, they had to be weeded regularly to keep them from being overwhelmed by the surrounding vegetation. All of this, too, was to be done "with as much serious intention to execute it well, as . . . planting Corn, or sowing Wheat,"[64] for in time the effort would be fully repaid by the huge savings in labor that would result.

Moreover, the labor saved would be slave labor, which to Washington almost certainly mattered more than anything else. His aversion to slavery had only grown stronger over the years. "There is not a man living who wishes more sincerely than I do, to see a plan adopted for the abolition of it," he had written Robert Morris in 1786.[65] Yet the only "proper and effectual" means of doing so would be "by Legislative authority," and for the purposes of advocating such a step Washington found himself, as president, in an increasingly awkward position. The Republicans had made their greatest inroads in the South, and the least hint that he was trying to bring about the end of slavery was sure to weaken the Federalist cause even further in the region.

He could at least try to reduce his own dependence on slavery, however, which ultimately was what he hoped to achieve with projects such as the round barn and live fences. As worthwhile as that would be for its own sake, too, it had a corollary that was even more appealing. Amid the rising din of political conflict, what better way could there be of demonstrating his moral worth—of proving, perhaps most importantly to himself, that he was in fact a virtuous man—than by freeing Mount Vernon from the scourge of slavery? In the long run, of course, it would take more than live fences to do that, but they were a start.

Unfortunately, his campaign to establish hedgerows at Mount Vernon got nowhere. Despite his endless warnings about tending the plants, they regularly vanished into dense thickets of faster-growing weeds. Over the years there would be sporadic revivals of interest in the project, but the early months of 1793—just as the opposition to his administration was emerging into the open—marked the peak of Washington's passion for "live fences." After that his enthusiasm trailed off. At the same time, however, a far more radical solution to Mount Vernon's problems was forming in his mind.

In December 1793 Washington wrote the noted British agricultural reformer and author Arthur Young, asking for help in finding "substantial farmers, of wealth and strength" to lease four of the five farms at Mount Vernon. The rent would be a dollar an acre a year, and the leases could run for as long as ten years. The letter described each of the four farms in detail. Only the Mansion House Farm would be held back for Washington's own "residence, occupation and amusement in agriculture." If necessary he was prepared to rent to groups as well as individuals, even to divide the farms among several different renters. His primary concern was having "*good* farmers" as tenants. In explaining to Young why he had decided to rent the farms, he mentioned a desire to bring in regular income and "a wish to live free from care, and as much at my ease as possible" for the remainder of his life.[66]

But there was part of the story Young was not told. Along with his new plans for Mount Vernon, Washington had stepped up efforts to sell his western lands, and for both projects he gave Tobias Lear the same reasons he had given Young—plus one other, which he described as "more powerful than all the rest." With the added cash from the land sales and a fixed income from Mount Vernon, he hoped to be able to free his slaves, or as he put it, "to liberate a certain species of property which I possess, very repugnantly to my own feelings."[67]

Renting out four fifths of Mount Vernon and freeing its slaves! To let go of what he had spent a lifetime acquiring, building, and improving was for Washington a radical step, as he well knew. For the moment he wanted his intentions kept absolutely secret. In his letter to Lear he marked the sentence about freeing his slaves "Private," and he omitted it altogether from the copy kept at Mount Vernon. Still, the unthinkable had taken shape in his mind: he had conceived a vision of Mount Vernon dramatically unlike anything that had preceded it. And more than anything else his feelings about slavery had brought him to that point.

In an earlier letter to Arthur Young discussing the cost of agricultural labor in America, Washington had compared the "hired labor" used in the North and the "black Servants" who constituted the bulk of the southern workforce. White labor was more expensive than in other countries, he wrote, "whilst blacks, on the contrary, are cheaper," especially those owned by the wealthy, who, he candidly admitted, were "not always as kind, and as attentive to their [slaves'] wants and usage as they ought to be," often feeding them "upon bread alone." But if slave labor cost less, it had the disadvantage of being less satisfactory than free labor in other ways. "Blacks are capable of much labour, but having (I am speaking generally) no ambition to establish a *good* name, they are too regardless of a *bad* one; and of course, require more of the masters eye than the former."[68]

Washington's point about slaves' inability to establish a "good name" was one he made on several occasions. It reflected his fundamental understanding of human behavior, and it represented his mature sense of slavery's greatest single flaw as a system of labor. People strove to do well in life to win the respect of others, or so he believed, and certainly that was true of his own behavior. But slaves had no opportunity to win respect or earn good reputations; hence their lack of "ambition" and the inferior quality of their work. Who could tell what they might not accomplish as freemen? The question seemed implicit in Washington's line of reasoning, and it was a question remarkably free of the usual racist assumptions of his society.

The poor work habits of unmotivated slaves also spread like a contagion to the rest of the Mount Vernon labor force, even those in the most responsible positions. Describing to William Pearce what he expected of Thomas Green's replacement, Washington stressed that he wanted the new man "cautioned against an error which I have felt no small inconvenience from; and that is that . . . they will fall into the slovenly mode of executing work which is practiced by those, among whom they are." One of the worst offenders in this respect, Washington continued, was Anthony Whiting, Pearce's predecessor as manager, who, "tho' perfectly acquainted with every part of a farmers business . . . yet, finding it a little troublesome to instruct the Negros, and to compell them to the practice of *his* modes, he slided into theirs."[69] Here was still another problem eliminating slavery would solve.

In practical terms, Washington's hope was that the slaves he freed would find work on the soon-to-be-leased Mount Vernon farms. That would mean they could stay where they were, which in turn would help resolve a major issue posed by their liberation. Over the years Washington's slaves and Martha's had intermarried freely. Though southern masters did not always recognize slave marriages, Washington never seems to have doubted they were valid and binding. Legally, however, Martha could not dispose of her slave property; in effect she had only a life interest in it. Thus if Washington freed his slaves, many couples would find themselves split between slavery and freedom, but at least if the freed slaves remained at Mount Vernon the pain would be lessened.[70]

Yet months went by and no one stepped forward to lease Washington's farms. At first that may not have seemed so troubling, but by 1795 he was growing impatient to see his plan implemented. His second term as president was drawing to a close, and he would soon be returning to Mount Vernon. Meanwhile, the problems he faced as president had only deepened. Taking stock during his final year in office, he could have congratulated himself that the new government had survived, that the economy had recovered, and that the nation remained at peace in a world of war. But American neutrality still hung by the slenderest of threads, and the division between the Federalists and the Republicans was now clearly irreparable. Also, the personal attacks on Washington continued with unabated ferocity. "As some gazettes of the United States have teemed with all the Invective that disappointment, ignorance of facts, and malicious falsehoods could invent, to misrepresent my politics and affections; to wound my reputation and feelings; and to weaken, if not entirely destroy the confidence you had been pleased to repose in me," he wrote in an early, eventually discarded, version of his Farewell Address, "it might be expected at the parting scene of my public life that I should take some notice of such virulent abuse. But, as heretofore, I shall pass them over in utter silence."[71]

In a fresh effort to resolve the future of Mount Vernon and its slaves, Washington finally decided early in 1796 to advertise publicly the availability of three of his farms for lease at the rate of one and a half bushels of wheat per acre, or the equivalent in cash. At the same time, he announced that he would accept offers on thirteen tracts of western lands totaling forty-one thousand acres.[72] To friends around the country and abroad whom he asked to arrange for the publication of his ad, he stressed that he wanted only the best, most careful farmers as leaseholders at Mount Vernon. "I have no idea of frittering the farms for the accommodation of our country farmers, whose knowledge, [or] practice at least, centre in the destruction of the land, and very little beyond it."[73] He also made clear to those closest to him his continuing desire to do something about his slaves.[74]

From Mount Vernon, William Pearce reported receiving several inquiries about the term leases. Nevertheless, when the Washingtons finally left Philadelphia after seeing John Adams inaugurated as president, the farms remained unrented. And with no prospects in sight and the spring planting season already upon him when he reached Mount Vernon, Washington went ahead and gave instructions for getting in another year's crops.[75] He also began writing about life under his vine and fig tree again, and the steady parade of visitors resumed.[76]

Fortunately there were other, more rewarding diversions awaiting him. Despite his constant admonitions, the eight years of his presidency had not been kind to Mount Vernon. The main house needed dozens of repairs, and for months he had been sending instructions about projects he wanted completed before his return, including the addition of shutters ("outside Venetian blinds") to the west front of the house.[77] But the bulk of the work remained to be done, and now he would be there to supervise it himself, something he had always enjoyed.

By the end of March the painters had arrived—too soon, it turned out, because close inspection revealed "some joiners work" that should have been done beforehand. The marble around the fireplaces in several of the ground-floor rooms also had to be replaced. "I find myself almost in the Situation of a new beginner, so much does my houses, and every thing about them, stand in need of repairs," Washington wrote in April. "What with Joiners, Painters, Glasiers, etc. etc. I have scarcely a room to go into at present, that is free from one, or other of them."[78]

Once the carpentry and painting were finished, a quantity of new furniture—sent from Philadelphia on the sloop laden with the rest of the family's possessions—had to be unpacked and placed in the refurbished rooms. Outside the house, too, every day revealed new "decays . . . in the out buildings and Inclosures" that needed remedying.[79] Little by little it all got done, though not without the usual complaints about the people doing the work. "Workmen in most countries, I believe, are necessary plagues," wrote Washington. "In this, where entreaties as well as money must be used to obtain their work . . . they baffle all calculation."[80]

Even with the last mirror and fence rail in place and "the Music of hammers" and "the odoriferous smell of paint" fading, however, some things about Mount Vernon remained exactly as they had been before. The mansion house stood spanking clean and freshly painted, the elegant desk Washington had used as president was safely lodged in his study, and the "Vistoes" he had envisioned though all those years away stretched out across the landscape; but the fields and meadows were still tended by slaves, the soil they labored over was still badly in need of replenishing, and there was still no plan for passing Mount Vernon on to another generation.

The effort to lease the three farms also seemed to be languishing. Then, toward the end of 1797, Richard Parkinson wrote from England about the possibility of renting River Farm.[81] The author of *The Experienced Farmer,* he was exactly the sort of person Washington hoped to have as a tenant, and the following year Parkinson actually appeared at Mount Vernon and spent the better part of a day riding over the land. Washington was away at the time, but the Englishman returned later, and the two had a long talk. It must have been a humbling experience. Parkinson had decided not to rent River Farm. As gently as he could, he explained that the soil was far too inferior to support the kind of farming he was used to. His father grew ten times as many bushels of wheat per acre as Washington did.[82]

So much for the dream of making Mount Vernon a model of the latest and best British agricultural techniques. But if that was not to be, what alternatives were there, what else could be done with the place and its people? Over the years Washington had used it in different ways at different times. As his needs had changed, he had managed to shape and reshape it to meet them. Now he wanted to simplify its management and eliminate what he had come to see as a great blight upon it, the presence of slavery. Yet there seemed to be no way of doing either—of cutting through the layered complexities of the world he had created to give it, this one last time, a fresh set of contours.

But perhaps after all he was not cutting deeply enough.

CHAPTER 10

To Give and Bequeath

THE LAST YEAR of George Washington's life, like so many others at Mount Vernon, mixed the commonplace liberally with the momentous. Typical of the former was Parson Latta's visit. On July 3, 1799, without warning and describing himself simply "as a young clergyman from Pennsylvania traveling to see the country," he made his way up the drive hoping to see the Washingtons' "improvements." Since "the General" was off on his daily rounds, Martha dutifully pointed the way to the gardens. Several hours later Washington returned to find Latta still on the premises, having toured the grounds and viewed the house from every possible angle. Introductions were exchanged, and Latta was offered and drank a glass of cold punch. Still he lingered. Finally Washington invited him to dinner, and yet another kindness followed that one. As a rule meals at Mount Vernon went forward without any formal blessing, but on this occasion Latta was asked, as he put it, "to officiate in my clerical character" both before and after dinner.[1]

With his visit at last over, Latta departed, apparently satisfied in every way by his encounter with the noble—and pious—hero/statesman. And however Washington felt about having his food prayed over in such circumstances, he too could be satisfied. He had not quite caught the young man's name (recording it later in his diary as "Lattum"), but every courtesy had been shown him. The scene was played exactly as it should have been.[2]

Still, it must have been a relief that not all the less consequential moments under Washington's vine and fig tree were like this one—that occasionally the pattern broke, as it had a year earlier when a passel of Fitzhughs traveling from Alexandria unexpectedly appeared at Mount Vernon. Being old friends, they were invited to dinner even though the house was already full of people. Tables were set up in the new room and laid with Sevres porcelain, and all through the long meal that followed, the company laughed and joked. Mrs. Festus Fitzhugh, a vast woman of prodigious appetite, was described by one of the other guests as sweeping through "one platter after another," while her husband gleefully encouraged her with the words "Betsy, a little more, a little more." And Washington was reported to be in equally "high spirits . . . and full of attention to everyone."[3]

If the Reverend Latta's presence at Washington's table signified what Mount Vernon had become, dinner with the Fitzhughs represented its past: the ample hospitality; the ease with which the public spaces of the house could be thrown open to welcome guests; the artfully concocted blend of formality and informality; the Sevres porcelain and the good-natured, ravenous Mrs. Fitzhugh; and, of course, presiding over it all, the gracious host himself. Here indeed were pleasure and power mixed and held, however fleetingly, in the kind of balance Washington seems to have envisioned when he planned the rebuilding of the house before the Revolution.

But in the summer of 1799 it remained Mount Vernon's future, not its present or its past, that most concerned him.

The season had begun on a portentous note, with a dream of Washington's that seemed to foretell Martha's death. In describing it to her afterward, however, he remarked that dreams often predicted "a contrary result" and added: "I may soon leave you." Several days later Martha found evidence on scraps of paper in his study that led her to believe he was rewriting his will.[4] She was right. At the time Washington was in excellent health for a man of sixty-six years. Still, something had moved him to act, and on July 7, 1799, he set his signature to a completely redrawn version of his final will and testament.

Carefully copied on sheet after sheet of fine, watermarked paper, the document ran to just over twenty-eight pages and was wholly the product of Washington's mind and hand. He alone conceived it, composed it, and copied it. Years of overseeing the affairs of assorted friends and relatives had taught him the proper forms to use, and by the time he sat down to the task he knew exactly what he intended to do. The result is as interesting and significant as anything he ever wrote.[5]

Some things were predictable. His modest debts were to be paid, and Martha was to have the full use of his estate during her lifetime. In the very next paragraph, however, came what he had long dreamed of doing: he declared that on Martha's death all of his slaves were to be freed. Moreover, he went beyond simple manumission, directing that among the freed slaves those too old or too young to be independent should be supported as long as necessary. The young were also to be taught to read and write and provided with "some useful occupation," and the will further stipulated that none of the freed slaves were to be transported out of Virginia "under any pretense whatsoever." All of this, too, Washington commanded his executors "most pointedly, and most solemnly" to fulfill "without evasion, neglect or delay."[6]

And so they did. Not until 1839, forty years after his death, would the carefully detailed accounts of Washington's estate show the final payment to the last of his former slaves receiving support, and except for teaching them to read and write, which Virginia law prohibited, everything was done as he wished.[7] To be sure, he had not cut completely through the knot. Martha's slaves would remain in bondage. But insofar as the choice was his to make, he had broken with the system that had for so long held his own inde-

162
1834

Dr Estate of General Washington

Dr | Cr

To balance due Estate brought over from page 161 — | 462 | 75

Oct. 15 To Cash pd to Edmond Johnson for Taxes of difficult run Land for 1833 & 1834 — | 1 | 06

To omitted Tax for and expenses in Building & repairs to houses on the land settled Edw Johnson — — — | 22 | 65

To over crediting the Estate in money paid by

" To Edmond I Lee's Clerks notes — — | 2 | 08

To furnishing Old free Negroes Suckey, Molly & Gabriel Clothing house & fuel Meal &c &c for the year 1834 at $25 each p year — — | 75 | ~

1834 To Taxes & repairs for house in Alexa from 1833 to 1834 see Entwisle's account — | 30 | 62

1835 To Cash pd Snowden as p receipt — | 3 | 25

1834 To Cash paid Commmr Moore — — — | 42 | 50

1835 To Do paid Wm Yeaton for enclosing &
Oct 29 repairing Vault at Mt Vernon — | 618 | 15

To debt paid Clerks Notes of Fairfax Co | 4 | 62

1836 To Do paid Dennis Johnson for a Coffin for Old Lucy — — — — | 3 | 00

To furnishing Old free Negros Suckey Molly & Gabriel at $25 pr year for 1834 & 1835 | 75 | 00

~~To ditto from 1835 to 1836 they have received half allowance of ~~ | |

 — — | 87½

To Taxes paid on Nansemond Land | |

~~To Raise Tax to Washington~~ — — — | |

To Tax paid Nansemond Land — — | | 95

To Coffin for Old Molly — — — | 3 | 00

 — — | 882 | 75

Page from the ledger of Washington's estate showing payments for the support and burial of several of his former slaves. Courtesy of the Chapin Library of Rare Books, Williams College.

pendence hostage to the denial of liberty to other human beings. He was free, and hence-forth his slaves would be free too—free to make of their lives whatever they could.

Placed at the beginning of a document that he knew would be published and widely read, Washington's decision regarding his slaves commands instant attention. Other sur-prises followed, however, for in many ways that one decision set the pattern for the entire will—for the dozens of bequests, large and small, that disposed of the great mass of pos-sessions Washington had spent a lifetime acquiring and conserving. The world in which he had grown to maturity and become a rich man accepted slavery; it was also a world that set a premium on keeping family wealth intact as it passed from generation to gen-eration. Yet that is exactly what Washington chose not to do.[8]

Significantly, his first bequests were for public purposes, all of which had to do with education: twenty shares of stock in the Bank of Alexandria to Alexandria Academy; one hundred shares in the James River Company to Liberty Hall Academy in Rockbridge, Virginia; and fifty shares in the Potomac Company to help establish a national university in the District of Columbia. The last project was particularly close to his heart. In the Constitutional Convention of 1787, founding such an institution had been proposed as one of the powers to be expressly granted to Congress, but then the idea was dropped. Washington had recommended it to Congress in 1790, however, and a site in the federal city was set aside for it. In his view, a national university was essential to stop the prac-tice of sending American youth abroad to be educated, causing them to "contract too frequently not only habits of dissapation & extravagance, but principles unfriendly to Republican Government, and to the true and genuine liberties of mankind." A national institution would also gather students together from across the country, thereby freeing them from "local prejudices and habitual jealousies . . . which, when carried to excess are never failing sources of disquietude to the Public mind and pregnant of mischievous consequences to this country."[9] The stock Washington earmarked for a national univer-sity had been given to him by the Commonwealth of Virginia; here was a way of repay-ing that debt and at the same time giving it broader relevance.

After the bequests for educational purposes came those to individuals, the most important of which, in monetary terms, occurred at the end of the will. There, after a series of smaller bequests, Washington outlined his intentions regarding the lion's share of his assets: a rich collection of holdings listed in a detailed "Schedule of property" that accompanied the will. Real estate predominated, including lands in Virginia, Maryland, Pennsylvania, Kentucky, and New York, as well as huge tracts farther west, in the valley of the Ohio River. There were also several city lots, the Mount Vernon livestock, and $35,000 worth of assorted bonds and shares. Meticulously estimating the value of each item, Washington put the total at $530,000.[10]

For the period this was an enormous sum of money, especially added to the value of the rest of the estate, which modern estimates set at roughly $250,000, not including, of course, the freed slaves. Plainly, if Washington had chosen to limit his bequests to two or three heirs, those individuals would have found themselves quite rich. Certainly, too, such a division would have satisfied Virginian standards of justice. His own father had divided his estate along sharply unequal lines, and if anyone felt aggrieved as a result, there is no record of the fact.

Yet here as well Washington's instructions to his executors could not have been clearer. Taking everything listed in the "Schedule of property," they were to divide or sell the individual items "as, in their judgment shall be most conducive to the interest of the parties concerned," and then distribute the results in twenty-three equal shares to the people he designated. Included as beneficiaries were Martha's four grandchildren and every one of his surviving nieces and nephews, as well as the children of those who were dead.[11]

In their legalistic blandness the words were straight forward enough, but their meaning was anything but routine. On Washington's death there would be no big winners. Instead, more than two dozen people would benefit financially from his will. The shares were large enough to be significant but too small to make anyone truly rich—and they were equal. In the end that was the standard Washington chose. The question is why.

Almost certainly had he not been childless, his will would have been more like his father's. Because he did not have children of his own, however, he had the chance to make his will more than just a means of transmitting lands and cattle and bank shares. On a personal level, to all those nieces and nephews who might have expected less but hoped for more, he offered a lesson in independence. Over the years several of them had turned to him for financial support, and that year had already brought at least one request for funds. As he generally did, Washington responded with a lecture—and a loan.[12] Earlier in the will he had excused most such debts. Now he added for each of Gus Washington's grandchildren a modest nest egg, an amount not unlike his own inheritance. That was the end of it, however. In the future, his nieces and nephews would have to fend for themselves.

But if that was the lesson Washington hoped to teach his heirs, his intentions could also be interpreted more broadly. To move from equality in family matters to equality in society at large was both an obvious step and a logical one. Nor was the logic simply a question of equal shares, equally distributed, for the most striking feature of the division Washington mandated in his will was that after he died his personal fortune, his wealth, would cease to exist. Division meant dispersal; dispersal meant extinction. It was that simple, and final.

Washington could have been suggesting that great wealth was undesirable, something to be eliminated if possible, yet it seems more likely that he had a different point in mind. Not wealth per se, but its perpetuation across time was what his will prevented. A society constructed along such lines would not be free of disparities in economic well-being, but they would be short-lived, impermanent. The struggle to acquire and possess would begin anew each generation, with everyone starting on the same footing. In short, equality of opportunity—that is what Washington seems to have been aiming at, a point reinforced by his concern for education. Did he in fact intend, through his will, to offer it to his fellow citizens as a general prescription? All we can be certain of is what he put on paper. There is another clue in the will, however, and that is the provision he made for Mount Vernon, the piece of property that meant more to him than any other on earth.

The "Schedule of property" to be distributed in the twenty-three-part division made no mention of Mount Vernon, but that did not mean Washington intended to preserve it as it was. On the contrary, in three earlier paragraphs in the will he had stipulated that his "Mansion house" and "upwards of four thousand acres" around it were to go to his nephew Bushrod Washington, who was also to receive Washington's papers; that another 2,077 acres of Mount Vernon land were to be split between the two sons of his nephew and former manager, George Augustine Washington; and that the remainder of the plantation, including his mill and distillery and 2,000 acres "more or less" was to go to Nelly Custis and her new husband, Lawrence Lewis, a nephew of Washington's.[13]

Mount Vernon too was to be divided, then. The acreage Bushrod would inherit amounted to less than half the total Washington had painstakingly assembled over the years. Even more telling, the will said nothing at all about how he was to operate and maintain his inheritance with so much of the land (and the most fertile parts, at that) gone and no slaves left to do the work. A rock-solid Federalist who had developed a successful legal practice in Richmond, Bushrod had been appointed the year before by John Adams to the U.S. Supreme Court. The position was an honorable one, but fulfilling its duties was unlikely to leave much time for plantation management, and the income was modest at best. Perhaps Washington imagined that Bushrod would bring in tenants to farm his share of the land, but he himself had had no success at finding tenants who would give the soil the care it needed.

The truth was that under the terms of the will, Mount Vernon would cease to be the kind of place it had been during Washington's lifetime. Intimately familiar with its problems, he knew what it had taken to hold it together for forty years. He was aware of what it cost—in time, effort, and money—to paint it and repair it, to keep the roof sound and the windows and doors tight. It is hard not to believe that he foresaw full well the future that awaited it: the slow, steady slide into decay that would carry his once grand home to the brink of ruin over the next fifty years. Yet if that was the future he envisioned, it was also a future of his own making. Leaving his slaves in bondage, keeping his assets intact, not dividing Mount Vernon, and settling it all on to one or two heirs would have produced a very different outcome. Washington chose to do none of those things, however. He had built Mount Vernon, and now he was apparently decreeing, all but literally, its destruction.

Nor did he make the least attempt to keep the contents of the house together. Earlier in the will he had bequeathed—one after another and each to a different person—all of the objects most intimately associated with him. Thus to various relatives went his swords, his "Spy-glasses," and several gold-headed canes, including one left to him by Benjamin Franklin; to Lafayette went a pair of elegant steel pistols "taken from the enemy in the Revolutionary War"; to his personal physician and old friend Dr. James Craik went his desk and chair, to Dr. David Stuart his shaving and dressing table and his telescope, and to Bryan Fairfax a Bible "in three large folio volumes, with notes, presented to me by the Right reverend Thomas Wilson, Bishop of Sodor & Man."[14]

So piece by piece Mount Vernon was to be taken apart, its contents scattered, its lands divided, its slaves freed, and the house itself left to slip into decrepitude. As a young man Washington had wanted the place to speak boldly of independence, and also of power, rank, and dominion, for to him all four of those things were essentially synonymous. After the Revolution he worked to soften Mount Vernon's impact, to make it less relentlessly imposing, but the impulse to do so had always had to struggle against his inborn passion for neatness and order. Now, with nature alone to point the way, his creation would soon enough fade into the bower of greenery he had caused to grow around it.

As he penned the relevant phrases, did Washington stop to wonder what those contentious souls, Mount Vernon's builders, would have made of his latest vision of the place? It had always been so much an expression of his indomitable will that it must have seemed he meant it to stand forever. The power to command such permanence, too, was emblematic of everything that separated him from the builders. Of necessity they calculated time, like the other components of their lives, in finite increments. To discover that Washington was prepared to do the same in the case of Mount Vernon would indeed have come as a surprise.

Would it have made the builders feel differently about him, lessened the animus that so often touched their relations? By mandating Mount Vernon's demise, Washington made it purely and simply his home, not a monument to him, or a memorial to anything. And by extension its builders, slave and free alike, became simply people who owed him their labor, and that debt had long since been paid. One thinks of Johann Ehlers returning to work at Mount Vernon after Washington's death, in Bushrod's time. Perhaps it was his way of making peace with the place and with his former master. Perhaps, too, Washington himself had something comparable in mind when he framed the provisions of his will as he did. He loved Mount Vernon and had spent a lifetime improving and embellishing it, but his involvement with the place had shaped more than bricks and wood and artfully planted drifts of trees; it had shaped his mind and soul as well. And the lesson it taught was that as long as other people lived by his sufferance, he would never be truly independent; that only in a world where everyone was free could he hope to be free too. This, then, was the result. In his will—the last of the several great farewells that punctuated his life—he chose not to project his personal world, with all its intricately encoded signs of status and power, forward into the future. Instead, in a stunning affirmation, he chose equality.

For the present, however, life at Mount Vernon would go on as usual. Pleading ill health, William Pearce had given up his duties as manager shortly before the Washingtons returned from Philadelphia.[15] His replacement, James Anderson, instituted several innovations, including the large-scale distilling of whiskey, which provided a convenient and profitable means of marketing the plantation's surplus wheat. But in other respects Anderson proved less satisfactory than Pearce. An unusually touchy individual, he announced that he was leaving when given suggestions for improving his performance. Hastily Washington backed off, and Anderson agreed to stay, at least for the time being.[16]

In a happier vein, Nelly Custis's decision to wed Lawrence Lewis, the son of Washington's sister Betty, once again joined George and Martha's families in marriage. The ceremony took place on Washington's birthday, "abt. Candle light," as he noted in his diary, and the festivities lasted for a full week afterward.[17] By the end of November the couple's first child had been born, and they were already making plans to build a house on the portion of Mount Vernon land Washington had set aside for them in his will.

Also in November, Bryan Fairfax returned from a long visit to England. He had gone carrying letters from both Washingtons to Sally Fairfax, who by then was living as a widow in Bath. In Washington's first communication with her in twenty-five years, he described the times he had spent in her company as "the happiest of my life."[18] Yet if this seemed to speak almost too plainly of the passions of his youth, the fact that Martha wrote as well emphasized the ties that later bound the Washingtons and Fairfaxes together as couples.[19]

Time had long since healed any strain the final break with England had caused between Washington and Bryan Fairfax, who continued to live nearby at Mount Eagle and who eventually inherited the family title, becoming "Lord Fairfax," as Washington carefully addressed him thereafter.[20] However, other, less easily resolved conflicts from the larger world kept intruding on "the more tranquil theater" Washington hoped to preserve at home. The year before, as relations between the United States and France deteriorated to the point where war seemed imminent, John Adams, without consulting him, had appointed Washington commander in chief of American forces.[21] Reluctantly, he accepted and for a time was caught up in a flurry of military preparations, including the ticklish business of choosing the officers who were to serve under him.[22] But within months the war fever began to abate, which can only have pleased Washington, though he had ordered a splendid new uniform, which unfortunately did not arrive in time for Nelly's wedding.[23]

In the end, Adams decided to take the initiative and send a special mission to France, a move that infuriated many of his fellow Federalists, who begged Washington to use his influence against the plan. Wisely he refused. While he continued to fear "some awful crisis" ahead, he noted that the ship of state remained afloat, adding that "as a Passanger only" he would "trust to the Mariners whose duty it is to watch, to steer it into a safe Port."[24]

Divisions over foreign policy were only part of what has been aptly described as the "congestion of divided purposes" that overtook the Federalists in their final years of national power.[25] An acute sense of being under siege, conflicting personal ambitions, and multiple disagreements over fundamental principles all played a role in shattering party unity and driving voters in growing numbers into the Republican camp. But in the long run even more damaging was the undeniable accuracy of the major charge the Jeffersonians leveled against the party of Adams and Hamilton. Locally, some Federalists proved quite adept at adjusting to the realities of partisan politics. On the national level, however, the party seemed irredeemably committed to the notion that power belonged in the hands of those who, by virtue of privileges like wealth and education, "deserved" to govern.

For his part, Washington remained a loyal Federalist, but he refused to speak out publicly in favor of either the party or its candidates. As for the issue of privilege, he had taken his stand on that unequivocally in his will. If, when the time came, the disposition he had made of his wealth appeared to place him closer to the Republicans than to the Federalists, then so be it. He had acted in full confidence that what he did was right. It also would have been easy to find precedents for his actions in the past: in his conviction that British measures before the Revolution threatened the liberties of all Americans alike, for example, or in the growing anger of a provincial army commander forced to defer to lesser men who had acquired with money and patronage the superior rank that should have been his.

For the rest, there seemed little left to do beyond putting the finishing touches on what he had already accomplished. On December 10, 1799, he completed an elaborate set of instructions, to be implemented over the next several years, for each of Mount Vernon's farms. In a covering letter to James Anderson he stressed that his plans were to be followed "most *strictly*, and *pointedly*" and urged that all accounts for the current quarter "be made final; as an entire new scene will take place afterwards."[26]

The following night there was a ring around the moon, foretelling stormy weather, but Washington rode out as usual the next morning and continued his tour of the farms even after it began to sleet and snow. On his return he did not bother to change his clothes but went directly into dinner. More than once in the past he had become seriously ill in similar circumstances, and though he seemed fine at dinner, the next day his throat was sore enough to confine him to the house in the morning, yet not too sore to keep him from spending the hour before sunset out in the snow, marking trees that he wanted cut down around the bowling green. That night he awoke in intense pain and was having trouble breathing but asked Martha to wait until morning to send for help, which she did.[27]

By then it was already too late, at least for the medical practices of that age. During the long day that followed, with three different physicians in attendance, Washington was repeatedly blistered and bled, but to no avail. Despite the anxiety of everyone present, he seemed calm, saying that he had "believed from the first attack it would be fatal" and asking only that the will he entrusted to Martha be kept safe and that he be allowed to "go off quietly." A little after ten that evening he drew his last, labored breath.

Contemplating the scene from this vantage point, it is hard not to see Washington playing his usual commanding role in it. Had he willed his own death? Surely not in any ordinary sense. But it is clear that he was prepared to die, had made all the necessary arrangements for it, and did nothing to prevent it from occurring when it did. This would not have been the first time he had formed a hypothesis and left events to confirm it or not, as fate decreed. In the past, too, fate had invariably proved him right.

And what was there left for him to do? He had fought and won a revolution and presided over the establishment of a new national government, which in spite of the perils of the moment remained on even keel. He had built a private world at home that he managed to use for the invaluable purpose of demonstrating that power in a properly constituted republic required clear limits. He had even, in his will, offered his fellow countrymen a memorable lesson in what later generations would speak of as democracy. Truly his life's work was finished. He liked to say that God's ways were "inscrutable, and irresistible." When the end came, however, he read his destiny well enough, for as always, he kept it firmly in his own hands.

Redivivus, 1800–Present

MARTHA WASHINGTON lived on at Mount Vernon for two and a half years after her husband's death. Preferring not to stay in the room the two of them had shared and where he had died, she moved to a small, third-floor room, in which a stove was installed for her comfort. But she was often ill and remained subdued and melancholy. Meanwhile, Mount Vernon began to deteriorate almost at once. With the soon-to-be freed slaves already wandering off, Martha sued in court to release the rest, income fell, and taxes took much of the money needed for repairs. When Abigail Adams visited at Christmastime in 1800, she thought the place seemed forlorn and neglected.

Following Martha's death from a sudden fever on May 22, 1802, an auction was held to dispose of the movables left at Mount Vernon after the bequests in the couple's wills had been carried out. Family members bought part of the livestock and several pieces of furniture, but most items went elsewhere. Altogether the sale raised more than $100,000, which was split into individual shares as stipulated in Washington's will.

With Martha dead and the house empty, the two grandchildren she and Washington had brought there to live—Nelly Custis Lewis and George Washington Parke Custis ("Wash")—moved on to new houses built on land they had inherited from him. Both led full lives. Nelly died in 1857 and her brother five years later. In 1831, the only one of his children to reach adulthood, Mary Anne Randolph Custis, married Lieutenant Robert E. Lee. Nelly's firstborn daughter, Frances Parke Lewis Butler, survived until 1875, becoming the last of the family members who lived with Washington at Mount Vernon to die.

As master of a much-reduced plantation, Bushrod Washington did what he could to keep Mount Vernon going. He even embellished it a bit, adding a balustrade around the roof of the piazza and a small porch, with a similar balustrade, at the south end of the house. But lacking the money to handle the mounting number of repairs all of the buildings needed, he could do little to stop the decay that had already begun when the place came to him. He spent only summers at Mount Vernon, living first in Philadelphia, then in Washington, D.C., the rest of the year.

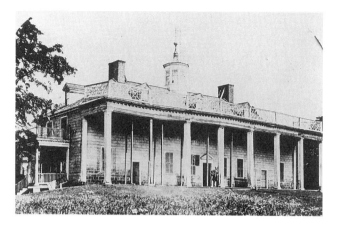

Left: *Mount Vernon, ca. 1855. Authors' collection.*

Right: *Ann Pamela Cunningham. Courtesy of the Mount Vernon Ladies' Association.*

Bushrod died without warning in 1829, and since he was childless, Mount Vernon was divided among several of his siblings' children and grandchildren, with the house itself going to John Augustine Washington, who died in 1843. After that it passed to his eldest son, another John Augustine Washington, who spent the next five years struggling in vain to restore the property he had inherited. Finally, in 1848, the dilapidated mansion house and a small parcel of land around it were offered for sale to the public for $200,000.

Though the price was high, it was eventually paid through the efforts of Miss Ann Pamela Cunningham and the extraordinary organization she founded. On hearing her mother describe the sorry state of Mount Vernon after a moonlit boat trip past it in 1853, Cunningham resolved to acquire and preserve it as a shrine to Washington's memory. The daughter of a wealthy South Carolina planter, she suffered from ill health throughout her adult life, but that did not stop her from working tirelessly to achieve her goal. In 1858 she signed a contract to purchase the house and 202 acres, secured by a down payment of $18,000. Two years later, with only $6,600 left to be raised on the price, John Augustine Washington relinquished the property.

Over the years, Cunningham was helped by many people, including Edward Everett, who personally donated more than $50,000 earned by giving addresses on Washington's character. Her chief support, however, came from a growing group of women she enlisted in the cause. At first she planned to involve only women from the South, but northern women asked to participate too. Formally chartered by the Virginia legislature in 1856 as the Mount Vernon Ladies' Association of the Union, the group became the first historic preservation organization in the United States and remains one of the most successful.

Representation in the Ladies' Association is by state, with each state representative holding the title of vice regent. As head of the organization, Cunningham became its first regent. For seven years during and after the Civil War she was in South Carolina taking care of her family's affairs. She returned to Mount Vernon as "resident director"—as well as regent—in 1867 and served until 1873. She died two years later, in South Carolina.

After Cunningham's time, the resident directorship became a separate position, and in recent decades an increasingly professional staff has taken responsibility not only for the day-to-day operation of Mount Vernon but also for framing discussions on how best to present and interpret Washington's home to the public. The result has been a deepening commitment both to making the physical aspects of what visitors see as accurate as possible and to broadening the range of experiences they have while there. Traditionally the focus has been on the Washingtons, the mansion house, and its contents; now the lives of the plantation's other residents—most notably the slaves—are featured as well. One also learns about Mount Vernon as a working agricultural enterprise. By any standard, the achievement is impressive.

What would Washington have thought of it all? We have argued that he had no desire to see Mount Vernon preserved. Yet if that was so, it is equally true that anyone who has ever been there has cause to be grateful that his wishes did not prevail, for the place continues to evoke the man more completely than anything else could. With the house in perfect repair, the grounds in far better shape than they ever were during his lifetime, and not a single slave in sight, this may not be the Mount Vernon Washington knew. It is, however, remarkably like one he dreamed of, the one that filled his imagination, ever receding before the reality—a fragment of a utopia that never was, but also, in its passing, a harbinger of another, better world to come.

House-Building in Eighteenth-Century Virginia

TO UNDERSTAND the changes George Washington made at Mount Vernon it is helpful to know not only why he did what he did but also how it was done—how stone, brick, mortar, metal, wood, plaster, and paint were transformed into finished houses in Virginia in the eighteenth century. In later years Washington was inclined to think it would have been better if he had built his house from the ground up, instead of working with an existing structure. In one sense he was right: some things were beyond changing when he set out to rebuild in the spring of 1758, or again in 1774. But the truth was that any major building project in that world was a highly complex affair, difficult both to plan and to complete.

To someone used to mobilizing military supplies and troops for battle, many of the problems would have seemed familiar. Dozens of artisans and laborers, working at various trades and crafts, had to be assembled, along with an even wider assortment of building materials. All of those components, too, came into play at different times, with separate teams of workers, using different materials, necessarily dovetailing their activities as the process of construction unfolded.

Fortunately, by the middle of the eighteenth century Virginia boasted an array of building practices capable of producing impressive results, but that had not always been so. Fifty years earlier William Fitzhugh complained bitterly to an English correspondent about his experience building a fully framed wooden house with local materials and labor:

> [I] should not advise to build either a great, or English framed house, for labour is so intolerably dear, & workmen so idle & negligent that the building of a good house, to you there will seem insupportable, for this I can assure you when I built my own house, & agreed as cheap as I could with workmen, & as carefully & diligently took care that they followed their work notwithstanding we have timber for nothing, but felling & getting in place, the frame of my house stood me in more money . . . than a frame of the same dimensions would cost in London, by a third at least where everything is bought, & near three times as long preparing.

When Fitzhugh made these remarks, most houses in Virginia were still being built, as they had been in the beginning, without permanent foundations or "English" frames. In time, as more people chose to build solider, longer-lived houses, levels of skill rose noticeably and costs at least stabilized. But such houses would never be inexpensive—by American or English standards.

Looking at a structure like the mansion house at Mount Vernon, what one sees is essentially a series of coverings. Strip those away, layer by layer, and you will reach the frame of the building, which in turn stands on the foundation—the point at which construction began.

Initially in Virginia, masonary foundations were made of stone where it was available, and in some places stone continued to be used for those sections that were below grade and thus would not show. But brick was the preferred material for foundations, as it was for chimneys. It was also occasionally used, as at Mount Vernon, to buttress earlier stone foundations.

An ancient craft, brickmaking was widely practiced by the Romans, who introduced it to England. After they left it fell into disuse, but in the late Middle Ages it was revived, and by the seventeenth century building with brick had become common. Brickmasons were on the first ships arriving in Jamestown in 1607, and in time brick became the building material of choice for wealthy Virginia planters.

Because of its high clay content, the soil in Virginia lent itself well to brickmaking. In fact, bricks could usually be made at or near the building site itself, often with the dirt taken from the cellar excavation. In addition to clay, sand was essential, and if the soil contained less than 30 percent sand it had to be carted to the site—usually from a nearby riverbed—and added. It was also important to be close to large supplies of water and wood. At Monticello, Thomas Jefferson was uncertain where to put his brick kilns because of the lack of a ready source of water at his mountaintop building site. At one point he considered locating the kilns by a spring on the mountainside and having the bricks hauled up once they were burned. In the end, however, he calculated that it would be more efficient to dig a well at the site itself.

After being shoveled together in a shallow pit, the sand and clay were soaked with water and left to sit for a while to make them more pliable. For small jobs, the mixture would then be turned with hoes. If the project was larger, the brickmakers might use heavy paddles mounted on a wheel towed by mules or oxen treading the periphery of a ring pit. When the mixture was thoroughly tempered, it was scooped up and squeezed into wooden molds partitioned into sections to form standard-size bricks. To keep the mud from sticking to the molds they first were doused in water or dusted with sand. An efficient worker could mold up to five thousand bricks a day.

Once they were filled, the molds were scraped along the top to get rid of excess clay and placed on planks to dry partially. Next the bricks were slid out of their molds and set on their sides to dry further in the sun. In good weather they could air-dry in five days, but even with the added protection of wooden planks, a sudden rain squall could ruin the work. When the bricks were dry, they were stacked and layered, with air spaces

A modern depiction of an eighteenth-century brick kiln, showing the "eyes" (covered) at the bottom used for stoking the kiln, and freshly molded bricks drying in the foreground. Courtesy of the Colonial Williamsburg Foundation.

between, in wood-filled piles roughly eight to ten feet high, making up the temporary "clamps" or kilns in which they were to be burned. Bell-shaped "eyes," or tunnels, ran through the kilns from end to end, with the number of eyes depending on the size of the kiln. A large kiln might contain as many as thirty-six eyes, and about three thousand bricks could be fired per eye. As soon as the bricks were in place, the outside of the kiln was plastered with mud to hold in the heat, and the firing began.

In all, it took about five cords of hardwood and five days of stoking the fires through the eyes of the kiln for the temperature inside to rise to the requisite 2,500° F. On the first day of firing, heavy clouds of steam and black smoke poured from the top of the kiln as the moisture and impurities in the mud packs were burned off. As the temperature continued to rise during the following days and the mud was transformed into brick, the top of the kiln glowed red. Gauging the inside temperature was an art more than a science; it all depended on the judgment and knowledge of the brickmaker. Generally, when the top of the kiln began to slump, it was time to plug up the holes and let the bricks cool down gradually, but several more weeks had to pass before the kiln could be dismantled and the bricks sorted.

Brick-burning was an imperfect process at best. Brickmakers had to estimate the number of bricks needed for the work to be done, aided perhaps by tables written down and passed along through time. Not all the bricks in a given batch were evenly burned; typically only half were well hardened and usable. Of those, the bricks closest to the fire or rimming the eyes of the kiln were glazed and could be used decoratively. A common pattern, known as Flemish bond, alternated ends of glazed brick with lengths of regular ones to give a checkered effect. Softer bricks from the outside of the kiln were sometimes used along with straw and mud as nogging, or filling, between the studs of a framed structure, providing added protection against vermin, fire, and cold.

The mortar to bond the bricks together during construction was made from lime, sand, and water. In the interior of Virginia, quarries could furnish stone to burn for lime. Near the coast it was easier to use oyster shells, which a number of petty entrepreneurs, including ferrymen, sold by the bushel. When the brick kiln was dismantled, its remains were often kept in place for burning lime, although lime was also burned in special kilns made of layers of logs interspersed with layers of oyster shells. The burned lime and sand were then mixed together in fixed portions to make the mortar, which generally sat for two or three days before being mixed again. When the mortar was finally tempered, it was mixed with water, shoveled into wooden scuttle-shaped troughs, loaded onto a carrier's shoulder, and taken to the bricklayers.

Laying brick properly took considerable skill. With a thumb resting on the handle of a triangular-shaped trowel, the bricklayer dipped the edge of the trowel into the mortar, applied it to the end of a brick held in the other hand, pressed the brick firmly into the mortar bedded on the top row of bricks, and scraped off the excess at the joint. Thus the work proceeded in swift, repetitive strokes along each course. Because the bricks were rough, almost half an inch of mortar was packed between them, and before it hardened, the bricklayer used a straight edge to flatten the surface, then scored a line along the middle of it with a jointer. Jointing not only helped pack in the mortar and prevent cracking; it also gave the uneven brick surface a more regular appearance.

If the house was to be built of wood on brick foundations, as Mount Vernon was, the next major step was the addition of the frame. But even as the foundation rose, a crew of carpenters, working under the direction of an undertaker if the project was one of any size, would have been preparing the framing. This was possible because the frames of wooden buildings were independent structures. Rather than being attached to a foundation, they rested on it, deriving their stability from their own interlocking parts. Weight and counterweight; balanced stresses and strains; timbers strong enough to bear the pressure; tenons and mortises thick enough to do their job, yet positioned so as not to weaken the structure; braces and trusses holding the sides of the house and its roof rafters tightly in place: it all went together like a well-made jigsaw puzzle, its strength greater than the sum of its parts.

Frames were made of wood, and some kinds of wood were stronger and more durable than others. Virginia builders tended to favor yellow pine, poplar, and, less frequently, oak. Landon Carter used both sweet gum and oak in building Sabine Hall, and Carter Burwell, gathering the framing timbers he would need for Carter's Grove, bought fifty poplar trees from a neighbor. Having the right kind of wood was particularly important in Virginia, where buildings were continually plagued by rot, as Washington discovered to his great annoyance on more than one occasion.

Having the right tools was also essential if a frame was to be properly constructed. The owners of large plantations routinely took stock of their tool supply when writing out orders for English goods. Before a large building project, everything from felling axes to planes for fine benchwork, if not supplied by the artisans themselves, had to be on hand or the work might suddenly come to a stop. Iron produced locally was good enough for making horseshoes, latches, and pots, but it lacked the temper for more demanding uses. Of the carpenters' tools available in the colonies, only those with English-made steel blades held their edge.

In cutting, shaping, and fastening together the wood for a frame, the workers followed detailed formulas, with the building's size and use determining the numbers, lengths, and thicknesses of the timbers required. For example, whether or not a beam running down the midline of a structure—sometimes called a "summer" beam—was needed depended on the depth of the building. Similarly, the placement of windows, doors, chimneys, and staircases altered the pattern of the upright studs and horizontal joists that fit between the heavier timbers of the building's skeleton. The first order of business, always, was to draw up a plan listing the framing members required, and it behooved owners as well as carpenters to know the basic rules for constructing a frame. Builders' guides like Joseph Moxon's *Mechanick Exercises* were well known and much used.

Various arrangements were made for felling trees and cutting them to size for the frame. Timber cut on the plantation itself could be hauled directly to the building site, or it could be pitsawn or watersawn, either on the place or at a local sawmill. Lumber for weatherboards, flooring, doors, windows, and trim—all added later in the building process—was generally obtained from a sawmill.

A tree trunk measuring twenty-four to thirty inches in diameter could furnish a builder with four sills and four joists, plus whatever studs or secondary rafters could be made from the limbs. Once felled, the tree was cut into appropriate lengths, which were then jockeyed across two other logs so they could be hewn on one or more sides. The first step in hewing was to "snap" a line along the timber using a reel with twine dipped in red ocher, or keel. Next, standing on top of the timber, with the same ax used to cut down the tree, the hewer began making deep cuts through the bark, splitting off slabs between each cut, still working well outside of the marked line. Then, from the ground, a second series of cuts was made, penetrating to the line, after which an ax with a short handle and a broad blade sharpened on one side was used to chisel out the excess wood, thereby roughly squaring off the side. If the surface had to be finished more smoothly, the hewer, standing again on the timber, made repeated cuts toward his feet with an adz—a sharp, hoe-shaped tool. An even smoother finish could be obtained later, with a fore plane.

A log hewn on one or two sides might then be pitsawn, which was done either literally over a long pit deeper than a person's full height or using specially built wooden staging. While the log rested on its flat side, one sawyer, standing on top of it, was responsible for guiding the saw along a line. The saw itself was set in a frame, and as the sawyer above pulled upward, the sawyer below prepared to pull downward in a reciprocating action, coping as well as possible with the shower of sawdust constantly falling from above.

Where water power was available, logs could be watersawn. On Occoquan Creek below Mount Vernon, John Ballendine owned and operated two sawmills using water power to produce the plank he sold. When a log was watersawn, it was placed length-wise in a carriage and moved along either by a pulley system using weights on ropes, or by a ratchet that advanced the log at each cut. The saw was fixed in a sash—powered by a water wheel—that moved up and down in greased grooves. Two or more blades could be set parallel, thereby increasing the number of cuts made at once. Once the log was fully cut, the planks were moved away and stacked, and the carriage was dragged back to its starting position.

After being cut and stacked, wood had to season, and different woods dried at different rates. Softwoods such as pine could dry sufficiently in several months; hardwoods like oak took much longer. If worked too soon, most wood tended to split or warp, yet carpenters knew better than to season some woods completely: locust, for example, had to be worked green to be worked at all. Occasionally builders attempted to shorten the time it took for wood to dry, but the process was precarious. After looking in vain for seasoned wood, Thomas Jefferson's joiner constructed a kiln that he hoped would dry wood more speedily, but it burned down, destroying all the plank that had been reserved for Monticello's doors and sashes.

When the timbers for a frame were finally collected at a site, they were sorted, matched, and shaped. Many of them would eventually fit together with tenons or mortises, and fashioning those was exacting work. After careful measurement, lines were scored on three sides of the wood with a pricker. Next, holding a mallet in one hand and a broad chisel in the other and working well outside of the lines, the joiner made the first rough cuts. Considerable care had to be taken when working along the grain of the wood not to split and spoil the piece. When the sides were pared smooth to the marked lines, the joiner measured the companion piece for the finished joint and tried the pieces together at intervals until arriving at an exact fit. Holes were then bored in each of the pieces, and tapered pins were made with a paring chisel to hold them together. Once all of this was done, the timbers were labeled and stacked, ready for assembling. The labeling was crucial, since almost every piece of framing had to be mortised, tenoned, or notched, and each tenon was intended for a particular mortise.

There was also a logical order to assembling the various sections of the frame, beginning with the sills, which rested immediately on top of the foundation. Typically, for a double-pile house, sills were ten to twelve inches thick and could be either mortised and tenoned together or half-lapped. If they were mortised and tenoned, the mortise was cut into the longer sills at the front and rear. If a summer beam was to be used, it was fitted into the end sills and girders—the heavier crosspieces connecting the front and rear sills. Next came the thinner floor joists, called sleepers, set from one and a half to two feet apart, for the interior flooring to rest on. Sometimes floor joists were mortised and tenoned, sometimes simply notched; in either case they were all carefully prepared beforehand so they could be slid into place and then secured with wooden pegs.

With the horizontal framing on top of the foundation complete, the upright pieces of the frame—usually assembled first on the ground in sections—were raised into place. Thickest of all were the corner posts, which were buttressed by braces angled up from the sills, meeting the posts at unequal heights so as not to weaken them. Between the corner posts and above each girder, at regular intervals of perhaps nine or ten feet, were

Illustration of work on the framing of a building, starting with the sawing of the timbers, and ending with the construction of the frame itself. From Denis Diderot, Encyclopédie *(Paris, 1751–72). Courtesy of the Library of the Sterling and Francine Clark Art Institute, Williamstown, Massachusetts.*

additional posts, and at regular intervals between them came the lighter studs to which the weatherboarding would later be nailed. On top of the posts and studs, in the horizontal plane, went the girders and joists that held the structure together above. Above those came the plate—the boards forming the platform on which the roof would rest.

Raising a frame into its upright position required skill, teamwork, and careful preparation. Not only were the individual sections heavy, but also when fully upright, they were out of reach. Thus after being pushed up by hand as far as possible, they had to be raised the rest of the way with poles or pikes. In addition someone had to hold a rope looped over the top of the section so it would not fall over on its other side. In this way, section by section, moving from one end of the house to the other, the frame was raised, guided onto the sills, and secured with temporary braces. Finally came what was perhaps the most difficult maneuver of all: lifting the joists and heavier girders, which could weigh as much as 650 pounds each, and fitting them into place on top of the structure.

In the North, a farmer might call on neighbors to raise the frame of a house or barn. On Virginia plantations, the undertaker would arrange for friends to help crews of slaves assembled on the place. But throughout the colonies a successful raising—perhaps because it was dangerous, and certainly because it involved teamwork and camaraderie— was customarily followed by feasting, often with a bottle of rum smashed against one of the uppermost timbers. Quantities of rum were also consumed in the usual way, offering everyone, slaves included, a momentary respite from work.

Once the plate, which rimmed the top of the frame, and the upper girders and joists were in place, the roof rafters could be positioned. Common rafters of equal size were sufficient for smaller houses, but roofs covering a large span required the support of principal rafters as well. Principal rafters were sometimes as much as seven inches thick at their base, and they were trussed with king posts at the center or queen posts on either side. The lighter common rafters were spaced at regular intervals between the principal ones.

The timbers for the roof were cut and assembled into trusses on the ground. Then teams of carpenters, working from one end of the building to the other, raised each truss, temporarily bracing it before hammering home the pegs to secure it at the base. The trusses were further secured by being connected to one another with horizontal purlins, which in turn supported the secondary rafters. At the ridgeline, all the rafters were tenoned and mortised and pegged. Any gables called for in the plan had to be framed into the slope of the roof as well, and gambrel roofs with double slopes called for two sets of rafters, plus a curb plate where the angle of the pitch changed. A hipped roof involved not two but four slopes and was that much more complex.

When the rafters were attached at the ridgeline, the frame was complete and ready to be covered both inside and out, but it was the exterior that usually received attention first. In the South, wooden building frames could rot beyond repair in a single season if left open to the weather.

Outside walls could be quickly and cheaply covered with riven, or split, boards, feathered at the ends so they would lap each other for a weathertight fit. If the house was to be of any distinction, however, it was likely to be weatherboarded with more finely finished overlapping clapboards. Often purchased from a sawmill and then reworked by carpenters at the site, clapboards were first planed to produce a smooth, slightly tapered surface, then frequently trimmed with a beaded edge across the bottom to help prevent splintering and to give them a decorative touch.

The weatherboarding was fastened to the studs of the frame with wrought iron rose head nails, which could be made by plantation blacksmiths. The process was relatively simple, even though each nail was cut, shaped, and finished by hand. Thin rods were usually available from an ironmonger, and the blacksmith only had to put one end of a rod in the fire while an apprentice or slave pumped the bellows. When the end of the rod was hot enough to work, the smith placed it on an anvil and, measuring the desired length by eye, hammered that section on all sides to create a square, tapered shape. Next, the rod was cut almost through with the pointed top of the hammer, after which the end of the rod was jammed into a small hole bored in the anvil. The smith then severed the rod at the cut, and, as a final step, hammered out the head of the nail.

Local merchants also sold nails, but finding adequate supplies of them always seemed to be problematic for Virginians. In the seventeenth century a legislative act had prohibited people from burning down their houses in order to salvage the nails. Also, the prevailing opinion among plantation owners was that nails for a major undertaking had to be British-made because they were sharper, a situation that changed after the Revolution. By 1788 Clement Biddle was writing Washington from Philadelphia: "The impor-

tation of Nails is nearly at an End, that Article being manufactured here of Better quality than the English in very large quantities & Can be shipped to Virginia without paying Duty."

Even before the weatherboarding went on, the trim around the doorways and windows would have been set in place. And simple or fancy, such details required both skill
and a considerable arsenal of specialized tools. Planes, fitted with razor-sharp blades pro-
truding from their bottoms or "soles," were especially important. When a carpenter
pushed or drove a plane the length of a board, the shape of the imprint mirrored that of
the blade. There were many different kinds of planes: bench planes for rough, unrefined
work; long planes for floorboards; and smoothing planes—also called trying, or trueing
planes—for final finishing. Fitting planes carved out rabbets, or grooves, on the edges of
boards, and myriads of molding planes—from wide cornice planes to narrow bead
planes—were used for decorative work.

With the right planes, a carpenter could reproduce particular patterns continuously
and as often as necessary. A series of planes could be used to make a combination of cuts
in steps and curves from a single piece of wood. Some cuts were so wide that the plane
had to be guided by one person while another pulled it with a rope. Most planes, however, could be operated with one or two hands, and much of the work was done at a
bench, where the wood could be tightly secured. Using a plane to good effect (and keeping it sharp) took an experienced hand. It was also important to know how hard or soft
different woods were, and how their grains ran. "You must examine the temper of your
stuff, by easy Trials, how the Plane will work upon it" and "set your iron accordingly,"
was Joseph Moxon's advice to the readers of his builder's guide.

The use of fine molding planes was particularly important in crafting the exterior cornice, which extended around the entire building and had to be uniform in profile
throughout its length. The cornice protected the seam at the eaves under the roof against
the weather, but it was also an important decorative detail instantly visible to anyone
approaching the building. Typically, the cornice on an aspiring planter's house would be
designed to include elements of classical taste, such as running courses of modillions or
dentils, small bracketlike projections attached to the soffit—the flat underside of the
overhanging portion of the roof above. Presumably the builder also selected a combination of convex and concave curves for the moldings that slanted away from the weather.
Designs for cornices could be found in any one of a growing number of imported English pattern books, but it is just as likely that the owner or the carpenter chose to copy a
cornice from a nearby house or church.

If details like modillions were to be added to the cornice, they were shaped and cut
before being attached to the soffit with nails and glue. The glue was made from a mixture of the hides and hooves of horses, pulverized and boiled with water to form a binding agent about the consistency of raw egg white. Since the glue had to be used while still
warm (otherwise it congealed), it was kept in a lead pot as it was brushed on each of the
pieces of wood to be joined together. For a reliable bond, the grains of the connecting
pieces had to run in the same direction.

As soon as the cornice was finished, the carpenters could turn their attention to the
roof. Modest houses were often roofed with riven oak boards, but people who could

afford to do so built roofs of overlapping, wooden shingles, nailed in rows to lath. A shingled roof was more watertight and better at keeping out the summer heat.

Most builders of means purchased shingles rather than having them made on site, since they were widely available. The cypress shingles Washington liked were especially good, but shingles were also made of juniper, yellow pine, oak, and chestnut. The process itself was not complicated. Sitting astride a stool that braced a block of wood and using a mallet in one hand and a froe (a knife with a long blade perpendicular to its handle) in the other, the worker cut through the block, riving, or shaving off, a fairly thin slice of it. Then on a device known as a "shingle horse" a second worker placed the piece in a clamp operated by a foot pedal and, using a drawknife, tapered the piece down to a thickness of less than an inch. Sometimes as a last step the corners of the shingle were hacked off with a hatchet to retard warping. Shingles thus "butted" were more expensive, but they lasted longer.

The shingles were nailed in rows to the lath, which was made of one-by-three-inch strips of yellow pine or some other readily available wood. Running horizontally from one rafter to the next, the strips were closely spaced for the first two feet above the eaves and then spread as far as six inches apart toward the ridgeline. Beginning at the bottom of the roof, the carpenters first put in place a row of shorter, square-butted shingles that overhung the cornice by an inch or more. The next row covered this one entirely, but thereafter the shingles were nailed so they overlapped one another with the bottom third of each shingle left exposed. At any given point, therefore, the shingling covering the house was three layers deep. Commonly in Virginia shingles were eighteen inches long, which meant that six inches were exposed. And so it went, with shingle overlapping shingle as the carpenters made their way up the slope of the roof. At the top, the final row on one side extended above the peak so that the seam at the ridgeline lay away from the prevailing wind. As a last step, the carpenters gave the roof a protective coating of either pine tar or Spanish brown paint. Made from pulverized iron ore and linseed oil, the same paint was often used as a primer for new weatherboards. It was both cheap and readily available.

With the weatherboarding, cornice, and roof finished, the house was largely closed in, but before moving inside, the carpenters would have to finish the doors and windows if that had not been done earlier. Windows were among the most costly elements of a house. There had been several attempts to make glass in the colonies, including one in Jamestown in the early seventeenth century and another announced in a 1752 issue of the *Virginia Gazette*, but most window glass used in Virginia before the Revolution was imported from England. Generally it came precut in eight-by-ten-inch panes, packed in wooden boxes. The best window glass, called "crown glass," was formed by spinning molten glass on a rod to create a flat, four-foot-wide circular disk. When the disk was cool, a glazier scored it with a diamond blade to break it into the prescribed sizes for windowpanes. The "bull's-eye" in the center could not be used (unless in a transom above eye level), nor could the thick edges of the disk, so there was a good deal of waste, which was reflected in the price.

In Europe before the seventeenth century, glass panes were fixed in lead between thick stone mullions; later mullions and sashes were made of wood. Christopher Wren

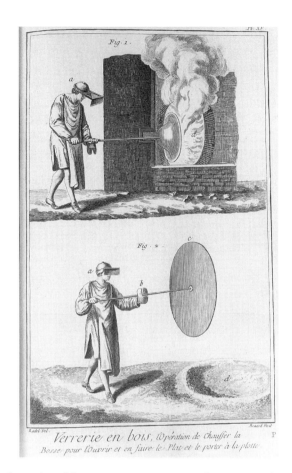

Illustration of window-glass blowing. From Denis Diderot, Encyclopédie *(Paris, 1751–72). Courtesy of the Library of the Sterling and Francine Clark Art Institute, Williamstown, Massachusetts.*

may have introduced double-hung, movable-sash, wooden windows to England when designing a country house in Hertfordshire in 1669. Soon afterward, sash windows with pulleys and weights were installed in the royal apartments at Hampton Court and Kensington Palace, and by the early 1700s double-hung sash windows were widely used on both sides of the Atlantic. In the colonies, the upper sash was often fixed in place, and the lower sash had to be propped open with sticks. Only lead was heavy enough to act as a counterweight for the window sash and still fit in the relatively narrow pockets in the frame, but lead weights had to be imported from England and were expensive; hence the tendency to omit them. The sash itself was made by carpenters on the site, using planes and one-inch boards and fastening the pieces at the corners with wooden pins. Putty to hold the glass in the sash was yet another item regularly ordered from London mercantile houses.

Exterior doors were also made up on the site, usually of two-inch plank, which for added effect could be worked into panels. If the opening to the main entrance was more than four feet wide, the builder was likely to install a pair of doors. Porches were still relatively rare, but for larger, more expansive frame houses, carpenters sometimes fashioned pilasters for either side of the entrance and added a pediment above, perhaps taking the design from a pattern book. If brass hinges, latches, and locks were to be used instead of wrought iron ones they too had to be imported from abroad.

As a last exterior embellishment, most frame houses had one or two stone steps leading to the exterior doors. The best quarries in Virginia were in the Piedmont or farther west, but the stone could be ferried down secondary creeks to the major rivers. Once landed, it had to be hauled to the site and set in place by a mason.

———

Inside the house, the work followed much the same pattern as outside. Basically it was a matter of applying successive layers of finishing material to the frame. If the house was closed in, the weather would be less of a factor, but the work still progressed in stages, with each stage dependent on those that had come before. And here too there was a tendency to begin at the bottom and work upward. Floors could be done first or later, but they had to be carefully planned for. To ensure that the plank was properly seasoned, Washington often tried to purchase it well beforehand.

The most commonly used wood for flooring was the heart of yellow pine, which was both hard and durable. One-and-a-quarter-inch thick and from five to eight inches wide, floor plank generally came from a mill. Once it reached the carpenter's hands, however, each board had to be hewn on the bottom to fit across the joists below and planed on the edges to fasten to the boards on either side of it. Also, a succession of smoothing planes, including one especially adapted for long strokes, was used to finish the topside of the plank. The finished boards were nailed to the joists with T- or L-headed nails to retard splitting, though occasionally and at considerable extra expense they were pegged to one another as well.

In modest houses, the finish of the interior walls was straightforward and for the most part quite plain. The carpenter installed baseboards and chair rails in all of the principal rooms and also added trim around the door and window openings. Simple ornamentation involved only planing, and the same was true of the wooden cornices, if there were to be any, placed where the walls met the ceiling. Chimneypieces might be a bit more elaborate, with the chimney breast reaching to the ceiling in the hall or parlor, the principal room used for entertaining.

If, however, the owner of the house moved or aspired to move in more exalted circles, the trim chosen could far exceed these modest enhancements. Walls could be partially or wholly paneled; doorways could be framed with pilasters and topped by pediments; cornices could become full, classical entablatures; and chimneypieces could be transformed into astonishingly rich confections of ornament, especially with English pattern books to point the way.

Such interiors often required not only the skills of a joiner, who could use a plane, but those of a woodcarver as well. The craft itself was an old one, developed in England during the fourteenth and fifteenth centuries. In the late seventeenth and early eighteenth centuries, with Grinling Gibbons's work, wood carving became a high art and was much in vogue. In the colonies it had similar appeal for those wealthy enough to afford it.

A woodcarver's tools consisted of a wooden mallet and steel chisels and gouges of various dimensions and shapes. Much of the work was performed on moldings and consisted of relatively simple patterns of cuts, repeated time and again. When a carver wrote "Thursday morning"—and then "noon"—on a plank of wood hidden behind a modillion in an elegantly trimmed house in Charleston, it may have been to document the time it took to complete an especially boring job. Occasionally, however, the opportunity to do something more ambitious presented itself: the capital of an Ionic or Corinthian column, for example, or free-flowing garlands of foliage for a chimneypiece, or an intricate frieze for a cornice. Hardwood was often used for elaborate woodwork inside the house, though pine was cheaper and easier to carve. Work done in pine was usually primed with Spanish brown paint before being installed.

One interior detail that had to be carefully planned from the beginning was the staircase, since the space it would occupy was delineated by the framing of the building. Each situation was different, with the precise configuration of the stairs necessarily depending on the amount of room available, the heights and positions of various doors within the house, and the ceiling height. Also, some calculations had to fall within prescribed parameters: the pitch of the stairs could not vary, nor could the heights of the risers or the depths of the treads. Generally the pitch of a "flying" (continuous straight) run was between forty-five and twenty-seven degrees. There could not be more than ten or twelve steps in a single run, or the climber might tire; nor could there be fewer than two. Moxon's *Builder's Dictionary* prescribed stairs for large houses that had risers from four to six inches high, treads from twelve to eighteen inches deep, and stairs that were from six to sixteen feet wide.

Once the general design of the staircase was determined, simple mathematical calculations were made by translating the height of the room from floor to ceiling into inches and then dividing by 4, 5, or 6 to arrive at the number of stairs. Next, by stretching a "going rod" (a measuring stick) across the floor, the carpenter could measure the distance from where the newel post would be positioned at the stairway's beginning, to a point directly below the spot where the newel post on the floor above would be located: Again the total was divided, this time by the number of stairs, to determine the depth of each tread. By positioning the newel posts, the angle, or the "going of the flight," could also be determined.

On the basis of all these calculations, the stringboards—planks to which the risers and treads would eventually be attached—could be fashioned. Since the dimensions of the steps had been established, a triangular pattern, representing the profile of a single step, was cut and set on the edge of the stringboard so that the slope, or pitch side, of the triangle lay along the top of the plank. After the plank had been marked for the requisite number of steps, it was sawed. For narrow flights of stairs two stringboards were sufficient, but for a stairway wider than four feet, a third, positioned underneath in the middle, gave additional support. When the stringboards were fixed in place, the treads and risers were added. Stair treads were made of yellow pine. Risers were tongued at both edges into treads. An extra piece of molding just below the nosing on the tread added support and gave the joint a more finished look. Further support could be provided by attaching triangular blocks of wood underneath the tread where it met the riser.

In most houses in the South, stair runs were straight, with only simple handrails and no more decoration than a single stringpiece running up the side. In large houses, however, stairways could become highly dramatic focal points, with complex runs—involving several landings—and an abundance of decorative detail. Thus a broad, open well around the stairway might provide space for a carved frieze. Carved designs could also be used on the end of each step, and the newel posts, as well as the balusters supporting the railing, could be carved or turned on a lathe, or both.

Just as house carpenters often worked as joiners and carvers, some were skilled at turnery as well. A turner operating a lathe usually began with a full-size pattern, which could be transferred to a block of wood using a compass and calipers. For something as repetitive as stair balusters, a template and jig with pins to do the measuring and score the wood at appropriate intervals was probably also used. Then as the block rotated toward him, the carpenter cut into its surface with a chisel steadied on a horizontal rest. It was important to cut gently at first, so as not to catch the tool or split the wood. The lathe itself was usually powered by a foot pedal, but someone who specialized in the business might use one driven by a large wheel operated, in the South, by slave power.

After all of the interior woodwork, including the staircase, was in place and covered with an initial coat of paint, the carpenters were free to prepare the ceiling and walls for plastering. As a first step they had to make lath of riven strips of wood roughly a quarter of an inch thick, one to one and a half inches wide, and four to eight feet long. The strips were fastened to the studs with rose head nails, leaving about a quarter of an inch between the boards to provide a "key" to hold the plaster when it was applied.

Brickmasons often did the interior plastering of houses. A first coat, made of sand mixed with a small amount of slaked lime and animal hair, was troweled on; then came a second coat, almost entirely made of lime and much thinner, which gave the walls and ceiling a smooth, white surface. The first and second coats together were typically three-quarters of an inch thick. It took several weeks for plaster to dry once it was applied. Thereafter it needed only occasional whitewashing, though other coverings could be used.

When the plastering was finished, the wood trim could be given its final coat of paint. The key ingredient in paint was whatever coloring agent was used, and pigments imported from England were thought to be superior to local ones. Prussian blue pigment was especially expensive and perhaps for that reason was the most prestigious color, followed by green. Formulas for mixing paint varied from painter to painter, but it took a knowledgeable artisan to mix the ingredients correctly and arrive at the desired color and consistency. The work was done at the site, as the paint was needed. The pigments came in cakes, which had to be ground dry, then thoroughly reground with boiled linseed oil. This mixture, in turn, was ground in the desired amounts with white lead previously ground with linseed oil. Occasionally spirits of turpentine and other chemical agents, such as arsenic, were added. It was the linseed oil—made in the colonies from flax seed but routinely imported by planters—that gave the paint its protective, glossy surface.

Working with a round brush, a painter could vary the shade and intensity of some colors by altering the amount of pressure put on the brush while the surface was being coated. Sometimes, too, stenciled decoration was added, using patterns cut from cork—"on what figure you please"—dipped in a contrasting color and pressed on the wall. It was also fashionable to imitate marble or woodgraining with paint, which took additional skill and artistry.

As an alternative to having rooms paneled or painted, some innovative house owners after 1750 began to have their walls partially or fully covered with cloth or paper hangings. Most often the papers, which depicted everything from architectural elements and floral and geometric patterns to scenes of Roman ruins, were imported from England. Toward the end of the century "wallpaper" in plain colors, particularly blue and green, became popular, along with figured paper borders. Even after the Revolution, Virginia planters continued to import English papers, but by the 1790s one New York dealer offered "4000 elegant Paper Hangings with rich borders to suit" for the "southern market."

Wallpaper often came in rectangular pieces rather than continuous rolls. Both could be either tacked or pasted to the wall. The composition of the paste varied as painters and upholsterers (who often installed wallpaper) experimented with what worked best on a particular wall, but typically the mix consisted of flour and water with some alum added. Frequently, instructions for making up the paste and applying it came with the paper.

Plaster ceilings could also be embellished. One method was to use decorative plaster or stucco ornaments formed in molds and left to harden before being applied. As a less expensive alternative, papier-mâché imitations of architectural detail suitable for ceilings were sold along with wallpaper and paper borders. The customer had only to provide the dimensions of the room; the merchant would then customize the design accordingly—or that was the hope.

Whether it was when the painter finished coating the final length of cornice or when the last piece of wallpaper was hung, at some point construction would end. Even then, the house probably was not finished, at least in the eyes of its owner. More than likely there was work to be done on the adjacent outbuildings, not to mention the surrounding grounds. Also, the rooms in the house had to be furnished and, if the owner could afford them, provided with amenities like curtains and carpets. Still, the basic process of building had run its course.

Sources: Much of our information about building houses in eighteenth-century Virginia comes from contemporary accounts. In Washington's papers are such particulars as his instructions for laying shingles and his method of painting boards to resemble stone. His diary entries include observations about firing brick, and a letter in 1773 from his undertaker, Going Lanphier, lists the scantling needed for the south addition. We have used the Mount Vernon ledgers to discover where Washington found materials such as plank, oyster shells, stone, and cypress shingles. Correspondence with Robert Cary & Sons includes orders for imported items like axes, molding planes, nails, glue, paint ingredients, locks and hinges, window glass, putty and lead for constructing sash, and wallpaper and papier-mâché ornaments. And in a larger sense, his letters serve as an excellent example of the complex relationship between Virginia planters and mercantile houses in a metropolis some thirty-five hundred miles distant.

We have also relied on two building manuals commonly used in eighteenth-century Virginia: *The Builder's Dictionary: or, Gentleman and Architect's Companion* (London, 1734, 1981 rep.); and Joseph Moxon, *Mechanick Exercises: or the Doctrine of Handy-Works applied to the Arts of Smithing Joinery Carpentry Turning Bricklayery* (London, 1703) for such details as how to work a lathe, and how stairways were built.

Vestry instructions for the workers recruited to build Pohick Church include George Mason's formulas for making mortar for both bricklaying and interior plasterwork. Landon Carter writes of things like rotten sills and posts—"though of oak"—in his diary. See *The Diary of Colonel Landon Carter of Sabine Hall, 1752–1778,* Jack P. Greene, ed. (Charlottesville, Va., 1965). Also indicative of the degree of perseverance required to build a substantial house in Virginia is John Carlyle's colorful comment in a letter to his brother: "So much Trouble that If I had Suspected . . . What I have meet with, I believe I Shoud made Shift with a Very Small house." See James D. Munson, *Colonel John Carlyle, Gent.: a True and Just Account of the Man and His House* (Alexandria, Va., 1986), which reinforces William Fitzhugh's similar remarks made in the seventeenth century, quoted in Camille Wells, "The Eighteenth-Century Landscape of Virginia's Northern Neck," *Northern Neck of Virginia Historical Magazine* 38 (1987): 4217–55.

Several present-day sources have been especially useful to us as we have explored unknown territory. For a straightforward and informative description of the steps involved in building a frame house in eighteenth-century Virginia we are particularly indebted to Paul E. Buchanan, "The Eighteenth-Century Frame Houses of Tidewater Virginia," in Charles E. Peterson, ed., *Building Early America: Contributions Toward the History of a Great Industry* (Radnor, Pa., 1976), 54–73. Marcus Whiffen, *The Eighteenth-Century House of Williamsburg: A Study of Architecture and Building in the Colonial Capital of Virginia,* rev. ed. (Williamsburg, Va., 1984), offers a clear explanation of such details as the kinds of nails used, paint ingredients, bench planes, chisels and gouges, framing, and sash windows. Similarly, we have relied on Jack McLaughlin's account of the different phases of construction—most notably his vivid description of brickmaking—in *Jefferson and Monticello: The Biography of a Builder* (New York, 1988). Daniel D. Reiff's discussion in *Small Georgian Houses in England and Virginia: Origins and Development through the 1750s* (London and Toronto, 1986), of the relation of pattern books to actual building practice, is provocative, as is the rest of the book, although it focuses on brick rather than frame houses. On paints and painting we have learned a great deal from Matthew Mosca's "The House and Its Restoration," *Antiques Magazine* 135, no. 2 (1989):462–73; and for a thorough treatment of the wallpaper trade, we consulted Catherine Lynn's *Wallpaper in America: From the Seventeenth Century to World War I* (New York, 1980). Kenneth M. Wilson, "Window Glass in America," in Peterson, ed., *Building Early America*, 150–64; Harley J. McKee, "Brick and Stone: Handicraft to Machine," ibid., 74–95; and Diana S. White, "Roofing for Early America," ibid., 135–49, are all informative. And last, to better visualize such processes as sawing plank in a water mill, hewing logs, and making shingles, we have found the text and line drawings in Edwin Tunis's *Colonial Living* (Cleveland and New York, 1957) and his *Colonial Craftsmen and the Beginnings of American Industry* (Cleveland and New York, 1965) extremely useful.

Notes

The following abbreviations are used throughout the notes:

GW   George Washington

GWD   *The Diaries of George Washington*, Donald Jackson, ed., Dorothy Twohig, assoc. ed. (Charlottesville, Va., 1976–79), 6 vols.

GWW   *The Writings of George Washington from the Original Manuscript Sources, 1745–1799*, John C. Fitzpatrick, ed. (Washington, D.C., 1931–44), 30 vols.

PGW   *The Papers of George Washington,* William W. Abbot, ed., Dorothy Twohig, ed. (Charlottesville, Va., 1983–), in progress.

PGWp   Papers of George Washington project, offices, Alderman Library, University of Virginia, Charlottesville, Virginia.

ViMtvL   Mount Vernon Ladies' Association Library, Mount Vernon, Virginia.

Chapter 1

1. Bryan Fairfax to GW, 29 March 1778, copy, PGWp.

2. Peter Stephen DuPonceau to Anna L. Garasche, 9 Sept. 1837, copy, ViMtvL. Ponceau, who served as von Steuben's secretary and aide-de-camp, was confiding his memories to his granddaughter in old age.

Chapter 2

1. Douglas Southall Freeman, *George Washington: A Biography* (New York, 1948), 1:15, also 527–29. Freeman provides the fullest scholarly account of the Washington family's early years in America. For briefer versions see James Thomas Flexner, *George Washington: The Forge of Experience (1732–1775)* (Boston, 1965), 9–17, and John E. Ferling, *The First of Men: A Life of George Washington* (Knoxville, Tenn., 1988), 3–8.

2. Freeman, *Washington*, 1:15–29.

3. Ibid., 7, n. 26, summarizes the relevant Virginia statutes.

The best analysis of Virginia's economy and society during the first three quarters of the seventeenth century is contained in Edmund S. Morgan's pathbreaking *American Slavery, American Freedom: The Ordeal of Colonial Virginia* (New York, 1975), 3–292. Allan Kulikoff offers a fine short account in *Tobacco and Slaves: The Development of Southern Cultures in the Chesapeake, 1680–1800* (Chapel Hill, N.C., and London, 1986), 23–44. On the developing shape of the colony's social structure and the increasing prominence in it of a small number of families that included the Washingtons, see also Bernard Bailyn, "Politics and Social Structure in Virginia," in James M. Smith, ed., *Seventeenth-Century America: Essays in Colonial History* (Chapel Hill, N.C., 1959), 90–115.

4. William Fitzhugh to Nicholas Hayward, 30 Jan. 1680, 81, quoted in Freeman, *Washington*, 1:11.

5. Ibid., 20–21.

6. Ibid., 22, as well as the lengthy appendix tracing the history of the proprietorship to 1745, 447–513.

7. Henry Hartwell, James Blair, and Edward Chilton, *The Present State of Virginia and the College* (1697), quoted in Charles C. Wall, "Notes on the Early History of Mount Vernon," *William and Mary Quarterly*, 3rd ser., 2 (1945):175. See also John Stilgoe, *Common Landscape of America, 1580 to 1845* (New Haven, Conn., 1982), 65.

8. Worthington Chauncey Ford, *Wills of George Washington and His Immediate Ancestors* (Brooklyn, N.Y., 1891), 77ff.

9. Freeman, *Washington*, 1:29–31.

10. Wall, "Early History of Mount Vernon," 175.

11. Ibid., 174–75 and 186–87. A more recent analysis of the evidence is contained in the excellent, highly detailed "Historic Structure Report" prepared for the Mount Vernon Ladies' Association by Mesick, Cohen, Waite, Architects (1993), 75–78, MSS, ViMtvL.

12. Ford, *Wills*, 36.

13. Ibid., 35–37.

14. On the radical restructuring of Virginia's economy and society brought about by the spread of slavery see Morgan, *American Slavery*, 295–387; Kulikoff, *Tobacco and Slaves*, 37–435; and Darrett B. Rutman and Anita H. Rutman, *A Place in Time: Middlesex County, Virginia, 1650–1750* (New York and London, 1984), 164–203. The changing position of the gentry and its relation to the rest of Virginia society is also discussed in Rhys Isaac, *The Transformation of Virginia, 1740–1790* (Chapel Hill, N.C., 1982), 11–138. And for a telling picture of how these developments manifested themselves in the life of a single individual, see Kenneth A. Lockridge, *The Diary and Life of William Byrd II of Virginia, 1674–1744* (Chapel Hill, N.C., and London, 1987).

15. Freeman, *Washington*, 1:10–14.

16. Leonidas Dodson, *Alexander Spotswood: Governor of Colonial Virginia, 1710–1722* (Philadelphia, 1932), 278–303.

17. Freeman, *Washington*, 1:37.

18. Ibid., 38ff.

19. Ibid., 33–42 and 48–56.

20. *Estate of Capt Augustine Washington, Inventory, July, 1743* (Fredericksburg, Va., n.d.).

21. Earthfast construction is effectively described by Cary Carson, Norman F. Barka, William M. Kelso, Gary Wheeler Stone, and Dell Upton in "Impermanent Architecture in the Southern American Colonies," *Winterthur Portfolio* 16 (1981):135–96.

See also Fraser D. Neiman, "Domestic Architecture at the Clift's Plantation: The Social Context of Early Virginia Building" in Dell Upton and John Michael Vlach, eds., *Common Places: Readings in American Vernacular Architecture* (Athens, Ga., and London, 1986), 294–307; Daniel D. Reiff, *Small Georgian Houses in England and Virginia: Origins and Development Through the 1750s* (London and Toronto, 1986), 192–94; and Camille Wells, "The Eighteenth-Century Landscape of Virginia's Northern Neck," *Northern Neck of Virginia Historical Magazine* 37 (1987):4217–55.

22. The most detailed treatment of early eighteenth-century gentry houses in Virginia is Reiff's *Small Georgian Houses*. See especially 13–18 and 221–316. Reiff concludes that the typical brick, five-bay-wide, hipped-roof house built in the colony before 1750 was more an expression of local, vernacular building traditions than direct British design influence, either through published sources or specific models.

Two other studies—though not of gentry houses per se—that stress the continuing centrality of vernacular building traditions in Virginia yet also point to sharp changes in building design during the eighteenth century are Henry Glassie, *Folk Housing in Middle Virginia: A Structural Analysis of Historic Artifacts* (Knoxville, Tenn., 1975) and Dell Upton, *Holy Things and Profane: Anglican Parish Churches in Colonial Virginia* (Cambridge, Mass., and London, 1986).

For interpretations of gentry house design emphasizing European influences see Thomas T. Waterman, *Mansions of Virginia: 1706 to 1776* (New York, 1945), 29–241, and William H. Pierson's admirable *American Buildings and Their Architects: The Colonial and Neo-Classical Styles* (Garden City, N.Y., 1970), 61–78. Mills Lane covers much the same ground in *Architecture of the Old South: Virginia* (Savannah, Ga., 1987), 10–89.

On the social uses and significance of the new house type see Isaac, *Transformation of Virginia*, 34–42 and 70–79, and for broader perspectives: James Deetz, *In Small Things Forgotten: The Archaeology of Early American Life* (Garden City, N.Y., 1977), 92–117; Richard L. Bushman, *The Refinement of America: Persons, Houses, Cities* (New York, 1992), 100–138; and Kevin M. Sweeney, "High-Style Vernacular: Lifestyles of the Colonial Elite," in Cary Carson, Ronald Hoffman, and Peter J. Albert, eds., *Of Consuming Interests: The Style of Life in the Eighteenth Century* (Charlottesville, Va., and London, 1992), 1–58.

In addition there are a number of studies comparing the material world of the gentry with that of their less affluent neighbors or providing information that makes it possible to do so. See, for example, the Rutmans, *Place in Time*, 188–95; Richard L. Bushman, "American High-Style and Vernacular Cultures," in Jack P. Greene and J. R. Pole, eds., *Colonial British America: Essays in the New History of the Early Modern Era* (Baltimore, 1984), 416–55; and Carole Shammas, *The Pre-Industrial Consumer in England and America* (New York, 1990). Also, Jack P. Greene, in *Pursuits of Happiness: The Social Development of Early Modern British Colonies and the Formation of American Culture* (Chapel Hill, N.C., 1988), offers a variety of penetrating insights into the role such matters played as agents of cultural change and definition.

23. The building of the Governor's Palace in Williamsburg and subsequent alterations to it are described in Marcus Whiffen, *The Public Buildings of Williamsburg, Colonial Capital of Virginia: An Architectural History* (Williamsburg, Va., 1958), passim, and Waterman, *Mansions of Virginia*, 29–61. In *The Governor's Palace in Williamsburg: A Cultural Study* (Williamsburg, Va., 1991), Graham Hood provides an extensive analysis of life in the Palace, structured around a close reading of an inventory of the property of Governor Norborne Berkeley, Baron de Botetourt, prepared following his death in 1770. The study is a model of recent approaches to the analysis of material culture.

24. Freeman, *Washington*, 1:14, and Kulikoff, *Tobacco and Slaves*, 276.

25. Ford, *Wills*, 41–51.

26. Kenton Kilmer and Donald Sweig, *The Fairfax Family in Fairfax County: A Brief History* (Fairfax, Va., 1975), 24–33.

27. For descriptions and conjectural drawings of Belvoir see ibid., 30, and Waterman, *Mansions of Virginia*, 330–32.

28. Freeman, *Washington*, 1:447–513. GW's biographers are in general agreement that contact with the Fairfaxes was a transforming influence in his life. See Flexner, *Forge of Experience*, 24–25, and Ferling, *The First of Men*, 8–10. Even after GW's star began to rise, he continued to do everything in his power to cultivate the Fairfaxes, and while he was away at the front urged his younger brother, John Augustine, whom he had left in charge at Mount Vernon, to do the same. "I should be glad to hear that you live in perfect Harmony and good fellowship with the family at Belvoir, as it is in their power to be very serviceable upon many occasions to us as young beginner's" (GW to

John Augustine Washington, 28 May 1755, *PGW*, Col. Ser., 1:289).

29. Freeman, *Washington*, 1:228ff.

30. Ibid., 71, 229, 236, and 239. For a concise account of the formation and early history of the Ohio Company see also *PGW*, Col. Ser., 1:58–59, n. 1. Ultimately the company failed to achieve its objectives, and opinions differ about the broader consequences of the effort. Writes Francis Jennings in his sweeping, passionate history of the Seven Years' War: "What must be contemplated seriously . . . is that the heedless greed of these few headstrong men lit a fire in the wilderness that spread to become a conflagration throughout the world. That they lost money in the process is only a crowning irony." See Jennings, *Empire of Fortune: Crowns, Colonies, and Tribes in the Seven Years' War in America* (New York and London, 1988), 13.

31. Mesick, Cohen, Waite, "Historic Structure Report," 79, and accompanying drawings, MSS, ViMtvL.

32. Lawrence Washington's inventory, MSS, ViMtvL.

33. See Mesick, Cohen, Waite, "Historic Structure Report," drawings following 82, MSS, ViMtvL.

34. Mesick, Cohen, Waite configure the ground-floor rooms of Lawrence's house differently than we have, arguing that "the likely location" of the room listed as "the Hall" in his inventory was the northwest corner of the building rather than the southeast corner, as we suggest. They also date the present finish of the room in the southeast corner from GW's first rebuilding of the house in 1757–58, during which, as the evidence clearly indicates, the other ground-floor rooms were refinished ("Historic Structure Report," 80–81 and 389–91, MSS, ViMtvL). This dating and Mesick, Cohen, Waite's placement of Lawrence's hall are supported by Dennis J. Pogue, the current director of restoration of Mount Vernon, in his excellent overview of the development of the plantation during the forty-five years of GW's proprietorship. See Dennis J. Pogue, "Mount Vernon: Transformation of an Eighteenth-Century Plantation System," in Paul A. Shackel and Barbara J. Little, *Historical Archaeology of the Chesapeake* (Washington, D.C., 1994) 101–14, esp. 104.

The reasons for our earlier dating of the southeast corner room's finish and our designation of it as Lawrence's hall—in addition to its location next to the entrance on the side of the house facing the river, a means of reaching Mount Vernon probably more used at that time than the road from Alexandria, which was only just being established as a town—are: (1) the differences in finish and design between this room and those refinished as part of GW's 1757–58 rebuilding of the house; and (2) evidence behind the present interior walls of the room indicating that a different sequence of steps was followed in refinishing it than the one used in the 1757–58 rebuilding.

The chief differences in design and finish involve the chair rail and the molding surrounding the doors and windows of the room, all of which are unlike those elsewhere at Mount Vernon. The window and door surrounds are notably plainer and narrower, and the chair rail has an altogether different profile—basically rounded, whereas the chair rails throughout the parts of the house refinished or newly built in 1757–58 are flat on the top, with a shelflike profile. Waterman notes the latter anomaly in *Mansions of Virginia* and argues that the chair rail in the room in question is of an earlier style, indicating an earlier date for the room's finish.

The major piece of evidence regarding the steps followed in refinishing the southeast corner room results from the fact that three of the ground-floor rooms in the part of the house built by Lawrence, instead of being stripped to the studs before being refinished, were covered with entirely new interior walls firred out from the originals by a few inches. Only in the case of the southeast corner room, however, was the existing plaster removed from the lath before this was done. In the two rooms on the west side of the house, which the evidence clearly indicates were refinished during GW's 1757–58 remodeling, both the original plaster and the lath were left intact behind the new walls. In a relatively recent excavation of a trash midden eighty feet south of the house, a large layer of plaster was discovered, which undoubtedly came from stripping a room. Fragments of plaster later found in the walls when the ceiling of the southeast corner room was replaced match those in the midden. Unfortunately it is impossible to date the layer containing the plaster more closely than sometime between 1748 and 1769. (We are grateful to Dennis Pogue, who, with characteristic generosity, has shared this information with us.)

A final point that should be mentioned regarding our designation of the southeast corner room as Lawrence's hall concerns the size of the room. As the ground floor emerged from the 1757–58 rebuilding of the house, this room was noticeably smaller than either of those on the west side of the building, including the one that became GW's best room, the west parlor. Why did Lawrence choose a smaller room for

his hall? One answer could be that both the rooms on the east side of the house may originally have been larger than they are now. The evidence clearly indicates that the present passage was divided by a wall running across its width in line with the west walls of two rooms on the east side of the house. The form of the dividing wall is not known, but it seems at least possible that: (1) the passage may have run initially only from the west wall of the house to the line of the division; and (2) the two rooms to the east may have adjoined one another. Both rooms in that case would have been larger than they are now. In this plan the northeast room would have been the one designated as the "Parlour" in Lawrence's inventory, a configuration that among other things would help explain the curious treatment of the "Parlour & Passage" as a single room in the inventory.

Admittedly all of this is conjectural, but the evidence at many points is missing or at best ambiguous. Mesick, Cohen, Waite place Lawrence's parlor where we do ("Historic Structure Report," 81, MSS, ViMtvL), but Dennis Pogue believes it was in the southwest corner of the house ("Mount Vernon," Shackel and Little, eds., *Historical Archaeology of the Chesapeake,* 104). We would add in support of our version of the configuration of Lawrence's rooms that it closely resembles the original ground-floor plan of the Governor's Palace in Williamsburg.

35. On the changing uses and designations of rooms in eighteenth-century Virginia houses see Neiman, "Domestic Architecture at Cliffs Plantation," 307–12, and Dell Upton, "Vernacular Domestic Architecture in Eighteenth-Century Virginia," in Upton and Vlach, eds., *Common Places,* 315–35. Of halls Upton writes: "What had in the seventeenth century been a general-purpose living and working place became in the eighteenth century the focus of . . . institutionalized conviviality." However, Upton also notes that "institutionalized conviviality" was no helter-skelter affair. "The elegance and formality of the entertaining room set the tone for sociability at the same time that it made the participants aware of the limits. Visually, everything about the planter's hall said 'this far but no farther'" (ibid., 321). On all counts the room we have identified as Lawrence Washington's hall would seem to fit the pattern Upton describes.

36. Lawrence Washington's inventory, MSS, ViMtvL.

37. Freeman, *Washington,* 1:263–64.

38. Lawrence Washington's will, MSS, ViMtvL.

39. See John Mercer's letter defending his son

George Mercer, "the carpenter," *Virginia Gazette*, 12 Sept. 1766. For someone of Mercer's standing to bind his son to a tradesman was unusual to say the least, and the arrangement was eventually terminated.

40. "The Estate of Lawrence Washington Esq. Deceased," Settlement Papers of Lawrence Washington, 1752–1756, MSS, ViMtvL. John North was a joiner who lived on a farm that either abutted Lawrence's property or was part of it. William Sewell was working with William Waite, according to Lawrence's estate accounts (MSS, ViMtvL), probably as an apprentice carpenter.

41. Lawrence Washington's will, MSS, ViMtvL.

42. Freeman, *Washington*, 2:1ff.

43. *PGW,* Col. Ser., 1:232–34.

44. Both Flexner and Freeman describe GW's childhood at length. His formal schooling probably ended in Fredericksburg when he was not yet twelve (Freeman, *Washington*, 1:64). On his reading, dancing instruction, card playing, and clothes taken to Belvoir see ibid., 229; and on his prowess at riding and his copying of Hawkin's *Rules* and passages from the *Spectator*, Flexner, *The Forge of Experience*, 22–38. Among the maxims GW copied were: "Every action done in company ought to be with some sign of respect to those that are present. . . . Cleanse not your teeth with the tablecloth. . . . Keep to the fashion of your equals. . . . [and] Labor to keep alive in your breast that little spark of celestial fire called conscience" (ibid., 22).

In *George Washington: The Virginia Period, 1732–1775* (Durham, N.C., 1964), Bernhard Knollenberg—who writes with the stated intention of refraining from "undue glorification" of his subject and applying "the critical approach to Washington's own statements as to other evidence"—also covers GW's childhood, but reaches essentially the same conclusions other biographers have (ibid., 3–10). More striking is David Hackett Fischer's analysis in *Albion's Seed: Four British Folkways in America* (New York, 1989). In discussing Virginia's "Child Ways," he uses GW as a prime example of the tension between the "stoic mastery of self" instilled in Virginia youth and the emphasis on "boisterous feelings and manly passions and a formidable will." That tension, he argues, "became a coiled spring at the core of Virginia's culture," though in GW's case "Virginia's system of child-drearing had a spectacular success" (ibid., 311–18).

45. An excellent discussion of GW's work as a surveyor and a list of the surveys he did between July 1749 and October 1752 appear in *PGW,* Col. Ser., 1:8–37.

46. "A Journal of my Journey over the Mountains began Fryday the 11th of March, 1747/8," *GWD,* 1:6–23.

47. Ibid., 1:91.

48. On Dinwiddie's service as lieutenant governor of Virginia see Louis Knott Koontz, *Robert Dinwiddie: His Career in American Colonial Government and Westward Expansion* (Glendale, Calif., 1941) and John Alden, *Robert Dinwiddie: Servant of the Crown* (Charlottesville, Va., 1973). Prior to the governorship of Lord Botetourt, which began in 1768, the position of chief executive in Virginia was routinely filled by the lieutenant governor, while the individual serving as governor remained at home in England.

49. Invoice from John Ridout, 23 Oct. 1754, *PGW,* Col. Ser., 1:217–18.

50. *The Journal of Major George Washington, Sent by the Hon. Robert Dinwiddie, Esq; His Majesty's Lieutenant-Governor, and Commander in Chief of Virginia, to the Commandant of the French Forces on Ohio. To Which are Added, the Governor's Letter, and a Translation of the French Officer's Answer* (Williamsburg, Va., 1754), repr. in *GWD,* 1:130–60.

51. For Dinwiddie's instructions to GW see *PGW,* Col. Ser., 1: 65. The question of GW's rank and pay is aired in GW to Richard Corbin, n.d., ibid., 70; GW to Robert Dinwiddie, 18 May 1754, ibid., 98–100; Dinwiddie to GW, 25 May 1754, ibid., 102–4; and GW to Dinwiddie, 29 May 1754, ibid., 107–13.

52. The incident is described in GW's letter of 29 May 1754 to Dinwiddie (ibid.), but only after nine paragraphs devoted to the pay issue.

53. GW's account of his surrender of Fort Necessity, as well as the Articles of Capitulation he signed on 3 July 1754 and two other accounts presumed to have been written by him—one in 1757 and the other in 1786—are reprinted in ibid., 157–73.

54. GW to William Fitzhugh, 15 Nov. 1754, ibid., 226.

55. Despite his decision to quit the military, GW still felt moved to declare at the end of his letter to Fitzhugh: "My inclinations are strongly bent to arms" (ibid.).

56. Lease, 17 Dec. 1754, ibid., 232–34.

57. The expenditures mentioned are recorded in Ledger A, 49 and 37, copy, PGWp.

58. For an account of the campaign see Paul E. Kopperman, *Braddock at the Monongahela* (Pittsburgh, 1977). In *Empire of Fortune* Jennings offers a notably more critical view (109–68, passim).

59. GW to John Augustine Washington, 6 May

1755, *PGW*, Col. Ser., 1:266–67. On GW's status as a volunteer and the issue of rank see GW to William Byrd, 20 April 1755, ibid., 249–51; to Carter Burwell, same date, ibid., 252–53; and to John Robinson, same date, ibid., 254–57.

60. GW wrote a brief account of the battle to his mother, noting that he "had four Bullets through my Coat, and two Horses shot under me" (GW to Mary Ball Washington, 18 July 1755, ibid., 336–37).

61. GW's commission and two accompanying memoranda from Dinwiddie appear in ibid., 2:3–8. For his conflicted feelings about accepting the appointment see GW to Warner Lewis, 14 Aug. 1755, ibid., 1:360–63.

62. Among the many communications on the subject of Dagworthy's claim to outrank GW and the other senior officers of the Virginia Regiment, the most complete statement of GW's position is contained in the letter he wrote Dinwiddie, 14 Jan. 1756, asking for permission to appeal to Shirley in person (ibid., 2:283–86; for Dinwiddie's reply, granting permission for the trip, see ibid., 290–91).

63. Joseph Chew to GW, 14 March 1757, ibid., 4:115–16.

64. Chew to GW, 13 July 1757, ibid., 301–3.

65. See Freeman, *Washington*, 2:157–68, for a detailed account of the trip. On Shirley's career as a colonial official and military commander see John A. Schutz, *William Shirley: King's Governor of Massachusetts* (Chapel Hill, N.C., 1961).

66. Carl Bridenbaugh treats Harrison's life and work in *Peter Harrison: First American Architect* (Chapel Hill, N.C., 1949). On the Redwood Library see 48–53; also Pierson, *American Buildings*, 142–50. Shirley's house in Roxbury is described in W. W. Cordingley, "Shirley Place, Roxbury, Massachusetts, and Its Builder, Governor William Shirley," *Old-Time New England: The Bulletin of the Society for the Preservation of New England Antiquities* 12 (1921):51–63. Antoinette F. Downing discusses the possibility that Harrison designed the house in "Harrison, Peter," in Adolf K. Placzek et al., eds., *Macmillan Encyclopedia of Architects* (London and New York, 1982), 2:321–22. In addition to its use of rusticated boards, Shirley Place incorporated three other prominent features that were later to appear at Mount Vernon: a cupola, a large ground-floor Palladian or "Venetian" window, and a two-story "Saloon" or entertaining room.

Also adding to the likelihood that this particular trip influenced GW's thinking about architecture is the fact that one of his traveling companions was Captain George Mercer—the same George Mercer who had earlier been apprenticed by his father, John Mercer, the Washingtons' lawyer, to William Waite, an Alexandria house carpenter, in the hope that he might turn his skill at drawing into a career as an architect.

67. GW to John Campbell, earl of Loudoun, 10 Jan. 1757, *PGW*, Col. Ser. 4:79–93. See also GW to James Cuninghame, 28 Jan. 1757, ibid., 105–7.

68. GW to Richard Washington, 6 Dec. 1755 and 15 April 1757, ibid., 2:207–8 and 4:132–35.

69. Ibid.

70. GW to Robert Dinwiddie, 10 March 1757, ibid., 112–15. Alden, in *Robert Dinwiddie: Servant of the Crown*, argues that Dinwiddie consistently supported GW's appeals for preferment until Nov. 1756, when he ceased doing so (90–117).

71. Ledger A, 38, copy, PGWp.

72. In contrast to most of his biographers, Ferling discounts the depth of GW's attachment to Sally Fairfax, at least in the beginning, describing him as "too self-absorbed to have instituted the kind of warm relationship that he believed he wanted" (*The First of Men*, 34–35, 51, and 53–54).

73. Editorial Note, *PGW*, Col. Ser., 6:202.

74. GW to Richard Washington, 15 April 1757, ibid., 134.

Chapter 3

1. GW to John Alton, 5 April 1759, *PGW*, Col. Ser., 6:200. John Alton had been GW's body servant in the Braddock campaign and worked at Mount Vernon in various capacities, including farm overseer, until his death in 1785 (ibid., 200, n.).

2. GW to Richard Washington, 15 Apr. 1757, ibid., 4:132–34; invoice from Richard Washington, 10 Nov. 1757, ibid., 5:49–50.

3. GW to Richard Washington, 15 Apr. 1757, ibid., 4:134.

4. Humphrey Knight to GW, 16 June 1758, ibid., 5:217; John Patterson to GW, 17 June 1758, ibid., 222.

5. George William Fairfax to GW, 1 Sept. 1758, ibid., 437.

6. John Patterson to GW, 17 June and 2 Sept. 1758, ibid., 222 and 449–50; Humphrey Knight to GW, 13 July 1758, ibid., 284–85; and George William Fairfax to GW, 25 July 1758, ibid., 328–29.

7. Of the four contenders for the seat in the House of Burgesses, GW came away with the most votes. "Treats" (furnished by the candidate and consumed by the voters) totaled 160 gallons of beer, rum, cider,

and wine, which came to more than a quart and a half per voter (Freeman, *Washington*, 2:317–21). For an excellent description of Virginia elections during the colonial period, including the time-honored custom of treating, see Charles S. Sydnor, *American Revolutionaries in the Making: Political Practices in Washington's Virginia* (New York and London, 1965), 21–73.

8. George William Fairfax to GW, 25 July, 5 Aug., and 15 Sept. 1758, *PGW*, Col. Ser., 5:328–29 and 371–72, and 6:19–20; and John Patterson to GW, 13 Aug. 1758, ibid., 5:390–91.

9. GW to George William Fairfax, 25 Sept. 1758, ibid., 6:38–40.

10. John Patterson to GW, 13 Aug. 1758, ibid., 5:390.

11. Ibid. These closets remain a major mystery at Mount Vernon since no drawing or plan showing them survives, and almost all traces of them were covered by GW's later additions to the house. See Mesick, Cohen, Waite, "Historic Structure Report," 85–86, MSS, ViMtvL.

12. The conclusion that rusticated boards were used on the exterior of Mount Vernon as early as 1758 is based on the discovery of such siding on portions of the walls covered in the 1770s when the house was extended northward (Charles C. Wall, "Restoration Repainting," report for the Mount Vernon Ladies' Association of the Union, 1956, Mount Vernon Reference Notebook 10, "Building Materials," ViMtvL). On the subject of adding sand to the paint, GW wrote to William Thornton: "Sanding is designed to answer two purposes, durability, and presentation of Stone; for the latter purpose, and in my opinion a desirable one; it is the last operation, by dashing, as long as any will stick, the Sand upon a coat of thick paint" (GW to William Thornton, 1 Oct. 1799, *GWW*, 37:387).

13. George William Fairfax to GW, 1 and 15 Sept. 1758, *PGW*, Col. Ser., 5:436–37 and 6:19–20.

14. John Patterson to GW, 13 Aug. 1758, ibid., 5:390.

15. George William Fairfax to GW, 1 Sept. 1758, ibid., 436–37.

16. George William Fairfax to GW, 1 Sept. 1758 (the second letter of this date), ibid., 438–39.

17. John Patterson to GW, 2 Sept. 1758, ibid., 449–50.

18. George William Fairfax to GW, 15 Sept. 1758, ibid., 6:19–20.

19. Freeman, *Washington*, 2:352.

20. Ibid., 306–7. After hearing the previous spring that he was to serve under Forbes, GW had written to Brigadier General John Stanwix asking him "to mention me in favorable terms to General Forbes . . . as a person who would gladly be distinguished in some measure from the *common run* of provincial Officers; as I understand there will be a motley herd of us" (GW to John Stanwix, 10 April 1758, *PGW*, Col. Ser., 5:117–18).

21. GW to Sally Cary Fairfax, 25 Sept. 1758, ibid., 6:41–43.

22. In contrast to most of GW's biographers, Bernhard Knollenberg has high praise for Forbes, describing him as "an indomitable and successful leader [who] has generally received less credit than he deserves . . . because of Washington's unfavorable letters concerning him" (*Washington: The Virginia Period*, 69).

23. See "Address from the Officers of the Virginia Regiment" to GW, 31 Dec. 1758, *PGW*, Col. Ser., 6:178–81; and GW's reply, "To the Officers of the Virginia Regiment," 10 Jan. 1759, ibid., 186–87; also "Resolution of the House of Burgesses," 26 Feb. 1759, ibid., 192.

24. The ceremony took place on 6 Jan. 1759 (Freeman, *Washington*, 3:1–2).

25. Ibid., 2–12.

26. GW to Robert Cary & Co., 1 May 1759, *PGW*, Col. Ser., 6:315–18.

27. Ledger A, 72, copy, PGWp.

28. Ibid., 58.

29. Ibid., 49.

30. Ibid., 54. GW was not the only person to have trouble with Winter. On 22 June 1760 John Fendall ran the following advertisement in the *Maryland Gazette*: "Ran away from the Subscriber, a Convict Servant Man named *John Winter*, a very compleat House Painter; he can imitate Marble or Mahogany very exactly, and can paint Floor Cloths as neat as any imported from *Britain*. . . . He is a very impertinent Fellow, pretty tall, and very red about the Nose and Face" (*Maryland Gazette*, quoted in *PGW*, Col. Ser., 6:329–30, n. 11).

31. As we indicated above (chap. 2, n. 34), our designation of the rooms at Mount Vernon during Lawrence's time there differs both from the configuration Mesick, Cohn, Waite describe ("Historic Structure Report," 79–82 and the drawings following 82, MSS, ViMtvL) and the plan outlined by Dennis Pogue ("Mount Vernon," Shackel and Little, eds., *Historical Archaeology of the Chesapeake*, 104). The four also see no change in the orientation of the house occurring as a result of GW's 1757–58 rebuilding of it, nor, to our knowledge, has anyone else proposed such a theory.

In addition to the reasons already given for our

placement of Lawrence's hall and parlor on the east side of the house—and thus the reorientation by GW in the 1757–58 rebuilding, when the rooms to the west were transformed into a new parlor and dining room—we would note two other points here. First, the usual pattern in Virginia gentry houses was for the stairway to be placed at the opposite end of the passage from the main entrance to the building. Since Lawrence located his stairway to the west, the implication is that the main entrance lay to the east, unless he had decided to depart from the standard placement of those two important features, and we can see no reason why he would have done that.

As for why GW did not change the location of the stairway—if indeed he was changing the orientation of the house—the fact is that he could not have done so without further extensive rebuilding of the structure as it came to him from Lawrence. Given the location of the wall running through the building on the north–south axis, there is not enough room to place a grand staircase at the east end of the passage and still preserve access from it to the two rooms on the east side of the house. Under the circumstances GW chose the easier, more economical solution and rebuilt the stairway, but left it at the west end of the passage.

Also substantiating our view, we believe, are GW's instructions of April 5, 1759, to John Alton, on the eve of the family's arrival at Mount Vernon and Martha Washington's first view of her new home. In asking Alton to "get two of the best Bedsteads put up—one in the Hall Room, and the other in the little dining Room that use to be," it seems most unlikely that he had in mind placing beds in the newly refinished west parlor and dining room, since together with the passage they were meant to be the cynosure of the rebuilt mansion. The rooms in which he must have wanted the beds placed, then, were the other two on the ground floor—those to the east—and his own designations would seem to make their former uses clear. They were a "Hall Room and a little dining Room that use to be." There is also the suggestion here that during the years GW lived in the house before the 1757–58 rebuilding, he had already begun changing the functions of those rooms, making either Lawrence's original parlor or his hall into a "dining Room" (a designation not used in the 1753 inventory of his estate) and leaving the other a "Hall Room." In any case, we are confident that the two rooms in question were on the east side of the house, making it highly Probable that the principal entrance in Lawrence's time was there as well.

32. Freeman, *Washington*, 1:193ff.

33. GW to Richard Washington, 10 Aug. 1760, *PGW*, Col. Ser., 6:452–53.

34. Although some shipments of tobacco were still consigned to Richard Washington over the next five years, no more goods were ordered from him, and GW's correspondence with him seems to have ended in 1765 (ibid., 319, n.).

35. For a brief description of the tobacco trade see Freeman, *Washington*, 3:42–44; and for two fuller treatments, Arthur P. Middleton, *Tobacco Coast: A Maritime History of Chesapeake Bay in the Colonial Era* (Newport News, Va., 1953) and Jacob M. Price, *Capital and Credit in British Overseas Trade: The View from the Chesapeake, 1700–1776* (Cambridge, Mass., 1980).

36. See, for example, GW to Richard Washington, 15 April 1757, and to Robert Cary & Co., 1 May and 20 Sept. 1759, and 28 Sept. 1760, *PGW*, Col. Ser., 4:134, and 6:317–18, 352–55, and 459–64.

37. There is a large and steadily growing body of historical literature on the consumer revolution of the eighteenth century in both Britain and America. Three fine collections of essays on the subject are: Neil McKendrick, John Brewer, and J. H. Plumb, *The Birth of Consumer Society: The Commercialization of Eighteenth-Century England* (Bloomington, Ind., 1982); John Brewer and Roy Porter, eds., *Consumption and the World of Goods* (London and New York, 1993); and Carson, Hoffman, and Albert, eds., *Of Consuming Interests*. In GW's case we also find particularly apt Colin Campbell's approach in *The Romantic Ethic and the Spirit of Modern Consumerism* (Oxford and New York, 1987), which emphasizes issues of self-definition and character as opposed to the more usual focus on the emulative aspects of consumption.

38. GW to Robert Cary & Co., 1 May, 12 June, and 20 Sept. 1759, *PGW*, Col. Ser., 6:317–18, 327–28, and 352–55.

39. Invoice from Robert Cary & Co., 6 Aug. 1759, ibid., 332–36.

40. Invoice from Robert Cary & Co., 15 March 1760, ibid., 392–402. In this case the total charges amounted to £353.15.9, and the goods shipped came from thirty-two different London establishments.

41. Ibid., 399–400.

42. GW to Robert Cary & Co., 28 Sept. 1760, ibid., 459–61.

43. GW to Robert Cary & Co., 10 Aug. and 28 Sept. 1760, ibid., 448–50 and 459–61.

44. Ibid., 461–63.

45. Invoice from Robert Cary & Co., 31 March 1761, ibid., 7:22–29.

46. GW to Robert Cary & Co., 1 Aug. 1761, ibid., 61–62.

47. *GWD*, 1:258. For an interesting discussion of the outbuildings at Mount Vernon before GW's time and during the early years of his proprietorship see Pogue, "Mount Vernon," Shackel and Little, eds., *Historical Archaeology of the Chesapeake*, 104–6. He concludes that the four outbuildings to the west of the house, evidences of which were found in archaeological excavations by Morley J. Williams in the 1930s, were probably all built by Lawrence Washington. The additional structures built at GW's direction, Pogue suggests, may have been a pair of privies on the east side of the house. However, to us this seems unlikely given GW's designation of the location of the two "houses" he contracted with the Tripletts to build in 1760. Again, according to his diary, they were to go "in the Front" of the main house, which by that date indicated a location to the west of it.

48. Ibid., 267. Although it is unclear exactly where the brickyard was located, years later, when he was choosing trees to be transplanted elsewhere on the grounds, GW refers to "the old Brick kiln" near the wharf (ibid., 4:75). The locations of two other brickyards at Mount Vernon—behind the present Regents' Quarters and near the West Gate, in no. 1 field—have been documented. One pre-Revolutionary brick kiln was still standing in 1939 (Mount Vernon Reference Notebook 10, "Building Materials," ViMtvL).

49. *GWD*, 1:268.

50. Ibid., 256, 260–61, 263, and 269.

51. GW to Robert Cary & Co., 1 May 1759, *PGW*, Col. Ser., 6:317–18.

52. On the garden at Gunstan Hall and others of the same type that would have been familiar to GW see C. Allan Brown, "Eighteenth-Century Virginia Plantation Gardens: Translating an Ancient Idyll," in Therese O'Malley and Marc Treib, eds., *Regional Garden Design in the United States* (Washington, D.C., 1995), esp. 145–54. Brown also provides a brief analysis of the gardens at Mount Vernon (ibid., 154–57).

53. This version of the entrance drive and gardens at Mount Vernon—now almost totally obscured by later changes—is described by Morley J. Williams in "Washington's Changes at Mount Vernon Plantation," *Landscape Architecture* 27, no. 2 (1938): 62–73. The remains of the first front gate lie close to the center of what became the bowling green. For a general description of the grounds as they emerged from GW's efforts over the years see Elizabeth Kellam de Forest, *The Gardens & Grounds at Mount Vernon: How George Washington Planned and Planted Them*

(Mount Vernon, 1982). These subjects are also covered in detail, with additional archaeological evidence, in Pogue, "Mount Vernon," Shackel and Little, eds., *Historical Archaeology of the Chesapeake*, 101–14, and the same author's "Giant in the Earth: George Washington, Landscape Designer," in R. Yamin and K. Besherer, eds., *Landscape Archaeology: Reading and Interpreting the American Historical Landscape* (Knoxville, Tenn., 1996).

54. *GWD*, 1:297.

55. Ibid., 304.

56. Ledger A, 130, copy, PGWp.

57. *GWD*, 1:306–7.

58. Ledger A, 130, copy, PGWp.

59. *GWD*, 2:120.

60. GW to Robert Cary & Co., 15 Nov. 1762, *PGW*, Col. Ser., 7:164–67; invoice from Robert Cary & Co., 13 Feb. 1764, ibid., 287–95.

61. GW to James Gildart, 5 June 1764, ibid., 310–11.

62. GW to Robert Cary & Co., 1 May and 12 June 1759, ibid., 6:317–18 and 327. For a useful list, with descriptions, of most of GW's agricultural books see Alan Fusonie and Donna Jean Fusonie, *Selected Bibliography on George Washington's Interest in Agriculture* (Davis, Calif., 1976).

63. GW, Survey Notes of 1–2 Oct. 1759, quoted in Freeman, *Washington*, 3:28.

64. The additions GW made to his land holdings at Mount Vernon are summarized in John H. Rhodehamel, "The Growth of Mount Vernon," Mount Vernon Ladies' Association, *Annual Report, 1982*, 18–24.

65. On Mount Vernon's changing slave population see the 1760 and 1772 Lists of Tithables, *PGW*, Col. Ser. 6:428 and 9:54–55. Between 1754 and 1772 GW bought forty-six slaves. See also Worthington Chauncey Ford, *Washington As an Employer and Importer of Labor* (New York, 1971), 8–9; and for an instance when GW financed slave purchases with drafts on Cary, GW to Robert Cary & Co., 1 Aug. 1761, *PGW*, Col. Ser., 7:61–62.

66. See GW to Robert Cary & Co., 18 Sept. 1762, ibid., 153–55, mentioning the "incessant Rains" of the summer of 1760; also 20 June 1762, ibid., 140, noting: "We have had one of the most severe Droughts in these parts that ever was known . . . Our Plants in spite of all our efforts to the contrary are just destroyed"; and 22 Jan. 1764, ibid., 284, stating: "My crops upon Potomack are vastly deficient, in short a wet Spring, a dry Summer, and early Frosts have quite demolished me."

67. *GWD*, 1:266, 283, 296, and 300.

68. GW to Cary, 26 April 1763, *PGW*, Col. Ser., 7:202–4. The problem of the prices GW received for his tobacco was a perennial one. Two years earlier he had written Cary: "I am at a loss to conceive the Reason why Mr. Wormeleys, and indeed some other Gentlemen's Tobacco's should sell at 12d. last year and mine . . . fetch 11 1/2. . . . Certain I am no Person in Virginia takes more pains to make their Tobo fine than I do and tis hard then I shoud not be as well rewarded for it" (GW to Robert Cary & Co., 13 April 1761, ibid., 34). In addition to the discussion of GW's problems with tobacco in the standard biographies, Bruce A. Ragsdale provides a thoughtful analysis in "George Washington, the British Tobacco Trade, and Economic Opportunity in Prerevolutionary Virginia," *Virginia Magazine of History and Biography* 97 (1989):133–62.

69. For a penetrating discussion of tobacco-growing, the selling of the crop, and the way those things affected the attitudes of Virginia's wealthiest citizens see T. H. Breen, *Tobacco Culture: The Mentality of the Great Tidewater Planters on the Eve of Revolution* (Princeton, N.J., 1985). Breen argues that good tobacco prices were a vital matter of self-esteem for planters. Ultimately his concern is with how such feelings, together with the details of the marketing of the tobacco crop and the resulting indebtedness of many of the great planters, helped "crystallize elements in a political ideology" that led them to support the patriot cause. For the most part we find his conclusions provocative and convincing.

70. Cary's letter has not survived (Was it shredded in a fit of pique?), but GW refers subsequently to "The Copy of your Letter of the 13th of February," noting the high balance (GW to Robert Cary & Co., 1 May 1764, *PGW*, Col. Ser., 7:305–6).

71. GW to Robert Cary & Co., 10 Aug. 1764, ibid., 323–31. According to Breen *(Tobacco Culture*, 84–157) a standard planter response to indebtedness was to interpret it as the result of some sort of plot or conspiracy among the merchants. This line of reasoning, in turn, Breen argues, made the planters all the more susceptible to seeing the political conflict with England over taxation in similar terms.

For other treatments of Virginia, its elite, and the coming of the American Revolution see: Lawrence H. Gipson, "Virginia Planter Debts before the American Revolution," *Virginia Magazine of History and Biography* 69 (1961):275–77; Emory G. Evans, "Planter Indebtedness and the Coming of the Revolution In Virginia, "*William and Mary Quarterly,* 3rd ser., 19 (1962):511–33; Thad W. Tate, "The Coming of the Revolution in Virginia: Britain's Challenge to

Virginia's Ruling Class," ibid., 323–43; Morgan, *American Slavery, American Freedom*, 369–87; Jack P. Green, "Society, Ideology, and Politics: An Analysis of the Political Culture of Mid-Eighteenth-Century Virginia," in Richard M. Jellison, ed., *Society, Freedom, and Conscience: The American Revolution in Virginia, Massachusetts, and New York* (New York, 1976), 14–76; Isaac, *Transformation of Virginia,* esp. 179–269; Herbert Sloan and Peter Onuf, "Politics, Culture, and the Revolution in Virginia," *Virginia Magazine of History and Biography* 41 (1983):259–84; Kulikoff, *Tobacco and Slaves,* 390–413; Warren M. Billings, John E. Selby, and Thad W. Tate, *Colonial Virginia: A History* (White Plains, N.Y., 1986), 251–335; and John E. Selby, *The Revolution in Virginia, 1775–1783* (Williamsburg, Va., 1988), 1–54.

Though they differ about details, most of these authors see the gentry successfully uniting, in support of the patriot cause, a society that had become increasingly divided along class lines. In the process, the group not only further solidified its position at the top of the social order but also appeared to regain the confidence lost in the years of political controversy and economic uncertainty that followed 1750. Key elements in this formulation are readily apparent in GW's personal experience through the period.

72. GW to Stewart & Campbell, 4 Sept. 1766, *PGW*, Col. Ser., 7:461–62.

73. See ibid., 360–61, n., regarding GW's contract with Carlyle & Adam, wheat merchants in Alexandria. GW was not alone among Chesapeake planters in switching from tobacco to wheat as his primary crop; others were doing so and many more would in the future, as part of a generalized diversification of the region's economy. See David C. Klingaman, *Colonial Virginia's Coastwise and Grain Trade* (New York, 1975); Paul G. E. Clemens, *The Atlantic Economy and Colonial Maryland's Eastern Shore: From Tobacco to Grain* (Ithaca, N.Y., 1980); and Peter V. Bergstrom, *Markets and Merchants: Economic Diversification in Colonial Virginia, 1700–1775* (New York, 1985).

74. Freeman, *Washington*, 3:243. See also Ledger A, 299, copy, PGWp, and James Wharton, "Washington's Fisheries at Mount Vernon," *Commonwealth* (Aug, 1952), 11–13 and 44.

75. Freeman, *Washington*, 3:242–44.

76. GW to Robert Cary & Co., 10 Aug. 1764, 20 Sept., 25 Oct., and 6 Nov. 1765, and 23 June 1766, *PGW*, Col. Ser., 7:327–28, 402–4, 409–11, and 447–49.

77. GW to Robert Cary & Co., 20 Sept. 1765, ibid., 398–402.

78. Ibid. See also GW to Francis Dandridge, ibid., 395–96.

79. In addition to the standard biographies, Paul K. Longmore, in *The Invention of George Washington* (Berkeley and Los Angeles, Calif., and London, 1988), provides an excellent analysis of the personal, political, and ideological factors shaping Washington's stance in the growing conflict between England and America. Longmore finds him, throughout the period, "politically shrewd, closely in touch with the beliefs, aspirations, and fears of his contemporaries, a consummate political leader and public actor who sought to embody and to be perceived as embodying their highest ideals" (ibid., x).

The ideals to which Longmore refers are those associated with the classical republicanism that Bernard Bailyn and so many historians since his seminal work, *The Ideological Origins of the American Revolution* (Cambridge, Mass., 1967), have seen as the intellectual heart of the patriot movement. Two other studies cited here that owe much to Bailyn's formulation, yet also modify it in important respects, are Breen's *Tobacco Culture* and Gordon S. Wood, *The Radicalism of the American Revolution* (New York, 1991).

80. GW to George Mason, 5 Apr. 1769, *PGW,* Col. Ser., 8:177–80. Mason, GW's longtime friend, neighbor, and political mentor, was seven years his senior. He was the fourth member of his family to bear the name and together with the others is the subject of Pamela C. Copeland and Richard K. MacMaster's *The Five George Masons: Patriots and Planters of Virginia and Maryland* (Charlottesville, Va., 1975). See also Helen Hill Miller, *George Mason, Gentleman Revolutionary* (Chapel Hill, N.C., 1975). To GW's letter of 5 Apr. Mason replied: "Our all is at Stake, & the little Conveniences of Life, when set in Competition with our Liberty, ought to be rejected" (Mason to GW, 5 Apr. 1769, *PGW,* Col. Ser., 8:182–83). On later phases of the nonimportation movement see Donald M. Sweig, "The Virginia Nonimportation Association Broadside of 1770 and Fairfax County: A Study in Local Participation," *Virginia Magazine of History and Biography* 87 (1979):316–25.

81. GW to George Mason, 5 Apr. 1769, *PGW,* Col. Ser., 8:177–80. For an interesting analysis of how patriot protest over taxation resonated with American attitudes toward consumer goods see T. H. Breen, "'Baubles of Britain': The American and Consumer Revolutions of the Eighteenth Century," in Carson, Hoffman, and Albert, eds., *Of Consuming Interests,* 444–82; also his "An Empire of Goods: The Anglicization of Colonial America, 1690–1776," *Journal of British Studies* 25 (1986):467–99.

82. GW to Robert Cary & Co., 25 July 1769, *PGW,* Col. Ser., 8:229–30.

83. William Byrd II to Mr. Beckford, 6 Dec. 1735, quoted in Freeman, *Washington,* 1:172.

84. Stretching over a period of several years there was a great deal of correspondence on "the bounty lands," as they were called. See in particular GW to Charles Washington, 31 Jan. 1770; to Governor Lord Botetourt, 5 Oct. 1770; and Petition to the Governor and Council and related papers, 1–6 Nov. 1771, *PGW,* Col. Ser., 8:300–303, 388–90, and 533–47. Freeman, who provides the most detailed discussion of the subject (*Washington,* 3:245–304), puts GW's total acquisitions at 32,884 acres.

Unlike Freeman, most of GW's biographers have been uncomfortable with the relentlessness of his pursuit of the bounty lands (e.g., buying up the rights of other, less knowledgeable claimants and appearing to reserve the best acreage for himself), and several have been quite critical. Writes Flexner: "We know that as a general rule Washington was not avaricious. However . . . there rises the unmistakable impression that in this one aspect of his career he acted as an oversharp business man" (Flexner, *Forge of Experience,* 303). See also Knollenberg, *Washington: The Virginia Period,* 99–100.

85. Freeman, *Washington,* 3:296.

86. *PGW,* Col. Ser., 8:468, n. 1.

87. Freeman, *Washington,* 3:287.

88. *GWD,* 3:108–9.

89. GW to Robert Adam, 22 Nov. 1771, *PGW,* Col. Ser., 8:550–52.

90. Freeman, *Washington,* 3:306–7.

91. The next day GW wrote to Martha's brother-in-law: "Yesterday removd the Sweet Innocent Girl into a more happy, & peaceful abode than any she has met with, in the afflicted Path she hitherto has trod. . . . This Sudden, and unexpected blow, I scarce need add has almost reduced my poor Wife to the lowest ebb of Misery" (GW to Burwell Bassett, 20 June 1773, *PGW,* Col. Ser., 9:243).

92. GW to Robert Cary & Co., 10 Nov. 1773, ibid., 9:374–75; also, Freeman, *Washington,* 3:326 and 341–42. Despite GW's efforts to clear his balance with Cary, the bank stock from Patsy's estate with which he hoped to do it was not finally sold until after the Revolution (GW to Robert Cary & Co., 1 June 1774, *PGW,* Col. Ser., 10:84, n. 3).

93. GW to Robert Cary & Co., 26 July 1773, ibid., 9:289.

94. Cash accounts, Aug. 1773, ibid., 293–94.

95. GW to Cary, 6 Oct. 1773, *PGW*, Col. Ser., 9:343.

96. GW, west elevation of the mansion, unsigned, undated MSS, ViMtvL.

97. *GWD*, 3:136–37. On the growth of Annapolis and its merchant class during this period and the eventual decline of both see Edward C. Papenfuse, *In Pursuit of Profit: The Annapolis Merchants in the Era of the American Revolution, 1763–1805* (Baltimore and London, 1975).

98. On the proliferation of architectural pattern books and their increasing use in America see: John Archer, *The Literature of British Domestic Architecture* (Cambridge, Mass., and London, 1985), esp. 3–148; Eileen Harris and Nicholas Savage, *British Architectural Books and Writers, 1556–1785* (Cambridge, Eng., 1990); Reiff, *Small Georgian Houses*, 173–81 and 275–83; Helen Park, *A List of Architectural Books Available in America Before the Revolution* (Los Angeles, 1973); Janice G. Schimmelman, *Architectural Treatises and Building Handbooks Available in American Libraries and Bookstores Through 1880* (Worchester, Mass., 1986); and the articles in Mario di Valmarana, ed., *Building by the Book*, 3 vols., (Charlottesville, Va., 1984–90).

99. The fullest account of Buckland's life and career is Rosamond Randall Beirne and John H. Scarff, *William Buckland 1734–1774: Architect of Virginia and Maryland* (Baltimore, 1958, repr. 1970). See also Pierson, *American Buildings and Their Architects*, 150–56; Barbara A. Brand, "William Buckland, Architect in Annapolis," in Valmarana, ed., *Architecture by the Book*, 3: 65–99; and on Maryland architecture in general, including Buckland's work, Mills Lane, *Architecture of the Old South: Maryland* (New York, London and Paris, 1991), 12–73.

100. Philip Slaughter, *The History of Truro Parish in Virginia* (Philadelphia, Pa., 1974), 72ff. The notion that GW drew up the original plan and elevations for Pohick Church, which Benson Lossing includes in his *Home of Washington, or Mount Vernon and Its Associations, Historical, Biographical, and Pictorial* (New York, 1859), 87–88, is discounted by Upton in *Holy Things and Profane*, 14–15 and 32–33.

101. *GWD*, 3:193.

102. Going Lanphier to GW, 16 Oct. 1773, *PGW*, Col. Ser., 3:348–50. The letter was written from "New Church"—presumably Pohick.

103. At least one of GW's visitors expressed considerable admiration for the skill and energy with which he supervised construction projects. "The General has a great turn for mechanics. It's astonishing with what niceness he directs everything in the building way, condescending even to measure the things himself, that all may be uniform." See John Hunter, diary entry for "November 17, 1785," *Pennsylvania Magazine* 17, no. 1 (1893):76, copy, ViMtvL.

Chapter 4

1. The building of Washington's houses in "the Federal City" is described by John P. Riley in "George Washington's Capitol Hill Townhouses," *Mount Vernon Ladies' Association Annual Report, 1990*, 31–35. On William Thornton's life and career see *Dictionary of American Biography* (New York, 1928–37), 18:504–7. GW's strong partiality to the "grandeur, simplicity and beauty" of Thornton's plan for the Capitol was conveyed in a pair of letters to the Federal City commissioners written 31 Jan. and 3 Mar. 1793 (*GWW*, 32:325 and 363).

2. GW to William Thornton, 20 Dec. 1798, ibid., 37:6.

3. William Thornton to GW, 25 Dec. 1798, copy, PGWp.

4. GW to William Thornton, 30 Dec. 1798, *GWW*, 37:79.

5. William Hogarth, *Analysis of Beauty*, quoted in Rudolph Wittkower, *Palladio and English Palladianism* (New York, 1983), 202.

6. David Hume, *Of the Standard of Taste*, quoted in ibid., 200. Such sentiments, Wittkower points out, were diametrically opposed to the intellectual underpinnings of classicism—the "classical-idealistic framework of references focused on absolute standards," which had first been formulated by Leon Battista Alberti in the fifteenth century (ibid., 193).

7. William Pierson, in *American Buildings and Their Architects*, goes so far as to assert that "most colonial buildings were not designed at all, but were simply built by local craftsmen who worked with available materials and skills in the established tradition" (ibid., 141). In contrast, Upton in *Holy Things and Profane* emphasizes the precision of the planning process—at least in the case of parish churches—and its complexity. "The responsibilities that we customarily assign to the professional architect . . . were handled by a bewildering variety of people. . . . If we cannot conceive of traditional craftsmen reeducated by cultivated gentlemen, we cannot locate design entirely in the builder to the exclusion of his client either. Who designed the churches? They all did. The fracture of high style and vernacular, of design and execution, along clear class or craft lines is impossible" (ibid., 28).

8. Batty Langley, *The City and Country Builder's*

and Workman's Treasury of Designs: Or the Art of Drawing and Working the Ornamental Parts of Architecture, repr. (New York, 1967), Plates 51, 38, 54, 49, and 55. Mesick, Cohen, Waite, "Historic Structure Report," MSS, ViMtvL, contains a brief but comprehensive analysis of the use of printed architectural sources at Mount Vernon (121-29).

9. *Inventory of the Contents of Mount Vernon, With a Prefatory Note by Worthington Chauncey Ford* (Cambridge, Mass., 1909). For the listing of books see 14-40. Complete titles, arranged by subject, can be found in *A Catalogue of the Washington Collection in the Boston Athenaeum* (Boston, 1897), comp. and annotated by Appleton P. C. Griffin, Appendix, 482-565. For further identification and description of the relevant titles see Archer, *Literature of British Domestic Architecture;* Park, *Architectural Books;* and Schimmelman, *Architectural Treatises and Building Handbooks.*

10. "John Mercer's Library," Appendix K, C. Malcolm Watkins, *The Cultural History of Marlborough, Virginia* (Washington, D.C., 1968), 198-208. The titles on architecture include "Hoppne's Architecture, Salmon's Palladio Londinencio, Palladio's Architecture, Langley's City and Country Builder . . . Noblemen's Seats by Kip . . . Willis' Survey of the Cathedrals . . . [and] Churches, Palaces and Gardens in France." It is possible that Mercer may have been selling these and other books in his "library."

11. On the design and building of Pohick Church see Slaughter, *History of Truro Parish* and Upton, *Holy Things and Profane*, 14-15, 26, 32-33, 89-91, and 94. Slaughter includes the full text of the agreement with the original undertaker for the project, Daniel French, which specifies in considerable detail the exterior and interior finish of the building, down to stipulating both the use of "the Ionic Order" for the "Alter Piece" and its dimensions (75).

12. Waterman, *The Mansions of Virginia*, 268-98.

13. *Maryland Gazette,* May 22, 1751. The pattern book in question, William Adam, *Vitruvius Scotius; Being a Collection of Plans, Elevations, and Sections of Public Buildings, Noblemens and Gentlemen's Houses in Scotland: Principally from the designs of the Late William Adam, Esq. Architect* (Edinburgh, 1750), appears neither in Park, *Architectural Books* nor in Schimmelman, *Architectural Treatises and Building Handbooks.* Among the other houses Waterman attributes to Ariss—based on similarities to plates in *Vitruvius Scotius*—are Mount Airy in Richmond County and John Carlyle's house in Alexandria. In tracing Ariss's ancestry, Waterman surmises that he

was the great-grandson of Nicholas Spencer, who purchased, with John Washington, the land on which Mount Vernon was eventually built.

For a discussion of the architectural planning process at Mount Vernon that stresses the variety of sources Washington relied on and the importance of the role he himself played see Walter M. Macomber, "Mount Vernon's 'Architect,'" *Historical Society of Fairfax County, Virginia* 10 (1969):1-10.

14. On Harrison's influence on Mount Vernon see Chap. 2, supra, 39; on Buckland's, Chap. 3, 70-71.

15. Mark Girouard, *Life in the English Country House: A Social and Architectural History* (New Haven, Conn., 1978), 2.

16. Ibid., 3.

17. Medieval country houses and households are described in ibid., 13-80. On developments during the Tudor, Elizabethan, and Jacobean periods see 81-118, and John Summerson, *Architecture in Britain, 1530-1830* (London, 1983), 23-111.

18. Ibid., 113-56. See also Giles Worsley, *Classical Architecture in Britain: The Heroic Age* (New Haven, Conn., and London, 1995), 1-20, which offers a revisionist analysis of Jones's work, describing him as "working hard, and with considerable success, among fellow architects and builders to achieve a broad-based Classical revolution." In general Worsley challenges the standard view—most effectively developed in Summerson's *Architecture in Britain*—of the neat, sequential, and "inevitable" progression of architectural styles over time.

19. A lively discussion of the growing importance of learning and culture among the English upper classes can be found in Lawrence Stone, *The Crisis of the Aristocracy, 1558-1641* (Oxford, 1965), 672-724. "In the long run," Stone argues, "the enthusiastic, though belated, adoption of the new educational pattern by the aristocracy was a major cause of their survival as a ruling elite" (ibid., 722).

20. Girouard classifies houses designed to function in this way as a distinct type—"formal houses"—and places their heyday between 1630 and 1720 (*Life in the English Country House*, 119-62).

21. In *An Open Elite? England 1540-1880* (Oxford, 1984), 375, Lawrence and Jeanne C. Fawtier Stone estimate that in the three counties they surveyed, as few as one quarter of the country houses where significant construction occurred between 1700 and 1819 were wholly new.

22. For three brief accounts of English neo-Palladianism see Summerson, *Architecture in Britain*, 319-82; James S. Ackerman, *The Villa: Form and Ideology of Country Houses* (Princeton, N.J., 1990),

134–58; and Worsley, *Classical Architecture in Britain*, 85–151. In line with his general views, Worsley seeks to deemphasize both the abruptness and the distinctiveness of the neo-Palladian "revolution." The buildings themselves tend to support his point, even as the rhetorical pronouncements of the neo-Palladians challenge it.

More detailed analysis can be found in James Lees-Milne, *The Earls of Creation: Five Great Patrons of Eighteenth-Century Art* (London, 1962); Wittkower, *Palladio and English Palladianism;* John Harris, *The Palladians* (London, 1981); and Robert Tavenor, *Palladio and British Palladianism* (London, 1991). And in *The Palladian Rivival: Lord Burlington, His Villa and Garden at Chiswick* (New Haven, Conn., and London, 1994), John Harris offers a splendid study of what remains the single greatest icon of English neo-Palladian architecture.

23. Colen Campbell, *Vitruvius Britannicus,* quoted in John Archer, *The Literature of British Domestic Architecture, 1715–1842* (Cambridge, Mass., 1985), 245.

24. Andrea Palladio, *The Four Books of Architecture* (New York, 1965), Second Book, 46–48. Palladio was by no means alone among sixteenth-century Italian writers in celebrating the joys of rural life. See Ackerman, *The Villa,* 108–33, and Archer, *Literature of British Domestic Architecture,* 56–59.

The literature on Palladio and his villas is enormous. Two of the standard sources are by Ackerman: *Palladio* (Harmondsworth, Eng., 1966) and *Palladio's Villas* (New York, 1967). See also Georgina Masson, *Italian Villas and Palaces* (New York, 1959); Lionello Puppi, *Andrea Palladio* (Boston, 1975); Howard Burns, ed., *Andrea Palladio, 1508–80* (Boston, 1975); Donata Battelotti, *The Villas of Palladio* (Milan, 1990); and Bruce Boucher, *Andrea Palladio: The Architect in His Time* (New York, 1994). Three books, largely comprised of photographs but which nonetheless contain interesting if brief texts, are: Joseph C. Farber and Henry Hope Reed, *Palladio's Architecture and Its Influence: A Photographic Guide* (New York, 1980); Philip Trager, Vincent Scully, Renato Cevese, and Michael Graves, *The Villas of Palladio* (New York, 1986); and Manfred Wundram, Thomas Pape, and Paola Marton, *Palladio* (Cologne, 1992).

In *The Palladian Landscape: Geographical Change and Its Cultural Representations in Sixteenth-Century Italy* (University Park, Pa., 1993), Denis E. Cosgrove provides an intriguing analysis of Palladio's architecture in its contemporary physical and cultural settings. He concludes: "From whichever angle we approach the Palladian landscape . . . representations of utopia are never far from the surface" (see ibid., 242–43).

On the spread of English Palladianism generally and to America in particular see ibid., 378–82; Pierson, *American Buildings,* 110–56; Walter Muir Whitehill, *Palladio in America* (New York, 1978); Roger G. Kennedy, *Architecture, Men, Women and Money in America 1600–1860* (New York, 1985); and Worsley, *Classical Architecture in Britain,* 278–87.

25. The historical literature on this subject continues to grow. Two pioneering studies that remain highly useful are Caroline Robbins, *The Eighteenth Century Commonwealthman: Studies in the Transmission, Development, and Circumstances of English Liberal Thought from the Restoration of Charles II until the War with Thirteen Colonies* (Cambridge, Mass., 1959), and Isaac Kramnick, *Bolingbroke and His Circle: The Politics of Nostalgia in the Age of Walpole* (Cambridge, Mass., 1968). See also J. G. A. Pocock, *The Machiavellian Moment: Florentine Political Thought and the Atlantic Republican Tradition* (Princeton, N.J., 1975); Perez Zagorin, *The Court and the Country: The Beginning of the English Revolution* (London and Henly, Eng., 1969); John Brewer, *Party Ideology and Popular Politics at the Accession of George III* (Cambridge, Eng., and New York, 1981); and Kramnick, *Republicanism and Bourgeois Radicalism: Political Ideology in Late Eighteenth-Century England and America* (Ithaca, N.Y., and London, 1990).

26. Again, the literature on this subject is vast. H. F. Clark, *The English Landscape Garden* (London, 1948), is a standard, full-length study. Three excellent shorter treatments are Edward Hyams, *The English Garden* (New York, 1964), 7–103; Wittkower, *Palladio and English Palladianism,* 177–204; and Ackerman, *The Villa,* 159–84. Also helpful is John D. Hunt and Peter Willis, eds., *The Genius of the Place: The English Landscape Garden, 1620–1820* (London, 1975).

27. Summerson, *Architecture in Britain,* 348.

28. The National Trust, *Saltram, Devon* (n.p., 1986), contains a description of the house as well as a history of its building and biographical information about the Parkers.

29. National Trust, *Saltram,* 38.

30. The duchess of Devonshire, quoted in ibid., 51.

31. See Chap. 1, supra, 5.

32. Jack Crowley in "Inventing Comfort: The Piazza" (which the author was good enough to share with us as an unpublished essay in 1994) provides a

fine discussion of the initial appearance of and possible sources for porches on American houses. His view is that West Indian influences were less important than the "stoops" found on houses in areas settled by the Dutch. Crowley describes Mount Vernon's piazza as "innovative" and notes that Washington "intended it to be a social space, not a token of Palladian style."

33. Mesick, Cohen, Waite, "Historic Structure Report," 123. The source for the details of the pillars (though not of their proportions) was Langley's *Treasury of Designs*, Plate 51, where they appear as part of the design used for the Venetian window at the north end of Mount Vernon.

For a more extensive discussion of the use of the Tuscan order at Mount Vernon see Scott Campbell Owen, "George Washington's Mount Vernon as British Palladian Architecture" (unpublished master's thesis, School of Architecture, University of Virginia, 1991). James S. Ackerman, in "The Tuscan/Rustic Order: A Study in the Metaphorical Language of Architecture," *Journal of the Society of Architectural Historians* 42 (1983):15–34, provides a provocative discussion of the symbolic connotations of the Tuscan order. Of such matters, however, GW was almost certainly ignorant.

34. The most comprehensive treatment of the subject in these terms is Hood's *Governor's Palace*. See especially 38–115.

35. Ibid., 80.

36. See Sweeney, "High Style Vernacular," in Carson, Hoffman, and Albert, eds., *Of Consuming Interests*, 19–20; also Kulikoff, *Tobacco and Slaves*, 263, and Isaac, *Transformation of Virginia*, 26.

37. The most complete account of Monticello and its building is Jack McLaughlin's excellent *Jefferson and Monticello: The Biography of a Builder* (New York, 1988). Though none of them provides as much detail as McLaughlin's book, other thoughtful treatments of the subject are: Paul Wilstach, *Jefferson and Monticello* (Garden City, N.Y., 1925); Frederick Doveton Nichols and Ralph E. Griswold, *Thomas Jefferson, Landscape Architect* (Charlottesville, Va., 1978); William Howard Adams, *Jefferson's Monticello* (New York, 1983); Pierson, *American Buildings and Their Architects*, 287–316; Lane, *Architecture of the Old South: Virginia*, 90–125; Ackerman, *The Villa* (Princeton, N.J., 1990), 185–213; and Worsley, *Classical Architecture in Britain*, 285–87. An earlier version of the comparison between Mount Vernon and Monticello in these pages can be found in Robert F. Dalzell, Jr., "Constructing Independence: Monticello, Mount Vernon, and the Men Who Built Them," *Eighteenth-Century Studies* 26 (1993):543–80.

38. On Jefferson's architectural books see William Howard Adams, ed., *The Eye of Thomas Jefferson* (Washington, D.C., 1976), 98–99.

39. Individuals who assembled collections of this sort in England were regularly described as "virtuosos," a term that according to the earl of Shaftesbury referred to "real fine gentlemen . . . lovers of art and ingenuity." On the virtuosos, their collections, and cabinets of curiosities see Girouard, *Life in the English County House*, 172–74. (The earl of Shaftesbury is quoted in ibid., 172.)

40. Anna Maria Thornton, quoted in Jack McLaughlin, *Jefferson and Monticello*, 5. Anna Maria Thornton was the wife of William Thornton.

41. While granting the similarity of the garden front of Monticello to the Hôtel de Salm in Paris—a comparison frequently made by other architectural historians—Giles Worsley asserts that Lord Burlington's villa at Chiswick "is a closer source," adding: "To see Jefferson as an innovative neo-Classicist breaking the trammels of British architecture to create a new independent style worthy of a young republic is grossly to misrepresent his work" (Worsley, *Classical Architecture in Britain*, 286). For a sharply different and more closely reasoned view see Pierson, *American Buildings and Their Architects*, 287–334.

42. Thomas Jefferson, *Notes on the State of Virginia*, William Peden, ed. (Chapel Hill, N.C., and London, 1982), 153.

Chapter 5

1. GW to Bryan Fairfax, 4 July 1774, *PGW*, Col. Ser., 10:109–10. The letter also contained a lengthy paragraph responding to Fairfax's statement to GW that the colonies ought to petition "the throne" yet again. GW doubted that there was even "the most distant hope of success" from such a petition and ended by asking: "Ought we not, then, to put our virtue and fortitude to the severest test?" (ibid.; see also Bryan Fairfax to GW, 3 July 1774, ibid., 106–8).

2. *GWD*, 3:250–52. In the same spirit, presumably, the morning of the day Dunmore dissolved the Burgesses GW rode out with the governor to inspect his farm "and Breakfasted with him there" (ibid., 251).

3. Lund Washington's Account Book, MSS, ViMtvL.

4. *GWD*, 3:269–70; and "Inventory of House Furniture bought by Col. George Washington at Col. Fairfax's Sale of Belvoir, 15 Aug. 1774," copy, PGWp. Altogether GW spent £169.17.6 at the sale.

5. GW to Bryan Fairfax, 24 Aug. 1774, *PGW*, Col. Ser., 10:154–56. In his letter to GW, Fairfax had said:

"I am very sorry we happen to differ in opinion. I hope however that our Sentiments will again coincide as in other Matters" (Bryan Fairfax to GW, 5 Aug. 1774, ibid., 143–50).

GW's remarks to Fairfax give particular point to Edmund Morgan's analysis of the affinities between slavery and republicanism. "Virginians may have had a special appreciation of the freedom dear to republicans, because they saw every day what life without it could be like" (Morgan, *American Slavery, American Freedom*, 376).

6. Ibid.

7. Freeman, *Washington*, 3:392. See also Flexner, *Forge of Experience*, 324–28; Cunliffe, *Man and Monument*, 57–58, and Ferling, *The First of Men*, 102–7.

8. GW to John Augustine Washington, 25 Mar. 1775, *PGW*, Col. Ser., 10:308.

9. Spotsylvania Independent Company to GW, 26 Apr. 1775, ibid., 346–47; Freeman, *Washington*, 3:411–12.

10. On 29 May John Adams wrote: "Colonel Washington appears at Congress in his uniform, and, by his great experience and abilities in military matters, is of much service to us" (Adams quoted in ibid., 426, also n. 41, same). Freeman observes that this is the first reference to GW's wearing his uniform to Congress but speculates that he may have done so earlier, perhaps even "from the beginning of the session" (ibid.).

11. Longmore notes that "George Washington's chief biographers have depicted him as a sort of compromise candidate for command of the Continental Army" but argues persuasively that "Congress never seriously considered anyone but Washington for the command," and further that: "He himself not only anticipated the impending call, but made his availability apparent" (Longmore, *Invention of George Washington*, 160).

12. GW to Martha Washington, 18 June 1775, ibid., 3–6.

13. GW to Lund Washington, 20 Aug. 1775, ibid., 337.

On the overall aims, character, and organization of the American war effort during the Revolution see: Dave Richard Palmer, *The Way of the Fox: American Strategy in the War of Independence* (Westport, Conn., 1975); John Shy, *A People Numerous and Armed: Reflections on the Military Struggle for American Independence* (New York, 1976); Robert K. Wright, Jr., *The Continental Army* (Washington, D.C., 1983); Don Higginbotham, *The War of American Independence: Military Attitudes, Policies, and Prac-*

tice, 1763–1789 (Boston, 1983); E. Wayne Carp, *To Starve the Army at Pleasure: Continental Army Administration and American Political Culture, 1775–1783* (Chapel Hill, N.C., 1984); and John Keegan, *Fields of Battle: The Wars for North America* (New York, 1996), 135–86.

As is the case in other instances, Freeman provides the fullest coverage of GW's activities as commander of the Continental forces in the war (Freeman, *Washington*, 3:460–586, and Vols. 4 and 5), followed by Flexner in *George Washington in the American Revolution, 1775–1783* (Boston, 1968), which, if less encyclopedic, is both reliable and eminently readable. Also of particular value in the vast literature on the subject are the following: George Athan Billias, ed., *George Washington's Generals* (New York, 1964); Don Higginbotham, *George Washington and the American Military Tradition* (Athens, Ga., 1985); and John Shy, "George Washington Reconsidered," in Henry S. Bausum, ed., *The John Biggs Cincinnati Lectures in Military Leadership and Command, 1986* (Lexington, Va., 1986). And for a brief but highly perceptive evaluation that touches on a variety of issues see in addition Edmund S. Morgan, *The Genius of George Washington* (New York and London, 1980), esp. 3–18. According to Morgan, GW's greatest achievement occurred not on the battlefied but in defining for his fellow citizens—in terms compatible with broader aims of the Revolution—the proper relationship between civil and military authority. "He was fighting," Morgan argues, "a people's war, and he knew that he would lose what he was fighting for if he tried to take more power than the people would freely give" (ibid., 10 and 13–14). Higginbotham reaches much the same conclusion. "It was a Washington-shaped army, and when it complained, it wanted pay not power. To some of his troubled countrymen, it looked too much like a European army, but it had not sought traditional Old World objectives of empire and glory" (Higginbotham, *Washington and the American Military Tradition*, 104).

Part of Washington's success in these respects may well have resulted from the fact that in certain very palpable ways—and most notably, perhaps, in his continuing concern for the rebuilding of Mount Vernon—he never lost touch with mundane realities of civilian life.

14. GW to Samuel Washington, 30 Sept. 1775, *PGW*, Rev. Ser., 2:72. GW's anxiety was not idly expressed. In detailing its causes he wrote: "I learn by my last Letters from home, that neither Mrs. Washington, nor Lund, had received a Line from me since the 27th of July, although I have never missed writing

by any Week's Post since I came to this place, to both of them" (ibid.). On Dunmore's military operations in Virginia see Selby, *The Revolution in Virginia*, 41–79 and 124–27.

15. Lund Washington to GW, 15 Oct. 1775, ibid., 172.

16. GW to Lund Washington, 20 Aug. 1775, *PGW*, Rev. Ser., 1:335.

17. Lund Washington to GW, 14 Nov. 1775, ibid., 375.

18. Lund Washington to GW, 5 Nov. 1775, ibid., 306.

19. Lund Washington to GW, 5 Dec. 1775, ibid., 480. "Liberty is sweet," commented Lund.

20. Surprisingly enough, there is no record of the name of this individual, one of the most gifted artisans to work at Mount Vernon. On the arrangements for his coming see Fielding Lewis to GW, 23 Apr. 1775, ibid., Col. Ser., 10:343 and n. 2.

21. Waterman, *Mansions of Virginia*, 285–90. See also Mesick, Cohen, Waite, "Historic Structure Report," 125–26, MSS, ViMtvL.

22. Lund Washington to GW, 29 Sept. 1775, *PGW*, Rev. Ser., 2:65.

23. Ibid.

24. Lund Washington to GW, 22 Oct. and 5 Nov. 1775, ibid., 219 and 306.

25. Lund Washington to GW, 12 Nov. 1775, ibid., 355–56.

26. Lund Washington to GW, 24 Nov. 1775, ibid., 421–22.

27. Lund Washington to GW, 29 Sept., 5 and 15 Oct., 5, 12, 14, and 24 Nov., and 3 and 23 Dec. 1775, ibid., 64, 116, 172–73, 307, 356, 374, 422, 477–78, and 594–95.

28. By the end of the year GW was apparently thinking of using the fourth outbuilding as a kind of infirmary to house the sick (Lund Washington to GW, 23 Dec. 1975, ibid., 594–95). His instructions about the stone chimneytops for the outbuildings came in a letter that has not survived. See, however, Lund Washington to GW, 14 Nov. 1775, ibid., 374. Work on the outbuildings continued into the next year (Lund Washington to GW, 8 Feb. 1776, ibid., 3:271).

29. In his letter to John Hancock, the president of the Continental Congress in Philadelphia, officially informing him of the British evacuation of the city, GW added, as a personal aside, a piece of information that he himself would surely have wanted to have had he been in Hancock's position: "I have a particular pleasure in being able to inform you Sir, that your house has reciev'd no damage worth mentioning. Your furniture is in tolerable Order and the family

pictures are all left entire and untouch'd" (GW to John Hancock, 19 Mar. 1776, ibid., 490).

30. Lund recommended going ahead with the addition to the north end of the house in February, and though the letters GW wrote home that winter have not survived, he himself was clearly intent on doing so (Lund Washington to GW, 22 Feb. 1776, ibid., 355).

31. Lund apparently wrote of the shortage of nails on 14 Aug. 1776, in a letter that has not survived. See GW to Lund Washington, 26 Aug. 1776, ibid., 6:136.

32. Ibid.

33. GW to Lund Washington, 19 Aug. 1776, ibid., 84–85.

34. GW to Lund Washington, 30 Sept. 1776, ibid., 441–42.

35. Ibid.

36. GW to Robert Morris, 13 Jan. 1777, copy, PGWp.

37. Lund Washington to GW, 28 Jan. 1778, copy, PGWp.

38. Bryan Fairfax to GW, 29 Mar. 1778, copy, PGWp.

39. Lund Washington to GW, 18 Mar. 1778, copy, PGWp.

40. Ibid.

41. GW to Lund Washington, 18 Dec. 1778, *GWW*, 13:427–28. On the progress of the work in general see Lund Washington to GW, 22 Apr., 19 Aug., and 2 Sept. 1778, copies, PGWp. Hours of labor at Mount Vernon are credited to Lanphier's account throughout the following year, but they all seem to have been for "your man" rather than for any work of Lanphier's own (Lund Washington's Account Book, MSS, ViMtvL).

42. Regarding the years between Monmouth and Yorktown, Cunliffe writes: "There was never to be another time at which Washington, or the cause he stood for, could be smashed at a blow" (Cunliffe, *Washington: Man and Monument,* 90).

43. GW to Lund Washington, 28 Mar. 1781, *GWW*, 21:386.

44. Jonathan Trumbull, Jr., quoted in Freeman, *Washington,* 5:327.

45. GW to Lund Washington, 21 Nov. 1782, *GWW*, 25:362; also 12 Feb. and 11 June 1783, ibid., 26:126–27, and 27:2–3.

46. GW to Clement Biddle, 2 Oct. 1783, ibid., 175–76.

47. GW to George William Fairfax, 10 July 1783, ibid., 57–60. The letter was a reply to one Fairfax had written GW congratulating him "on the favourable termination of the War." Although the Fairfaxes did not return to America, George William and GW did

continue to correspond until George William's death in 1787, and in one particularly poignant letter GW wrote: "I took a ride [to Belvoir] the other day to visit the ruins—& ruins indeed they are. . . . When I viewed them—when I considered that the happiest moments of my life had been spent there—when I could not trace a room in the house (now all rubbish) that did not bring to my mind the recollection of pleasing scenes; I was obliged to fly from them; & came home with painful sensations, & sorrowing for the contrast" (GW to George William Fairfax, 27 Feb. 1785, *PGW*, Con. Ser., 2:387–88).

48. Disinclined, as he said, "to send to England (from whence formerly I had all my goods) for any thing I can get upon tolerable terms elsewhere," GW had asked Lafayette to purchase the silver plate even before returning home to Mount Vernon after the war. The list of items he wanted included "A large Tea-Urn," two teapots with stands, a coffeepot and stand, a creampot, a tea chest, two large trays, two smaller trays, two bread baskets, a set of coasters, "A Cross or Stand for the centre of the Dining table," twelve salts, eight "Bottle sliders," six large goblets, twelve candlesticks, and three pairs of snuffers, plus "any thing else which may be deemed necessary, in this way." And if the items could be engraved "I should be glad to have my arms thereon, the size of which will, it is to be presumed be large or small in proportion to the piece on which it is engraved" (GW to Lafayette, 30 Oct. 1783, *GWW*, 27:215–18). In his eagerness to acquire silverplated ware, which was a relatively new product on the market, GW also placed at least one other order for some of the items he commissioned Lafayette to buy and later tried to cancel the order he had given the Frenchman. By then it was too late, however. The goods (costing £129) had been shipped to America and eventually arrived at Mount Vernon with the help of Thomas Jefferson. As a result, much to his annoyance GW ended up owning duplicates of several items (GW to Lafayette, 1 Feb. 1784; to Thomas Jefferson, 24 Mar. 1784; Thomas Jefferson to GW, 31 Mar. 1784; GW to Lafayette, 4 Apr. 1784; Daniel Parker to GW, 21 June 1784; and GW to Melancton Smith, 20 Dec. 1784, *PGW*, Con. Ser., 1:88, 231, 244, 257, 467, and ibid., 2:223–24).

49. In an early use of the phrase, in a letter written before the end of the Revolution, GW referred to being "set down under our Vines and fig Trees" (GW to Bartholomew Dandridge, 18 Dec. 1782, *GWW*, 25:443–46).

50. GW to Lafayette, 1 Feb. 1784, *PGW*, Con. Ser., 1:87–88.

51. For a penetrating discussion of GW, retirement, and republican ideology see Garry Wills, *Cincinnatus: George Washington and the Enlightenment* (Garden City, N.Y., 1984), esp. 3–25. Wills aptly describes GW as "a virtuoso of resignations" and observes: "He perfected the art of getting power by giving it away" (ibid., 3).

52. GW to Lund Washington, 15 Aug. 1778, *GWW*, 12:326–27.

53. GW to Lund Washington, 24 Sept. 1779, ibid., 14:148.

54. GW to Lafayette, 5 Apr. 1783, ibid., 26:300. Lafayette had written of the project: "Such an example as yours might render it a general practice; and if we succeed in America, I will certainly devote a part of my time to render the method fashionable in the West Indies" (ibid., n. 10). In his reply GW wrote: "I shall be happy to join you in so laudable a work," but suggested they wait until they met again to discuss the details "of the business" (ibid.). The following year Lafayette visited GW at Mount Vernon, and they may well have spoken of the matter then. If so, however, nothing further came of it, at least as far as GW's involvement was concerned.

55. GW to William Hamilton, 15 Jan. 1784, *PGW*, Con. Ser., 1:47–48. Hamilton was a noted horticulturalist GW had come to know in Philadelphia before the Revolution (ibid., n.).

56. GW to Samuel Vaughan, 14 Jan. 1784, ibid., 45. The style of decoration Vaughan had described to GW owed its origins to the work of Robert Adam and his brother James in England. For a brief discussion of the subject see Summerson, *Architecture in Britain*, 427–43.

57. GW to Lund Washington, 13 Aug. 1783, copy, PGWp.

58. GW to Samuel Vaughan, 14 Jan. 1784, *PGW*, Con. Ser., 1:45.

59. Ibid.

60. GW to Clement Biddle, 13 Aug. 1783, *GWW*, 27:102.

61. GW to Tench Tilghman, 24 Mar. 1784, *PGW*, Con. Ser., 1:232; and to John Rumney, Jr., 3 July 1784, ibid., 484. In elaborating on his wishes to Tilghman, GW wrote: "If they are good workmen, they may be of Assia, Africa, or Europe. They may be Mahometans, Jews, or Christian of any Sect—or they may be Athiests—I would however prefer middle aged, to young men, and those who have good countenances & good characters on ship board, to others who have neither of these to recommend them—altho, after all, the proof of the pudding must be in the eating" (ibid.).

62. GW to Samual Vaughan, 6 Apr. and 20 June 1784, ibid., 273 and 466.

63. *GWD*, 4:114.

64. GW to Samuel Vaughan, 5 Feb. 1785, *PGW*, Con. Ser., 2:326.

The views we express in the following discussion owe much to Pauline Maier's *The Old Revolutionaries: Political Lives in the Age of Samuel Adams* (New York and London, 1990) and to her insightful reflections in that book on the ways in which the American Revolution shaped the experience of some of its more notable participants. While she finds their later lives "full of complications and contradictions," she does see a common thread running through them—one, too, that cuts across the classical republican/liberal dichotomy that has played so large a role in recent historical debate about the nature of the Revolution. In the introduction to the most recent edition of the book she writes that though the revolutionaries of 1776 were indeed intent on establishing a republic and one they often described in classical terms, they "uniformly associated Independence and the foundation of a republic less with restoration or stasis than with change; the Revolution began a 'novus ordo seclorum,' a new order of the ages. Essential to that new order was the establishment of a meritocratic basis of rank and the abandonment of legal privilege, an enhanced respect and opportunity for individuals of humble origin, and a new and more broad-based prosperity, which would itself be the natural fruit of freedom" (ibid., x). Although GW is not one of Maier's old revolutionaries, he did in fact come to understand independence in terms quite close to these. He did not reach that point in a single bound, however. In the 1780s he still had a ways to go, which tends to confirm another of Maier's observations: "One of the greatest strengths of the biographical approach to history lies precisely in its capacity to undercut the distorting reductionism to which more abstract arguments are prey" (ibid., xi).

65. William Fitzhugh to GW, 2 and 13 May 1785, *PGW*, Con. Ser., 2:529 and 554–55. GW to William Fitzhugh, 21 May 1785, ibid., 3:7.

66. Richard Boulton to GW, 4 June 1785, ibid., 34–35. See also GW to Richard Boulton, 24 June 1785, ibid., 79; and to William Fitzhugh, 14 and 16 July 1785, ibid., 119 and 128–29.

67. "Rawlings & Barnes" advertised themselves in the *Maryland Gazette* on 14 Feb. 1771 as able to do "Ceilings and Cornices on the shortest notice." They worked, along with William Buckland, on the Chase–Lloyd house in Annapolis, for which they were paid £208:13:0 by Edward Lloyd (Beirne and Scarff, *William Buckland*, 83). Rawlins (as his name had come to be spelled) wrote GW on 20 Aug. 1785 (*PGW*, Con. Ser., 3:192, n.).

68. GW to John Rawlins, 29 Aug. 1785, ibid., 207–8.

69. GW to Tench Tilghman, 29 Aug. 1785, ibid., 208–9; also 14 Sept. 1785, ibid., 249.

70. GW to Tench Tilghman, 2 Nov. 1785, ibid., 339.

71. GW to Edward Newenham, 25 Nov. 1785, ibid., 387–88. Newenham's letter to GW about Tharpe has not survived (ibid., 145, n).

72. John Rawlins to GW, 15 Nov. 1785; Tench Tilghman to GW, 18 Nov. 1785; GW to John Rawlins, 30 Nov. 1785; GW to Tench Tilghman, 30 Nov. 1785; Tench Tilghman to GW, 30 Dec. 1785; GW to Tench Tilghman, 7 Jan. 1786; Tench Tilghman to GW, 16 Jan. 1786; GW to Tench Tilghman, 22 Feb. 1786; Tench Tilghman to GW, 1 Mar. 1786; and GW to Tench Tilghman, 10 Mar. 1786: ibid., 359, 371, 421–22, 424–26, 482–83, 497–98, 507–8, 571, 576–77, and 595. The protracted correspondence on the subject of Rawlins consisted of negotiations, conducted through Tilghman, over the terms of GW's agreement with him. GW reluctantly conceded most of the points at issue, including the price—£168—which he considered far too high. In addition he agreed to pay £13.10 for Rawlins's traveling expenses, as well the cost of transporting Rawlins's workmen, their tools, and the molded plaster ornaments to Mount Vernon. He also had to pay the cost of materials. (The articles of agreement are quoted at length in ibid., 576–77, n. 1.) As little as Washington liked the terms, he wrote Tilghman, "rather than encounter further delay—perhaps a disappointment—or ask the favor of a stranger to engage an undertaker to cross the Atlantic, who might be troublesome to me thereafter, I submit to this imposition as the lesser evil" (GW to Tench Tilghman, 7 Jan. 1786, ibid., 498).

73. "I shall essay the finishing of my Green Ho. this fall; but find that neither my own knowledge, or that of any person abt me, is competent to the business," GW had written Tench Tilghman in August 1784, asking him to send dimensions and a description of Mrs. Charles Carroll's greenhouse at Mount Clare, outside of Baltimore. Margaret Carroll was a relative of Tilghman's, and he responded promptly with answers to GW's questions (GW to Tench Tilghman, 11 Aug. 1784, and Tench Tilghman to GW, 18 Aug. 1784, ibid., 2:30–31 and 42–44). In spite of his reference to "finishing of my Green Ho," GW's questions make it clear that construction had barely begun in

1784. Supplies were issued to workmen throughout the summer of 1787 for finishing the building (Mount Vernon Store Book, 1787, MSS, ViMtvL).

For an interesting discussion of the hegemonic functions of greenhouses see Anne Yentsch, "The Calvert Orangery in Annapolis, Maryland: A Horticultural Symbol of Power and Prestige in an Early Eighteenth-Century Community," in William M. Kelso and Rachel Most, eds., *Earth Patterns: Essays in Landscape Archaeology* (Charlottesville, Va., 1990), 169–87. Mark P. Leone presents similar views regarding a broad spectrum of gentry material culture in his provocative essay "The Georgian Order as the Order of Merchant Capitalism in Annapolis, Maryland," in Leone and Parker B. Potter, Jr., eds., *The Recovery of Meaning: Historical Archaeology in the Eastern United States* (Washington, D.C., 1988), 235–61.

74. *GWD*, 4:78.

75. See supra, chap. 3, 58–59.

76. *GWD*, 4:80–81.

77. Ibid., 75.

78. Ibid., 86–87, 89, and 91–99.

79. Ibid., 167, 181, 184, 190, 193, 199, 202–3, and 205.

80. Ibid., 190, 199–200, and 202.

81. Ibid., 200 and 203–4. As further proof of his eagerness to do a statue of GW, Houdon had agreed to a fee of 1,000 guineas, plus expenses, for the commission, which was far less than he had originally asked (ibid., 200, n.).

82. Ibid., 271 and 293–95.

83. Ibid., 291 and 298.

84. Ibid., 313–14.

85. Ibid. Tench Tilghman died about this time, so we lack what would no doubt have been GW's scathing commentary to him on Rawlins's method of fulfilling his obligation.

86. GW to John Rumney, 15 May 1786, *PGW*, Con. Ser., 4:53; *GWD*, 4:334–36.

87. Ibid., 5:29–30.

88. GW to John Rawlins, 13 Apr. 1787, *PGW*, Con. Ser., 5:141. On GW's agreement with Tharpe see *GWD*, 4:345.

89. GW to George Augustine Washington, 1 July 1787, *PGW*, Con. Ser., 5:243.

90. GW to Robert Townsend Hooe, 27 Nov. 1786, ibid., 4:400; GW to George Digges, ibid., 480–85.

91. John Rawlins to GW, 10 Mar. 1787, ibid., 5:82; GW to George Augustine Washington, 1 and 29 July, 1787, ibid., 243 and 276. In the first four months of 1787 Mathew Baldridge worked a total of 22 1/2 days on the new room (Weekly Reports for 1786–1787, MSS, ViMtvL). A payment of £219.3.6 was made to Rawlins on 29 Mar. 1787, and another to Thomas Hammond "for friezes & mouldings for the New Room" on 23 July (Ledger B, 222 and 246, copy, PGWp).

92. Freeman, as usual, provides the fullest treatment both of GW's anxious brooding on the subject and of his role at the convention (Freeman, *Washington*, 5:78–116).

93. GW to George Augustine Washington, 1 and 29 July and 1 Aug. 1787, *PGW*, Con. Ser., 5:243, 276, and 287–88.

94. GW to Joseph Rakestraw, 20 July 1787, ibid., 267.

Chapter 6

1. *GWD*, 1:232–33.

2. Much has been written on American slavery and the complex relationship between masters and slaves in the South. For a sense of the range of historical debate on the subject see Eugene D. Genovese, *The Political Economy of Slavery: Studies in the Economy and Society of the Slave South* (New York, 1965); also his *Roll, Jordan, Roll: The World the Slaveholders Made* (New York, 1974); and Robert William Fogel and Stanley L. Engerman, *Time on the Cross*, 2 vols. (Boston, 1974). Two earlier studies that nonetheless contain much useful information as well as sharply differing points of view are Ulrich Bonnell Phillips, *Life and Labor in the Old South* (Boston and Toronto, 1922) and Kenneth M. Stampp, *The Peculiar Institution: Slavery in the Ante-bellum South* (New York, 1956). The best treatments of the establishment and spread of slavery in colonial Virginia are Morgan, *American Slavery, American Freedom,* the Rutmans, *Place in Time,* and Kulikoff, *Tobacco and Slaves.* Kulikoff provides as well a thoughtful analysis of slave families and the role of slaves generally in plantation life. See also Herbert Gutman's pathbreaking *The Black Family in Slavery and Freedom, 1750–1925* (New York, 1976), and for a notably different point of view, Brenda E. Stevenson's fine *Life in Black and White: Family and Community in the Slave South* (New York and Oxford, 1996).

In addition we found two studies dealing largely with the nineteenth century quite helpful: Charles B. Dew, *Bond of Iron: Master and Slave at Buffalo Forge* (New York, 1994), which describes the organization of a slave labor force to carry on complex, nonagricultural forms of production; and James Oakes, *Slavery and Freedom: An Interpretation of the Old South* (New York, 1990). Oakes's primary concern is with "the relationship between slavery and liberal capitalism." Southerners, he argues, "took their definition of freedom from the liberal capitalist world which produced them and of which they remained a part, and this could only mean that *southern* slavery was defined as the denial of the assumptions of liberal capitalism" (ibid., xi and xiii). To pose the conflict between the two systems so starkly might seem problematic, but in the long run GW himself came to feel that there was no reconciling slavery and freedom and chose between them accordingly.

To date there have been two book-length treatments of GW's relations with his workers, slave and free: Worthington C. Ford, *Washington as an Employer and Importer of Labor* (Brooklyn, N.Y., 1889), and Walter Z. Mazyck, *George Washington and the Negro* (Washington, D.C., 1932). See also Ellen M. Clark, "George Washington and Slavery at Mount Vernon," 1988, copy, ViMtvL.

3. For Lawrence Washington's slaves see "Memorandum. A division of slaves made, and agreed to, between Colo. George Lee and the Brothers of the deceased Majr Lawrence Washington," 10 Dec. 1754, *PGW*, Col. Ser., 1:229–30 and n.; also "Lease of Mount Vernon," ibid., 232–34. Although the slave named George was allotted to Lee, he apparently was one of the nineteen slaves who stayed on at Mount Vernon under the terms of the lease agreement between Anne Fairfax Washington Lee and GW. Two slaves named Tom were allotted to GW from the brothers' portion: one was four months old at the time of the division, and the other measured four feet, one inch in height. For the Custis slaves see "Settlement of the Daniel Parke Custis Estate: Appendix III, List of Artisans and Household Slaves in the Estate," ibid., 6:282 and n. The list is in GW's hand, and most of the slaves included accompanied Martha Washington to Mount Vernon. On "Billy" see Ford, *Washington as an Employer*, 8, which refers to GW's purchase of Hannah and a child for £80 in 1759.

4. Information on GW's slave holdings through the years is recorded in a series of lists, beginning with those cited in the note immediately preceding this one. Following them in sequence are the lists of tithables he recorded annually from 1760 through 1774, and after those come two other lists, dated 1786 and 1779.

Tithables were counted for tax purposes and included all free males (but not free females) above age sixteen as well as all slaves, male *and* female, over sixteen. As a rule, in recording Mount Vernon's tithables GW listed "House Servants," "Tradesmen," and slaves assigned to the outlying farms in separate groups. The complete run of lists of tithables is as follows: May 1760, *PGW*, Col. Ser., 6:428; 4 June 1761,

ibid., 7:45; 9 June 1762, ibid., 139; 10 June 1763, ibid., 227; 17 June 1764, ibid., 313; 2 July 1765, ibid., 376; 16 June 1766, ibid., 442; 15 June 1767, ibid., 515; 20 June 1768, ibid., 8:104; 20 June 1769, ibid., 220; 16 July 1770, ibid., 356; 14 June 1771, ibid., 479; 10 June 1772, ibid., 9:54; 9 June 1773, ibid., 238; 10 July 1774, ibid., 10:137.

The 1786 list of slaves was recorded by GW in his diary on 18 Feb. and includes individuals of every age. Occupations are given for all adults except those "past labour." Children's ages and their mothers' names are listed. Also, the slaves at the "Home House," the "Children House," and each of the outlying farms are listed together in groups, making it possible to tell not only what a particular person did but also where he or she lived. In addition, GW placed a mark beside the name of each of the "dower slaves"—those who had come to Mount Vernon as part of the Custis inheritance. Under Virginia law Martha could not alter the status of the dower slaves, and heavily intermarried as they were with GW's own slaves, they represented the greatest obstacle to any plan to end slavery at Mount Vernon. The fact that GW singled them out in the 1786 list suggests that he may have been mulling over the problem as early as that date (*GWD*, 4:277–83).

The 1799 list of slaves is undated but seems to have been drawn up just before GW drafted his last will and testament. It is organized in much the same way as the 1786 list and includes the same information, except that there is an added column of "Remarks" indicating marital status and spouse's name, if any, for each of the adult slaves. The ages of adult slaves are also given, which was not done in 1786, and GW's slaves and the dower slaves are listed in separate columns (*GWW*, 37:256–68).

5. Cash Accounts, May 1772, *PGW*, Col. Ser., 9:35.

6. GW to Daniel Jenifer Adams, 20 July 1772, ibid., 70.

7. See Allan Kulikoff, *Tobacco and Slaves*, 73, on the rate of natural increase for African Americans. To arrive at mortality rates for slave children he compared the plantation records of Robert Lloyd in the 1740s and 1750s and Robert Carter in the 1790s.

8. See, for example, Lund Washington to GW, 5 and 15 Oct. 1775, *PGW*, Rev. Ser., 1:117 and 174; also Kulikoff, *Tobacco and Slaves*, 327. Death rates of slaves in New Kent County, Virginia, between 1651 and 1746 rose during the fall months and were highest in February.

9. GW to Anthony Whiting, 14 Oct. 1792, *GWW*, 32:184.

10. Lund Washington to GW, 2 Sept. 1778, copy, PGWp.

11. Ledger B, 156, copy, PGWp.

12. See GW to Charles Lee, *GWW*, 29:460–61.

13. GW to Lund Washington, 30 Apr. 1781, ibid., 22:14 and n.

14. "Mr. Barnes's Davy brot. home my Negroe fellow Boson who Ran away on Monday last." Davy was paid 10s. for his trouble. *GWD*, 1:269 and n.

15. "Advertisement for Runaway Slaves," 11 Aug. 1761, *PGW*, Col. Ser., 7:66. Two of the slaves had been bought from an African ship two summers before.

16. GW to Joseph Thompson, 2 July 1766, ibid., 453–54. "He may, with your good management, sell well, if kept clean & trim'd up a little when offerd to Sale," GW wrote (ibid.).

17. GW to the secretary of the Treasury (marked "private") 1 Sept. 1796, *GWW*, 35:201. "Enclosed is the name, and description of the Girl I mentioned to you last night," GW wrote. "She has been the particular attendent on Mrs. Washington since she was ten years old. . . . We have heard that she was seen in New York . . . and since in Portsmouth."

18. GW to Frederick Kitt, 10 Jan. 1798, ibid., 36:123–24.

19. GW to Gilbert Simpson, 23 Feb. 1773, *PGW*, Col. Ser., 9:185.

20. Lund Washington to GW, 18 Feb. and 4 Mar. 1778, copy, PGWp. The following year, when GW was considering selling slaves to raise cash, he made it clear in a letter to Lund that whatever was done he would not split up slave families. "If these poor wretches are to be held in a State of Slavery, I do not see that a change of masters will render it more irksome, provided husband & wife, and Parents & children are not separated from each other, which is not my intention to do" (GW to Lund Washington, 24–26 Feb. 1779, *GWW*, 14:148).

21. Lund Washington to GW, 8 Apr. 1778, copy, PGWp.

22. GW to Anthony Whiting, 2 Dec. 1792, *GWW*, 32:248.

23. For a detailed account of the changing configuration of Mount Vernon's farms see John H. Rhodehamel, "The Growth of Mount Vernon," Mount Vernon Ladies' Association of the Union, *Annual Report, 1982*, 18–24.

The work on the farms was further divided into tasks performed by different slaves at different times of the year. As on other plantations, too, the increasing diversification of crops and activities that occurred as GW shifted from tobacco-growing to grain, fishing, and the production of as many plantation necessities as possible had a major impact on the ways in which the slave labor force was organized. Work by individual slaves on specific tasks tended to replace work in gangs, and the division of labor between sexes became much more pronounced. For a general discussion of these developments see Philip D. Morgan, "Task and Gang Systems: The Organization of Labor on New World Plantations," in Stephen Innes, ed., *Work and Labor in Early America* (Chapel Hill, N.C., and London, 1988), 189–220; and Lois Green Carr and Lorena S. Walsh, "Economic Diversification and Labor Organization in the Chesapeake, 1650–1820," ibid., 144–88. The latter concludes with a useful appendix—based on GW's 1786 list of slaves and his diary for that period—categorizing tasks performed by slaves at Mount Vernon according to age, sex, and season (ibid., 185–88). As presented, the data effectively support the authors' contention that, in general, female slaves fared less well than males as a result of economic diversification and changing patterns in the organization of plantation labor in the Chesapeake.

24. "Negroes Belonging to George Washington," June 1799, *GWW*, 37:256–68.

25. List of slaves, 18 Feb. 1786, *GWD*, 4:277–83, and "Negroes Belonging to George Washington," June 1799, *GWW*, 37:256–68.

The nature and stability of slave families is a subject that continues to provoke scholarly debate. For the past twenty years the standard view has been the one Gutman outlined in *The Black Family in Slavery and Freedom,* which emphasizes the success of slaves at building and sustaining family bonds, chiefly in nuclear families, but recently that view has been challenged with considerable force by Stevenson, in *Life in Black and White.* She argues that the slaves' "most discernable ideal for kinship organization was a malleable extended family," not the conventional nuclear unit derived "from long-term monogamous marriages" (ibid., 325). Though she concentrates on the nineteenth century, she includes an (ibid., 209–12) analysis of data drawn from GW's records—principally the 1799 list of slaves—and in detail her conclusions do not differ from our own. We question, however, whether such an analysis supports the view that something other than the nuclear family can be considered the slaves' "ideal" form of family structure. Except to indicate that a significant number of GW's slaves were married, the data Stevenson uses offer no information about slave preferences or ideals. What would seem to do so are the strongly expressed desires of couples to remain together recorded in GW's correspondence, which she does not discuss. To be sure, she is using Mount Vernon primarily as an example of "the physical context" in which slaves lived on large plantations, and to that end she provides a detailed description of GW's system of individual farms. In at least one instance, however, she mistakes the distance that separated the farms. River Farm lay across Little Hunting Creek from the main body of Mount Vernon, not, as Stevenson asserts, "across the Potomac River" (ibid., 211). On the other hand, we do agree with another, far more important point Stevenson makes: "The slave family was not a static, imitative institution that necessarily favored one form of organization over another. Rather, it was a diverse phenomenon, sometimes assuming several forms even among the slaves of one community," to which she adds, "the slave family's enormous adaptive potential, often was instrumental in allowing the slave and the slave family's survival" (ibid., 324–25).

26. In a lengthy letter to a new overseer, GW warned against such abuses. "You may use every precaution . . . this is too much practiced and is one, if not the primary cause of my loosing a number of horses" (GW to William Pearce, 22 Dec. 1793, *GWW*, 33:204–5).

27. GW to William Pearce, 25 Jan. 1795, ibid., 34:104.

28. Kulikoff argues that as the tobacco economy in the Chesapeake matured and slaves were increasingly concentrated on large plantations, they had greater opportunities for communal interaction, and this led to the maintenance of an identifiable African-American culture. For a similar argument, presented in greater detail, see John W. Blassingame, *The Slave Community: Plantation Life in the Antebellum South* (New York, 1979). On the other hand, Jean Butenhoff Lee challenges this line of interpretation, citing evidence of larger numbers of slaves, working in more isolated groups on smaller plantations, than previous studies have shown. Lee also points out that communal interactions—subject to the whims and financial circumstances of slave owners—were constantly being disrupted as slaves were sold or otherwise moved from place to place (Jean Butenhoff Lee, "The Problem of Slave Community in Eighteenth-Century Chesapeake," *William and Mary Quarterly*, Series 3, 43, no. 3 [1986]:333–61). Because of Mount Vernon's large size and relative stability during GW's lifetime, it seems likely that its slave community experienced less disruption than those on many plantations.

29. On typical food rations on Virginia plantations see Kulikoff, *Tobacco and Slaves*, 392 and n. GW's own correspondence is particularly revealing on such

points. "In the most explicit language I desire they may have plenty; for I will not have my feelings again hurt with complaints of this sort, nor lye under the imputation of starving my negros and thereby driving them to the necessity of thieving to supply the deficiency," he wrote home at one point (GW to Anthony Whiting, 28 Apr. 1793, *GWW*, 32:437–38). See also GW to Arthur Young, 18 June 1792, ibid., 65, for his thoughts on slave care by other masters. "The common food of them (even when well treated) being bread, made of the Indian Corn, Butter milk, Fish (pickled herrings) frequently, and meat now and then. . . . In addition to these, ground is often allowed them for gardening, and privilege given them to raise dung-hill fowls for their own use." But, he added, "the wealthy," who owned large numbers of slaves, were "not always as kind, and as attentive to their wants and usage as they ought to be; for by these, they are fed upon bread alone."

GW's remark about not wishing to have his "feelings hurt again by complaints" about lack of food suggests that the slaves had complained to him personally, which in turn implies the use of a time-honored tactic employed by slaves on many plantations: going to the master over the heads of overseers, thereby undermining their authority. More often than not, too, according to Genovese, the tactic worked. "Any sensible master, notwithstanding all pretensions and professions, trusted his slaves against his overseer. Overseers came and went; the slaves remained" (Genovese, *Roll, Jordan, Roll,* 17). An overseer quoted by Stampp attests to much the same thing: "Your Negroes behave badly behind my back and then run to you and you appear to beleave what they say" (unnamed overseer quoted in Stampp, *Peculiar Institution,* 108).

30. Julian Ursyn Niemcewicz, *Under Their Vine and Fig Tree: Travels Through America in 1797–1799, 1805, With Some Further Account of Life in New Jersey,* Metchie J. E. Budka, trans. and ed. (Elizabeth, N.J., 1965), 100–101. Niemcewicz, a Polish publisher and writer in exile, was known for his championship of Poland's independence from Russia. His record of his ten-day visit to Mount Vernon provides more details about the slaves than most other visitors' accounts. For general descriptions of slave housing in Virginia see Kulikoff, *Tobacco and Slaves,* 368 amd 339; also John Stilgoe, *Common Landscape of America, 1580–1845* (New Haven, Conn., 1982), 67–68.

31. Charles Cecil Wall, "Housing and Family Life of the Mount Vernon Negro," Oct. 1954 report to the Mount Vernon Ladies' Association, MSS, ViMtvL.

According to Wall's reconstruction of the evidence, the two greenhouse wings were probably meant to house sixty-five to seventy-five slaves. Both wings had two rooms, each with an outside door and a fireplace. The walls were probably lined with berths for sleeping. In 1799 as many as ninety-six slaves may have been housed in the greenhouse wings.

32. Niemcewicz, *Under Their Vine and Fig Tree,* 101.

33. Recent excavations of the cellar under the "House for Families" (predecessor to the greenhouse wings) at Mount Vernon provide rich evidence for the slaves' diet. See Dennis Pogue, "Slave Lifeways at Mount Vernon," Mount Vernon Ladies' Association of the Union, *Annual Report, 1989,* 35–40.

34. "Davy's lost lambs, carry with them a very suspicious appearance," GW wrote William Pearce on 5 July 1795. "If the lambs had been poisoned, or had died a natural death, or their deaths had been occasioned by an accident, their bones would have been forthcoming" (*GWW,* 34:230). Even if his managers were not ever vigilant on such details, GW himself was. "By your last Weeks Report, I perceive 80 Bushels of Wheat was sent from River Plantation to the Mill and 79 only received" (GW to Anthony Whiting, 4 Nov. 1792, ibid., 32:204). See also GW to George Augustine Washington, 31 Mar. 1789, ibid., 30:257. And Niemcewicz, in *Under Their Vine and Fig,* 97, remarks: "One sees . . . Corrents, Rasberys, Strawberys, Gusberys, quantities of peaches and cherries . . . which the robins, backbirds and Negroes devour before they are ripe."

35. GW to the overseers at Mount Vernon, 14 July 1793, ibid., 33:10.

36. GW to William Pearce, 7 June 1795, ibid., 34:212. Even locks had a way of disappearing. "They are bought, used a few weeks, then lost or stolen" (GW to Howell Lewis, 25 Aug. 1793, ibid., 33:65).

37. GW to William Pearce, 4 Dec. 1796, ibid., 36:306. GW was also always on the lookout for signs of slowdowns. "The dificiency of Stockings is another instance of the villainy of those I have about me" (GW to Anthony Whiting, 18 Nov. 1792, ibid., 32:232). Similarly: "It is observed, by the Weekly reports, that the Sewers make only Six shirts a week, and the last week Caroline (without being sick) made only five; Mrs. Washington says their usual task was to make nine . . . tell them therefore from me, that what *has* been done, *shall* be done . . . for their own reputation, and for the sake of peace and quietness, otherwise they will be sent to the several Plantations, and be placed as common laborers" (GW to Anthony Whiting, 23 Dec. 1792, ibid., 32:227).

38. William Pearce to GW, 19 Oct. 1793, copy, PGWp.

39. GW to William Pearce, 27 Oct. 1793, *GWW,* 33:142–43.

40. The "Mount Vernon Farm Accounts," copy, ViMtvL, contain scattered weekly reports beginning in the mid-1780s. GW studied the reports with great care, and he was distressed when he did not receive them or when they were so vague he could not understand them. "No letter nor Report was receivd from you yesterday. . . . I am always anxious to hear once a week from home." In the same letter he also remarked: "I have seen no account in any of the Reports, of the number of Bricks at Dogue-run" (GW to Anthony Whiting, 2 Dec. 1792, ibid., 32:245–47). And still later, to a new manager he wrote: "Buy in Alexandria a proper (bound) book . . . this is intended as a register of the proceedings on the farms. . . . Suffer no excuse therefore for [the overseers'] non-compliance every Saturday night" (GW to William Pearce, 22 Dec. 1793, ibid., 33:196).

41. GW to the overseers at Mount Vernon, 14 July 1793, ibid., 33:11.

42. Gunner was added to GW's tithables in 1774 (*PGW,* Col. Ser., 10:137). In 1781, he was among the slaves taken by the British (enclosure from Lund Washington to GW, Apr. 1781, *GWW,* 22:14 n.). He was recovered in Philadelphia during the war, and in 1789 it was noted that he was making bricks for a barn with Tom Davis (GW to George Augustine Washington, 31 Mar. 1789, ibid., 30:258). He was mentioned again in Dec. 1792, "Throwing up Brick earth" for George Augustine Washington's house (GW to Anthony Whiting, 9 Dec. 1792, ibid., 32:259). In 1799 he and his wife, Judy, were both listed as "Passed Labour" ("Negroes Belonging to George Washington," June 1799, ibid., 36:256).

43. Ibid.

44. "Settlement of the Daniel Parke Custis Estate: Appendix III, List of Artisans and Household Slaves in the Estate," *PGW,* Col. Ser., 6:282. Most of the slaves appear on the list of tithables the following year (list of tithables, May 1760, ibid., 428).

45. GW's "Memorandum of Carpentry Work to be Done," June 1791 (*GWW,* 31:307–9) includes, for example, building cornhouses, moving three houses, salvaging materials from older buildings, repairing roofs, making doors and dormers for the granaries, building a stable and a new barn, repairing the icehouse, making posts for the circle in front of the house, working on gravel walks in the garden, weeding, planting and trimming trees, "getting up" the soil in the vineyard, and more. On other kinds of work

done by the carpenters see *GWD,* 2:67: "My Carpenters & House People went to Planting Corn at Doeg Run after they had finishd fishing." Or a few weeks later: "My Carpenters & House People went to Work at my Mill repairing the Dams—hightening of them—& opening the Race" (ibid.). See also the "Mount Vernon Farm Accounts," MSS, ViMtvL; and for carpentry work hired out to neighbors, Humphrey Knight to GW, 16 June 1758, *PGW,* Col. Ser., 5:217, and Ledger A, 14 and 72, copy, PGWp.

46. Ibid., 49.

47. Humphrey Knight to GW, 2 Sept. 1758, *PGW,* Col. Ser. 5:447–48.

48. List of tithables, July 1774, ibid., 10:137. See also enclosure from Lund Washington to GW, 30 Apr. 1781, *GWW,* 22:14n.

49. Ledger B, 86, copy, PGWp.

50. Cash accounts, May 1772, *PGW,* Col. Ser., 9:35.

51. Sambo Anderson, as he eventually chose to be known, was remembered in the neighborhood as late as the 1840s. He was reputed to be the son of a king. His face was tattooed, and he wore in his ears rings that he claimed were "made of real Guinea gold." GW is supposed to have given him land to build a house on Little Hunting Creek across from Mount Vernon. After GW's death Sambo earned his livelihood hunting game and eventually bought two slaves himself. "Mount Vernon Reminiscences," *Alexandria Gazette,* 18, 22, and 25 Jan., copy, ViMtvL.

52. Enclosure from Lund Washington to GW, 30 Apr. 1781, *GWW,* 22:14, n.

53. On the part slave carpenters played in building another well-known Virginia house see Jack McLaughlin, *Jefferson and Monticello,* 96; and on Jefferson's handling of his slaves generally, Lucia Stanton, "'Those Who Labor for My Happiness': Thomas Jefferson and His Slaves," in Peter S. Onuf, ed., *Jeffersonian Legacies* (Charlottesville, Va., 1993), 147–80. Stanton observes that Jefferson had better luck with his slave artisans than GW did and for the most part treated his slaves well. But she also points to other, less happy developments. "The constant tension between self-interest and humanity seems to have induced in him a gradual closing of the imagination that distanced and dehumanized the black families of Monticello. . . . His unsuccessful early efforts to curb or end slavery were followed by years in which he uttered simultaneous protestations of the impracticability of emancipation and cries of alarm about the consequences of inaction. . . . His insights into the kinds of behavior caused by enslavement were forgotten and his suspicions of racial inferiority gained the upper hand, perhaps serving as a defense against

stings of conscience" (ibid., 162–63).

54. See the lists of Mount Vernon's tithables, 1760–74, cited in full, supra, n. 4.

55. Genevese, *Roll, Jordan, Roll,* 327ff, discusses the higher status of the more "polished" slaves working in or around the main house. One slaveowner's son he quotes wrote his father: "Will you please keep George . . . about the house . . . as I do not wish that he should forget his training, I want him to acquire a *house* look" (ibid., 329).

56. "The mulattoes are ordinarily chosen for servants." Niemcewicz, *Under Their Vine and Fig Tree,* 101.

57. GW to Anthony Whiting, 19 May 1793, *GWW,* 32:463.

58. In 1776 Morris was transferred as overseer to Dogue Run, which had been experiencing a steady turnover in white overseers up to that point. Michael was transferred to Ferry Farm in 1771 and then brought back again in 1774.

59. GW to Anthony Whiting, 24 Feb. 1793, ibid., 357.

60. GW to William Pearce, 16 Feb. 1794, ibid., 33:275.

61. Ibid.

62. GW to Anthony Whiting, 29 Aug. 1791, ibid., 31:350. Even fences were fair game. If they were not constructed "in a very substantial manner," the posts and rails could be pulled apart and used for firewood (GW to William Pearce, 16 Feb. 1794, ibid., 33:269).

63. GW to Anthony Whiting, 3 Feb. 1793, ibid., 32:330. He added, "If they can be applied to other uses, or converted into cash, rum, or other things, there will be no scruple in doing it."

64. GW to William Pearce, 20 Mar. 1796, ibid., 34:502–3.

65. Ledger B, 86, copy, PGWp.

66. See, for example, weekly reports for 29 Apr., 6 Aug., and 24 Oct. 1786, "Mount Vernon Farm Accounts," MSS, ViMtvL.

67. GW, "Memorandum of Carpentry Work to be Done," June 1791, *GWW,* 31:307.

68. For weekly rum allowances see "Rum—CR.," Mount Vernon Store Book, 1 Jan. to 31 Dec. 1787, MSS, ViMtvL.

69. In 1786 Kitty was listed as a spinner (list of slaves, 18 Feb. 1786, *GWD,* 4:277–83). By 1799 she was milking cows, still at the home plantation ("Negroes Belonging to George Washington," June 1799, *GWW,* 37:256).

70. "By Carpenter Isaac pd him for 8 Galls. honey and a balance for chickens 11.25" (entry for 21 Aug. 1799, Ledger C, 53, copy, PGWp).

71. GW to William Pearce, 30 Aug. 1795, *GWW*, 34:291.

72. GW to Anthony Whiting, 16 Dec. 1792, ibid., 32:263. "He must have left the fire in a very unjustifiable situation, or have been a fine time absent from it," GW wrote. "I wish you to inform him, that I sustain injury enough by their idleness; they need not add to it by their carelessness."

73. Humphrey Knight to GW, 2 Sept. 1758, *PGW*, Col. Ser., 5:447.

74. *GWD*, 1:259. In *Roll, Jordan, Roll*, 12–22, Genovese provides a thoughtful discussion of the complexities and ambiguities confronting overseers on southern plantations, a subject that has attracted surprisingly little scholarly attention. Among other things, he notes that overseers were let go "much more often" for treating slaves too harshly than for treating them too leniently. Yet undue leniency could also be a problem. "No master wanted his overseer to get too close to the slaves" (Genovese, *Roll, Jordan, Roll*, 17). See also William Kauffman Scarborough, *The Overseer: Plantation Management in the Old South* (Baton Rouge, La., 1966), which argues that overseers as a group have been unfairly maligned by historians, just as they were by their employers.

GW's contracts with his overseers were generally specific on a variety of points, including treatment of the slaves working under them. Thus Nelson Kelly was obliged to agree that he would "take all necessary and proper care of the negroes committed to his management, treating them with humanity and tenderness when sick, and preventing them when well, from running about and visiting without his consent; as also to forbid strange negroes from frequenting their quarters without lawful excuses for so doing" (agreement with Nelson Kelly, quoted in Ford, *Washington as Employer*, 33).

75. GW, indenture with John Askew, 1 Sept. 1759, *PGW*, Col. Ser. 6:340.

76. GW, agreement with Benjamin Buckler, 21 Feb. 1771, quoted in Ford, *Washington as Employer*, 42.

77. GW, agreement with Caleb Stone, 8 Feb. 1773, *PGW*, Col. Ser., 9:341, n. 5.

78. *GWD*, 1:295. "Agreed to give Turner Crump one Sixth part of what he can make by my Carpenters this Year," GW wrote. See also Ledger A, 60, copy, PGWp.

79. GW, indenture with John Askew, 1 Sept. 1759, *PGW*, Col. Ser., 6:340.

80. GW, agreement with John Askew, 22 Oct. 1761, ibid., 7:93–94; also Ledger A, 60, copy, PGWp.

81. *GWD*, 1:259.

82. Ledger A, 121, copy, PGWp.

83. Ibid., 60 and 182. See also "An Account of Days Work Don by John Askew" in "Carpenters & Work . . . from 1760 to 1765," MSS, ViMtvL. According to GW's tabulations the absentee record was stunning. In 1763, for instance, Askew worked for three days in May and did not show up again until July 6.

84. Ledger A, 60, copy, PGWp.

85. GW to George William Fairfax, 25 July 1763, *PGW*, Col. Ser., 7:233–34.

86. Ibid.

87. "An Account of Days Work Don by John Askew," in "Carpenters & Work . . . from 1760 to 1765," MSS, ViMtvL; also Ledger A, 60 and 182, copy, PGWp; and GW's cash accounts, May, June, and Sept. 1764, May, July, and Aug. 1766, and Jan. 1767: *PGW*, Col. Ser., 7:304, 309, 332, 439, 452, 458, and 481.

88. Ibid., 9:341, n. 5.

89. Progress on the outbuildings can be followed in Lund Washington's letters to GW 5 Oct. and 5, 15, and 24 Nov. 1775, ibid., Rev. Ser., 2:65, 116, 307, 374, and 422.

90. Lund Washington to GW, 3 Dec. 1775, ibid., 480.

91. Ledger A, 59ff, copy, PGWp.

92. See William Stone, will, witnessed 5 Sept. 1777, Fluvanna County, Virginia, Will Book 1, O.S.:5. Courthouse, copy, PGWp. Also the inventory taken 24 Aug. 1778, which, in addition to carpentry tools, listed sides of shoe leather and shoemaking equipment, a gun and saddle, a healthy number of cows (including a bull), sheep, and hogs, furniture that included a small desk, and a Bible, a prayer book, and a book of sermons.

93. Fluvanna County, Virginia, Will Book, O.S.:118.

94. Ronald Vern Jackson, *First Census of the United States, Virginia: Records of the State Renumeration: 1782–1785* (Bountiful, Vt., 1978), 86, 1785, copy, ViMtvL. In addition to the buildings, Caleb Stone listed seven whites in his household.

95. List of Taxable Property in Truro Parish, Edward Payne's District, 1815, copy, ViMtvL. Items listed for Caleb & Sons also included a silver watch and a clock but no mahogany furniture.

96. Will, Caleb Stone, 7 Jan. 1807, Fluvanna County, Virginia, Will Book 2, O.S.:52. Also his inventory, recorded 28 May 1810, ibid., 55.

97. Washington to Anthony Whiting, 6 Jan. 1793, *GWW*, 32:293. "You will see by the enclosed to Thomas Green . . . on what footing I have placed his continuance," GW wrote. "It is necessary . . . to con-

sider how the business can be carried on without him, or some other White-man . . . for I am sure, none of my Negro Carpenters are adequate to the framing, and executing such a Barn as I am about to build at D: run."

98. GW to William Pearce, 18 Dec. 1793, ibid., 33:194; also GW to George Augustine Washington, 1 July 1787, ibid., 29:240, and to Anthony Whiting, 3 Mar. 1793, ibid., 32:365.

99. GW to Anthony Whiting, 4 Nov. 1792, ibid., 32:205.

100. See, for example, the agreement made with Green at the end of 1787 in which he promised that he would "not absence himself" and would "be honest sober, and faithful . . . behaving himself upon all occasions orderly and quietly," (articles of agreement, 6 Dec. 1787, copy, ViMtvL); or GW's reference to a new agreement drawn up in the fall of 1793: "I have engaged the person who superintends [the carpenters] at present to look after them another year. He is a good workman himself, and can be active; but—as he is fond of drink . . . I place no great confidence in him. He has, however, promised" (GW to William Pearce, 27 Oct. 1793, ibid., 141–42).

101. "Codicil," 26 Mar. 1787, copy, ViMtvL.

102. Thomas Green to GW, 15 May 1788, copy, PGWp.

103. GW to Thomas Green, 31 Mar. 1789, *GWW,* 30:262–64.

104. GW to William Pearce, 18 Dec. 1793, ibid., 33:194.

105. GW to Anthony Whiting, 3 Mar. 1793, ibid., 32:365.

106. GW to William Pearce, 16 Feb. 1794, ibid., 33:270.

107. GW to Thomas Green, 23 Dec. 1793, ibid., 212–14.

108. "I cannot bear the thought of adding to the distress I know they must be in by turning them a drift," GW wrote, "and to mix them among the Negros would be attended with many evils. . . . It would be better therefore on all accounts if they were removed to some other place even if [I] was to pay the Rent" (GW to William Pearce, 2 Nov. 1794, ibid., 34:13). On Sally Green's plans to move to Alexandria see William Pearce to GW, 11 Nov. 1794, copy, PGWp, to which GW replied: "Caution Sally Green against dealing with my negros after she is fixed in Alexandria" (GW to William Pearce, 30 Nov. 1794, *GWW,* 34:48). But when Washington learned later that she was not doing well, he wrote: "If Mrs. Green and her family are really in distress, afford them some

relief . . . in my opinion it had better be in anything than money, for I very strongly suspect that all that . . . is applied more in rigging herself, than in . . . useful necessities for her family" (GW to William Pearce, 4 Apr. 1796, ibid., 35:13).

109. John C. Fitzpatrick, ed., *The Last Will and Testament of George Washington and Schedule of his Property, to which is appended the Last Will and Testament of Martha Washington* (Mount Vernon, 1992), 18.

110. Thomas Green's estate, which included a walnut table, a small chest, a trundle bed, and tools, was assessed at a total value of £13.4.6 (inventory, recorded 7 Dec. 1797, Fairfax County, Virginia Will Book G-1, 1794–99, 327–28).

111. GW to William Pearce, 18 Dec. 1793, *GWW,* 32:191. Apparently Anthony Whiting had not been an exemplary predecessor. "[He], it is said, drank freely, kept bad company at my house and in Alexandria, and was a very debauched person" (ibid., 192).

Chapter 7

1. Since fewer than twenty-one thousand English registrations for bond servants immigrating to the colonies are still extant, the figure given for the total number is an estimate derived from several different studies. See David Galenson, *White Servitude in Colonial America: An Economic Analysis* (Cambridge, Eng., London, and New York, 1984), 16–17. Galenson's study of bonded servants in the colonies, including their migration patterns, population characteristics, and occupations is based on English registrations recorded in three leading ports: London, Bristol, and Liverpool. Richard S. Dunn, in "Servants and Slaves: The Recruitment and Employment of Labor," in Jack P. Greene and J. R. Pole, eds., *Colonial British America: Essays in the New History of the Early Modern Era* (Baltimore and London, 1984), 159, estimates that roughly half of all English immigrants came as bonded servants. The English tended to immigrate as single males or females, and Germans as families (ibid., 14ff.). Bernard Bailyn's study of registrations from Dec. 1773 to Mar. 1776 points to the high preponderance of single males and females (as opposed to families) immigrating to the upper South. See his *Voyagers to the West: A Passage in the Peopling of America on the Eve of the Revolution* (New York, 1968), 205ff.

2. Carl Bridenbaugh, *The Colonial Craftsman* (Chicago and London, 1961), 1–2. Galenson calculates—using, again, specific sets of registration records—that the percentage of self-professed crafts-

men immigrating to the colonies was 19 percent to 41 percent (Galenson, *White Servitude,* 71ff.).

3. For a concise explanation of the guild system in London see Roger W. Moss, Jr., "The Origins of the Carpenters' Company of Philadelphia" in Charles E. Peterson, ed., *Building Early America: Contributions Toward the History of a Great Industry* (Radnor, Pa., 1976), 35–53.

4. Ibid. Artisans in Philadelphia are also covered in a number of solidly researched, recent studies: Sharon V. Salinger, *"To Serve Well and Faithfully": Labor and Indentured Servants in Pennsylvania, 1682–1800* (New York, 1987); Billy G. Smith, *The "Lower Sort": Philadelphia's Laboring People, 1750–1800* (Ithaca, N.Y., 1990); and Ronald Schultz, *The Republic of Labor: Philadelphia Artisans and the Politics of Class, 1720–1830* (New York, 1993).

For developments—in some ways similar and in other ways not—in what grew to be the leading urban center of the upper South, see Charles G. Steffen, *The Mechanics of Baltimore: Workers and Politics in the Age of Revolution, 1763–1812* (Urbana and Chicago, Ill., 1984); also Christine Daniels, "From Father to Son: Economic Roots of Craft Dynasties in Eighteenth-Century Maryland" in Howard B. Rock, Paul A. Gilje, and Robert Asher, eds., *American Artisans: Crafting Social Identity, 1750–1850* (Baltimore and London, 1995), 3–16; and Tina H. Sheller, "Freemen, Servants, and Slaves: Artisans and the Craft Structure of Revolutionary Baltimore Town," in ibid., 17–32. The Carpenters' Society of Baltimore was organized in 1791 (Steffen, *Mechanics of Baltimore,* 102–3).

5. W. J. Rorabaugh, in *The Craft Apprentice: From Franklin to the Machine Age* (New York and London, 1986), 4ff., discusses the failure of the guild system to develop fully in the colonies. On the upper South see Bridenbaugh, *Colonial Craftsman,* 7–21; and Steffen, *Mechanics of Baltimore,* 27–48. Morgan provides a vivid account of mortality in seventeenth-century Virginia in *American Slavery, American Freedom,* 158–79. See also Bailyn, *Voyagers to the West,* 99ff. And on artisans becoming planters see Kulikoff, *Tobacco and Slaves,* 33–37; Daniel D. Reiff, *Small Georgian Houses in England and Virginia,* 191–92; and Michele K. Gillespie, "Planters in the Making: Artisanal Opportunity in Georgia, 1790–1830" in Rock, Gilje, and Asher, eds., *American Aritsans,* 33–47.

6. The slow growth of towns in Virginia and the politics of setting up town centers to encourage trade and manufactures in the colony are discussed in Kulikoff, *Tobacco and Slaves,* 104ff., and the Rutmans, *Place in Time,* 204–33.

7. Hunter D. Farish, ed., Henry Hartwell, James Blair, and Edward Chilton, *The Present State of Virginia and the College* (Williamsburg, Va., 1940), 9–10, quoted in Bridenbaugh, *Colonial Craftsmen,* 9.

8. See Jean B. Russo, "Self-Sufficiency and Local Exchange: Free Craftsmen in the Rural Chesapeake Economy" in Lois Green Carr, Philip D. Morgan, and Jean B. Russo, eds., *Colonial Chesapeake Society* (Chapel Hill, N.C., and London, 1988), 389–432. Russo takes issue with the contention that the plantation system was altogether unhospitable to independent craftsmen trying to make a living.

9. Mary G. Powell, *The History of Old Alexandria, Virginia From July 13, 1749 to May 24, 1861* (Richmond, Va., 1928), 29ff. GW was one of the surveyors laying out the new town in 1749. Lawrence Washington was a trustee, as were George William Fairfax and John Carlyle. When the lots were put up for sale at public auction, it was agreed that no one would be allowed to buy more than two contiguous lots. In the event, lots in prime locations (the center of town and the waterfront) were taken up by each of the three men. Most of the original lots were sold by 1754.

10. William Waller Hening, *The Statutes at Large of Virginia,* 6:286–87. The law was passed in February 1752.

11. GW had the deeds drawn up for two lots in Alexandria at the end of 1765. See Ledger A, 222a, copy, PGWp. He became one of the trustees of the town the following year and built a small house (since demolished) at Cameron and Pitt Streets (Powell, *History of Old Alexandria,* 159). In Sept. 1769 he noted in his diary: "I rid to Alexandria to see how my House went on" (*GWD,* 2:128). On the town's growth see also Kulikoff, *Tobacco and Slaves,* 124–25.

12. Waite was one of the carpenters who had witnessed Lawrence's will. He had an account with Ramsay & Dixon as early as 1753 (Account Book of the Merchantile Partnership of Williams Ramsay & John Dixon, Alexandria, Virginia, 1753–57, Lloyd House, Alexandria Public Library).

13. Ibid. "John Paterson, Joyner," began making purchases at Ramsay & Dixon's store in 1754. Lanphier was charged for goods bought there the year before. Ibid.

14. William Ramsay, Robert Adam, and Carlyle & Dalton to GW and John West, 16 May 1774, *PGW,* Col. Ser., 10:61.

15. Kulikoff, *Tobacco and Slaves,* 124–25.

16. See Penny Morrill, *Who Built Alexandria? Architects in Alexandria 1750–1900* (Alexandria, Va., 1979), 28, in which she notes that in 1873 a Car-

penters' Society had been in existence for "over a century."

17. The notice ran as follows: "ONE DOLLAR REWARD—for the CHEAP CARPENTER—The subscriber will give the above reward . . . to any person who will bring to his house in Duke Street, that underhanded chap, who advertises to work for 25 per cent less than rates established by the Carpenters' Society—as he intends to indulge him in his fondness for *cheap work,* by giving him a sound drubbing, *gratis*" (*Alexandria Gazette,* quoted in ibid., 28).

18. Carpenters and Joiners' Society of Alexandria, *The Builders' Price Book* (Alexandria, 1812), Lloyd House, Alexandria Public Library. The notice at the beginning of the book states that by "having the prices of their work equitably established . . . upon true and mathematical modes of measurement" the members of the society would help ensure "a good understanding amongst each other, and that their customers may be equally and justly charged."

19. Morrill, *Who Built Alexandria?,* 1.

20. Town of Alexandria, Board of Trustees, Minutes, 16 Feb. 1770 and 29 Nov. 1771, copy, Lloyd House, Alexandria Public Library.

21. On the cost of transporting servants see Edwin J. Perkins, *The Economy of Colonial America* (New York, 1988), p. 92; and on the economic plight of English workers and the appeal of immigrating to the colonies, Dunn, "Recruitment and Labor," 160–62. The subject of indentured servants is also treated in detail in Peter Wilson Coldham, *Bonded Passengers to America* (Baltimore, 1983).

22. Galenson, *White Servitude,* 192–93.

23. On recruiting servants and the roles played by crimps, statute fairs, and register offices, including one next to the gates of the London Exchange known as "kidnapper's walk," see Bailyn, *Voyagers to the West,* 296–323. Perkins, in *The Economy of Colonial America,* 92, discusses the percentage of those who came voluntarily versus those who were sentenced, and J. R. T. Hughes, in *Social Control in the Colonial Economy* (Charlottesville, Va., 1976), 109, estimates that forty-five hundred convicts were shipped to America between 1661 and 1700 and as many as thirty thousand from 1700 to 1776. Bailyn, in *Voyagers to the West,* 295, observes that many so-called criminals were only down-and-out tradesmen "caught in the extraordinarily fine mesh of the eighteenth-century criminal laws, which classified equally as capital offenses both murder and the theft of a handerchief." A. Roger Ekirch provides a comprehensive treatment of the subject in *Bound for America: The Transporta-* tion of British Convicts to the Colonies, 1718–1775 (Oxford, 1987). See also Peter Wilson Coldham, *Emigrants in Chains: A Social History of Forced Emigration to the Americas of Felons, Destitute Children, Political and Religious Non-Conformists, Vagabonds, Beggars, and other Undesirables, 1607–1776* (Surrey, Eng., 1992), which draws together a wealth of anecdotal information about transported criminals and concludes on the subject of their treatment: "Felons exiled into the colonies were frequently spoken of, both by themselves and by their jailers, as having been sold into slavery. That this was not just a figure of hyperbole becomes evident upon contemporary accounts based on personal experience" (ibid., 115).

24. Ibid., 313. By the late eighteenth century the forms were printed in duplicate: one copy for the servant, and the other for the buyer (usually the ship captain until the servant was sold). The servant also had to signify that his or her labor was not already bound to another owner.

25. Galenson, *White Servitude,* 13–15; Perkins, *Economy of Colonial America,* 95–96.

26. Bailyn, in *Voyagers to the West,* 316–23, provides a vivid description of the crowded and unsanitary conditions on shipboard, including Janet Schaw's account of being locked in below the hatches during a twelve-day storm and standing continuously in the deep pools of water in order to keep from drowning.

27. On the importance of the timing of arrivals in the colonies see ibid., 313–15.

28. Ibid., 324–50. Harry Piper, a merchant in Alexandria dealing in the servant trade, complained in his letters home of "the disagreeable business of Servants." After the sale of one shipload of servants among whom there were only a few tradesmen, he wrote his superiors: "The Volunteer Servants from Dublin are really very sorry, they being brought up to no sort of Business, & Men & Women are both very great Blackguards. . . . I wish had been hanged." There was also duplicity to contend with. "Two that I sold in Frederick had been sold there, a little while before, so you see what villains these are . . . [and] many of these servants disputed, & some of them the number of Years appear to be altered, which does not look well." Added to that was the problem of accepting credit from purchasers "that one is not well acquainted with, & I find that the best deceive" (Harry Piper to Dixon & Littledale, 10 Aug. and 12 Sept. 1768, Harry Piper Letter Book, Douglass Family MSS, Lloyd House, Alexandria Library).

29. Tench Tilghman to GW, 15 July 1784, *PGW,* Con. Ser. 1:529–30. Tilghman had just tried to pur-

chase two tradesmen, a bricklayer and a carpenter, for GW. "There was a Bricklayer, who could not say much for himself, and several Carpenters, but they would not engage for any certain time, neither would they take less than the high daily Wages given to such Tradesmen here" (ibid.).

30. Galenson, *White Servitude*, 97–102.

31. Thomas Spear, or Spears, a twenty-two-year-old carpenter and joiner, was bought off a ship from Bristol for a four-year term (*PGW*, Col. Ser., 10:366, n. 3). John Broad, a convict, was bought for a seven-year term for £45 Maryland currency (ibid., 9:314, n. 1). He was provided with tools and clothing in Mar. 1774 (Lund Washington's account book, p. 9, MSS, ViMtvL). Henry Young was paid for and provided with clothing in Aug. 1774 (ibid., 11). And William Webster, a convict from Scotland, was indentured and provided with tools and clothing three months earlier (ibid.).

32. Advertisement for runaway servants, 23 Apr. 1775, *PGW* Col. Ser., 10:341–42 and n. Four different people were paid for pursuing Webster and Spear. Spear was back at Mount Vernon by the following February, working on the "House opposite the Store" (Lund Washington to GW, 8 Feb. 1776, ibid., Rev. Ser., 3:271). See also Lund Washington's account book, 44, MSS, ViMtvL, for payment to the tailor for making breeches for Spear. Webster had been apprehended the spring before (cash accounts, Apr. 1774, ibid., Col. Ser., 10:19).

33. Lund Washington to GW, 17, 25, and 31 Jan. and 15 and 22 Feb. 1776, ibid., Rev. Ser., 3:129, 188, 232–33, 271, 318, and 355.

34. *Maryland Gazette*, 26 June 1760; also Ledger A, 54, copy, PGWp.

35. Lund Washington to GW, 29 Sept., 5 Nov., and 3 Dec. 1775, *PGW*, Rev. Ser., 2:64, 306, and 479.

36. Knowles and his wife, Rachel, were acquired by GW in Dec. 1773 for £45.6.8 (Ledger B, 119, copy, PGWp). They received their freedom dues in Dec. 1777. GW hired Knowles in 1786, and again in 1789 and 1790, as a stonemason (ibid., 226 and 314).

37. Donald Sweig, "White Indentured Servitude in Fairfax County: New Evidence Is Discovered," *Fairfax Chronicles* 2, no. 2 (1978):1–4. Mahoney was indentured for a two-year term for £16. On his attempt to get a raise in pay, see Thomas Mahoney to GW, 3 Apr. 1788, copy, PGWp. For GW's answer see Tobias Lear to Thomas Mahoney, 4 Apr. 1788, ibid; also GW and Thomas Mahoney, Articles of Agreement, 15 Apr. 1788, ibid. References to Mahoney's work are sprinkled throughout the Mount Vernon records. For example, the Weekly Reports for 1785–1786, 54, MSS, ViMtvL, indicate that he was working on shingling the salthouse. The following year, while Matthew Baldridge, another joiner, was working on the new room, Mahoney (along with Green) was detailed to the greenhouse (Mount Vernon Store Book, 1787, MSS, ViMtvL). Mahoney and Green also worked together on framing a barn floor in 1788 (*GWD*, 5:332–33). And Ledger B, 236, 331 (copy, PGWp) indicates Mahoney was paid wages until the end of May 1792.

38. McDermott was indentured to GW for a two-year term (Sweig, "Indentured Servitude in Fairfax County," 1–4; also John A. Cantwell, "Imported Indentured White Servitude in Fairfax and Prince William Counties 1750–1800," M.A. thesis, George Mason University, 1986, 70). On 1 Aug. 1786 he signed on for another year as a "Stone Mason, Bricklayer, and (when not employed in either of these) in other jobs which he may be set about" (*GWD*, 4:191, n.; see also ibid., 5:227; weekly reports for 1785–1786, 60, copy, ViMtvL; and on GW's desire to have McDermott return to Mount Vernon, GW to Tobias Lear, 25 Mar. 1797, *GWW*, 34:425).

39. GW to Captain Nathaniel Ingraham, 22 Mar. 1788, ibid., 29:445.

40. Ehlers had ended his term as an apprentice at the royal garden at Montbrillant in 1767, and at that point had been provided with a certificate bearing the seal of George III. Thereafter he worked at Herrenhausen as well as at Montbrillant. See Elizabeth Rosemary Norton, "A Penchant for Noble Patronage," *Daughters of American Colonists* (1962), 4:12.

41. GW to Hendrick Wilmans, 12 Oct. 1789, *PGW*, Pres. Ser., 4:166.

42. GW to Margaret Tilghman Carroll, 16 Sept. 1789, ibid., 43. Mrs. Carroll, whose greenhouse and stock of exotica in Maryland were well known, gave generously. Otho H. Williams, her gardener, charged with shipping the plants to Mount Vernon, wrote—much to GW's anxiety—"As some of [the trees] are large and bear a good deal of fruit and as their boxes are of considerable weight, it will be necessary to procure [a] commodious Vessel and a trusty Navigator." In the end, after considerable negotiation, only small plants were sent (ibid., 44–47, n.).

43. "Articles of Agreement made this twelfth of April Anno Domini one thousand seven hundred and eighty-seven by and between Geo. Washington Esq. . . . and Philip Bater, Gardener," reprinted in *Old Farmer's Almanac*, 1985, 209–10. Bater was also to be provided annually with "a decent suit of cloth-

ing befitting a man in his station; to consist of a Coat, Vest, and breeches; a working Jacket and breeches, of homespun . . . besides: two white shirts; three check Ditto; two pair of yarn stockings; two pair of thread Ditto; two linnen pocket handkerchiefs; two pair of linnen overalls; as many pair of Shoes as ar actually necessary" (ibid.).

44. Tobias Lear to Clement Biddle, 16 Sept. 1789, *PGW*, Pres. Ser., 4:42. See also George Augustine Washington to GW, 16 July 1790, ibid., 5:91–92, in which he states: "the Gardner is very desirous of getting a Dutch and English Dictionary to perfect himself in the English language as Alexandria does not afford one I promised to write you for one"; and Tobias Lear to Clement Biddle, 17 Aug. 1790, ibid., 272, asking for a "German & English Dictionary for the Presidents German Gardner." GW mentions to Howell Lewis sending "A Dutch News Paper . . . for the Gardener" (4 Aug. 1793, *GWW*, 33:42, n. 56).

45. At Martha Washington's direction Catherine Ehlers was given charge of the spinners. "Put her in a good and regular mode, and keep her to the exercise of it. An allowance will be made her for the trouble," GW wrote Anthony Whiting, 14 Oct. 1792 (ibid., 32:183–84). And on the subject of accommodations he remarked: "The Garderner . . . seemed earnestly to wish, that he might be removed from the House he now lives in [to Butler's house] . . . on acct. of its having a room to lodge in above (which a decent Woman would require) and another below to Cook in" (GW to Anthony Whiting, 28 Apr. 1793, ibid., 437). At some point, arrangements had been made for Ehlers and his wife to eat at the servants' table in the cellar of the main house. Later they asked to be allowed to prepare their own meals and apparently shared them with Johann Lotz, the young German gardener hired to help Ehlers (GW to William Pearce, 18 Dec. 1793, ibid., 33:200).

46. De Forest, *The Gardens & Grounds at Mount Vernon*, 59. The pitcher GW gave Ehlers and that subsequently passed down through his family is described in Norton, "A Penchant for Noble Patronage," *Daughters of American Colonists* (1962) 5:12. At the time it was in the possession of the author, a descendant of Ehlers's adopted daughter. It was exhibited at Gadby's Tavern in 1956, and its mate is still at Mount Vernon (ibid.).

47. See agreement made up in Germany before Ehlers undertook the voyage to Virginia, 24 June 1789, *PGW*, Pres. Ser., 3:63–64 and 64–65, n. According to his initial contract with GW, Ehlers was to receive 12 guineas for the first year, with a raise of

1 guinea every year thereafter for the next four years, in addition to being given room and board. Four years later, probably in an attempt to keep him at Mount Vernon, GW promised him a horse to ride six times a year into Alexandria and "continued use of the garden." Two years after that, in 1795, the terms included the following as well: "The Gardener may go on with his nursery, and be told that he shall be allowed the fifth of what are sold, or raised" (GW to William Pearce, 25 Jan. 1795, *GWW*, 34:103).

48. George Augustine Washington to GW, 5 Mar. and 16 July 1790, *PGW*, Pres. Ser., 5:204–5, and 6:91–92. "He is really industrious and very obliging and as to a knowledge of his business I am persuaded he possesses it very sufficiently," wrote George Augustine of Ehlers (ibid.). Visitors were invariably impressed by the variety and beauty of exotic plants at Mount Vernon. Mentioned were espaliated apricot, lime, orange, and fig trees, and also a Sago palm and a century plant. On the lima bean and artichoke seeds see GW to Anthony Whiting, 3 Feb. 1793, *GWW*, 32:327; and GW to William Pearce, 21 Sept. 1794, ibid., 33:503.

49. GW to William Pearce, 15 May 1796, ibid., 35:47.

50. Benjamin Henry Latrobe, "Through Virginia to Mount Vernon: Extracts from the Journal of Benjamin Henry Latrobe," *Appleton's Booklovers Magazine* 6, no. 1 (1905):10–11.

51. Norton, "A Penchant for Noble Heritage," *Daughters of American Colonists* (1962) 4 and 5:12; and 7:11.

52. GW to Anthony Whiting, 4 Nov. 1792, *GWW*, 32:201.

53. GW to Anthony Whiting, 23 Dec. 1792, ibid., 275.

54. GW to Johann Christian Ehlers, 23 Dec. 1793, ibid., 33:215.

55. GW to Anthony Whiting, 26 May 1793, ibid., 32:476.

56. Norton, "A Penchant for Noble Heritage," *Daughters of American Colonists* (1962) 4:6 and 5:12.

57. Robert Stewart to GW, 14 May and 3 June 1760, *PGW*, Col. Ser., 6:418 and 431; also *GWD*, 1:216.

58. Fielding Lewis to GW, 7 Feb. 1757, *PGW*, Col. Ser., 4:107–8; and on GW's sharing workmen with his neighbors, Ledger A, 61, copy, PGWp, GW to George William Fairfax, 25 July 1763, *PGW*, Col. Ser., 7:233–34.

59. See, for example, *GWD* 2:52, 212, 223, and

332. Between 21 and 31 Dec. 1771 GW spent five days hunting with the Tripletts. On one of those days William Triplett dined at Mount Vernon, on another both Tripletts dined at Mount Vernon, on a third GW dined at Thomas Triplett's, and on yet another he dined at William Triplett's (*GWD*, 3:77–78).

60. Thomas Triplett Russell, "Family Chronicle: A History of the Triplett Family, Their Relatives, and Friends in England and Virginia 1560 to 1800" (unpublished typescript, incomplete at the time of the author's death n.d.), 1–2, which includes a transcription of Francis's first land patent and the names of the servants he brought over, at least five of whom were in-laws (see also ibid., genealogical chart no. 2, n.p.).

61. Ibid., 80.

62. Ibid., 93, 153ff.

63. Ibid., 80.

64. Ibid., 101.

65. Thomas Triplett, William and Thomas's father, died in 1737, at the age of 36.

66. George William Fairfax to GW, 1 Sept. 1758, *PGW*, Col. Ser., 5:438–39.

67. Ledger A, 72, copy, PGWp. Triplett was not alone in using Mount Vernon's blacksmiths; several of Washington's other neighbors did so too. For a detailed discussion see Dennis J. Pogue, "Blacksmithing at George Washington's Mount Vernon: 1775–1800," *Northern Neck of Virginia Historical Magazine* 46, no. 1 (1996): 5378–95.

68. George William Fairfax to GW, 15 Sept. 1758, *PGW*, Col. Ser., 6:19. See also John Patterson to GW, 13 Aug. and 2 Sept. 1758, ibid., 5:390 and 450. "I layd befor him the disappointment that may accrue from the Work not being finish'd," wrote Patterson (ibid.).

69. Plan of Pohick Church in Slaughter, *History of Truro Parish*, following 82. The significance of pew assignments is discussed by Upton in *Holy Things and Profane*, 175–83. The location of the most desirable pews varied from church to church, he notes, adding: "Although some locations were traditionally preferred, almost any place would do so long as the honor was understood" (ibid., 182).

70. Russell, "Family Chronicle," MSS, 194.

71. William Triplett, inventory and additional inventory, 1803, and sale of estate, 14 Dec. 1803, Fairfax County, Virginia, Will Book I, 1801–6, 352, 363, 374, copy, PGWp.

72. GW to William Triplett, 25 Sept. 1786, *PGW*, Con. Ser., 4:268–71, and 24 Sept. 1797, *GWW*, 36:35–39.

73. Russell, "Family Chronicle," MSS, 298. As early as 1760, GW and William Triplett were vying with each other over a piece of land near GW's Dogue Run Farm. In the end, they split it (*GWD*, 1:268 and n.).

74. GW to Lund Washington, 28 Mar. 1781, *GWW*, 21:385. On the eventual settlement of the matter see *GWD*, 4:93 and 141, in which GW wrote: "Rid to Alexandria . . . exchanged Deeds in Court with Mr. Willm. Triplett for the Lands we had swapped" (ibid.).

75. GW attended Sarah Triplett Manley's funeral "at the plantation of Mr. Willm. Triplett" on 9 Oct. 1785 (ibid., 203). See also ibid., 5:33, in which he notes: "I set out for Mr. Triplets . . . he agreed to sell me Manley's Land on the following terms."

76. Russell, "Family Chronicle," MSS, 278.

77. Ibid., 193.

78. Jackson, *First Census of the United States, 1790, Virginia*, 85; also Russell, *Family Chronicle*, 193.

79. Ibid., 272; also Charles W. Stetson, *Washington and His Neighbors* (Richmond, Va., 1956), 216; Robert A Rutland, *The Papers of George Mason 1725–1792* (Chapel Hill, N.C., 1970), 1:cii; and Lund Washington to GW, 29 Sept. 1775, *PGW*, Rev. Ser., 2:64–65. (The editor's note accompanying Lund's letter identifies the Triplett in question as William, which may be incorrect, since it describes an election of militia officers and William was not a member of the Fairfax Independent Company.)

80. *GWD*, 3:271.

81. David John Mays, ed., *The Letters and Papers of Edmund Pendleton 1734–1803* (Charlottesville, Va., 1967), 1:98.

82. Russell, "Family Chronicle," MSS, 278, 283–84, and 193.

83. Charles H. Callahan, *Washington the Man and the Mason* (Washington, D.C., 1913), 300.

84. See supra, n. 71.

85. According to family genealogical records, Sears immigrated to Virginia "being engaged in some business in connection with Lord Fairfax's land grant." See Samuel Pierce May, *The Descendants of Richard Sares (Sears) of Yarmouth, Massachusetts, 1638–1888* (Albany, N.Y., 1890), Appendix, "Some Other Families Called Sears," 605. However, Sears was more than likely "Seers," the convict sentenced to seven years' transport to the colonies, listed in *Proceedings on the King's Commission of the Peace* (London, 1752, as repr. in Coldham, *Bonded Passengers in America*, 236). See also Mesick, Cohen, Waite, "Historic Structure Report," MSS, ViMtvL.

86. For a full treatment of Sears's work with Buck-land and at Gunston Hall—including an analysis of the distinctive features of his carving, see Luke Beck-erdite, "William Buckland and William Bernard Sears: Designer and Carver," *Journal of Early Southern Decorative Arts* 8, no. 2 (1982):7–41; and on the furniture made by the two, the same author's "Architect-designed Furniture in Eighteenth-Century Virginia: The Work of Williams Buckland and William Bernard Sears," in Luke Beckerdite, ed., *American Furniture 1994* (Hanover, N.H., and London, n.d.), 29–48.

87. Ibid., 8. In a suit brought against him by a journeyman in 1763, Buckland was charged for a "Pare shoes to Bernard Sears" purchased in 1759.

88. Beirne and Scarff, *William Buckland,* 36. The evidence that Buckland worked on Mount Airy's interior is circumstantial but compelling.

89. Beckerdite, "William Buckland and William Bernard Sears," 16–19.

90. May, *Descendants of Richard Sares,* Appendix, "Some Other Families Called Sears," 605.

91. Daniel French, who was appointed by the Truro Vestry to serve as contractor for building Pohick Church, died before the work was completed. His estate records provide details of the construction work, including the names of those individuals compensated for boarding workers (Fairfax County Will Book C-1, 1767–76, 196–212; see also Truro Parish, *Minutes of the Vestry,* 134–36).

92. Beckerdite, "William Buckland and William Bernard Sears," 29.

93. For a discussion of prescribed elements in Anglican churches such as church furniture and scriptures lettered on tablets on interior walls—in place of explicit religious imagery—see Upton, *Holy Things and Profane,* 118ff.

94. Apparently there was some confusion on the latter point that had to be ironed out later. "Whereas it appears that the Dimentions of the Alterpiece mentioned in the Articles with the undertaker for building the New Church, are not according to the proportions of Architecture, the said undertaker is authorised and desired to make the same according to the true proportions of the Ionick order notwithstanding" (Truro Parish, *Minutes of the Vestry,* 121–22).

95. Upton, *Holy Things and Profane,* 132–33, 137–38, and 248, n. 41.

96. Ibid., 138.

97. Sambo Anderson, quoted in "Mount Vernon Reminiscences," *Alexandria Gazette,* 22 Jan. 1876, copy, ViMtvL.

98. J. A. Simpson and E. S. C. Weiner, eds., *The Oxford English Dictionary* (Oxford and New York, 1989), 15:513.

99. Susan Annie Plaskett, *Memories of a Plain Family* (Washington, D.C., 1936), 197.

100. Truro Parish, *Minutes of the Vestry,* 133–35. At the same meeting the Vestry agreed to pay Sears an extra £58.19. "for carved Work done by him . . . being additional work directed and agreed to by the Vestry and not inserted in the Undertaker's Articles" (ibid., 134).

101. Lund Washington to GW, 29 Sept. 1775, *PGW,* Rev. Ser., 2:65.

102. Lund Washington to GW, 12 Nov. and 10 and 17 Dec. 1775, ibid., 356, 527, and 571.

103. That Sears boarded at Mount Vernon while working there is based on the assumption that his own home was too far to travel back and forth to on a daily basis. Lund refers to Sears's "own home" in a letter to GW, 22 Oct. 1775, ibid., 219.

104. Lund Washington to GW, 3 Dec. 1775, ibid., 480.

105. May, *Descendants of Richard Sares,* Appendix, "Some Other Families Called Sears," 605. Support for the patriot cause among American artisans generally ran high and was closely associated with what historians have described as a widespread "artisanal republican faith" that remained a powerful force for decades afterward. Among the many studies of the subject see, for example, Steffen, *Mechanics of Baltimore,* esp. 53–168 and 276–83; also Paul Gilje, "Introduction, Identity and Independence: The American Artisan, 1750–1850," in Rock, Gilje and Asher, eds., *American Artisans,* xi–xx.

106. May, *Descendants of Richard Sares,* Appendix,"Some Other Families Called Sears," 605. The same source mentions that he opposed the War of 1812. Apparently Sears was vocal enough about his political views to be remembered for them.

107. Sambo Anderson, quoted in "Mount Vernon Reminiscences," *Alexandria Gazette,* 22 Jan. 1876, copy, ViMtvL.

108. *Alexandria Gazette and Daily Advertiser,* 2 May 1818. It is worth quoting from Sears's obituary at length. "Died, at his residence in Fairfax County, Va., on the 27th day of April, in the 87th year of his age, William B. Sears, Sen., a native of England. Mr. Sears, tired of oppression of his own country, visited the United States, and contributed by his efforts, as well as by his astonishing mechanical talents, to the independence of the country, and that character it so justly deserves, for being a century in advance of

Europe in the mechanical arts. . . . Mr. Sears has reared and well educated a large family of children, who will transmit their father's fair name to posterity. Peace be to the names of those men, who, leaving the oppressions of feudal Europe, have planted scions in this land of liberty, where every man can sit under the shadow of his own vine and fig tree and can say there is none to hurt us." The concept of independence lay at the heart of artisanal republicanism, and it would be difficult to find a more evocative expression of it than this one. The fact that it echoes, in the vine and fig tree image, GW's favorite representation of his own independence makes it doubly striking.

109. May, *Descendants of Richard Sares*, Appendix, "Some Other Families Called Sears," 605.

110. GW to the commissioners of the District of Columbia, 20 Feb. 1797, *GWW*, 35:396.

111. *Alexandria Gazette and Daily Advertiser*, 2 May 1818.

112. On Rawlins's method of practicing his trade and GW's troubled relationship with him see supra, 119–21.

Chapter 8

1. On the background and status of undertakers in Virginia see Upton, *Sacred Things and Profane*, 23–29.

2. GW to Bryan Fairfax, 4 July 1774, *PGW*, Col. Ser., 10:109. GW's role was active enough to be commented on by a visitor after the war. "He . . . often works with his men—strips off his coat and labors like a common man." See John Hunter, diary entry for "November 17 1785, *Pennsylvania Magazine* 17, no. 1 (1893):76, copy, Mount Vernon Library; also Sambo Anderson's references to GW's "perfect plumb ball" eye in "Mount Vernon Reminiscences," *Alexandria Gazette*, 22 Jan. 1876, copy, ViMtvL.

3. John Patterson to GW, 17 June 1758, *PGW*, Col. Ser., 5:222.

4. Robert Campbell describes house carpentry in *The London Tradesman, Being a Compendious View of All the Trades, Professions, Arts, both Liberal and Mechanic, Now Practiced in the Cities of London and Westminster* (Devon, 1969 repr. of 1747 ed.), 161. Petterson also proudly identified himself as a joiner. On that craft, which went well beyond simple carpentry, see Joseph Moxon, "The Art of Joinery" in *Mechanick Exercises, or the Doctrine of Handy-Works Applied to the Arts of Smithing Joinery Carpentry Turning Bricklayery* (London, 1703), 63.

5. John Mercer to George Mercer, 22 Dec. 1767–28 Jan. 1768, Lois Mulkearn, ed., *George Mercer Papers Relating to the Ohio Company of Virginia* (Pittsburgh, 1954), 204. Mercer identifies Patterson as "Bramley's apprentice." "Bramley" was undoubtedly William Bromley, who was responsible for the interiors at Marlborough.

6. John Mercer and his sons are mentioned frequently in Freeman's *Washington*. See, for instance, 2:2, pertaining to Mercer's role in settling Lawrence Washington's estate; also, ibid., 1:382, referring to George Mercer's service in the French and Indian War; and ibid., 2:118, on Charles Mercer's appointment as aide-de-camp. Another brother, John Fenton Mercer, served under GW and died in a skirmish with the enemy in April 1756 (*PGW*, Col. Ser., 3:18, n. 1). Their uncle, James Mercer, had served under Lawrence Washington in the Caribbean in 1740 (Freeman, *Washington*, 1:66). On John Mercer's relationship to George Mason see Copeland and MacMaster, *The Five George Masons*, 69ff. and 76ff. On Mercer's library see ibid., 72 and 76ff.; also C. Malcolm Watkins, *The Cultural History of Marlborough, Virginia* (Washington, D.C., 1968), 36 and 189–204.

7. The fullest description of the building of Marlborough is to be found in ibid., 34–39.

8. Account book of Ramsay & Dixon, copy, Lloyd House, Alexandria Public Library.

9. William Munday (whose work Mercer found generally unsatisfactory) may have been related to Richard Munday, who worked as a carpenter on Carter's Grove.

10. It is not known precisely when John Patterson and Susannah Lanphier were married.

11. Payments in GW's ledger to Patterson suggest that he was working regularly at Mount Vernon by 1757. See Ledger A, 49, for a cash payment of £20 to him at the end of the year, presumably for work completed earlier.

12. The indenture was entered into for a five-year term, with freedom dues amounting to £40. It was recorded at court 15 Mar. 1757. See Fairfax County, Virginia, Deed Book D, 1755–61, 378, copy, PGWp.

13. Ledger A, 49, copy, PGWp.

14. In 1758 Patterson brought an Irish servant joiner to court for having "absented himself eight days and cost his master 745 pounds of tobacco to recover." The servant was sentenced to serve additional time. Fairfax County, Virginia, Minute Book, 1756–63, Part 1, 21, quoted in Messick, Cohen, Waite, "Historic Structure Report," 118, n. 85, MSS, ViMtvL.

15. Ledger A, 49, copy, PGWp.

16. John Carlyle to GW, 22 Aug. 1758, Col. Ser., 5:408.

17. John Patterson to GW, 2 Sept. 1758, ibid., 449.

18. Thomas Waterman gives the interior details of Patterson's rooms high marks, writing that they are "perhaps the most satisfactory of the house . . . in good scale, well designed, and well executed, conditions which are not entirely true of the 1773–87 work." Waterman, *Mansions of Virginia,* 281–82.

19. He did, however, receive two small payments listed later in GW's cash accounts for making pump boxes (*PGW,* Col. Ser., 7:105 and 107). Also, he was among the twenty-two men designated as managers of a plan to improve navigation on the Potomac River that GW enthusiastically supported (ibid., 177, n.), and in July 1765 he voted for GW in the Burgess elections for Fairfax County (ibid., 381).

20. Fairfax County, Virginia, Deed Book, 1755–61, Part 2, 693–95, copy, PGWp.

21. Alexandria Trustee Minutes, copy, Lloyd House, Alexandria Public Library, 68–69.

22. Fairfax County, Virginia, Minute Book, 1756–63, 792, copy, PGWp.

23. Truro Parish, *Minutes of the Vestry,* 5 Oct. 1761, 83.

24. John Patterson's inventory—recorded at court more than five years after his disappearance—included, aside from the unfinished set of drawers, three female slaves and a small girl, wool and cotton cards, and a quilting frame. Inventory, 24 May 1770, Fairfax County, Virginia, Will Book C-1, 1767–76, 80–81, copy, PGWp. See also Susannah Patterson's inventory listing wooling wheels and cards, linen wheels, and an old loom, recorded 20 Jan. 1800 (Fairfax County, Virginia, Will Book H-1, 1779–1801, 82–83, copy, PGWp).

25. Messick, Cohen, Waite, "Historic Structure Report," 104 and 118, n. 85, MSS, ViMtvL.

26. See John A. Cantwell, "Imported White Servitude in Fairfax and Prince William Counties 1750–1800," M.A. thesis, George Mason University (1986), 51.

27. For an account of the Lanphiers' correspondence with their Uncle William and their expectations of the estate see Harry Piper to John Dixon, 24 Oct. 1767, Harry Piper Letter Book, Douglass Family MSS, University of Virginia. Piper and Dixon eventually became involved in trying to help the family claim the estate.

28. John Patterson, will, 6 Oct. 1765, Fairfax County, Virginia, Will Book B-1, 1752–57, 94, copy, PGWp.

29. Mulkearn, ed., *George Mercer Papers,* 204.

30. Ibid.

31. John Patterson, inventory, 24 May 1770, Fairfax County, Virginia, Will Book C-1, 1767–76, 80–81, copy, PGWp.

32. Venus Lanphier, will, 14 Feb. 1769, recorded 24 Nov. 1769, Fairfax County, Virginia, Will Book C-1, 1757–76, 68–70, copy, PGWp.

33. "Mrs. Patterson sends a letter to her Uncle Lanphier,—her Sister is dead & has left her her part of the money if it is recovered—Going Lanphier, I believe will never go home." Harry Paper to John Dixon, 18 Dec. 1769, Harry Piper Letter Book, Douglass Family MSS, University of Virginia.

34. Harry Piper to John Dixon, 24 Oct. 1767, ibid.

35. Harry Piper to John Dixon, 18 Dec. 1769, ibid.

36. Harry Piper to John Dixon, 3 Nov. 1770, ibid.

37. The Lanphier family history has been compiled and preserved by several of Going's descendants. A copy of the MSS was made available to us by Elizabeth A. Livingston.

38. See Robin D. Gwynn, *Huguenot Heritage: The History and Contribution of the Huguenots in Britain* (London, 1985), 17ff., for a useful account of the Huguenot movement in France, the persecution of its adherents, and their exodus to England.

39. A brief history of the county of Wiltshire is available in *Encyclopædia Britannica* (Chicago and New York, 1973), 23:556.

40. On the repressive actions against the Huguenots in England see Grace Lawless Lee, *The Huguenot Settlements in Ireland* (London and New York, 1936), 10ff.

41. For a concise analysis of the campaign see Nicholas Canny, "The Marginal Kingdom: Ireland as a Problem in the First British Empire," in Bernard Bailyn and Philip D. Morgan, eds., *Strangers Within the Realm: Cultural Margins of the First British Empire* (Chapel Hill, N.C., 1991), 35–66.

42. On Cork see Charles Smith, *The Ancient and Present State of the County and City of Cork* (Cork, 1815), 2:234. While it is not known exactly where Going Lanphier's family lived in County Cork, both the names Guin and Lampriere appear in the church registers of St. Mary's in Youghal as well as on lists of Youghal freemen. See ibid., 72; Reverend Canon Hayman, "The Huguenot Settlers at Youghal," *Journal of the Cork Historical and Archaeological Society,* 1984, 3:262–64; and Lee, *The Huguenot Settlements in Ireland,* 80–81. Youghal's economy is described by Justin Callaghan Condon, "Trade and Commerce of the Town of Youghall," *Journal of the Historical Society of Cork,* ser. 2, 9 (1904): 117–20.

43. Cohb is twenty-five miles from Youghal.

44. State of Maryland, Prerogative Court, Inventories, 36:126–28, and Testamentary Proceedings, 32:171 and 187, Maryland State Archives. According to family legend, Thomas Lanphier had arrived on Maryland's shores with £40,000 and a retinue of eleven servants. His inventory presents a sharp contrast to such affluence, listing as it does only modest household goods, many of them described as "old," "middling," or "broken."

45. Fairfax County, Virginia, Will Book B-1, 1752–57, 113, copy, PGWp.

46. Account book of William Ramsay and John Dixon, copy, Lloyd House, Alexandria Public Library. Further evidence that Lanphier was working as a carpenter as early as 1754 is in his discharge of an apprentice, George Tarvin, in the spring of that year. See Fairfax County, Virginia, Order Book, 1754–56, 1:77. Also, the following year he brought two runaway servants to court. Ibid., 214, and 2:294 and 310.

47. Fairfax County, Virginia, Deed Book D-1, Part 1, 197, copy, PGWp.

48. Cash accounts, Aug. 1759, PGW, Col. Ser., 6:331.

49. Fairfax County, Virginia, Minute Book 1756–63, 652, copy, PGWp.

50. Morrill, *Who Built Alexandria?*, 3 and 15.

51. Lund Washington's account book, 64 and 85, MSS, ViMtvL.

52. Ibid.

53. Fairfax County, Virginia, Order Book, 1770–72, 308, copy, PGWp. On Boggess sawing plank for the benches for the new church see the estate accounts of Daniel French, Fairfax County, Virginia, Will Book D-1, 1776–82, 34, copy, PGWp. Boggess also boarded the two workers who constructed the horse blocks and benches for the church.

54. Harry Piper to John Dixon, 3 Nov. 1770, Harry Piper Letter Book, Douglas Family MSS, University of Virginia.

55. Ibid.

56. Lund Washington's account book, 64, MSS, ViMtvL.

57. Truro Parish, *Minutes of the Vestry*, 129, 133, and 134; also estate accounts of Daniel French, Fairfax County, Virginia, Will Book D-1, 1776–82, 34–36, copy, PGWp.

58. Going Lanphier to GW, 16 Oct. 1773, PGW, Col. Ser., 9:348. On the cover of the letter Lanphier wrote, "By favor of Mr. Willm Copon."

59. Lund Washington to GW, 12 Nov. 1775, ibid., Rev. Ser., 2:356.

60. Lund Washington to GW, 11 and 18 Mar. and 22 Apr. 1778, copies, PGWp.

61. "The wheels which was here are very much out of repair—they were sent early in the summer to Lanphier to mend, he promiseg to do them immediately, but findg he woud not do them, I sent them to Alexandria." Lund Washington to GW, 29 Sept. 1775, PGW, Rev. War. Ser., 2:64.

62. GW to Lund Washington, 13 Aug. 1783, copy, PGWp; also GWD, 4:298.

63. Alexandria City, Hustings Court Records, Deed Book B, 302, copy, Lloyd House, Alexandria Public Library.

64. Lanphier family history, MSS. He is also supposed to have lived for a while at "Green Hill" in Fairfax County.

65. Ibid.

66. *Alexandria Gazette*, 26 Jan. 1797.

67. *Alexandria Daily Advertiser*, 13 Mar. 1806.

68. Ibid., 22 June 1804.

69. Ibid., 19 Feb. 1806. In the same year, Robert Goin Lanphier bought a piece of property at 518 King Street, which he sold at a substantial profit seven years later, after building a house on it. See Jeanne F. Butler, *Competition 1792: Designing a Nation's Capitol* (Washington, D.C., 1976), 43–44.

70. See Mary Dorsey Adams to Mrs. F. F. Beirne, 23 Mar. 1962, Mount Vernon Reference Notebook 34, "Overseers and Artisans," ViMtvL, 2. That he designed and engraved the seals for both houses of Congress is family tradition.

71. Butler, *Competition*, 43–46.

72. See ibid., 43.

73. GW to Anthony Whiting, 14 Oct. 1792, PGW, 32:184.

74. Lund's position was not unique. Managers with similar duties were employed on other large plantations, but even less scholarly attention has been paid to them than to overseers. For a brief discussion see Scarborough, *The Overseer*, 178–94. Scarborough uses the term "steward," which was probably more prevalent than GW's "manager."

75. GW's younger brother, John Augustine (Jack), managed Mount Vernon during the French and Indian War, and his son, GW's nephew, George Augustine Washington, managed the place after Lund's tenure.

76. GWD, 2:37, n.

77. Ibid.

78. Russell, "Family Chronicle," MSS, 354.

79. See, for instance, GWD, 2:36, 45, 120, and 207; also 3:76 and 157.

80. Ibid., 2:27 n. See also Lund Washington to GW, 22 Aug. 1767, *PGW*, Col. Ser., 8:20, in which he writes: "My Compliments to Mrs. Washington & let her know that her Children are as well as I ever saw them."

81. GW to Charles Washington, 31 Jan. 1770, ibid., 302.

82. GW to Jonathan Boucher, 20 Apr. 1771, ibid., 448.

83. Slaughter, *History of Truro Parish*, diagram following 82.

84. See, for example, Lund Washington to GW, 15 Feb. 1776, *PGW*, Rev. Ser., 3:319. His earlier letters were signed "your most Obedient & Humble Servt" (Lund Washington to GW, 17 Aug. 1767, ibid., Col. Ser., 8:18). See also GW to Lund Washington, 19 Aug. 1776, ibid., Rev. Ser., 6:86; and for another example of GW's letters, which varied, GW to Lund Washington, 26 Aug. 1776, ibid., 137, where he signs himself "I am sincerely and truly Dr. Sir Yr Most Affecte Go: Washington."

85. GW to Lund Washington, 26 Nov. 1775, ibid., 2:431.

86. Ibid., 9:397, n. 16.

87. Lund Washington's account book, 43, MSS, ViMtvL.

88. See, for instance, Lund Washington to GW, 29 Sept. 1775, 25 Jan. and 29 Feb. 1776, 24 Dec. 1777, and 11 Mar. 1778: *PGW*, Rev. Ser., 2:64 and 187; 3:396; and (for the last two) copies, PGWp; also, GW to Lund Washington, 15 Aug. 1778, *GWW*, 12:326, in which he writes of "the high prices of every article of produce, & the redundancy of circulating paper."

89. Lund Washington to GW, 11 Mar. 1778, copy, PGWp. Lund's hopes of being able to sell corn and flour elsewhere are described in a letter to GW, 29 Feb. 1776, *PGW*, Rev. Ser., 3:395.

90. Lund Washington to GW, 15 and 29 Oct. 1775, and 31 Jan. 1776, *PGW*, Rev. Ser., 2:174–75 and 257 and 3:231.

91. Lund Washington to GW, 24 Dec. 1777, copy, PGWp.

92. Ibid. On an earlier occasion, Lund had written, "This House has been so Crouded with company since Mrs Washington came home that I fear many things is left undone that shoud have been done before she left home—I write in haste and a little confuse'd" (Lund Washington to GW, 14 Nov. 1775, *PGW*, Rev. Ser., 2:376).

93. Lund Washington to GW, 17 Jan. 1776, ibid., 3:129.

94. Lund Washington to GW, 29 Oct. 1775, ibid.,

2:257. For his own part, Lund was as anxious as GW about letting debts go unpaid. The following winter he wrote: "It wou'd give me an infinite deal of Satisfaction if I cou'd by any means find money to pay of several demands against you, for I cannot bear to be ask'd for money on your Ac[oun]t and not be able to pay it" (Lund Washington to GW, 8 Feb. 1776, ibid., 3:269).

95. See ibid., 116, n. 2; also Lund Washington to GW, 17 Jan. 1776, ibid., 126–27 and 131, n. 3; and GW to Lund Washington, 25 Dec. 1782, *GWW*, 25:470.

96. "From the Accounts I have from Loudon Prince William, & some other Countys, there is very little hopes of Collectg money from Tenants, they say it is Cruel in the Land Holders to expect their Rents when there is no market for the produce of the Land—& if there shoud be no market before the present Crop spoils upon there hands, it woud be the height of Injustice ever to expect to be paid for that years Rent," Lund wrote GW, 30 Dec. 1775 (*PGW*, Rev. Ser., 2:621); and later: "If I thought Mt Vernon wou'd stand where it does, when I returnd I wou'd take a Ride to them my self—perhaps if they had money I cou'd get some from them" (Lund Washington to GW, 15 Feb. 1776, ibid., 3:317). Shortly before GW was due to come home, Lund did make a trip to collect rents but met with no success. "I have not been able to collect one shilling from those of our Tenaments over the Ridge" (Lund Washington to GW, 1 Oct. 1783, copy, PGWp).

97. Lund Washington to GW, 29 Oct. 1775, *PGW*, Rev. Ser., 2:258.

98. GW's letter has not survived. See, however, Lund Washington to GW, 14 Nov. 1775, ibid., 375.

99. Lund Washington to GW, 22 Oct. and 5 and 12 Nov. 1775, ibid., 219, 306, and 355–56.

100. Lund Washington to GW, 15 Oct. 1775, ibid., 172–73.

101. Lund Washington to GW, 14 Nov. 1775, ibid., 374.

102. "I am really at a loss for the just proportion of each particular part, nor have I any body to direct me," Lund wrote, "I have once or twice talk'd to Lanphier about it but he mouths & talks in such a way that I do not understand him" (Lund Washington to GW, 12 Nov. 1775, ibid., 356).

103. Lund Washington to GW, 22 April 1778, copy, PGWp.

104. Lund Washington to GW, 24 Nov. 1775, *PGW*, Rev. Ser., 2:421.

105. Lund had written on one occasion, "I shoud

be much better Satisfy'd if you woud give Possitive direction in many things, rather than leave me in a State of uncertainty . . . as I woud wish to do that which I thought woud best please" (Lund Washington to GW, 29 Feb. 1776, ibid., 3:393–94).

106. GW to Lund Washington, 11 June 1783, *GWW*, 25:2.

107. GW to Lund Washington, 12 Feb. 1783, ibid., 26:126–27.

108. GW to Lund Washington, 28 Feb. 1778, ibid., 10:530.

109. GW to Lund Washington, 15 Aug. 1778, ibid., 12:327.

110. GW to Lund Washington, 20 Aug. 1775, *PGW*, Rev. Ser., 1:335–36.

111. GW to Lund Washington, 30 Sept. 1776, ibid., 6:441.

112. GW to Lund Washington, 26 Nov. 1775, ibid., 2:431.

113. Lund Washington to GW, 3 Dec. 1775, ibid., 480.

114. Lund Washington to GW, 15 Feb. 1776, ibid., 3:317.

115. Russell, "Family Chronicle," MSS, 352–53, sketches Elizabeth (Betsy) Foote's background. See also William Buckner McGroarty, "Elizabeth Washington of Hayfield," *Virginia Magazine of History and Biography* 33 (1925):154–65.

116. Elizabeth Foote Washington, Journal, "Summer, 1784," MSS, copy, ViMtvL. Searching, thoughtful, and candid if relatively brief, Elizabeth Foote Washington's journal is cited by Mary Beth Norton several times in *Liberty's Daughters: The Revolutionary Experience of American Women, 1750–1800* (Boston and Toronto, 1980). It is Norton's conclusion that Lund's wife's ultimate concern was for his happiness, on which in turn she believed her own happiness depended, making their marriage an example of tranditional, "hierarchical organization" (ibid., 62–64).

117. Although the house was finished in 1784, the property was not formally deeded over to Lund until a year later. *GWD*, 4:80–81, n.

118. Elizabeth Foote Washington, Journal, "October, 1785," MSS, copy, ViMtvL.

119. Russell, "Family Chronicle," MSS, 375.

120. Elizabeth Foote Washington, Journal, "September, 1788," MSS, copy, ViMtvL. The difficulty Elizabeth Washington had with her slaves was characteristic of the complexities that Elizabeth Fox-Genovese ascribes to such relationships in *Within the Plantation Household: Black and White Women of the Old South* (Chapel Hill, N.C., and London,

1988). "Neither women's history nor women's identities can responsibly be abstracted from the social relations of class and race in the society and communities with which we are here concerned," she writes.

121. Ibid. Quoting Elizabeth Washington specifically, Norton finds such descriptions of marital happiness "genuine and deeply felt," as well as typical for the period (Norton, *Liberty's Daughters*, 64–65).

122. Elizabeth Foote Washington, Journal, "Winter, 1792," MSS, copy ViMtvL.

123. Ibid., "July 17, 1796."

124. GW to Lund Washington, 20 Nov. 1785, *PGW*, Con. Ser., 3:374.

125. McGroarty, "Elizabeth Washington of Hayfield," *Virginia Magazine* 33 (1925):164.

126. The histories of John Patterson, Going Lanphier, and Lund Washington would seem to offer abundant support for Gordon Wood's argument in *The Radicalism of the American Revolution* (New York, 1992) about the transformative character of the struggle for independence. "In 1760," he writes of Americans, "the less than two million monarchical subjects who lived in these colonies still took for granted that society was and ought to be a hierarchy of ranks and degrees of dependency." Yet scarcely half a century later the same people had become "the most liberal, the most democratic, the most commercially minded, and the most modern people in the world" (ibid., 6–7).

Chapter 9

1. GW to Mary Ball Washington, 15 Feb. 1787, *PGW*, Con. Ser., 5:33–36.

2. Jan Lewis in *The Pursuit of Happiness: Family and Values in Jefferson's Virginia* (Cambridge, Eng. 1983), stresses the importance of inclusiveness and reciprocity in gentry social activities and notes that the practice of meticulously recording in diaries lists of visitors and people visited—something Washington did all his life—was common (21–24). In a somewhat different vein, in *Sacred Things and Profane*, Upton discusses the tension between the openhandedness of gentry hospitality and its heavy emphasis on status, positing two types as embodiments of the opposing sides in the conflict: the Christian gentleman and the Virginia gentleman (see 165–68). In Washington's case the Christian gentleman would seem to have gained increasing prominence over time. See also Isaac, *Transformation of Virginia*, 70–79, and, on the material aspects of gentry entertaining, Mark R. Wenger, "The Dining Room in Early Virginia," in Thomas Carter and Bernard L. Herman, eds., *Per-*

spectives in Vernacular Architecture 3 (Columbia, Mo., 1989), 149–59.

The fullest account of family and social life at Mount Vernon is Paul Wilstach, *Mount Vernon: Washington's Home and the Nation's Shrine* (Garden City, N.Y., 1916). Miriam Anne Bourne, *First Family: George Washington and His Intimate Relations* (New York and London, 1982) also contains useful information.

3. Flexner, *Forge of Experience*, 234.

4. *GWD*, 3:243–48.

5. "An Inventory etc. of Articles at Mount Vernon With the Appraised Value Annexed," MSS, ViMtvL. See also *Inventory of Mount Vernon with a Note by W. C. Ford*, 1–61. The furniture in the west parlor was valued at $842, with the most highly valued single item being a family portrait of the Lafayettes. The total for the dining room was $337.50, and for the passage $179.

Christine Meadows provides an excellent introduction to the furniture of Mount Vernon in "The Furniture," *Antiques* 135, no. 2 (1989), an issue of the magazine devoted to Mount Vernon. See 480–89; and for information on other aspects of the house's contents: Robert G. Stewart, "Portraits of George and Martha Washington," 474–79; Ellen McCallister Clark, "George Washington's Study," 490–95; Susan Gray Detweiler, "The Ceramics," 496–591; Wendy Wick Reaves, "The Prints," 502–11; and Martha Gandy Fales, "The Jewelry," 512–17, and "The Silver," 518–23. Fuller treatments of two of these subjects can be found in Susan Gray Detweiler, *George Washington's Chinaware* (New York, 1982) and Kathryn C. Buhler, *Mount Vernon Silver* (Mount Vernon, 1957).

Another useful article in the same issue of *Antiques* is Matthew John Mosca's "The House and Its Restoration," 462–73, which contains a concise discussion of the paint colors currently used on the interior of Mount Vernon, colors that replicate those in the house at the time of GW's death. For a more detailed treatment of the subject see the same author's "The Paint Analysis Reports: Mount Vernon," MSS, ViMtvL.

6. Wenger, "The Central Passage," 139–44.

7. "Inventory of Articles at Mount Vernon," MSS, ViMtvL. Altogether there were twelve likenesses of family members hanging in the room.

Richard Bushman writes tellingly that formal parlors in eighteenth-century American gentry houses "meant more than that the owners were rich or in touch with English culture. . . . Creating parlors as a site for a refined life implied spiritual superiority" (*The Refinement of America*, 120 and 182).

On the all-important business of making, serving, and drinking tea see Rodris Roth, *Tea Drinking in Eighteenth-Century America: Its Etiquette and Equipage*, U.S. National Museum Bulletin 225 (Washington, D.C., 1961), 61–91. Noting both its practical and its symbolic aspects, Kevin Sweeney writes on the subject: "By the 1720s tea drinking at home had established itself as the preeminent genteel ritual. . . . As the participants moved and conversed, they evaluated potential business partners, potential marriage partners, and possible political allies. Through their participation in these ceremonies they also convinced others, and themselves, of their own gentility and status" (Sweeney, "High-Style Vernacular," 9–10).

8. Wenger, in "The Dining Room," traces the increasing frequency with which this space appears in Virginia houses and includes a description of a table setting with the obligatory dishes of meat in the center (150–59). See also Upton, "Vernacular Domestic Architecture," 318–35.

9. Joshua Brooke, "A Dinner at Mount Vernon, 1799: From the Unpublished Journal of Joshua Brooke (1773–1859)," *New-York Historical Society Quarterly* 21 (1947):75.

10. Isaac Ware, quoted in Whiffen, *Public Buildings of Williamsburg*, 143.

11. Girouard in *Life in the English Country House* discusses both the growing fashion for such rooms and the altered style of entertaining they were designed to accommodate. Ultimately, he argues, the result of such changes was the emergence of an entirely new house type, which he labels "the social house" (180–212).

12. Whiffen, *Public Buildings of Williamsburg*, 143–44. On "the relentless sociability" the new wing featured—and fostered—see Hood, *The Governor's Palace*, 173–93.

13. The library at Mount Vernon has extensive holdings of visitors' accounts of their experiences at Mount Vernon (see Mount Vernon Reference Notebook 15, "Early Descriptions ante 1800," ViMtvL).

14. On the attitudes of GW's contemporaries toward power and retirement see Wills, *Cincinnatus*, 17–25; also Barry Schwartz, *George Washington: The Making of an American Symbol* (New York and London, 1987).

15. GW to George Augustine Washington, 25 Oct. 1786, *PGW*, Con. Ser., 4:308. *GWW*, 30:28, prints the word "manner" as "mansion." Both printings are

based on copies of the original, which no longer survives. The earlier of the two copies is the one used in *PGW*. Both versions make sense in the context of the paragraph and the letter as a whole.

16. GW to Mary Ball Washington, 15 Feb. 1787, *PGW*, Con. Ser., 5:33.

17. GW to James Anderson, 10 Dec. 1799, *GWW*, 37:462. Washington described the situation "as almost beyond belief."

18. Joseph E. Fields, comp., "*Worthy Partner*": *The Papers of Martha Washington* (Westport, Conn., and London, 1994), brings together all of the extant correspondence to and from Martha Washington as well as her other papers. A fine Introduction by Ellen McCallister Clark includes a concise biographical account. Of the several full-length biographies, the most recent is Alice Curtis Desmond, *Martha Washington* (New York, 1951). See also Elswyth Thane, *Washington's Lady* (New York, 1860) and Anne Hollingsworth Wharton, *Martha Washington* (New York, 1897).

19. Jonathan Boucher to GW, 18 Dec. 1770, *PGW*, Col. Ser., 8:414. Boucher lived and taught school in Annapolis, and Jackie Custis had been sent to him as a pupil and boarder (*GWD*, 3:172 n.).

20. In *Virginians at Home: Family Life in the Eighteenth Century* (Williamsburg, Va., 1952), Edmund S. Morgan provides a thoughtful overview of the subject, including a chapter on childrearing (5–18) that pays particular attention to education. Daniel Blake Smith, in *Inside the Great House: Planter Family Life in Eighteenth-Century Chesapeake Society* (Ithaca, N.Y., and London, 1980), is more concerned with the internal dynamics of family relationships. On childrearing practices see esp. 25–34, where he makes a strong case for the pervasiveness of Martha Washington's approach to parenting. Smith's conclusion, however, is disputed by Jan Lewis in *The Pursuit of Happiness* (30 and 237, n. 47). See also Philip Greven, *The Protestant Temperament: Patterns of Child-Rearing, Religious Experience and the Self in Early America* (New York, 1977), Part Four, which generally supports Smith's view; and, for yet another interpretation, David Hackett Fischer, *Albion's Seed*, 311–20, which points to a complex pattern combining in something like equal measure permissive and disciplinary elements. In the case of the Custis children it is possible to see how Martha and GW, separately and individually, might have assumed responsibility for the two sides of this fractured approach to childrearing. If so, Martha's influence definitely remained the stronger of the two.

21. Freeman, *Washington*, 6:295.

22. Benjamin Henry Latrobe, "Through Virginia to Mt. Vernon: Extracts from the Journal of Benjamin Henry Latrobe," *Appleton's Booklovers Magazine* 6, no. 1 (1905):15.

23. Niemcewicz, *Under Their Vine and Fig Tree*, 85.

24. Brooke, "A Dinner at Mount Vernon," 74. Brooke also noted that Martha reminded him of "my dear mother" (ibid.).

25. Abigail Adams to Mary Cranch, 28 June 1789, *New Letters of Abigail Adams, 1788–1801*, Stewart Mitchell, ed. (Boston, 1947), 13. Mary Cranch was Abigail Adams's sister.

26. Abigail Adams to Mary Cranch, 12 July 1789, ibid., 15.

27. The practice is briefly described in Fields, comp., *Papers of Martha Washington*, xxxi. In several cases both the letters as sent and the drafts in GW's hand survive. See, for example, Martha Washington to Elizabeth Powell, 1 and 20 May and 18 Dec. 1797, ibid., 301–3 and 309–10. Even when GW's drafts do not survive, however, the style of the letters identifies them unmistakably as products of his pen.

28. Martha Washington to Mercy Otis Warren, 26 Dec. 1789, ibid., 223–24.

29. Martha Washington to Fanny Bassett Washington, 1 July 1792, ibid., 239.

30. Martha Washington to Fanny Bassett Washington, 23 Oct. 1789, ibid., 220.

31. James Thomas Flexner, *Washington: The Indispensable Man* (New York, 1974), 371, n.

32. See supra, 107.

33. In 1789, on the other hand, GW had refused to appoint Bushrod U.S. district attorney for Virginia because, as he wrote, his nephew had yet to acquire the experience necessary to "justify" the appointment (GW to Bushrod Washington, *PGW*, Pres. Ser., 3:334).

34. Soon after George Augustine's marriage, GW had promised to leave him a large piece of land adjacent to Mount Vernon and urged him to build a house on it (GW to George Augustine Washington, ibid., Con. Ser., 4:307–9).

35. Ibid., Pres. Ser. 5:71–74, ns. 1, 2, and 3. GW agreed to pay $1,000 for a year's lease of the property, which had previously been occupied by the comte de Moustier, the French minister to the United States. He also arranged to purchase a great deal of Moustier's furniture. When the pea green carpet finally arrived eight months later, it was no longer wanted because the presidential household was about to move to Philadelphia.

36. Tobias Lear to Clement Biddle, 8 June 1789, copy, PGWp.

37. GW to Gouverneur Morris, 13 Oct. 1789, *PGW*, Pres. Ser., 4:177–78.

38. Gouverneur Morris to GW, 24 Jan. 1790, ibid., 5:48–56 and 57, n. 2. The "Plateaus" came in seven parts. For adorning them, there were two vases and twelve individual porcelain figures, as well as three larger "Groups" of figures, which could also be used (with glass covers) as "ornaments to the Chimney Piece of a drawing room."

39. GW to Gouverneur Morris, 15 Apr. 1790, *PGW*, Pres. Ser., 5:334.

40. GW to Clement Biddle, 29 Jan. 1798, *GWW*, 36:146; and "Inventory of Articles at Mount Vernon," MSS, ViMtvL.

41. In addition to the standard biographies of GW there are a number of studies of his role as president, most notably Forrest McDonald, *The Presidency of George Washington* (Lawrence, Kan., 1974), and Ralph Ketcham, *Presidents Above Party: The First American Presidency, 1782–1829* (Chapel Hill, N.C., 1984). See also Alexander DeConde, *Entangling Alliance: Politics and Diplomacy Under George Washington* (Durham, N.C., 1958); Louis M. Sears, *George Washington and the French Revolution* (Detroit, 1960); and Glenn A. Phelps, *George Washington and American Constitutionalism* (Lawrence, Kan., 1993).

Among the biographies of others, the most useful are Dumas Malone, *Jefferson and His Time*, 6 vols. (Boston, 1948–81); Irving Brant, *James Madison*, 6 vols. (Indianapolis, 1941–61); and Forrest McDonald, *Alexander Hamilton: A Biography* (New York, 1979). Also invaluable are Joseph J. Ellis, *American Sphinx: The Character of Thomas Jefferson* (New York, 1997), and Drew R. McCoy, *The Last of the Fathers: James Madison and the Republican Legacy* (Cambridge, Eng., and New York, 1989).

On the emergence of party divisions see Joseph Charles, *The Origins of the American Party System: Three Essays* (Williamsburg, Va., 1956); Noble E. Cunningham, Jr., *The Jeffersonian Republicans: The Formation of Party Organization, 1789–1801* (Chapel Hill, N.C., 1957); John C. Miller, *The Federalist Era, 1789–1801* (New York, 1960); Donald H. Stewart, *The Opposition Press of the Federalist Period* (Albany, N.Y., 1969), and Drew R. McCoy, *The Elusive Republic: Political Economy in Jeffersonian America* (Chapel Hill, N.C., 1980). The ideological dimensions of the split are further covered from two very different perspectives in John Murin, "The Great

Inversion," esp. 404–28, and Joyce Appleby, *Capitalism and a New Social Order: The Republican Vision of the 1790s* (New York, 1984). See also the essays in that author's *Liberalism and Republicanism in the Historical Imagination* (Cambridge, Mass., 1992). As interesting as we find Appleby's attempt to place liberal capitalism at the core of Jeffersonian ideology, Murin's approach and the formulation of the issues in Stanley Elkins and Eric McKitrick's magisterial *The Age of Federalism: The Early American Republic, 1788–1800* (New York and Oxford, 1993) strike us as more compelling. See esp. ibid., 3–161, 195–208, 257–92, and 760–61, n. 31.

42. Thomas Jefferson to GW, 23 May 1792, Julian P. Boyd, ed., *The Papers of Thomas Jefferson* (Princeton, N.J., 1950), 23:535–40.

43. GW to Alexander Hamilton, 29 July 1792, *GWW*, 32:95–100; Alexander Hamilton to GW, 18 August 1792, Harold C. Syrett, ed., *The Papers of Alexander Hamilton* (New York, 1961–87), 12:228–58.

44. GW to Thomas Jefferson, 23 Aug. 1792, *GWW*, 32:130–32; GW to Alexander Hamilton, 26 Aug. 1792, ibid., 132–34.

45. For a detailed treatment of the subject see Thomas P. Slaughter, *The Whiskey Rebellion: Frontier Epilogue to the American Revolution* (New York, 1986), and also Richard Kohn, "The Washington Administration's Decision to Crush the Whiskey Rebellion," *Journal of American History* 59 (1972): 567–84.

46. The standard studies of this singularly devisive piece of diplomacy are Samuel F. Bemis, *Jay's Treaty: A Study in Commerce and Diplomacy* (New Haven, Conn., 1962), and Jerald A. Combs, *The Jay Treaty: Political Battleground of the Founding Fathers* (Berkeley, Calif., 1970).

47. Jefferson, quoted in James Thomas Flexner, *George Washington: Anguish and Farewell, 1793–1799* (Boston and Toronto, 1969), 218.

48. On Freneau see Freeman, *Washington*, "American Newspapers and Editorials Opinion, 1789–93," Appendix, 6:393–413; also ibid., 7:5–7 and 17–86 passim; and on Bache, James D. Tagg, "Benjamin Franklin Bache's Attack on George Washington," *Pennsylvania Magazine of History and Biography* 100 (1976):191–230. Tagg concludes that Bache "either wrote or published the vast majority of the attacks" of a direct, personal nature on GW (ibid., 194).

49. In fact, the split began even earlier. Mason, a delegate to the Philadelphia convention, had refused to sign the Constitution. Of the several biographies

available, Helen Miller's *George Mason* provides the fullest coverage of his final years. On the subject of the newly established government, she quotes him as saying: "Our new Government is a Government of Stockjobbing and Favourtism. It required no extraordinary Degree of Penetration, to forsee that it would be so, from its Formation" (ibid., 325).

50. GW to Anthony Whiting, 14 Oct. 1792, *GWW*, 30:177-85. See also GW to Anthony Whiting, 28 Oct., 4, 11, and 18 Nov., 2, 16, and 23 Dec. 1792, 6, 13, and 20 Jan., 3, 10, 17 and 24 Feb., 3 and 24 Mar., 28 Apr., 5, 12, 19, and 26 May, and 9 June 1793, ibid., 194-99, 201-5, 214-19, 227-33, 245-51, 261-63, 274-77, 292-96, 297-303, 303-7, 327-33, 338-41, 345-49, 356-59, 364-66, 400-402, 434-38, 441-47, 455-59, 463-70, 470-76, and 491-95. A similar list could be compiled for any nine-month period of GW's presidency after the summer of 1792, when his nephew George Augustine Washington became too ill to carry on as manager at Mount Vernon.

51. GW to Anthony Whiting, 3 Mar. 1793, ibid., 364-66.

52. GW to William Pearce, 7 June 1795, ibid., 34:211-12; 6 Oct. 1793, ibid., 33:111. The instructions regarding "the neatness of my Farms" were sent in the letter accompanying Pearce's initial employment contract.

53. GW to William Pearce, 12 Jan. 1794, ibid., 240.

54. GW to James Anderson, 21 Dec. 1797, ibid., 36:112-13. GW prefaced his remarks by asserting: "The man who does not estimate *time* as *money* will forever miscalculate."

55. Ibid.

56. See, for example, GW to Anthony Whiting, 16 Dec. 1792, ibid., 32:262, in which he states: "There is no Proverb in the whole catalogue of them more true, than that a penny saved, is a penny got." On "many mickels make a muckel" see GW to James Germain, 1 June 1794, ibid., 33:390, in which he describes the saying as "an old Scotch adage."

57. GW to William Pearce, 18 Dec. 1793, ibid., 30:194.

58. GW's instructions for building the barn are reproduced in ibid., 32:285-87.

59. GW to Anthony Whiting, 24 Feb. 1793, ibid., 357.

60. GW to Anthony Whiting, 28 Oct. 1792, ibid., 195.

61. GW to Anthony Whiting, 14 Oct. 1792, ibid., 180.

62. GW to Anthony Whiting, 11 Nov. 1792, ibid., 226.

63. GW to Anthony Whiting, 2 Dec., 1792, ibid., 249.

64. Ibid. Whiting apparently complained that he was too short of hands to do the hedging as quickly as GW wanted and suggested that they give up fishing for a year to make time for it. Washington hoped that such drastic measures would not be necessary (in many years, after all, fishing provided the extra cash that kept Mount Vernon from running in the red); still, he made his preference clear. "If there was an absolute necessity for refraining from Fishing with my own People, or Postponing my Hedging operations another year, I should not hesitate a moment in giving up the first" (GW to Anthony Whiting, 6 Jan. 1793, ibid., 294-95).

65. GW to Robert Morris, 12 Apr. 1786, *PGW*, Con. Ser., 4:16.

66. GW to Arthur Young, 12 Dec. 1793, *GWW*, 33:174-83.

67. GW to Tobias Lear, 6 May 1794, ibid., 357-60.

68. GW to Arthur Young, 18-21 June 1792, ibid., 32:65-66.

69. GW to William Pearce, 25 Jan. 1795, ibid., 34:103-4.

70. On the problem posed by the "dower slaves," as they were called, see GW to David Stuart (marked "Private"), 7 Feb. 1796, ibid., 452-53.

71. The initial draft of the address is reproduced in ibid., 35:51-61. The language in question was eventually dropped at the urging of Hamilton. For further analysis of the subject see Victor H. Paltsits, *Washington's Farewell Address* (New York, 1935); the essays in Burton I. Kaufman, ed., *Washington's Farewell Address: The View from the 20th Century* (Chicago, 1969); and Elkins and McKitrick, *Age of Federalism*, 489-528.

72. "Advertisement," 1 Feb. 1796, ibid., 34:433-47. On the subject of slavery the advertisement stated: "Although the admission of Slaves with the Tenants will not be absolutely prohibited; it would, nevertheless, be a pleasing circumstance to exclude them; If not entirely, at least in a great degree: To do which, is not among the least inducements for dividing the farms into small lots" (ibid., 444).

73. GW to David Stuart, 7 Feb., 1796, ibid., 453.

74. Ibid.; also GW to William Pearce, 20 Mar. 1796, ibid., 501-2.

75. In addition he began looking for a new gardener (GW to Dr. James Anderson, Apr. 1797, ibid., 35:431-34; Dr. James Anderson should not be con-

fused with the Mount Vernon manager of the same name).

76. Appropriately enough, his letter asking Dr. James Anderson to help him find a new gardener had included the vine and fig tree refrain. See also GW to David Humphreys, 26 June 1797, ibid., 480; to the earl of Buchan, 4 July 1797, ibid., 488; to the earl of Radnor, 8 July 1797, ibid., 493; and to Sir Edward Newenham, 6 Aug. 1797, ibid., 36:4.

77. GW to William Pearce, 14 Nov. 1796, ibid., 279–80.

78. GW to George Lewis, 9 Apr. 1797, ibid., 434–35.

79. Ibid.

80. GW to Reverend William Gordon, 15 Oct. 1797, ibid., 49.

81. Parkinson first wrote GW in 1797, stating that he proposed to arrive in the United States the following March. However, not until 28 Aug. 1798 did he declare that he was about to depart from Liverpool, and he arrived accompanied by his family and a large quantity of livestock, including two stallions, which GW feared he meant to install at Mount Vernon. There was also a bill of £850 owed for freight on the ship that brought him over. Under the circumstances, GW hardly knew what instructions to send James Anderson. Room for the livestock, except the stallions, might be found at Mount Vernon, but there could be no question of paying the £850: GW simply did not have the money (GW to James Anderson, 1 and 3 Nov. 1798, ibid., 37:4 and 6–9). In the event, Parkinson appeared at Mount Vernon, but on finding that he could not unload there, went to Alexandria, where he made his own arrangements for the livestock and the freight charges.

82. For two somewhat different descriptions of the visit, based on an account of it subsequently published by Parkinson himself, see Freeman, *Washington*, 7:556–57, and Flexner, *Anguish and Farewell*, 451–52. Flexner asserts, "Parkinson was not a gentleman," but the Englishman seems to have been both candid and courteous in his dealings with GW.

Chapter 10

1. John E. Latta, unpublished journal, 3 July 1799, Mount Vernon Notebook in, "Early Descriptions," ViMtvL. (Latta's first name as recorded in the brief preface to the journal entry is probably incorrect. See below, n. 2.)

2. In his diary, GW wrote: "Doctr Stuart & a Parson Lattum from Pennsylvania dined here & left it in the afternoon" (*GWD*, 6:355). An editor's note iden-

tifies "Parson Lattum" as "probably Rev. James Latta (1732–1801), Presbyterian minister of Chestnut Level, Lancaster County, Pa. or one of his sons" (ibid.). Since Latta described himself as a "young" clergyman, it seems more likely that GW's visitor was a son.

3. Niemcewicz, *Under Their Vine and Fig Tree*, 106–7. Washington's diary contains the following entry for 13 June 1798: "Mr Fitzhugh, Lady & daughter—Mrs. Beverly Randolph with her daughter & Son in Law Randolph & his Sister dined here" (*GWD*, 6:301).

4. Martha Washington to an unnamed correspondent, 18 Sept. 1799, Fields, comp., *Papers of Martha Washington*, 321–22. The original letter has not survived, but Fields sees no reason to doubt its authenticity.

5. The will, with an accompanying "Schedule of property," is printed in full in *GWW*, 37:275–303, as well as in Eugene E. Prussing, *The Estate of George Washington, Deceased* (Boston, 1927), 42–85. It has also been published separately in John C. Fitzpatrick, ed., *The Last Will and Testament of George Washington and Schedule of his Property, to which is appended the Last Will and Testament of Martha Washington* (Mount Vernon, 1939). The last of these is usefully annotated, and is the version cited hereafter.

6. Ibid., 2–3.

7. Lawrence Lewis, "Executor's Ledger of the Estate of George Washington," MSS, Chapin Library, Williams College. In 1836 charges for three "old free Negroes"—Suckey, Molly, and Gabriel—were recorded; by 1839 only Gabriel was left, and he died in March of that year. Included were payments for housing, board, meat, meal, firewood, clothing, medical attention, nursing care, and at the end, coffins and grave-digging (ibid.). The list of GW's slaves compiled in 1799 contains two individuals named Suckey and two named Molly, so it is impossible to tell who the women in the ledger were. Gabriel (the only one of GW's slaves with that name) was thirty years old in 1799, lived at Muddy Hole Farm, and had a wife, Judy, at Dogue Run Farm ("Negroes Belonging to George Washington," June 1799, *GWW*, 37:256–68). See also Frank E. Morse, "More About General Washington's Freed Negroes," unpublished paper, 1968, copy, ViMtvL.

8. For two rather different treatments of inheritance patterns among the Virginia gentry see Smith, *Inside the Great House*, 231–48, and Kulikoff, *Tobacco and Slaves*, 189–92, 199–202, and 263–67.

Both historians note the presence of tension between, as Smith puts it, "the impulse to protect the family estate, to keep it intact in perpetuity . . . [and] the affectionate desire to provide for all children, dependent kin and close friends." Smith is inclined to emphasize the "affectionate" side of the equation, observing that after 1750, bequests beyond the immediate family became increasingly common. Such bequests, however, were largely confined to "gifts of cash, livestock, clothes," while "the most valuable parts of the estate—land and slaves" invariably went to children. Ideally there would be something for every child, but even then they were most often treated unequally (Smith, *Inside the Great House*, 232–36). Kulikoff stresses the latter point, arguing: "Ideal inheritance strategies depended upon family size: a man with few children might divide his fortune in a relatively equal manner . . . a man with many children, however, had to favor a few children or encourage several sons to stay single if even part of the family was to retain the family fortune" (Kulikoff, *Tobacco and Slaves*, 265).

Kulikoff's contention that keeping family wealth intact was an imperative gentry members ignored at their peril is strongly supported by David Fischer, who asserts that "even very rich men were forced to choose between the interests of individual children and the welfare of the family." He also points out (as statistics presented by Smith demonstrate) that over time "the custom of primogeniture grew stronger in Virginia" (Fischer, *Albion's Seed*, 381).

By any or all of these standards, the pattern of bequests in GW's will was most unusual, though neither Flexner nor John Alexander Carroll and Mary Wells Ashworth, who completed the final volume of Freeman's biography, seem to recognize the fact. Carroll and Ashworth describe GW's will aptly as "his greatest valedictory" but speak of his desire "to perpetuate" his "investment in a way of living" (Freeman, *Washington*, 7:583–94). Flexner asserts that despite GW's lack of a son "his approach remained dynastic" (Flexner, *Anguish and Farewell*, 453–55). On both points the facts appear to point strongly in the opposite direction.

9. Fitzpatrick, *Last Will and Testament of Washington*, 4–10. Alexandria Academy eventually merged with the city's public school system. Moved from its original location to Lexington, Virginia, Liberty Hall Academy in time became a collegiate institution, which survives to this day as Washington and Lee University. GW's hopes for a national university fared less well. His lead was not followed by Congress or other private benefactors, and by 1828 the shares of the Potomac Navigation Company he had earmarked for the project had become worthless (ibid., 31–32, ns. 7–12).

10. The item with the highest value was a group of tracts on the Great Kanhawa River, which GW listed at $200,000. Running for more than forty miles along the river and totaling 23,341 acres, these were the lands he had received in return for his service in the Virginia Regiment. There was already a conditional sales agreement for $200,000 for the entire holding, but it eventually fell through. In 1805 the heirs agreed to divide these and other tracts in the West and take title to them individually. How they were eventually disposed of is not known (ibid., 33, n. 21 and 55, ns. 9–10).

Where the amounts realized from sales of particular items in the estate are known, some exceed GW's estimates, but more than a few fall below the figures he listed in the "Schedule of property" (ibid., 30–40 and 50–54). "By way of advice," he urged his executors "not to be precipitate in disposing of the landed property . . . if from temporary causes the Sale thereof should be dull." In several cases this advice seems to have been ignored, which may account for some of the discrepancy between his estimate of what various holdings were worth and the prices they actually brought (ibid., 26). For further information see Prussing, *Estate of George Washington*, esp. 176–348.

11. Fitzpatrick, ed., *Last Will and Testament of Washington*, 24–26. If there were more than one of them in a family, the children of nieces or nephews who had died earlier received partial shares. As a result there were more people participating in the division than there were shares.

12. GW to Samuel Washington, 2 Apr. 1799, *GWW*, 37:172–74. Apparently Samuel Washington's slaves were about to be taken by court order and sold to cover his debts. "Nothing but the desire of preserving you, from what you say would be your ruin, has induced me to advance this money," declared GW.

13. Ibid., 19–23.

14. Ibid., 17–19.

15. According to GW, Pearce had decided to leave because of "an increasing Rheumatic affection [sic], which he says will not allow him to discharge his duty as he conceives he ought" (GW to James Anderson, 18 Aug. 1796, *GWW*, 35:182).

16. GW to James Anderson, 21 Dec. 1797, and 1 and 6 Feb., 22 May, and 11 June 1798: ibid.,

36:110–14, 151–55, 266–70, and 283–94. GW's chief objection to Anderson's performance of his duties was his lack of "system." He also objected to the suggestion that he ought to refrain from criticizing Anderson's work. "It is no gratification to me to hurt the feelings of any person living . . . but in matters which relate to my *own* concerns, I shall, most assuredly, express at all times my opinion of them." Nevertheless, in response to Anderson's hurt feelings and threats to quit, GW did offer to lighten his manager's workload (ibid., 283–84).

17. *GWD*, 6:335.

18. GW to Sarah Cary Fairfax, 16 May 1798, *GWW*, 36:262–64.

19. Martha Washington to Sarah Cary Fairfax, 17 May 1798, Fields, comp., *Papers of Martha Washington,* 314–15. The surviving draft of the letter is in Washington's handwriting (*GWW,* 36:265, n. 61).

20. GW to Reverend Bryan, Lord Fairfax, 26 Nov. 1799, ibid., 37:440. It was in fact to secure his title that Fairfax had traveled to England the year before.

21. On the shifting currents in Franco-American relations during this period see: Ralph A. Brown, *The Presidency of John Adams* (Lawrence, Kan., 1975); Albert H. Bowman, *The Struggle for Neutrality: Franco-American Diplomacy During the Federalist Era* (Knoxville, Tenn., 1974); William Stinchcombe, *The XYZ Affair* (Westport, Conn., 1980); and Elkins and McKitrick, *Age of Federalism,* 529–641.

22. GW to John Adams, 13 July 1798, *GWW*, 36:327–29.

23. GW to James McAlpin, 27 Jan. and 10 Feb. 1799, ibid., 37:111–12 and 128–29. As always GW specified in great detail what he wanted, down to the proper shade of buff "not inclining to yellow or Orange" for the facings of the coat.

Congress did not finally vote to disband the army until May 1800. For an interesting discussion of why the Federalists were so intent on prolonging its existence after the crisis had passed, see Elkins and McKitrick, *Age of Federalism,* 714–19.

24. GW to James McHenry, 17 Nov. 1799, *GWW,* 37:428–29.

25. Elkins and McKitrick, *Age of Federalism,* 732.

26. GW to James Anderson, 10 Dec. 1799, *GWW,* 37:459–72.

27. GW's final illness and death were most thoroughly described at the time by Tobias Lear, his secretary, who was present throughout the three days in question. Though the original manuscript of Lear's account has disappeared, a printed version can be found in Tobias Lear, *Letters and Recollections of Washington . . . With a Diary of Washington's Last Days* (New York, 1906).

For a modern medical analysis of the subject see "A Comparative Critique of Washington's Last Illness," Freeman, *Washington,* 7, Appendix II, 637–47. The consensus among the several physicians cited is that GW died of "septic sore throat, probably of streptococcic origin." To that cause one of the physicians added "the medical mistreatment he received" (ibid., 646–47).

◢ Index ◣

Page numbers in italic refer to illustrations. Within index entries "George Washington" is abbreviated as "GW."

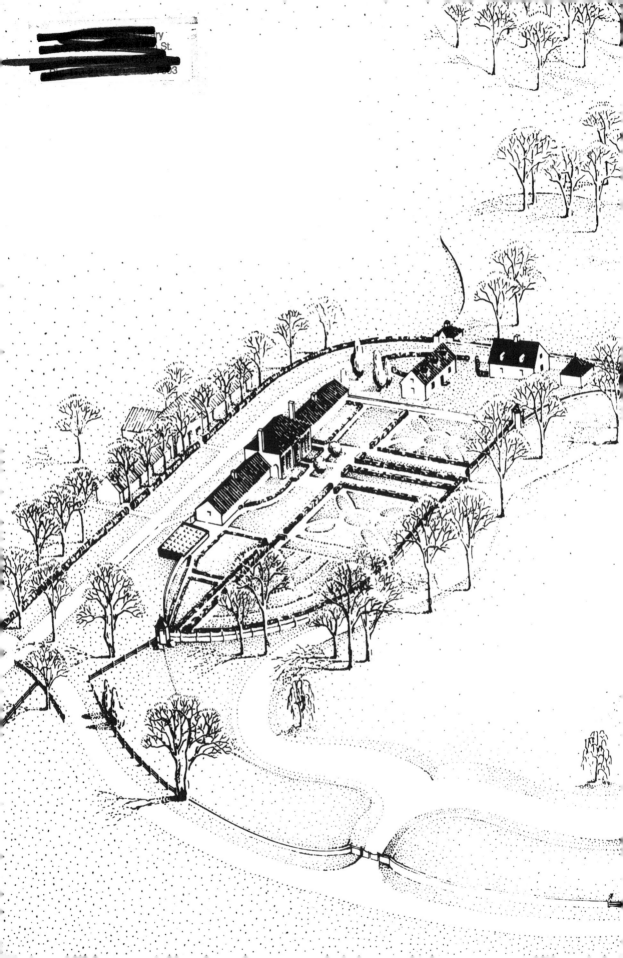